"This truly is a book of our time, which I believe every educationalist should read. This book gives voice to worldwide perspectives on education post-COVID from Early Years teachers in the Caribbean to menopausal women in the UK. It gives a fascinating perspective on both the challenges and positive impacts of COVID-19. The 'call for action' is a passionate challenge to re-think what it is to be a teacher, to nurture the autonomy of teachers and work together to support and care for each other. It has to be one of the most powerful books I have read in a long while and is likely to remain next to my desk to share and revisit repeatedly."

– **Jo Tregenza**, *Reader in Education at University of Sussex and Vice President of the United Kingdom Literacy Association*

"This is an important book. It explores the intersection between the professional and personal lives of teachers and academics and the focus on teachers' family life opens up big questions about the future of education globally, especially for the majority of the workforce who are women. Women educators and leaders work in an inequitable and inflexible system. Their voices are clearly expressed throughout the chapters and we need to hear them as it is clear the status quo is no longer adequate for women. This book will help to recalibrate the future of educational practice and it can't come soon enough for most of the education workforce."

– **Vivienne Porritt OBE**, *co-founder and Strategic Leader of #WomenEd, author, and Vice President of the Chartered College of Teaching*

TEACHERS AND TEACHING POST-COVID

Featuring a broad swathe of academic research and perspectives from international contributors, this book will capture and share important lessons from the pandemic experience for teaching practice and teacher learning more broadly.

Looking at core teaching values such as the facilitation of learning, the promotion of fairness and equality, and community building, the book centres the records of teachers' experiences from diverse educational phases and locations that illuminate how the complexity of teaching work is entangled in the emotional, relational, and embodied nature of teachers' everyday lives. Through rich, qualitative data and first-hand experience, the book informs the decisions of teachers and those who train, support, and manage them, promoting sustainable, positive transformation within education for the benefit of educators and learners alike.

This book will be of use to scholars, practitioners, and researchers involved with teachers and teacher education, the sociology of education, and teaching and learning more broadly. Policy makers working in school leadership, management, and administration may also benefit from the volume.

Katy Marsh-Davies is Senior Lecturer of Human Resource Management & Organisational Behaviour at Sheffield Hallam University, UK.

Cathy Burnett is Professor of Literacy and Education at the Sheffield Institute of Education, Sheffield Hallam University, UK.

TEACHERS AND TEACHING POST-COVID

Seizing Opportunities for Change

Edited by
Katy Marsh-Davies and Cathy Burnett

LONDON AND NEW YORK

Designed cover image: © Getty Images

First published 2024
by Routledge
4 Park Square, Milton Park, Abingdon, Oxon OX14 4RN

and by Routledge
605 Third Avenue, New York, NY 10158

Routledge is an imprint of the Taylor & Francis Group, an informa business

© 2024 selection and editorial matter, Katy Marsh-Davies and Cathy Burnett; individual chapters, the contributors

The right of Katy Marsh-Davies and Cathy Burnett to be identified as the authors of the editorial material, and of the authors for their individual chapters, has been asserted in accordance with sections 77 and 78 of the Copyright, Designs and Patents Act 1988.

All rights reserved. No part of this book may be reprinted or reproduced or utilised in any form or by any electronic, mechanical, or other means, now known or hereafter invented, including photocopying and recording, or in any information storage or retrieval system, without permission in writing from the publishers.

Trademark notice: Product or corporate names may be trademarks or registered trademarks, and are used only for identification and explanation without intent to infringe.

British Library Cataloguing-in-Publication Data
A catalogue record for this book is available from the British Library

ISBN: 978-1-032-39950-8 (hbk)
ISBN: 978-1-032-39949-2 (pbk)
ISBN: 978-1-003-35212-9 (ebk)

DOI: 10.4324/9781003352129

Typeset in Sabon
by codeMantra

CONTENTS

Acknowledgements   *xi*
List of contributors   *xiii*
Foreword   *xxi*
Jonathan Glazzard

Introduction   1

1 Teachers and teaching post-COVID   3
  Katy Marsh-Davies and Cathy Burnett

Priorities: Reassessing Roles and Responsibilities   23

2 Part-time women teachers-having it all?   25
  Suzanne Brown

3 Experiences of student-teacher mothers before
  and during COVID-19: Lessons in flexibility   43
  Joan Woodhouse

4 Teaching through the menopause: A flexible work paradox   64
  Belinda Steffan and Kristina Potočnik

5 Teacher well-being in times of COVID   87
  Chris Forde, Judith Hanks, and Rachel Mathieson

6 Stories found within higher education: Shifting
   professional identities of academics   106
   Kathryn Coleman, Melissa Cain, and Chris Campbell

7 Claiming professionalisation: Supporting Caribbean
   early childhood teachers' professional identities
   post-COVID-19   127
   Zoyah Kinkead-Clark and Sabeerah Abdul-Majied

Alliances: Relationships, Connections, and Community   143

8 "We're still trying to figure out every single day":
   Teaching since COVID-19   145
   Maxine Cameron and Sandra Schamroth Abrams

9 New ways of working and new opportunities: Early
   childhood leaders' professional practice post-COVID   163
   Wendy Boyd, Marg Rogers, and Margaret Sims

10 Pandemic parenting – balancing change, capabilities,
   and culture   181
   Kadia Hylton-Fraser and Kamilah Hylton

11 Stacking stories as inquiry into practice: Co-teaching
   an online literacy club for youth   202
   *Michelle A. Honeyford, Kelsey Collins-Kramble,
   and Jessica Neudorf-Wiebe*

Reimaginings: New Ways of Teaching and Being a Teacher   223

12 What the COVID-19 pandemic has taught us about
   becoming a teacher: Lessons for post-pandemic realities   225
   Benjamin Luke Moorhouse and My C. Tiet

13 Opportunities for modernising and revolutionising
   education systems post-COVID: Drawing on an
   international survey of teachers' experiences during the
   COVID-19 pandemic   242
   *Carol Hordatt Gentles, Marilyn Leask, and Mark
   Williams*

14 Sociomaterial perspectives on hybrid learning in
   primary classrooms during the COVID-19 pandemic   256
   Noreen Dunnett

15 Learning to read the (digital) room during the
   COVID-19 pandemic: Teacher perspectives   274
   Linda Laidlaw and Suzanna So Har Wong

16 Post-COVID pedagogy: Intersectional identities and
   technological spaces   291
   Ahmet Atay

Conclusion   307

17 COVID-19: A catalyst for change   309
   Katy Marsh-Davies and Suzanne Brown

Index   327

ACKNOWLEDGEMENTS

We wish to thank Emilie Coin, AnnaMary Goodall, and Kanishka Jangir at Taylor & Francis publishing for their support in producing this book. We thank all of our contributing authors, their institutions, and funders. We thank all who participated in the research that informed their chapters. We thank Sheffield Hallam University for the seed corn funding that allowed us to undertake small-scale research with teachers during the pandemic, which led us to this book project. Katy wishes to thank all the inspirational teachers in her life, including sister Jen, friend Erica, and cousins Zoe and Rebecca, and all of those who supported her during the compilation of this, her first book, including husband Lee, Mum, Dad, Sue, other brilliant sister Lucy, and everyone in the HROB subject group within Sheffield Hallam University. This is for her daughter Alex.

CONTRIBUTORS

Sabeerah Abdul-Majied is a lecturer and course coordinator of the Bachelor of Education Early Childhood Care and Education Programme and the Certificate in Early Childhood Development at The University of the West Indies (UWI) St. Augustine Campus. She has 33 years teaching experience mainly at the tertiary level. Her expertise is Early Childhood Teacher Education specialising in curriculum planning and development. She has published book chapters and authored and co-authored articles in international peer reviewed journals on Caribbean Children's Social and Emotional Development, Data Driven Decision making, STEM, and Early Childhood Teacher Professional development.

Ahmet Atay (Ph.D., Southern Illinois University-Carbondale) is Professor of Global Media and Communication at the College of Wooster. His research focuses on diasporic experiences and cultural identity formations; political and social complexities of city life, such as immigrant and queer experiences; the usage of new media technologies in different settings; and the notion of home; representation of gender, sexuality, and ethnicity in media; queer and immigrant experiences in cyberspace, and critical communication pedagogies. He is the author of *Globalization's Impact on Identity Formation: Queer Diasporic Males in Cyberspace* (2015) and the co-editor of several books. His scholarship appeared in a number of journals and edited books.

Wendy Boyd, Associate Professor, Southern Cross University, has made a significant contribution to early childhood education, internationally, and nationally, especially in the area of the early childhood workforce. Her research approach is grounded in achieving quality education delivered by effective teachers. She has a deep understanding of quality early childhood education having been a director of a large early childhood centre, which was consistently assessed as providing high-quality early childhood education and care.

Suzanne Brown is a Senior Lecturer of Initial Teacher Education at the Sheffield Institute of Education in the United Kingdom. Her research interests are around teacher recruitment and retention, with a particular interest in flexible working patterns in teaching – an area where little research exists. In 2022, she established and is the lead for the Effective Flexible Working in Schools Practitioner Network at the Sheffield Institute of Education, which encourages educational senior leaders and colleagues in education to share good practice around alternative working patterns.

Cathy Burnett is Professor of Literacy and Education at Sheffield Institute of Education, Sheffield Hallam University, UK. She has published widely for academic and professional readerships on teachers' professional lives and on relationships between children, digital media, and literacies within and beyond educational contexts. She has also led projects exploring the effects of research and data practices in education. She is a former president of the United Kingdom Literacy Association and a co-editor of *Journal of Early Childhood Literacy*. Her co-authored and co-edited books include *Undoing the Digital: Literacy and Sociomaterialism (2020)*, *New Media in the Classroom: Rethinking Primary Literacy (2018)*, *Unsettling Literacies: Directions for Literacy Research in Precarious Times* (2022), and *Research Mobilities in Primary Literacy Education: How Teachers Encounter Research in an Age of Evidence-Based Teaching* (forthcoming).

Melissa Cain is Senior Lecturer and National Head of Discipline (Secondary Initial Teacher Education) at Australian Catholic University (ACU). She also coordinates the secondary teaching courses in Queensland. Melissa's teaching and research focus on Initial Teacher Education, Inclusive Education, and Creative Arts, with a current focus on supporting equitable participation for students with vision impairment in mainstream schools.

Maxine Cameron is a Ph.D. student in the Curriculum and Instruction Ph.D. programme at St. John's University. Concerned about education in underserved and underfunded schools, Cameron focuses her research on the recruitment and retention of highly qualified teachers in marginalised school communities. Cameron has been an educator for 29 years, of which she has dedicated 16 years to being an administrator. For the past eight years, Cameron has served as Principal of the Roberto Clemente School in Brooklyn, New York. Cameron is recipient of the National Council of Negro Women Inc. Leadership & Educational Enhancement Award, the Beacon of Hope Award, and the New York State 19th Senatorial District 2020 Community Empowerment Award.

Chris Campbell is an Associate Professor and currently works in the Division of Learning and Teaching at Charles Sturt University. She is a Sub Dean (Learning Technology) and Science and Health Faculty Business Partner. Chris is the current President of ASCILITE. She has served on the Executive since 2014 and has been an active member of the ASCILITE community, having regularly attended ASCILITE conferences for many years.

Kathryn Coleman PhD, is the Committee Member (Communications) for Art Education Australia. She is Associate Professor in Visual Arts & Design Education at the Melbourne Graduate School of Education and University of Melbourne, and Petascale Campus Academic Convenor.

Kelsey Collins-Kramble is a teacher in Winnipeg, Manitoba, where she has taught in both senior year and middle year classrooms. She specialises in English Language Arts, Geography, and History, which she strives to teach through a lens of social justice. Kelsey is a member of the Manitoba Social Studies Teachers Association executive and journal team. In addition to her B.Ed., Kelsey holds a Master of Arts in Philosophy.

Noreen Dunnett is a Research Associate at the Centre for Research in Digital Education in the University of Edinburgh and online tutor/dissertation supervisor on the MSc in Digital Education programme. She has worked as an independent digital education consultant across all levels of education from primary to higher education. Over the course of the COVID-19 lockdowns in 2020–2021, she supported a small multi-academy trust in the Midlands, which comprised twelve primary schools. Her research interests include sociomaterial approaches to boredom and engagement in formal learning, technology, digital gaming, and the use of Twitter as a learning environment.

Chris Forde is Professor of Employment Studies in the Centre for Employment Relations Innovation and Change (CERIC) at Leeds University Business School. His research explores the changing nature of work and the consequences of changes for workers. He has interests in migration, restructuring, temporary and 'gig' or platform work, and well-being at work. He is currently Deputy Director of the ESRC Digital Futures at Work Research Centre, and Co-Director of CERIC.

Jonathan Glazzard is a Professor whose research focuses on mental health, well-being, and inclusion in education. He is a qualitative researcher and uses a broad range of approaches, including narrative methodology, visual/participatory methods, and more traditional interviews and focus groups. Jonathan's recent projects include exploration of head teacher resilience, teacher and child mental health, and the experiences of teachers who identify as LGBTQ+. Jonathan is a co-convenor of the British Educational Research Association Special Interest Group, Mental Health and Well-being in Education. He is also a member of the Excellence in International Transitions Research, which is led by Professor Divya Jindal-Snape. Jonathan is deeply committed to research that advances social justice. He has published widely on aspects of inclusion and social justice for marginalised groups and individuals, and he is deeply committed to research that improves the lives of individuals and research-informed teaching.

Judith Hanks is Associate Professor of Language Education at the School of Education, University of Leeds. Her research encompasses fully inclusive practitioner research (specifically Exploratory Practice) encouraging learners and teachers around the world to actively puzzle about their pedagogy, thus playing with researcher/learner/teacher identities and heightening engagement. A teacher, researcher, and teacher educator, she is interested in learner/teacher agency, intercultural issues in applied linguistics and language education, and issues of quality of life and well-being in educational settings. She is currently Chair of the cross-Faculty Research Ethics Committee for Business, Environment and Social Sciences.

Michelle A. Honeyford is an Associate Professor in Language and Literacy in the Faculty of Education at the University of Manitoba. Her research in language and literacies is deeply enmeshed in collaborative pedagogical inquiries committed to social justice, equity, diversity, and anti-oppressive practices in curriculum, teaching, and learning. Her work draws upon sociomaterial, transcultural, decolonial, multimodal, and critical theories, with current projects in areas of post-qualitative sociomaterial practitioner inquiry methodologies, place-writing, and assessment. Michelle is a co-founding director of the Manitoba Writing Project and is passionate about her work with teacher candidates designing innovative, interest-driven afterschool programmes for middle and high school students.

Carol Hordatt Gentles is a Senior Lecturer at the School of Education, UWI. Mona. She is a teacher education and teacher development specialist whose research focuses on the ideologies that inform the practice of teacher education with respect to pedagogical change, inclusion, critical pedagogy, ESD, preparation of teacher educators, and teacher professional development.

She is Chief Editor for the Caribbean Journal of Education and programme coordinator for the Masters in Teacher Education and Teacher Development offered by the School of Education at The UWI. Mona. She also currently serves as President of the International Council on Education for Teaching.

Kamilah Hylton is a Fulbright scholar from Jamaica who holds a PhD in environmental science from NJIT/Rutgers in New Jersey, USA. She also holds a postgraduate diploma in education from the University of Technology, Jamaica, and has almost 15 years of experience in higher education administration. Her research interests include STEM education and the leadership and management of sports education. She is currently the Dean of the Faculty of Science and Sport at Utech, Jamaica.

Kadia Hylton-Fraser is a Fulbright scholar from Jamaica who holds a doctorate in educational leadership from Lehigh University in Pennsylvania, USA, with over 20 years of classroom experience. Her research interests cover educational leadership, social justice leadership, and principal preparation. She is currently a member of council and the immediate past president of the Institute for Educational Administration and Leadership–Jamaica.

Zoyah Kinkead-Clark is a Senior Lecturer, researcher in Early Childhood Education, and Coordinator of the Graduate Studies Unit in the School of Education at The UWI, Mona. She also serves as the Manager of the Dudley Grant Early Childhood Resource Centre, which among other goals, provides professional development for early childhood teachers across the island of Jamaica and the wider Caribbean. Zoyah is engaged in a number of research initiatives in areas germane to early childhood development. Some of these initiatives include early childhood teacher education, parenting in the early years, and exploring how student transitions from pre-primary to primary school can be more readily supported (especially for children from low-resource communities and homes).

Linda Laidlaw is a Professor working on the area of early literacy in Language and Literacy Education at the University of Alberta. Formerly a classroom teacher, her research focuses on digital and mobile technologies in primary education, diversity, and the relationships between children's digital practices at home and their experiences at school. Her latest projects, funded by the Social Sciences and Humanities Research Council of Canada, working with teachers, parents, and children, investigates new pedagogical frames and strategies for literacy education in a changing world. In her own teaching and research, the COVID 19 pandemic has required her to rethink her own instructional methods and her research methodologies.

Marilyn Leask is a Professor with 40 years of experience in teaching and research. Her special research interests are teacher development and the use of digital technologies to support teaching and learning. In 1984, her classroom was connected via an early form of Internet with other schools. With others, she established the Education Futures Collaboration charity, which coordinates the creation of the freely available MESHGuide research summaries for teachers (www.meshguides.org), which are used in over 200 countries.

Katy Marsh-Davies PhD, SFHEA, is a management scholar with an interest in working lives, particularly professional identities and gender in neoliberal working contexts. She is currently a Senior Lecturer of Human Resource Management & Organisational Behaviour at Sheffield Hallam University, UK, and the conference track Co-Chair for the Identity track at the British Academy of Management. Her recent work on teachers during COVID led to publications, in Schools Week and The Conversation, and a keen interest in menopause and work. She has previously published in Gender, Work & Organisation and Employee Relations, written book chapters, and delivered numerous conference papers.

Rachel Mathieson is a teacher and educational researcher with a particular interest in teachers' experiences in the workplace. As Research Fellow in the School of Education, University of Leeds, and now a Visiting Research Fellow at the Leeds University Business School, she has worked on a number of projects investigating teacher well-being and related issues of recruitment and retention, as well as matters of post-16 education policy. Rachel is currently teaching Music and Modern Foreign Languages in a secondary school in West Yorkshire and is a Lead Evaluator for post-16 programmes at the National Centre for Excellence in the Teaching of Mathematics.

Benjamin Luke Moorhouse Ed.D, FHEA, is an Assistant Professor of English Language Education in the Department of Education Studies at Hong Kong Baptist University. He received his Doctorate of Education from the University of Exeter, UK. His research focuses on the lived experiences and competence of teachers, teaching young language learners, and the role of technology in language teaching and learning. His recent research has been published in journals such as *Educational Studies*, *Journal of Education for Teaching*, *Studying Teacher Education*, and *The Asia-Pacific Journal of Teacher Education*. He has authored three monographs, including Teaching abroad during initial teacher education (Springer, 2022).

Jessica Neudorf-Wiebe is a recent Bachelor of Education graduate who specialises in early years education and child development. She thrives in learning about the world around her by approaching her experiences with the art of curiosity. As a lifelong learner, collaboration and creativity drive her inquiries alongside her students.

Kristina Potočnik is Chair of Organisational Behaviour at the University of Edinburgh Business School. Her research interests cover occupational health and well-being, primarily focusing on healthy ageing in the workplace, as well as organisational resilience. She has published her work in different journals, including *Organization Science*, *Journal of Management*, *Journal of Vocational Behavior*, *Journal of Occupational and Organizational Psychology*, *International Journal of Management Reviews*, and *British Journal of Management*.

Marg Rogers is a Senior Lecturer in the Early Childhood Education team within the School of Education at the University of New England. Marg researches military families and professionalism in early childhood education and care. She is a Postdoctoral Fellow with the Manna Institute.

Sandra Schamroth Abrams Ph.D., is Professor of Adolescent Education and Director of the Ph.D. programme in Curriculum and Instruction at St. John's University, N.Y. Her research focuses on layered meaning making across digital and nondigital spaces. Abrams has published (or has in press) more than 85 scholarly works, and she has delivered more than 100 research presentations. Abrams is the recipient of national and international awards for her research and scholarship, including the St. John's University Excellence in Teaching and Scholarship Award and the United States Distance Learning Association Quality Paper Award for her co-authored article, Gamification and Accessibility. Abrams serves on multiple editorial boards and is an Associate Editor for the *International Journal of Multiple Research Approaches* and a founding co-editor of the Gaming Ecologies and Pedagogies book series.

Margaret Sims is a professor in Early Childhood Education and Care and has worked in the areas of family support and disabilities for many years. She researches in the areas of professionalism and the impacts of neoliberal policies in early childhood and higher education, families, disabilities, social justice, and families from culturally and linguistically diverse backgrounds. She is an Honorary Professor at Macquarie University.

Belinda Steffan is a Research Fellow at the University of Edinburgh Business School. Her research interests include how experiences of gendered ageing, age-related bias at work, and the appearance of bodily ageing influence continued labour force participation. She is particularly interested in the individual and individual differences within the organisational context of work. Her current research focus is the psychology of women's health at work, specifically menopause. Belinda has published her work in Human Relations and Gender, Work and Organization.

My C. Tiet Ed.D, is a Lecturer in the Faculty of Education (Teacher Education & Learning Leadership Unit) at The University of Hong Kong. She has taught in the USA and Hong Kong with extensive experience in the primary grades. Her research and passion focus on teacher education, reflective practices, and English language teaching and learning (curriculum design, assessment, literacy approaches, and methodologies). She is currently teaching undergraduate and postgraduate courses and is involved in supporting teachers in classrooms. She is particularly interested in the theory–practice integration and professional development for novice as well as experienced teachers.

Suzanna So Har Wong is a former early childhood educator now working as an Adjunct Professor and Assistant Lecturer of Language and Literacy Education at the University of Alberta. Her research focuses on young children's literacy practices at home and in school. Her current research project, *A longitudinal study of children's multiliteracy practices in 'out-of-school' settings*, focuses on children's literacy engagements in- and out-of-school environments and examines children's perspectives on these literacy practices. She has also been focusing during the pandemic on her work with pre-service teachers, who are learning how to rethink pedagogies for their own learning as well as their teaching in the future, using online approaches.

Mark Williams is a parent. He is also a former teacher and school governor. He has first-hand experience of the Special Educational Needs and Disabilities system in England.

Joan Woodhouse is Associate Professor and Co-Director of Research and Enterprise in the School of Education at the University of Leicester, UK. She was a secondary school teacher in the English Midlands for almost twenty years before becoming an Initial Teacher Educator at the universities of Canterbury Christ Church, Nottingham, and Leicester. She currently teaches on Master's programmes and supervises Master's and doctoral students. Her main research focus is on teachers' lives, aspirations, and careers. Her work has focused on the experiences and perceptions of women teachers and headteachers, student teachers, early career teachers, older teachers, and student teacher mothers.

FOREWORD

Jonathan Glazzard

The chapters of this book present research from across a wide range of global contexts, and this is one of the book's key strengths, along with several others. Each chapter is well-written using an accessible writing style. The authors have taken great care to theorise the content of their chapters, and rather than presenting the COVID-19 pandemic as a tragic event, there is a strong uplifting feel to the book. The book strongly focuses on reimagining education in a post-pandemic world. Although the authors present the adverse effects of the pandemic, there is a strong emphasis on what we have learned from educators' responses to it and the implications of this professional learning for teaching, leadership, and teacher development.

I found myself becoming absorbed in the narratives of the participants in the various research projects. The participant quotes and reflections demonstrated not only the adverse impacts of the pandemic but also the empowering effects of it. Some key cross-cutting themes emerge from the chapters. These include, but are not limited to, the following: the need for bold and empathetic leadership, the need to involve teachers in the process of change and share power with students (see Chapter 13), the need for teacher education to emphasise the core principles of teaching (see Chapter 12), and the need for flexible ways of working and teaching. A consistent approach to the presentation of chapters supported me to navigate the book, and the final chapter presents an effective synthesis of the key messages from across all chapters.

The book is an important contribution to knowledge. The first chapter sets out the educational context clearly. Education continues to operate within a quasi-market which has resulted in the prioritisation of commercialisation, an evidence-based discourse which privileges large-scale quantitative research and inequalities in the workforce. Prescriptive frameworks and the emphasis on datafication have resulted in increased burnout and high rates of teacher attrition. One of the strengths of this book is how it privileges the voices of teachers, teacher educators, and parent-teachers. The research studies that are presented in the chapters are largely qualitative (although not exclusively), and the findings are interesting and rich and have transferability. It is strikingly clear from reading the book that the impacts of the global COVID-19 pandemic were common across the different global contexts that the chapters explore. One theme that strongly emerged was that educators developed flexibility and demonstrated resilience as they negotiated their professional and personal responsibilities.

In Chapter 2, on part-time women teachers, Brown calls for more bold and empathetic leadership to support women teachers who need to work flexibility to balance their professional and personal commitments. Chapter 10 argues the need for social justice leadership across education, and the identification of these approaches to leadership invites further research into the principles and practices associated with these types of leadership. Similar themes also emerge in Chapter 3, although this chapter explores the needs of student teacher mothers in higher education. Higher education has given insufficient attention to the needs of this group of students, and the pandemic highlighted the challenges they faced more acutely perhaps than previously. Again, similar themes emerge in Chapter 4 which explores teachers' experiences of teaching during the menopause.

The pandemic demonstrated how teachers needed to return to the core essentials of teaching. These include a pedagogy of care which gives priority to children's holistic development. In Chapter 5, the authors illustrate how this gave teachers a new sense of determination to remain in the profession, and Chapter 8 also draws out the link between a pedagogy of care and student and teacher well-being. Chapters 7 and 9 explore the implications of the COVID-19 pandemic for early childhood teachers and leaders. They call for improved recognition and status given to the early childhood education sector, and Chapter 7 makes several recommendations which will improve the working conditions of early childhood educators.

The pandemic made it necessary for educators across all sectors of education to work more creatively, and Chapter 6 calls for academic teachers working within higher education contexts to acknowledge their creativity and resilience. I thoroughly enjoyed the style of writing in Chapter 11. It was accessible, personal, and took the reader through a professional journey of curriculum development. Key messages that are emphasised in the book are that disruption can present opportunities for innovation and change (see Chapter 15) and that the traditional classroom can be reimagined from being a physical and bounded space to allow official and unofficial teaching spaces to co-exist (see Chapter 14). The benefit of online learning presents new and existing learning opportunities (see Chapter 16), and the pandemic provides an opportunity to pause, reflect, and think differently about education.

The final chapter presents several calls for action, notably the need to develop and nurture teachers' professional autonomy and to cultivate cultures of care and empathy. Within a neoliberal marketised education system, these priorities have been arguably disregarded in recent years. In many countries, education policies have emphasised a culture of competition, and high academic achievement has been used as a proxy of a successful education system. At the same time, we have witnessed, globally, high rates of teacher attrition, poor teacher mental health, low job satisfaction, and burnout. Prescriptive policy frameworks have reduced teachers' professional autonomy, and the emphasis on a knowledge-based curriculum in some countries has reduced opportunities for rich, meaningful, and memorable learning experiences. This book is both uplifting and empowering. It provides educators with an opportunity to return to the core principles of teaching, and it calls for the voices of teachers to be prominent in key policy decisions. The pandemic demonstrated that teachers were resilient and adaptable agents of change. They focused on a pedagogy of care, and relationships between schools and communities were strengthened. Teachers were trusted to make judgements about the achievement of their students, rather than students being subjected to high-stakes examinations. This book calls for the education sector to pause, reflect, and consider what was learned during the pandemic and nudges policy makers, school leaders, and teachers to think differently, rather than returning to an education system that reflects pre-pandemic times. It is an excellent piece of scholarship which privileges the voices of practitioners from across the globe. I commend the authors and the editors for producing a text which makes a significant contribution to the body of knowledge.

Professor Jonathan Glazzard, Head of Department and Professor of Teacher Education, Faculty of Education, Edge Hill University, UK.

Introduction

1
TEACHERS AND TEACHING POST-COVID

Katy Marsh-Davies and Cathy Burnett

Introduction

Joanne: I think lockdown showed how important teaching is and how adaptable we are as a profession and how hard we work but also how wide our remit is, that it isn't just the learning in the classroom, it's the teachers that took lunch packs round to people and free school meals and all the safeguarding stuff that we did as a profession. Actually, it's wider than just the stuff in the classroom.

Joe: I know it's awful to talk about such a horrible time as being – well, I wouldn't have wanted to miss it, in some ways, to have missed the experience of being part of it and being involved with it and how much I've learnt about myself as a teacher, to how flexible and adaptable it's possible to be [...]. It's been just the most unique experience really to be teaching during COVID but also it's been a real privilege for me to be in a position of, I feel, making a difference in those children's lives. Being able to maintain those relationships, maintain that routine. So, yeah. For me, being a teacher, it's all been about connections, and communications, and empathy with emotions and feelings that people have been experiencing.

Helen: When I spoke to the Head [teacher] and I said that the reason I needed to care for my mum is she had a motor neurone virus, oh, maybe 20 years ago but it left her severely immunocompromised. My dad's over 70, diabetic and asthmatic so they needed a lot of support. They couldn't manage their house on their own, they're in a three-storey house and obviously when they had a cleaner coming in, when they had me and my brother that helped a lot, they were fine, but as soon as we hit lockdown they couldn't do that [...]. My Head [teacher] didn't seem to be taking any of it on board [...]. It still bothers me now. It still upsets me hugely and I still feel very resentful and this is why I think I definitely need to go... I can't let that resentment go... I think if I'd been more 'difficult' and said ... "I have dependents, my parents need me", I wonder whether they'd have just sucked it up but of course being an adult and having a mortgage and having a child I couldn't take the risk.

Extracts from Interviews with UK Teachers, 2020

At the time of writing (February 2023), the first teacher strikes for almost seven years have taken place in England. And yet only a few years before, in March 2020, teachers in almost all countries were embarking on an unprecedented attempt to maintain educational provision while their inhabitants stayed home. The COVID-19 pandemic halted formal school/campus-based teaching almost everywhere, at least for short periods, impacting 1.5 billion students – over 98% – across the world (UNESCO, 2022a). Education became primarily a remote practice due to the social distancing required to avoid the spread of the virus with digital technologies employed to teach online. While approaches varied across nations, many teachers had to combine teaching-at-a-distance with face-to-face teaching for some learners. In doing so, they had to find ways of maintaining the meaningful relationships and interactions so central to learning while managing social distancing, mask-wearing and sanitisation and risking infection themselves.

This crisis did much to increase the awareness of and respect for the work of teachers. Not only did parents and carers gain insights into the challenges of supporting learning but, as 'lockdowns' led to social isolation for many families, teachers facilitated vital sources of practical and emotional support (Borup et al., 2020). They worked to ensure that children could continue to learn and in many cases that their parents could continue to work. Many teachers, like Joanne above, also went from house to house to deliver vital supplies such as books, digital devices and meals. And teachers did all of this while also caring for their own families and grappling with their own experiences of disruption, fear, illness and bereavement. Helen, featured above, spent the first six weeks of lockdown living with and caring for her elderly parents, during which time she was apart from her young son. The inflexibility of her school during this period led to her questioning her future as a teacher (for a fuller analysis of this case, see Marsh-Davies & Burnett, 2021).

As academics with a longstanding involvement in working lives (Katy) and education (Cathy), we shared an interest in what all of this meant for teachers. Katy's doctoral research explored home-based work, and she was keen to understand how enforced home-working would be experienced across professions but in particular by teachers – having heard of the struggles of friends and family members who are teachers as well as observing her own child's educators via Zoom lessons. Cathy is an ex-primary teacher who has worked in a variety of educational contexts including initial teacher education. Her research often involves working closely with teachers to reflect on their experiences and collaborate to advocate for innovation in educational policy and practice.

In Spring 2020, we collaborated for the first time (virtually of course) and managed to gain a small grant from our institution[1] to allow us to conduct 14 interviews with UK teachers about their experiences of teaching during the pandemic (ibid). We invited them to share photos of their new working lives and locations and reflect on what it meant to be a teacher teaching from home during the crisis. We were interested in how the participants constructed their teacher identities and navigated their changing and often conflicting roles within the physical spaces of their homes and the practical and emotional work this necessitated of them.

The interview extracts that open this chapter were generated through this project. Joanne and Joe capture a sense of professional pride about teaching during the pandemic. For them, the pandemic experience seemed to animate – or perhaps re-awaken – a sense of fulfilment and self-respect. This however was not the whole story. Helen describes the incompatibility of her caring responsibilities with expectations of her as a teacher and the impossible tensions between her working life and family commitments. And her experience was echoed by other teachers who also told of anxieties associated with teaching at this time, anxieties that were often exacerbated by concerns for their families. As the chapters of this book explore, while many teachers responded to the COVID-19 outbreak with great ingenuity and resilience (see, for example, Chapters 6 and 15), many also faced significant struggles, leading to detrimental impacts on their well-being (see Chapter 5). The pandemic experience was important therefore not only in shedding light on the experience and achievements of teachers in unprecedented times but also in highlighting the complexity of teaching *at any time* and the tensions that many teachers were *already* experiencing between professional and personal commitments, tensions intensified by inflexible hours during the school day, workloads that stretch into evenings, weekends and holidays and difficulties in taking leave during term-time.

In this book, we explore the impacts of the pandemic on teachers by considering not just their professional practice but also their lives and 'landscapes' (Reynolds, 1996). There is a substantial body of work that considers the implications of personal beliefs and experiences for teaching (e.g. Mansour, 2009; Kagan, 1992) and that explores the emotional impact of teaching on teachers' well-being (e.g. Fried, 2011; Yin, 2016). Teachers' experience of teaching and their personal experience of their working lives however have tended to be addressed separately (Fayed & Cummings, 2021). In this book, we juxtapose insights into teachers' lives within and beyond teaching itself in order to examine the working lives of teachers in the round.

The chapters that follow feature research from across the Caribbean and from Australia, Canada, Hong Kong, the United States of America and the United Kingdom and focus on teachers at various stages of their career and working in different phases – in early childhood care and education (ECCE), in schools and in universities. Written from a variety of standpoints, they combine to account for the myriad roles that teachers play: as pedagogues, carers, workers, colleagues, leaders, innovators, administrators and managers. They also recognise the relationships between being a teacher and teachers' lives beyond teaching – their families, their commitments and interests, and their health and well-being. Together these chapters provide rich contemporary records of teachers' working lives that illuminate the diverse ways that the complexity of teaching work is entangled in the emotional, relational and embodied nature of teachers' everyday lives.

Beyond COVID

Before going further, we want to say a little about our use of the term 'post-COVID' in the title of this book and chapter. We recognise that the virus has not been eradicated, and so 'post' might in some ways seem inappropriate. At the time of writing, the World Health Organisation (2023) continues to talk in terms of a pandemic, and through the course of writing this book, new waves and variants have emerged. We use the term 'post-COVID' therefore in two ways.

Firstly, we use it to frame a period of time – specifically the period since the initial outbreak of COVID-19, from the earliest and most severe impacts through the various waves of infection and to the gradual easing of restrictions and concerns. As we write, we reflect that we have lived with the consequences of a coronavirus pandemic for over three years. These will be engrained in the life experience of all those studying, practising and leading teaching. This timeframe allows us to explore the impacts on teachers' lives and practice, to highlight where changes have taken place and where they have not, where COVID has spurred opportunity and innovation and where it has been impeding or retrogressive.

Secondly, we use 'post-COVID' as a provocation for change. Much has been written about the pandemic as a reflexive moment, an opportunity to rethink established ways of operating in many aspects of our lives. Roy (2020), for example, provides an evocative metaphor of the pandemic as a 'portal', while Arnove (2020, p. 43) contends 'it is a pathway that leads to a reconfigured future, one that must be different from the world we previously knew'. Within education, there are some signs that the pandemic experience has generated renewed ideas about how teaching can and should be practised (Fayed & Cummings, 2021). And the chapters of this book demonstrate how much teachers have to offer to such a project. They tell of what teachers learned and reflected upon as they adapted to changing circumstances, as they 'figured out' how to teach (see Chapter 8), adopted 'new ways of working' (Chapter 6) and thought 'outside the box' (Chapter 16). However, at the time of writing, memories of the pandemic experience seem to be fading fast amidst intensifying concerns about economic and national security. In the sphere of education, policymakers have focused primarily on the detrimental impacts of COVID (e.g. Chaturvedi et al., 2021). Rather than spurring debate, recognising teachers' innovations and involving teachers in shaping new educational futures, responses have tended to re-entrench existing approaches to pedagogy and schooling in the drive to recoup 'lost learning'.[2] As we explore in the next section, however, such approaches are ripe for change.

Challenges for teachers and teaching

Education systems, policies and practices differ across the world, and different societies revere and reward their teachers differently (Price & Weatherby, 2018). Nevertheless, recent years have seen the increasing effects of the neoliberal agenda on educational provision in many jurisdictions (for a helpful discussion around those impacted, and a few notable exceptions, see Hill & Kumar, 2009). Gilbert (2021) describes neoliberalism as 'a dominant ideological and discursive project that promotes deregulation, the privatization of the public sector, the eradication of unions and the welfare state, and the extension of market principles into all areas of life' (p. 444). In the context of neoliberalism, students and parents are positioned as consumers as market-driven criteria are mobilised and 'choice, competition, accountability, efficiency' (Nóvoa & Alvim, 2020, p. 37) are the watchwords for systems that claim to be effective through combining high accountability with low regulation.

While it is beyond the scope of this chapter to track the advance of the neoliberal agenda in education,[3] suffice it to say that its effects are widespread. They play out in a series of mutually reinforcing developments that include:

- prescriptive frameworks for teacher learning that undermine professional agency (e.g. Trelford, 2021);
- the 'datafication' of schooling as standardised test scores are leveraged for school improvement, and accountability (Bradbury & Roberts-Holmes, 2017);

- shifts from school governance by local authorities to the quasi-marketisation of schooling through movements such as academisation in England and Charter Schools in the USA (Hilton, 2019);
- the increasing influence of independent consultants and commercial organisations in leading schools, educational innovation and the production of educational resources and interventions (Gunter, Hall & Mills, 2015);
- an evidence-based education movement which rests on randomised controlled trials as the key source of evidence (Biesta, 2016);
- state-funded banks of teaching plans and resources ostensibly designed to save teachers time but which work in effect to marginalise teacher judgement (e.g. Oak Academy in England – https://www.thenational.academy/).

These trends have been the subject of considerable critique for over two decades, not least for perpetuating a narrowly conceived educational provision and exacerbating inequities for learners (Hayes et al., 2017). Their impact on teachers has also been well documented, from Ball's (2003) seminal work on the 'terrors of performativity' through to more recent research exploring the effects of a data-driven system on teachers' lives and work (Bradbury and Roberts-Holmes, 2017; Lewis & Holloway, 2019). Such developments have contributed to a narrow technicist view of teachers that underplays the complexities of teaching and marginalises professional agency (Priestley et al., 2016). They have also led to developments that undermine teacher professionalism overtly. Gilbert (2021), for example, presents an illuminating case study of North Carolina schools which insist on the use of a virtual time stamp of teachers' work, requiring them to 'clock on' and 'clock off' using software provided by a privately owned profit-making company.

Despite all of this, the work of teachers continues to be complex and teachers may exercise considerable professional agency in interpreting, contextualising and supplementing directives about curriculum, pedagogy and other aspects of their professional lives (Burnett, Merchant & Guest, 2021; Schaefer & Clandinin, 2019). However, as professional frameworks position teaching as primarily a technical activity, such subtle work becomes less visible. It is also likely to be diffused as strong accountability cultures channel energy towards measurable outcomes rather than the responsive and relational work of teaching (Lewis & Holloway, 2019). As such, many teachers find themselves at odds with the system in which they work, and it is perhaps unsurprising that there is a global recruitment and retention crisis in teaching (UNESCO, 2022b).

Resourcing issues have exacerbated post-pandemic in the sector in many countries, in a context where there were already significant recruitment and retention challenges. In England, for example, a third of teachers who qualified in the last decade have left the profession, according to Walker's (2023) analysis of Department for Education data. Worth & Faulkner-Ellis (2022) suggest that despite teacher retention rates improving substantially in England in 2020 due to economic uncertainty and lockdowns, they then decreased towards pre-pandemic levels in 2021. The overview for the British 'Teacher Recruitment and Retention Conference' (2023) suggests that 'a lack of competitive pay, unmanageable workloads and poor mental health are the leading reasons behind this trend'. As previously mentioned, unrest within the profession has led to strikes by school teachers, as well as university lecturers in the UK, and a telling article by Whittaker (2023) stresses that there might have been additional industrial action if teachers did not consider themselves already too poor to strike, i.e. unable to stretch to cover their basic living costs if losing even a day's pay.

This situation is further exacerbated due to inequalities within the teacher workforce. The UK reflects most nations in the gender composition of teaching and like most nations (WomenEd, 2023) has a gender pay gap. School workforce statistics (Education Statistics Service, 2021) show that in England, the early years workforce is almost exclusively female; primary schools are female-dominated; and secondary settings contain more female than male teachers. Only in higher education are males (very slightly) more prevalent in the teaching workforce (HESA, 2021). NAHT (the Union representing School Leaders in England, Wales and Northern Ireland) reported in 2021 that 'males earned on average 2.4% more at classroom teacher level, but 11.3% more (on average) than women head teachers'. NAHT (ibid) also reflect that there are pay and leadership gaps in relation to other characteristics such as race and sexuality, though issues may be less well documented due to underreporting which has been attributed to historical inequalities within the sector.

Ferjola & Hopkins (2013) discuss the workplace experiences of teachers in Australia. They suggest that schools have traditionally been 'hostile environments' for those who are lesbian and gay. Griffin & Tackie (2017, p. 2) consider racial inequalities in the US context, reporting that

> while school systems have made significant progress in recruiting and hiring more teachers of color [sic], they have done little to keep them in the classroom over time. Indeed, teachers of color [sic] tend to exit the profession at higher rates than other teachers.

It is clear that the intersections of gender, sexuality and race (as well as other attributes) with teacher identity can compound struggles faced by teachers, as well as presenting notable differences in experience (as can be seen in Atay's chapter, later in this book).

'Post-COVID research' – openings and gaps

The chapters in this book look to the future, drawing on research largely conducted during the pandemic,[4] to propose shifts in educational provision and in teachers' working conditions. Before outlining the scope and range of their contributions, we note that research is never a neutral endeavour but is always constrained and enabled by particular social and material conditions. It is therefore worth reflecting on the kinds of research that were possible (or not) during lockdowns and how these constrained and enabled certain *kinds* of insights about teaching. In what follows, we explore some reasons why the pandemic period may have offered particularly rich opportunities for investigating teachers' perspectives on their working lives. Many of the points we make here are rather speculative but are worth noting as they may go some way to explaining the distinctive contributions of the chapters that follow.

One of the effects of lockdowns was that academics around the world, finding themselves confined to their homes, at last found time for research and writing. Of course, this was not the case for all, particularly for those with young families or other caring commitments. But for many lockdowns did make time for research, and research provided a sense of purpose in uncertain times. From a practical perspective, educational researchers had to work out how to 'do research' while unable to visit schools or other settings or to meet with learners or teachers. Methods involving observation or 'sitting alongside' individuals or groups were out of the question, and researchers also had to ensure that research did not generate additional burdens for professionals or learners in those difficult times. This meant that plans for ongoing projects had to be adapted (e.g. see Laidlaw and Wong's chapter) and choices of methods for new projects were limited to those that were feasible to conduct online such as questionnaires (e.g. Hordatt Gentles, Leask & Williams), interviews and focus groups often using video conferencing software (e.g. Cameron & Abrams), autoethnography, reflective and experimental writing (e.g. Honeyford, Collins-Kramble & Neudorf-Wiebe), documentary analysis (e.g. Kinkead-Clarke & Abdul-Majied) and observation of online activity (e.g. Dunnett).

Given the limited range of available methods, it is perhaps unsurprising that so many educational researchers spent time eliciting the perspectives of teachers. There may also have been subtler reasons why this period was particularly fruitful in generating insights into teachers' lives. Research took place at a time when it was commonplace to reference mental or physical health in any kind of communication and to sign off emails and phone calls with the ubiquitous 'stay safe'. Teachers' and researchers' shared feelings of insecurity and uncertainty may have generated an intimacy and intensity that encouraged reflection, an intimacy heightened further as Zoom calls opened windows into one another's homes and family lives (Gourlay et al., 2021). It is possible that teachers' heightened sensitivity to mental and physical well-being led them to reflect deeply on their feelings about teaching and on their professional role in supporting the well-being of those they taught and worked alongside. It is also possible that teachers felt more inclined to talk as they themselves had more time to reflect and had much to say. As the strangeness of pandemic life threw teaching into sharp relief, it prompted reflexivity and critical reflection not just on what was happening as the pandemic unfolded but on teaching and teachers' lives more generally.

While recognising the important contribution that this book's chapters make to debates about teaching post-COVID, it is important to acknowledge that many voices are absent.[5] Teachers working in different countries, conditions and contexts will have had diverse experiences, and the perspectives featured here are inevitably selective. While many teachers talked with apparent candour about their experiences, their testimonies are inevitably shaped by the frameworks researchers provided and by teachers' perceptions of what they felt was *appropriate* to share. Also, by choosing to foreground teachers' perspectives, we leave out the voices of others. These include the children, young people and adults they taught and their families who may well have had very different perspectives on education post-COVID, perspectives with great potential to feed into frameworks for teaching in important ways (e.g. Chamberlain et al., 2021; Lee & Wenham, 2021; Children's Parliament, 2020). Despite these caveats, these chapters do, we suggest, provide nuanced insights into the complexity of teaching and being a teacher that offer much to debates about what teaching is and should be post-COVID.

Navigating this book

In curating this volume, we had initially planned to sort chapters into sections that disaggregated the work of teachers and teaching. We allocated chapters to sub-sections focused on: working lives, professional identity, teaching and learning and so on. Having reviewed the chapters, we found them hard to categorise in this way as so many authors presented teaching as a messy assemblage of commitments, values, politics, beliefs and feelings that spill *between* professional and personal lives. We realised that our initial attempts at categorisation reinforced the very notion we hoped to challenge – that different dimensions of teachers' lives should be understood and addressed as separate phenomena. We decided therefore to organise differently, mixing chapters that addressed pedagogy and professional commitments with those that addressed aspects of teachers' working and personal lives. We refer to these as *Priorities*, *Alliances* and *Re-imaginings*.

Priorities

As explored above, the pandemic experience was important in shedding light on the achievements of teachers and the complexity of teaching and in highlighting the tensions that many teachers experience between professional and personal commitments due to heavy workloads and inflexible working conditions. For many, it was a time when their commitment to learners and their families was reinforced as they gained new insights into the lives of the children they taught. Many of the chapters speak of reaffirmations of long-held beliefs, of reinvigorated commitments and of renewed enthusiasm for the work of teaching. At the same time, they attest to struggle, to managing the complex demands of personal and professional lives and to dissonance between deeply held beliefs about what matters and the demands of educational systems. Given all of this, the pandemic provided an impetus for interrogating priorities and, for some, time to revisit what mattered to them within and beyond their teaching role. In this section, we explore how the pandemic experience surfaced professional and personal priorities for teachers that were often at odds with the workings of educational systems.

Working part-time is often considered to be effective in providing work–life balance and enhanced well-being (see the review by Shiri et al., 2022), but Brown's chapter tells a different story as she warns that, for many of the women who did so in her research, the result was not so positive. The part-time workers she interviewed in England were regarded as less committed and professional, and their career progression was hindered. They struggled with a lack of clear boundaries and the stress of competing priorities. The pandemic provided an opportunity to experiment with new working practices – with many teaching from home for the first time, resulting in, not only a change in location, but also adaptations to the temporal regimes of their professional, and personal, roles. While the option of working fixed part-time hours was unsatisfactory for some, the new forms of flexibility afforded by the pandemic proved effective and popular, with many teachers not wishing to return to 'business as usual' (Marsh-Davies & Burnett, 2021). Perna (2022, n.p.) states that 'education has traditionally been considered a field where flexibility is just not possible', but the enforced online and hybrid approaches adopted during lockdowns have shown that some flexibility can generate successful learning. He proclaims that 'flexibility is the future of education' and proposes that it is another valuable approach to recruiting and retaining teachers.

We see the effects of increased flexibility in Woodhouse's chapter, also from England, which tells of the experiences of student teachers who are also mothers. Her sample consisted of those who embarked on initial teacher education before the COVID-19 pandemic yet completed the second half of their course during the 2020 lockdown. She describes how the lockdown period made it more possible for mothers to manage their multiple life roles and alleviated the necessity to juggle complex childcare interventions. Reflecting on her own experience as a teacher educator during the pandemic, she concludes 'the COVID-19 experience of teaching and preparing teachers has been challenging. Yet, it has opened up new possibilities, as we have become more aware of alternative ways of working that offer the potential to enrich students' experiences in lasting and meaningful ways'.

However, while such shifts may have happened at the local level, educational systems often remained obdurate. Kinkead-Clarke and Abdul-Majied call for a 'paradigm shift' in how ECCE teachers are valued, supported and renumerated. They describe how COVID impacted efforts to give professional status and improve pay and working conditions for ECCE teachers in the Caribbean. Hoped for improvements in pay and working conditions that would better reflect levels of qualification and the value of ECCE teachers' work did not materialise and professional and personal vulnerability linked to unstable and poor working conditions meant that some ECCE teachers were forced to seek alternative employment. This account reflects the low priority given to ECCE by policymakers in many jurisdictions, evident in low levels of funding and inadequate support for professionalisation. As with other chapters in this section, we see how professional and personal vulnerability is inextricably linked not just to the health and well-being of teachers but to the possibility of providing empowering and enabling education for all. Kinkead-Clarke and Abdul-Majied conclude with a set of recommendations for measures for ensuring that ECCE achieves the prioritisation it deserves.

Steffan & Potočnik follow up on the broad theme of teacher well-being by focusing on a more specific and often-unreported challenge for many teachers: menopause. Within the feminised teacher workforce, there is an exodus of people in their early fifties (Camden, 2015). The average age of menopause in the UK is 51 (NHS, 2023). This, Steffan & Potocnik propose, is no coincidence and highlights a women's health issue that desperately needs addressing as part of the teacher retention battle. They propose that 'the inflexibility of (pre and post-COVID-19) teaching presents a barrier to women accessing reasonable workplace adjustments to manage their menopause symptoms', which again points to the importance of flexibility for teachers post-COVID. Disappointingly, their participants had low expectations of gaining support from their employers for their well-being during menopause.

For some, a focus on greater flexibility in working conditions was also associated with greater flexibility in how and what to teach, and this in turn had further benefits for teacher well-being. Forde et al. found that some teachers reported improvements as they found respite from performance management, assessment and other energy- and time-consuming activities. Their participants reported that having more flexibility and control in their work became important for managing their well-being. They reveal that 'there were aspects of work during the crisis which enabled teachers to reinvigorate their sense of professionalism and allowed them to work according to the values which brought them into teaching'. This return, for some teachers, to the core principles of teaching contributed to enhanced teacher well-being and, Forde et al. propose, may hold the key to retaining teachers in the profession.

In a similar vein, Coleman, Cain and Campbell explored how the COVID-19 crisis prompted university educators to revisit professional priorities and gave them the time and space to do so. Using digital ethnography, they collected stories of teaching that were often written collaboratively across digital platforms. These stories highlighted various sites for shifting – or perhaps re-articulating – priorities linked to identities, epistemic beliefs, pressures, stress and self-efficacy; and to agility, risk and creativity. Together these stories of online teaching speak to a 'pedagogy of kindness' (Rawle, 2021) that involved navigating challenges around student well-being as they attempted to balance this with self-care. Coleman, Cain and Campbell provide powerful examples of the entanglement of personal and professional lives not least because students were more easily able to view their tutors 'as people who experience similar problems to them'. As well as highlighting the personal dimensions of professional life, they show how a focus on the personal had 'humanizing' effects, forged through empathy between teachers and learners and between teachers and their colleagues, effects that reflected and perhaps re-affirmed priorities marginalised in a datafied educational system.

Alliances

Many of the chapters in this book highlight the role of mutual support and relationships in navigating the pandemic. This is important as one of the effects of neoliberalism in education is to individualise teachers and learners by focusing on measuring progress and professional competence at an individual level (Bradbury & Roberts-Holmes, 2017). In this section, we feature chapters which foreground the role of partnership, collaboration and community in teaching. We use the term 'alliances' to evoke the shared sense of purpose that seemed to be central to so much of the work described and to acknowledge that many teachers faced challenging circumstances which were often exacerbated rather than eased by educational policy and resourcing issues.

Cameron and Abrams draw on interview data to explore how three elementary teachers and their principal in a New York Charter School faced the demands of meeting children's needs from day to day in an unfamiliar and unsettling context. They describe how this experience generated a high level of reflexivity which generated significant professional learning. This involved a considerable amount of flexibility in adapting teaching to the needs of children and families. Specifically, they describe how these educators shifted from an emphasis on the 'grit and grind' of data analysis, detailed forward planning and demonstrable progress to a focus on 'care and flexibility' that was responsive to children's needs and kept children's well-being to the fore – a shift in priorities similar to that described by Coleman, Cain and Campbell. Importantly, they highlight how this reflexive and responsive approach was galvanised by mutual support between colleagues and empathetic leadership that focused on the well-being of both students and staff.

Boyd, Rogers and Sims also highlight the central role of leaders – in their case in early childhood education (ECE) settings in Australia. Like Kinkead-Clarke and Abdul-Majied, they comment on the lack of consideration given to ECE, noting how early childhood practitioners in Australia slipped through the cracks during the pandemic as they were not recognised as essential workers by the government. Many faced financial hardship and their well-being suffered. Boyd et al. note how ECE leaders shielded staff from harm, recognised and valued their work and helped them to navigate difficult circumstances. Given this support, Boyd et al. found, their participants were able to adapt and experiment, finding new ways of working and enhancing their practice during this challenging time.

As well as alliances between colleagues, another aspect of pandemic education was a strengthening of relationships between home and school as parents and teachers became more aware of one another's roles and everyday lives (Moss et al., 2020). Hylton-Fraser and Hylton describe some of the challenges faced by parents and teachers, specifically teachers who are parents, in the context of the Jamaican education system. They note the challenges of juggling professional and familial responsibilities at a time when spaces and times for teaching and parenting merged and access to wider support networks was limited. One key implication for this work is that 'the pandemic has brought into sharper focus the need for parents and teachers to be greater collaborators in their children's learning process.'

Honeyford, Collins-Kramble and Neudorf-Wiebe reflect on their codesign and coteaching of the 'Read/Write/Share Club' – an online writing and book club for young teens in Canada held in the summer of 2020. Central to their work is the collaboration between the three authors. They exchanged experiences, thoughts and feelings through a process of 'stacking stories', which involved sharing and juxtaposing stories of their own experiences of teaching through lockdown. Their chapter is a compelling evocation of the role of community and togetherness in educational contexts, through which educators think not just 'about ourselves as teachers, but about what we are a part of with our students' and through doing so continually reflect on 'what matters most' in educational contexts. Their 'notice, think, wonder and share' rubric is a compelling invitation to think more widely about the purpose, form and impacts of teaching. As such this leads us to our last collection of chapters – 're-imaginings'.

Re-imaginings

As the chapters in the previous two sections illustrate, the stories and experiences featured in this book provide powerful accounts of aspects of teachers' lives that have often been marginalised in neoliberal education systems. They tell of how imperatives to demonstrate progress were to some extent, if not always, replaced by imperatives to attend to mental and physical well-being, to care and relationships and to collective effort and mutual support. In this section, we focus on chapters that offer ways to re-orientate to education through unsettling fundamental assumptions about how education is done and how the work of teachers is positioned.

Some chapters call for major reworkings of educational provision and how the work of teachers is conceived and supported. Moorhouse and Tiet, drawing on their experience as teachers and as teacher educators in Hong Kong, propose a radical revisioning of teacher education given that,

> 'the pandemic, as a destabilizing event, can provide us with important insights into becoming a teacher. First, it has reinforced the notion that 'being' a teacher, as part of a teacher's identity, is a dynamic construct that is unequivocally affected by personal as well as contextual factors (Pennington & Richards, 2016) and one which is continuously evolving and negotiated through experiences with those environmental changes (Sachs, 2005). Second, it has reminded us of the core role teachers ought to play in our communities. Not, just as disseminators of knowledge or assessors of skills, but as carers – someone with whom children within their care can trust and get support from in challenging times'.

Moorhouse and Tiet argue for developing approaches to initial teacher education that foreground the 'personal and contextual factors associated with 'being' a teacher' and build on three key ideas: (1) pedagogy of care (and self-care), (2) pedagogy of autonomy and partnership and (3) pedagogy of reflective practice.

Hordatt Gentles, Leask and Williams draw on the findings of their international research project to describe teachers as drivers of change during the pandemic. They observed a decentralising of power relations in education during the crisis, which some teachers expanded to shift the power dynamics of their (virtual) classrooms, giving more autonomy to learners. In the light of this analysis, they call for a 'democratization' of teaching post-COVID that fully recognises the agency and creativity of teachers.

Other chapters ease into the process of reorientation more gently but reflect similar ambitions. Many of these take digital technology as a starting point, but their implications go far beyond calls for the effective use of digital technologies in schools. Orientating in myriad ways to digital spaces, they foreground the embodied material work of teaching and characterise educational contexts as complex, problematic and ultimately fluid spaces. In doing so, they interrogate the very nature and purpose of education and consequently the role of the teacher.

Dunnett focuses on the ways in which teaching online altered the temporalities and spaces of teaching and required teachers to adopt new systems, language and routines. Dunnett reflects on these to question taken-for-granted classroom practices and teacher expectations in her socio-material analysis of teaching using Microsoft Teams. She notes how online teaching generates hybrid spaces in which physical and on-screen activity are overlayered and mutually entangled. From this perspective, she problematises notions of 'classroom' and 'school' and suggests there is much to learn from hybrid classrooms about what matters in teaching and learning and the kinds of approaches that are supportive to learners, not least through recognising and cultivating permeability between formal and non-formal learning.

Atay also explores the possibilities for recalibrating educational practice through teaching online. Leveraging a perspective as a transnational migrant queer scholar, Atay elegantly problematises the relationship between identity, pedagogy and being a teacher. Presenting stories of online teaching in the USA, Atay notes how the physical classroom can be a magical space for some but oppressive for others and concludes by arguing 'we need to understand how technology and online platforms facilitate learning for some and offer new ways of empowerment for others who are actively teaching in highly oppressive academic structures'. However, Atay's personal account is not just an argument for better more flexible use of technology. It attests to the 'slow violence' (see Aggarwal et al., 2021) of an unequitable, inflexible educational system and highlights the pressing need to attend to persistent and pernicious inadequacies of educational systems in which teachers do not simply act but are acted upon.

Laidlaw and Wong draw on a study of teachers' perspectives on teaching during the pandemic. They organise their analysis of teachers' innovations by drawing on Green's (1988, 2012) work to distinguish between operational-technical, cultural and critical orientations to teaching. Their argument is not so much about the challenges of teaching online – although they certainly speak of those, such as the difficulties of 'reading the room' online – but rather the 'unexpected learning' about teaching and learning more generally. As teachers became better acquainted with digital tools and the skills required to teach online (the operational-technical dimension), they grew in awareness of cultural dimensions of learning such as the need to acknowledge, value and build on children's own experiences and to make space for linguistic diversity. Importantly, their experiences also led them to systems-level critique and a questioning of the rhetoric on 'lost learning' and 'catch-up'. While this dominated debates about education during lockdown, it did not resonate with the needs of the children they taught. Instead, they argued that greater emphasis should be placed on ensuring children had plenty of time to connect with others in the light of the social experiences they missed. These reflections not only led to some feeling they had become 'better teachers' during the pandemic but generated pressing questions for teachers, educators and policymakers that could frame highly productive future discussions about educational priorities.

Final thoughts

As examples of 'post-COVID research', the chapters in this book speak to ongoing debates about teachers' well-being, identities, professional growth and professionalism and how teachers' working lives are managed, organised, celebrated and lived. In all cases, context matters and local and national policies combine with histories, social and cultural matters to inflect experience and conceptualisations of what might and could be possible. Together however these chapters suggest implications for teaching and for teachers' working lives, many of which we return to in the final chapter of this book. These include invitations to rework and rethink partnerships with parents and others, school leadership, pedagogy, more flexible working conditions and repositioning and validating the centrality of care both for teachers and for those they work with. Such recommendations recognise teachers as those with working lives that they must juggle with pressing personal concerns and pursue while managing bodily change and experiencing the effects of social injustice and marginalised and/or racialised identities. Perhaps most importantly, post-COVID, they offer insights that collapse the personal and the professional and move beyond a preoccupation with learning loss to re-imagine possibilities for teaching and being a teacher. We hope that as you read these chapters you are inspired by Honeyford et al.'s invitation to 'notice, think, wonder and feel' what teaching is and might be and to imagine possibilities that (re)position teachers as pedagogical innovators and activists, as respected professionals, as valued members of school and wider communities and as healthy individuals who lead fulfilling lives in and away from work.

Notes

1 This project was funded by Sheffield Hallam University's 'Research Institute Fund: Interdisciplinary Research and Innovation in Response to the COVID-19 Pandemic 2020–21'. Project activity code: L614.
2 We recognise that 'lost learning' is a contested and complex concept – see Moss et al. (2020) & Hargreaves (2021) for discussion.
3 A detailed account and analysis can be found in Hill & Kumar (2009).
4 Brown's chapter is the exception – but her research on part-time working teachers, conducted pre-pandemic, provides vital lessons on the challenges of flexible working for that are extremely pertinent post-COVID.
5 We recognise that the concept of 'voice' is problematic, as do Snaza & Lensmire (2006), but use it as they suggest, as a powerful metaphor for thinking about agency and representation in education.

References

Aggarwal, U., Mayorga, E., & Nevel, D. (2021) 'Slow violence and neoliberal education reform: reflections on a school closure', *Peace and Conflict: Journal of Peace Psychology*, 18 (2), pp. 156–164.

Arnove, R.F. (2020) 'Imagining what education can be post-COVID-19', *Prospects*, 49, pp. 43–46.

Ball, S. (2003) 'The teacher's soul and the terrors of performativity', *Journal of Education Policy*, 18 (2), pp. 215–228.

Biesta, G. (2016) 'Improving education through research? From effectiveness, causality and technology to purpose, complexity and culture', *Policy Futures in Education*, 14 (2), pp. 194–210.

Borup, J., Jensen, M., Archambault, L., Short, C.R., & Graham, C.R. (2020). 'Supporting students during COVID-19: developing and leveraging academic communities of engagement in a time of crisis', *Journal of Technology and Teacher Education*, 28 (2), pp. 161–169.

Bradbury, A. & Roberts-Holmes, G. (2017) *The datafication of primary and early years education*. London: Routledge.

Burnett, C., Merchant, G., & Guest, I. (2021) 'What matters to teachers about literacy teaching: exploring teachers' everyday/everynight worlds through creative data visualisation', *Teaching and Teacher Education*, 107. https://doi.org/10.1016/j.tate.2021.103480.

Camden, B. (2015) 'Over-fifties are fleeing the classroom', *Schools Week*, 10 July. Available at: https://schoolsweek.co.uk/over-50s-are-fleeing-from-the-classroom/#comments-start.

Chamberlain, L., Karlsen, M., Sinitsky, G., Bennett, S., Plowright-Pepper, L., & Vackova, P. (2021) *Coronavirus and my life: what children say. Children Heard.* Milton Keynes: The Open University.

Chaturvedi, K., Vishwakarma, D.K., & Singh, N. (2021) 'COVID-19 and its impact on education, social life and mental health of students: a survey', *Children and Youth Services Review*, 121, pp. 105866.

Children's Parliament (2020) *How are you doing? Public Health Scotland.* Available at: https://www.childrensparliament.org.uk/our-work/children-and-coronavirus/ (Accessed: 4 March 2023).

Educational Statistics Service (2021) *School workforce in England statistics.* Available at: https://explore-education-statistics.service.gov.uk/find-statistics/school-workforce-in-england (Accessed: 4 March 2023).

Fayed, I. & Cummings, J. (Eds.) (2021) *Teaching in the post COVID-19 era, world education dilemmas, teaching innovations and solutions in the age of crisis*. New York: Springer.

Ferjola, T. & Hopkins, L. (2013) 'The complexities of workplace experience for lesbian and gay teachers', *Critical Studies in Education*, 54 (3), pp. 311–324.

Fried, L. (2011) 'Teaching teachers about emotion regulation in the classroom', *Australian Journal of Teacher Education*, 36, pp. 1–11.

Gilbert, C. (2021) 'Punching the clock: a Foucauldian analysis of teacher time clock use', *Critical Studies in Education*, 62 (4), pp. 439–454.

Gourlay, L., Littlejohn, A., Oliver, M., & Potter, J. (2021) 'Lockdown literacies and semiotic assemblages: academic boundary work in the Covid-19 crisis', *Learning, Media and Technology*. doi:10.1080/17439884.2021.1900242

Green, B. (2012) Subject-specific literacy and school learning: a revised account. In: B. Green and C. Beavis, eds., *Literacy in 3D: An integrated perspective in theory and practice*. Melbourne: ACER.

Green, B. (1988) 'Subject-specific literacy and school learning: a focus on writing,' *Australian Journal of Education*, 32 (2), pp. 156–179. doi:10.1177/000494418803200203

Griffin, A. & Tackie, H. (2017) 'Through our eyes: perspectives from black teachers', *PDK International*, 98 (5).

Gunter, H.M., Hall, D., & Mills, C. (2015) 'Consultants, consultancy and consultocracy in education policymaking in England', *Journal of Education Policy*, 30 (4), pp. 518–539.

Hargreaves, A. (2021) 'What the COVID-19 pandemic has taught us about teachers and teaching', *FACETS*, 6, pp. 1835–1863.

Hayes, D., Hattam, R., Comber, B., Kerkham, L., & Thomson, P. (2017) *Literacy, leading and learning: beyond pedagogies of poverty*. London: Routledge.

HESA (2021) hesa.ac.uk. Available at: https://www.hesa.ac.uk/data-and-analysis/staff/working-in-he/characteristics (Accessed: 15 January 2023).

Hill, D. & Kumar, R. (2009) *Global neoliberalism and education and its consequences*. London: Routledge.

Hilton, A. (2019) *Academies and free schools in England: a history and philosophy of the Give Act*. Abingdon, Oxon: Routledge.

Kagan, D. (1992) 'Implications of research on teacher belief', *Educational Psychologist*, 27 (1), pp. 65–90.

Lee, C. & Wenham, L. (2021) "We just have to sail this sea all together until we find a shore': parents' accounts of home-educating primary-school children in England during COVID-19', *Education*, 51 (2), pp. 3–13.

Lewis, S. & Holloway, J. (2019) "Datafying the teaching 'profession': remaking the professional teacher in the image of data', *Cambridge Journal of Education*, 49 (1), pp. 35–51.

Mansour, N. (2009) 'Science teachers' beliefs and practices: issues, implications and research agenda', *International Journal of Environmental and Science Education*, 4 (1), pp. 25–48.

Marsh-Davies, K. & Burnett, C. (2021) 'Being a teacher during COVID-19', *British Academy of Management 2021: Virtual Conference Proceedings*. Available at: https://virtual.oxfordabstracts.com/#/event/1821/submission/207 (Accessed: 15 January 2023).

Moss, G., Allen, R., Bradbury, A., Duncan, S., Harmey, S., & Levy, R. (2020) *Primary teachers' experience of the COVID-19 lockdown – eight key messages for policymakers going forward*. London: UCL Institute of Education. Available at: https://discovery.ucl.ac.uk/id/eprint/10103669/1/Moss_DCDT%20Report%201%20Final.pdf (Accessed: 4 March 2023).

NAHT (2021) *naht.org.uk*. Available at: https://www.naht.org.uk/Our-Priorities/Our-policy-areas/Equality-diversity-and-inclusion/ArtMID/824/ArticleID/1414/Closing-the-Gender-Pay-Gap-in-Education-A-leadership-imperative#:~:text=Key%20findings,age%20and%20seniority%20in%20roles (Accessed: 15 January 2023).

Nóvoa, A. & Alvim, Y. (2020) 'Nothing is new, but everything has changed: a viewpoint on the future school', *Prospects*, 49, pp. 35–41.

NHS (2023) *NHS Inform*. Available at: https://www.nhsinform.scot/healthy-living/womens-health/later-years-around-50-years-and-over/menopause-and-post-menopause-health/menopause#:~:text=Perimenopause%20and%20menopause%20are%20a,to%20reach%20menopause%20is%2051 (Accessed: 30 July 2023).

Pennington, M.C. & Richards, J.C. (2016) 'Teacher identity in language teaching: integrating personal, contextual, and professional factors', *RELC Journal*, 47 (1), pp. 1–19.

Perna, M.C. (2022) 'Flexibility or Else: teacher retention in the brave new world of education', *Forbes*, 12 June. Available at: https://www.forbes.com/sites/markcperna/2022/07/12/flexibility-or-else-teacher-retention-in-the-brave-new-world-of-education/?sh=55d096db11a9 (Accessed: 15 January 2023).

Price, H.E. & Weatherby, K. (2018) 'The global teaching profession: how treating teachers as knowledge workers improves the esteem of the teaching profession', *School Effectiveness and School Improvement*, 29 (1), pp. 113–149.

Priestley, M., Biesta, G., & Robinson, S. (2016) *Teacher agency: an ecological approach*. London: Bloomsbury.

Rawle, F. (2021) 'A pedagogy of kindness: The cornerstone for student learning and wellness', *Times Higher Education*. Available at: https://www.timeshighereducation.com/campus/pedagogy-kindness-cornerstone-student-learning-and-wellness.

Reynolds, C. (1996) 'Cultural scripts for teachers: Identities and their relation to workplace landscapes', in Kompf, M., Bond, W.R., Dworet, D. & Boak, R.T. (Eds.), *Changing research and practice: teachers' professionalism, identities and knowledge*. London: The Falmer Press, pp. 69–77.

Roy, A. (2020) 'The pandemic is a portal', *Financial Times*, 3 April 2020.

Sachs, J. (2005). 'Teacher education and the development of professional identity', in Denicolo, P.M. & Kompf, M. (Eds.), *Connecting policy and practice: challenges for teaching and learning in schools and universities*. New York: Routledge, pp. 5–21.

Schaefer, L. & Clandinin, D.J. (2019) 'Sustaining teachers' stories to live by: implications for teacher education', *Teachers and Teaching*, 25 (1), pp. 54–68.

Shiri, R., Turunen, J., & Kausto, J. (2022) 'The effect of Employee-Oriented flexible work on mental health: a systematic review', *Healthcare*, 10 (883), pp. 1–14. doi:10.3390/healthcare10050883

Snaza, N. & Lensmire, T.J. (2006) 'Abandon voice? Pedagogy, the body, and late capitalism', InterActions, 2.

Teacher Recruitment and Retention Conference (2023) *governmentevents.co.uk*. Available at: https://www.governmentevents.co.uk/event/the-teacher-recruitment-and-retention-conference-2023/#overview (Accessed: 15 January 2023).

Trelford, H. (2021) 'Initial teacher education in peril: why the market review is about anything but 'world-class training'', *Forum*, 63 (3), pp. 58–65.

UNESCO (2022a) *Unesco.org*. Available at: UNESCO's education response to COVID-19 | UNESCO (Accessed: 15 January 2023).

UNESCO (2022b) *Unesco.org*. Available at: https://www.unesco.org/en/articles/world-teachers-day-unesco-sounds-alarm-global-teacher-shortage-crisis (Accessed: 27 February 2023).

Walker, P. (2023) 'Third of England's teachers who qualified in last decade 'have left profession'', *The Guardian*, 09 January. Available at: Third of England's teachers who qualified in last decade 'have left profession' | Teaching | The Guardian (Accessed: 15 January 2023).

Whittaker, F. (2023) 'I can't afford to strike but I can't afford to carry on like this', *Schools Week*. 20th Jan 23. Available at: https://schoolsweek.co.uk/i-cant-afford-to-strike-but-i-cant-afford-to-carry-on-like-it-is/ (Accessed: 27 February 2023).

WomenEd (2023) *womened.org*. Available at: https://womened.org/campaigns-resources/gender-pay-gap-for-women-in-education (Accessed: 27 February 2023).

World Health Organisation (2023) *who.int*. Available at: https://www.who.int/emergencies/diseases/novel-coronavirus-2019/situation-reports (Accessed: 15 January 2023).

Worth, J. & Faulkner-Ellis, H. (2022) *Teacher labour market in England: annual report 2022*. Slough: NFER.

Yin, H. (2016) 'Knife-like mouth and tofu-like heart: Emotion regulation by Chinese teachers in classroom teaching', *Social Psychology of Education* 19, pp. 1–22.

Priorities
Reassessing Roles and Responsibilities

2
PART-TIME WOMEN TEACHERS- HAVING IT ALL?

Suzanne Brown

Introduction

Being able to combine a successful career with family life is often referred to as 'having it all'. This notion is situated within the neo-liberal view of women regarded by Campo (2009, p. 65) as a 'much reduced and distorted message of feminism'. 'Having it all' for the part-time women teachers discussed in this chapter meant making difficult decisions and sacrifices about whose and which needs they should prioritise – often at the expense of their own careers and well-being. Decisions were shaped by expectations at work around professionalism, and at home by gendered expectations of motherhood. This left little scope for the questionable notion of 'free choice' (Hakim, 2006) in terms of how decisions around career were made.

Drawing on ideas from feminist research, this chapter discusses a body of life history research which I carried out within this epistemological stance. The life histories of part-time women teachers in relation to career progression are discussed. The context for working part-time is discussed, and issues related to well-being, motherhood, teacher recruitment and retention and excessive workload are discussed. The implications of the research findings are considered in relation to the post-COVID-19 era where flexible working is becoming a greater entitlement. The findings emphasise the importance of helping teaching mothers to combine a progressive career pathway with family life in post-COVID-19 times.

Teaching as a career might be perceived as being 'family friendly' due to the (false) perception of short working days and long holidays, yet too many teachers leaving the profession is a global issue (See et al., 2020). In England, in the 12 months to November 2021, the 'leavers rate' was 8.1%

DOI: 10.4324/9781003352129-4

of the state-funded teaching workforce. This equates to around 36,300 full-time equivalent qualified teachers, with around 32,000 leaving for reasons other than death or retirement (Long and Donechi, 2022). As most research around teacher recruitment and retention concerns early career teachers (Booth et al., 2021), there is a gap in the understanding of how to retain teachers further into their careers. Moreau (2018) argues that such 'friendliness' is underpinned by heteronormative and maternal views of women which do not consider what this might mean in terms of women's careers.

Compared to their proportion in the teaching workforce, women are under-represented at the senior leadership level (Gov.UK, 2017; Jerrim and Sims, 2019; European Union, 2020). Across the Organisation for Economic Co-operation and Development (OECD), whilst 68% of all teachers are female, only 47% of school principals are women (Jerrim and Sims, 2019). Ninety-six per cent of school principals work on a full-time basis (ibid, 2002). This context of inequality is important: being a woman and working part-time are factors which individually reduce the chances of achieving senior leadership in schools. Crucially, when combined, the chances of a part-time woman teacher becoming a senior leader are slim (Brown, 2019). The findings of the research discussed in this chapter provide a new contribution to understanding this inequality.

Literature review

For many women, their role as carers, and particularly as mothers, appears to be a major factor in making the decision to not work full-time (Hughes, 2002; Smith, 2012). Stubborn and persistent social expectations of women assuming the role as the primary carer to their children still exist (Coleman, 2002; Smith, 2012). Taking career breaks to look after children result in some women teachers' career patterns being misaligned with the advantageous (Moreau, Osgood and Halsall, 2005) continuous and linear model of progression. This can lead to women being overlooked for promoted positions because their career pathway is considered abnormal and indicative of a lack of commitment (ibid).

Heavy workload is also a common reason for teachers taking the decision not to work full-time. In the United Kingdom, sixty per cent of teachers mentioned caring responsibilities as their reason for working reduced hours, whilst 43% did so to try and manage their excessive workload (National Education Union, 2018), although some overlap may exist in the statistics. Part-time working may help to manage the workload alongside other responsibilities, yet this pattern of working does not necessarily resolve the difficulties for women teachers who work part-time because the workload is still too big (Brown, 2019).

Before the COVID-19 pandemic, teachers reported working around 46 hours per week (Worth and Faulkner-Ellis, 2022). Teacher working hours in the UK are higher than those reported in countries that took part in the OECD Teaching and Learning International Study in 2018 (Jerrim and Sims, 2019). Excessive workload is the most cited reason that ex-teachers give for leaving the profession and contributes to the difficulties in teacher recruitment and retention (Worth and Faulkner-Ellis, 2022). However, periods of lockdown during the COVID-19 pandemic saw teachers' working patterns change and a reduction in their working hours. Teachers were working around 40 hours per week – a figure similar to other professionals (Worth and Faulkner-Ellis, 2022). However, this reduction was short-lived, with working hours soon returning to pre-pandemic levels.

The issues around teacher recruitment and retention are highlighted by Sharp et al. (2019, p. 10) when arguing for greater opportunities for teachers to be able to adopt flexible working patterns:

> One of the ways of encouraging more teachers to remain in the profession for longer – and potentially to attract more to join the profession – is to ensure there are part-time or flexible working opportunities when teachers need them. Providing opportunities to keep teachers who would have left without being able to go part-time retains their expertise and reduces the risk of losing them from the profession permanently.

In the United Kingdom, as part of the Children and Families Act (legislation.gov.uk, 2014), everyone who has worked continuously for an employer for at least 26 weeks is entitled to request to work flexibly. However, teachers' flexible working requests are more likely to be refused than in the wider workforce. Sixty-six per cent of teachers are granted their requests compared to 80% in the wider workforce (NASUWT, 2016). Furthermore, most teachers who have management or senior leadership roles usually find their requests are refused (ibid.).

It can be seen from the points made above that working part-time, which is only one of many forms of flexible working (Gov.uk, 2014), is situated within a complexity of gendered expectations and workplace practices. Being able to adopt this pattern of working is not always a straightforward decision or a 'free' choice (Hakim, 2006). Instead, an individual's choice is situated within, and shaped by, the attitudes and expectations of a range of interested parties. Furthermore, having adopted a part-time rather than full-time pattern of working, the needs and priorities of others do not go away, as we shall see in this chapter. Stark and difficult examples of women being left to decide whether they should prioritise their own families, or the children at their school workplaces, are highlighted in the findings from this life history research. Bringing these difficulties under the spotlight helps to explain how trying to balance the needs and priorities of others leaves the women in this study with little time for free choice around career – and in one case fuels her exit from the profession. The life history approach taken in this study will now be explained.

Discussion for methodological approaches

Stanley and Wise (2002) reject arguments for one truthful and irrefutable social reality when discussing epistemology from a feminist perspective. The research discussed in this chapter is aligned with this epistemological stance and draws on ideas from feminist research. A life history approach (Goodson, 2008) was employed to gather women's differing and subjective truths or realities of working part-time and their relationships with career progression.

Methods

Six women, all of whom were white, married and mothers, agreed to be part of the study. They were each interviewed twice over a six-month period for around 90 minutes each time. Their schools were not aware of their participation. Headteachers or School Principals had been previously asked to advertise my request for women part-time teachers to participate in the research. The women were asked to reply to me directly. The methodological limitations arising from the lack of diversity within the group of participants were recognised and considered throughout the research. The cohort were of interest, however, due to the differences between them in terms of their education, histories of employment, management experiences, ages of their children and working patterns. More detailed vignettes of all the women's lives and experiences are found in Brown (2019).

At our first meeting, each participant was asked to talk about her life and career so far, including how part-time working was significant to her story. After the transcription of both recorded interviews, each participant was encouraged to check the transcriptions for accuracy, to make amendments and to add further points/clarifications. Measor and Sikes (1992) argue that 'respondent validation' is an important part of co-constructing life histories as well as being one of the best ethical safeguards.

Repeated and active readings of the transcripts took place alongside listening to the recordings to encourage familiarisation and immersion in the data. Prior to the second meetings, long pauses and periods of silence were noted on the transcripts from the first meetings (Goodson, 2008). These notes acted as a trigger for further exploration at our second meetings and supported the process of co-constructing the women's life histories (Biott, Moos and Moller, 2001).

Rich narratives emerged from the second meetings which involved exploring form and meaning together by highlighting potentially critical incidences (Measor, 1985). These were identified in the stories and highlighted on the transcripts from the first meetings in readiness for further exploration at the second meetings along with the silences and pauses. According to Measor (1985), critical incidences can indicate instances of change and choices being made in people's lives where priorities are re-assessed and hence yield an insight into how identities are built at various times of life.

The transcripts from both meetings with each participant were inductively coded (Denzin and Lincoln, 1994) as part of a thematic approach (Braun and Clarke, 2006). This chapter focuses on the theme of 'perceptions' (Brown, 2019) which emerged from the data.

Findings & discussion

All the women in the study were mothers, and this was a crucial influence in the stories they told and their decision-making. The stories of three of the women have been chosen for discussion in this chapter: Alice, Leah and Louise.

ALICE

Alice is married, white and in her thirties. Her husband became a headteacher between our two meetings. Alice has two young children, the eldest started school during this interval.

She felt unsupported in her first teaching job and left because she did not feel trained to teach outside her subject specialism. She taught her specialism in her second school but was refused part-time working after the birth of her second child. She left to work part-time at her current school.

At our first meeting, Alice explained that her mother stayed with the family for two consecutive days to provide childcare. She could attend to any emergency childcare issues whilst Alice worked. Alice appeared very happy with her working and childcare arrangements and felt supported at school. She said she had a good work–life balance.

However, at our second meeting, six months later, Alice said her school had become an academy and policy and procedure had changed. Her working days were no longer consecutive and so her mother was no longer able to childmind. Combined with her husband's new role and child starting school, Alice described feeling stressed and was struggling to cope with these changes. No longer feeling supported by the school, she decided to leave and was exploring possibilities outside of teaching.

> **LEAH**
>
> Leah, white and in her forties, is married to a deputy headteacher with three sons under the age of ten. Prior to motherhood, Leah occupied a middle-management position, spending long hours at work, explaining that her work had been her life. She considered herself to have had a voice in decision-making. She had volunteered as a sports coach.
>
> Returning full-time after her first maternity leave, she felt guilty for not spending time with her baby and for not devoting the previous amount of time to work. A second and difficult pregnancy quickly followed, making her transition back to work difficult. Not coping, her request for part-time working was granted with the condition that she relinquished her management position.
>
> Leah felt she needed to prove herself to the new head of faculty. She felt her opinions were no longer sought, and her voice was reduced. Leah participated in various community activities as a response to feeling guilty for not working full-time and to prove herself to her wider family, whom she regarded as being high-achieving.
>
> Leah aspired to future senior leadership but considered her current unwillingness to work full-time a barrier to her promotion.

> **LOUISE**
>
> Louise, white and in her late thirties, has three young children. Her husband occasionally works away from home.
>
> After graduation, Louise went straight into teaching, consecutively occupying two full-time teaching jobs before her current position. Louise involved her teaching union when her request to work part-time was initially refused after the birth of her first child.
>
> Louise now works three consecutive days each week, arriving early and leaving very late. She employed a nanny 36 hours a week to cover these days. This made financial sense to Louise.
>
> Having previously considered promotion, she had not pursued it as she felt her children were too young.

The discussion of the life histories begins with an exploration of the women's commitment to their paid work and families. In the first instance, this is done through Louise's story. From here, the women's experiences of juggling their paid work and responsibilities at home are considered, before exploring the outcomes and implications of prioritising their respective husband's careers.

The stories of Leah and Alice are included because they were both married to school leaders and interestingly had prioritised their husband's careers over their own. This prioritisation included the two women not working full-time. The accompanying detrimental impact on their careers and experiences at work is glaring. The notions of 'having it all' and choices around career are interwoven threads in these discussions along with how these findings can inform working practices in the post-COVID-19 era.

Commitment

This section begins with Louise describing how she felt when her commitment to her part-time teaching role was challenged by a male member of the senior leadership team (SLT). Louise's husband had gone to work before her and the children's nanny was late arriving, which resulted in Louise arriving late at her own place of employment:

> But he (the Senior Leader) brought up a couple of times that I'd been late in as well. I think he felt he had to address these, and I can remember it because, I remember the phrase that he used because it really obviously sort of hit me. He said, "Do you see teaching as a bit of a hobby?". It just made me realise that perhaps they do feel that I am less committed now. I mean the reasons for my being late those couple of times were that I was dealing with children at home, that's the only reason that ever causes me to be late into work when perhaps I wouldn't have been otherwise.
>
> *(Louise, second meeting)*

Because Louise had previously been late a couple of times due to prioritising her own children, her commitment and professionalism were questioned in a way which frustrated her. Her vignette highlights a previous issue around her part-time working which needed teaching union involvement before it was resolved. The language used by the SLT member implies that working part-time and being professional are mutually exclusive (Negrey, 1993). He angered Louise with his reference to a 'hobby'. This unfortunate event is aligned with the findings of Cockburn (2002) who found that many men in senior positions question the commitment of mothers, particularly those who work part-time. However, Gatrell (2005) found that women's sacrificing of their own time suggests their commitment to their paid work is greater than before they became mothers. The senior leader's inappropriate choice of language suggests he views Louise's part-time working as being voluntary and situated within a lack of commitment to full-time working (Durbin and Tomlinson, 2014). Louise's sense of marginalisation and lack of value is apparent from her comments.

Motherhood has its own powerful discourse which can act as a resistive parameter to decision-making (Smith, 2016). Louise was in a tricky situation with an expectation made clear by the senior leader that she should prioritise her work and the needs of the children at the school over her own children, despite a lack of childcare. Whilst lateness is not professionally advisable, what he imagined she should do with the three young children instead of waiting for childcare is not clear. The situation was clearly one he did not approve of and is suggestive of him thinking she should not be working if she can not fit within the rigidity of the normalised school day.

Louise's being late in the morning was an example of her sacrificing her own reputation and prioritising her husband's career. Essentialist constructions of men and women depict women as willing to assume the primary responsibilities for childcare and domestic issues (Moreau, Osgood and Halsall, 2007). Unlike men, this often results in women like Louise having to choose between their families and their careers (ibid.) or in this case between her own children and those at school. During COVID-19 times, this has become more apparent: women were more likely to pick up the gap in childcare, resulting from lockdown and beyond, with greater detrimental impacts on their employment than those experienced by men (Modestino, Lincoln and Ladge, 2021). The issue of prioritisation will be revisited later in the chapter.

Women's role as carers makes a valuable and wider economic contribution and helps to maintain the workforce (Hughes, 2002). Yet women's caring for their own children is considered low value; this is not the case when men assume this responsibility (Tronto, 1993). The COVID-19 pandemic has highlighted the importance of good and available childcare in enabling parents, especially women to remain in the workforce (Modestino, Lincoln and Ladge, 2021). Paying for childcare is expensive, this is illustrated by Louise's decision to pay for a nanny for her three children because this was less expensive than paying nursery fees. This type of childcare provision also gave Louise more flexibility to meet the demands of her paid work although this meant employing a full-time nanny for more hours than Louise herself was contracted to be at the school. On the three days, Louise was at work, she paid a nanny for 12 hours each day so that she could go to work early and stay until 7 pm so that she did not need to bring schoolwork home. Louise's comments highlight this arrangement was fallible: if the family nanny arrived late, then Louise picked up the slack at the cost of her own reputation.

Employing a nanny in this way was a more flexible option than those offered by many day nurseries, where opening hours are usually fixed around the typical working day. Start and finishing times vary between individual schools in the United Kingdom, with teachers expected to be in school early to prepare for the day and greet pupils. Care provisions which enable teacher-carers to do this are seemingly a crucial factor in enabling them to fulfil their professional commitments. Enabling teacher-carers to arrive in a good time at school to prepare for the school day requires care provision to be available even earlier than schools are, but this is not always the case.

Temporal arrangements around the organisation of the school day are inflexible, resulting in tensions (Brown, 2019). Meeting professional responsibilities alongside those of being a carer of young children, or indeed anyone requiring care, necessitates good, affordable and flexible care provision and/or more flexible working arrangements within schools. The COVID-19 pandemic was an unexpected and unwanted event, but it also served as a social experiment around responses and changes in working patterns and practices. Reported outcomes include the wider consideration and adoption of flexible working patterns within the wider workforce (Cranfield, 2022) and a greater desire from people to work flexibly (Chung et al., 2021). This puts pressure on the teaching profession to embrace alternative ways of working beyond the normalisation of a linear and full-time working pattern if it is not to lose more ground in terms of flexible working practices.

Discursive constructions of the part-time professional worker can lead to them being considered less committed due to the misalignment in professional assumptions around the ability and willingness to prioritise work (Dick, 2010). This is despite Jacobsen (2000) finding that in comparison to their full-time colleagues, part-time professionals are more affectively committed to their work. It may be obvious, but women can still be committed to their work even though they love their children (Gatrell, 2005). The women who are the focus of this chapter were committed to their work and wanted to maintain their professional reputations. They did not align themselves with the notions of deficiency or being less committed than their colleagues who worked full-time. Durbin and Tomlinson (2014) argue that the transition to part-time working is not about a lack of commitment but instead reflects the complexity of people's working lives at different life stages. This is particularly pertinent in the post-COVID-19 era where according to Vyas (2022, p. 1)

> The coronavirus pandemic has interrupted labor markets, triggering massive and instant series of experimentations with flexible work arrangements, and new relationships to centralized working environments. These approaches have laid the basis for the "new normal," likely extending into the organization of work in the post-pandemic era. These new arrangements, especially flexible work arrangements, have challenged traditional relationships with employees and employers, work time and working hours, the work–life balance (WLB), and the relationship of individuals to work.
>
> *(Vyas, 2022, p. 1)*

The shifts described in this excerpt illustrate how the pandemic has resulted in people thinking differently about when, where and how we work, meaning that flexible working is likely to be more widely enacted and normalised in the post-COVID-19 era (ibid). The women teachers discussed in this chapter experienced negative discourses around part-time working. Post-COVID-19, notions of deficiency and a lack of commitment linked to part-time working continue to be inappropriate but are now even more outdated. The featured women's commitment to both their paid work and non-paid work in the home was apparent from their stories. Both parts of their lives were 'greedy' (Edwards, 1993) in terms of the time they demanded. How the women tried to balance the different demands for the limited amount of time available to them is described in the next section.

The juggling act

Juggling the demands of motherhood and caring alongside the demands of their teaching roles caused the women in this study conflict, guilt and anxiety. The feelings they described illustrate their commitment to both their paid roles and roles at home. A lack of commitment would not lead to such affective responses. Between the two meetings, Alice's employer changed the days she worked each week without consulting her. This led to her childcare arrangements falling apart. In addition, her son started school. This meant he needed wrap-around care in the morning and after school, which she found difficult to arrange alongside her own working. Alice explains how her priorities became conflicted due to these two events:

> We need to get the bedtime routine done, I need to work, and I need to get prepared for the next day. Because school had split my days, I was only there two days, but really, I was in a working mind frame for at least four. I can't believe the amount of favours I've already had to call in when things have cropped up: could you take my son to school, could you be there to pick him up? This is ridiculous, it was meant to be easy, they're there, you pick them up, and they're there for the whole day. Yeah, massive, massive impact on me, massive impact on the family as a whole.
>
> *(Alice, second meeting)*

Alice's anxiety is palpable and illustrates how her decision-making involved a complex meshing of gendered expectations regarding motherhood and professionalism. Smith (2012, p. 95) makes the point that 'For a woman who is a mother, a professional career thus becomes an extra load, to be fitted in, around and on top of the maternal load'. This 'extra load' was too much for Alice, and she decided to leave teaching to prioritise her family life (Longhurst, 2008). Part-time working turned out not to be the solution Alice was hoping for when trying to combine a professional life with being a mother:

> I think that from a childcare point of view, going back full-time was never an option. I didn't want to, or I didn't see the point in having children,

to put them in full-time childcare. I wanted to spend time with them and also, I wanted to come back to work. I didn't want to lose my skills and I thought it was good for the children, seeing me as a role model, a working mum, because you can't have it all, but you can try, can't you. Work, be an adult and be a mum. So, yeah, that was the motivational thing for me, wanting the kids to see 'Yeah, mum is doing this, but looks after us as well'.

(Alice, second meeting)

Alice stated that her husband told her 'Your priority is the kids' when she was deciding whether to leave teaching due to her unhappiness. Alice worked part-time because she wanted a rewarding career and a happy family life, situated within the neo-liberal notion of 'having it all'. Trying to achieve these notions presented difficulties and had negative impacts on Alice's well-being. Campo (2009, p. 11) argues that:

> Perpetuating the narrative of 'having it all' feminism may make great copy in pages of newspapers that feed on controversy, but it does nothing for the millions of women who struggle daily in a society that still makes combining a career with family life heavy work.

Stress and guilt accompanied Alice's navigations of the competing priorities of work and family life, meaning that rather than 'having it all', life was 'heavy work'. In her taking of a feminist perspective to analysing care, Hughes (2002) argues that different types of care are given different prestige. Having the caring responsibility for an aspect of public life, such as being a headteacher, is seen to be valuable and important. In the private realm however, looking after family is considered relatively trivial.

Despite working part-time, the participants still felt the pressures of a heavy-paid workload. Leah expressed frustration that her employer did not recognise that her decision to work part-time meant that her willingness to give as much time to her job was reduced:

> So, thinking about my leaders, the ones that haven't got children would probably think that I'm not giving as much because I've got a family. Because I think, sadly, there's a culture in education that it is a vocation and you give your life to it, there's kind of no end to it. It's just relentless and if you haven't got other distractions then that can be how it is. I know leaders that haven't got families they do other things, but it's easier to plan that in I think, but the culture of education, the culture at my school, you know it's not said, but it's kind of, how could I put it? People will say to you, oh you shouldn't be working at the weekends, oh you shouldn't be working on your day off, but it never feels meant,

it always feels as if, what's the word, like a platitude, is that the correct word to use?

(Leah, second meeting)

Dick (2010) explains that employers do not always recognise the reduced temporal contribution accompanying people's decisions not to work full-time, with part-time workers expecting clearer boundaries between their working and private lives. In using the word *platitude*, Leah implies that the advice she was given was disingenuous because her workload was not reduced to enable the advice and so she still needed to work at weekends.

Walker, Sharp and Sims (2020) report that compared to research undertaken before the lockdown (Walker, Worth and Van den Brande, 2019), some teachers' workloads have become more manageable, although this was variable across distinct groups. Walker, Sharp and Sims (2020) report that younger teachers (aged 20–29) were more likely to say that their workload had become more manageable than people in their forties. Unpicking this finding through further research is important to ascertain what lessons can be learned about making workload perceivably more manageable in the post-COVID-19 era.

Walker, Sharp and Sims (2020) suggest that teachers in their forties were more likely to have school-aged children and were trying to meet the additional demands of home-schooling. They support this assertion by remarking that women teachers, with greater caring responsibilities, are more likely to regard their workload as being unmanageable. This chapter through its discussion of women teachers' day-to-day lived experiences offers insights into why this may be the case. Furthermore, it highlights that taking the decision to work part-time rather than full-time to try and mitigate the effects of excessive paid workload on family life does not provide the solution.

Even though the amount of time spent on domestic chores and childcare increased for both men and women during the lockdown (Soraya and Rondon, 2021), gender asymmetries in childcare and domestic chores became more apparent. Women were doing two-thirds of the childcare when schools and nurseries closed. Women reported being more psychologically distressed due to the increased number of hours spent on childcare and homeschooling (ibid). This suggests that gendered expectations and assumed responsibilities around care provision remain difficult to shift, despite unprecedented changes in the way lives were lived during the pandemic. Even when people were at home more, it was largely women who picked up these additional responsibilities. This reinforces the stubborn and gendered nature of expectations around care (Coleman, 2002). This leaves women teacher-carers who work part-time with heavy workloads both at home and at work.

For Leah and Alice, their husbands' heavy-paid workloads as school senior leaders were an additional factor in their decision-making regarding the assumption of the primary responsibility for childcare. This included the prioritisation of their respective husbands' careers. The implications of this on the women's lives and careers will now be discussed.

Prioritisation of careers

It is important at the outset of this discussion around prioritisation not to overlook the participants' commitment to their jobs and their husband's commitment to their families. To say otherwise would give an over-simplistic representation of how they described their day-to-day life experiences.

Both Leah and Alice made direct reference to how their respective husbands' careers had been given priority. Less explicit, however, is how their part-time working enabled their husbands to be continuously available to work and to follow a linear career pathway, both of which are highlighted by Moreau, Osgood and Halsall (2005) as being favoured by employers. Consequently, these men were in a better position than their wives to progress their careers.

The implicit assumption that she should be the one to respond to circumstances requiring unexpected childcare highlights the sacrificing of Leah's reputation to prioritise her husband's career:

> I worry about my husband's reputation at school, you know, I don't want him to be seen as the person that's having to shoot off for the kids all the time. I guess I think that that's frowned upon because that's something that I've seen at my school.
>
> *(Leah, second meeting)*

Leah made it clear her husband's reputation and career took priority over hers. Dick and Hyde (2006) make the point that a woman's prioritisation of her family is more culturally legitimate than if a man wishes to do the same. Leah did not want her husband to be considered problematic and deficient in the way she had been made to feel in the past by her school for prioritising her children. Seemingly, she was prepared to take the hit on her own reputation to protect her husband.

Both Leah and Alice were married to senior school leaders with higher salaries than them. This seemed to be important in their decision-making around priorities and arguably created the financial scope for them not to have to work full-time. Leah made the following point:

> Because we've prioritised his job basically. We as a family, as a couple have said, your job is more important because you're earning more money. If he has to come out of school, he will do. He has responded if the children have had an accident at school, you know he has been the

first person they've managed to get hold of sometimes, which I don't know why because I've tried to set it up so it's not, so it's me. But I think we just decided that he was in the more advanced position in his career, so he should carry on going up that career ladder.

(Leah, second meeting)

In addition to the influence of a higher salary, Leah and Alice had some insight of what their husbands' jobs involved and the necessity to be continuously available to work over a long working week. School leaders in the United Kingdom work more than 48 hours a week (Fuller et al., 2015). Alice made the following point which shows her growing disillusionment with how her husband working long hours was impacting their family:

He does work very, very long hours, which you know we knew, we knew. When he first started (as a headteacher) it was a bit of a novelty, we all sort of took it on as a family. The school's only up the road, it's absolutely beautiful, it's a gorgeous building, we used to go up at the weekend and play football because we could, close the gates and we just let the kids run around and we really, really took it on as a family. But that novelty's sort of worn off now as it does, and he does work some incredibly long hours.

(Alice, second meeting)

Leah and Alice each allude to the decision-making around career progression and prioritisation of their husbands' careers as a joint process with their respective husbands. It is clear, however, that they were also aware of the gendered expectations upon them as primary carers. The women knew they needed to be available to pick up the slack in terms of childcare if their husbands were to be enabled to be continuously available to work. The women were very aware of being stretched in terms of their own time and that additional time to progress their own careers was not available. They perceived that to progress their careers they would need to work full-time, which was not something they were prepared to do, along with a seeming acceptance of the negative implications of this decision for their careers (Brown, 2019).

Conclusions

This chapter has highlighted that for women teachers who work part-time alongside a family, 'having it all' was not what they hoped it would be. The impact of not working full-time on their careers was combined with the affective responses of guilt, stress and anxiety from juggling heavy workloads both at home and at work. The explorations have highlighted how being a mother and a part-time teacher influences choices and decision-making in relation to career progression. Importantly, working part-time appears to have exacerbated the negative effects of motherhood on career progression previously described by Smith (2016).

Reductionist assertions and assumptions of choices being 'free' (Hakim, 2000) are over-simplistic. Instead, in addition to an economic rationale, the women's decision-making was influenced by societal and gendered expectations around women's roles as primary carers and prioritisation of the needs and careers of others, often to their own detriment in terms of career progression and wellbeing. They walked the tightrope between showing commitment to their work and the 'moral minefield' of motherhood and the 'gendered moral rationalities' that shape mothering and paid work (Miller, 2017).

The findings of the study discussed in this chapter add a new dimension to the arguments of Moreau, Osgood and Halsall (2005) and Smith (2016) who challenged the commonly held perception that teaching is a good job to combine with having a family. Part-time working as a teacher does not necessarily provide women with the solution in terms of combining a career with having a family. Consequently, exploring other patterns of working flexibly are ever more important.

In the post-COVID-19 era where there has been greater adoption of flexible working patterns in the wider workforce (Forbes et al., 2020), schools still have a way to go to achieve at least parity with the wider workforce in adopting alternative working patterns. As teachers' pensionable age continues to rise in the United Kingdom (Teachers' Pensions, 2020), incidences of phased retirement seem likely to increase. People in new demographic groups will wish to work flexibly as part of this process. This chapter has shown that working part-time is not without its issues in terms of implications for both career and well-being.

Bold and empathetic leadership is required to ensure that the loss of teacher talent and potential is stemmed. This should include exploring different ways of being flexible in terms of where, when and how different aspects of the teachers' role and school leadership can be achieved. The COVID-19 era showed that when there is a need and a necessity for widespread change in terms of working practices, these can be made to happen quickly along with the removal of previously perceived barriers to change. This chapter has shown that changes are required in the way part-time teachers work if they are to be happy and successful in combining their workload with family life. The COVID-19 era has provided an unexpected momentum for such changes across the wider workforce which the teaching profession cannot afford to ignore if it is not to be left behind.

Note: Ethical approval for the research discussed in this chapter was granted by Sheffield Hallam University as part of a Doctoral Programme of study. The data discussed in this chapter are drawn from my Doctoral thesis (Brown, 2019).

References

Biott, C., Moos, L. and Moller, J. (2001) 'Studying Headteachers' lives: Getting the life history'. *Scandinavian Journal of Educational Research*, 45 (4), pp. 402–410.

Booth, J., Coldwell, M., Müller, L.-M., Perry, E. and Zuccollo, J. (2021) 'Mid-career teachers: A mixed methods scoping study'. *Education Sciences*, 11, p. 299. Available at: http://shura.shu.ac.uk/28758/1/Booth-Mid-CareerTeachers%28VoR%29.pdf

Braun, V. and Clarke, V. (2006) 'Using thematic analysis in psychology'. *Qualitative Research in Psychology*, 3 (2), pp. 77–101.

Brown, S. (2019) 'Part-time women teachers and their career progression: A life history approach.' EdD Thesis. Sheffield Hallam University. Available at: http://doi.org/10.7190/shu-thesis-00256

Campo, N. (2009) "Having it all' or 'had enough'? Blaming feminism in the Age and Sydney Morning Herald 1980–2004'. *Journal of Australian Studies*, 28 (84), pp. 63–72. Available at: http://doi.org/10.1080/144430509387992

Children and Families Act. (2014). http://www.legislation.gov.uk/ukpga/2014/6/contents/enacted

Chung, H., Birkett, H., Forbes, S. and Seo, H. (2021) 'Covid-19, flexible working, and implications for gender equality in the United Kingdom', *Gender and Society*, 35 (2), pp. 218–232. Available at: https://doi.org/10.1177/08912432211001304

Cockburn, C. (2002) Resisting equal opportunities: The issue of maternity, in S. Jackson and S. Scott (eds), *Gender: A sociology reader*. London: Routledge.

Coleman, M. (2002) *Women as headteachers: Striking the balance*. Oakhill: Trentham Books.

Cranfield (2022) *Employers more open to part-time working post Covid-19, report finds*. Available at: https://www.cranfield.ac.uk/press/news-2022/employers-more-open-to-part-time-working-post-Covid-19 (Accessed 18 September 2022).

Denzin, N.K. and Lincoln, Y.S. (1994) *Handbook of qualitative research*. London: SAGE.

Dick, P. (2010) 'The transition to motherhood and part-time working: Mutuality and incongruence in the psychological contracts existing between managers and employees'. *Work, Employment and Society*, 24 (3), pp. 508–525.

Dick, P. and Hyde, R. (2006) 'Consent as resistance, resistance as consent: Re-reading part-time professionals' acceptance of their marginal positions'. *Gender, Work and Organization*, 13 (6), pp. 543–564.

Durbin, S. and Tomlinson, J. (2014) 'Female part-time managers: Careers, mentors and role models'. *Gender, Work and Organisation*, 21 (4), pp. 308–320. Available at: https://doi.org/10.1111/gwao.12038

Edwards, R. (1993) *Mature women students: Separating or connecting family and education*. London: Taylor & Francis.

European Union. 2020. *At a glance teaching: A woman's world*. Available at: https://www.europarl.europa.eu/RegData/etudes/ATAG/2020/646191/EPRS_ATA(2020)646191_EN.pdf (Accessed 17 November 2022).

Forbes, S., Birkett, H., Evans, L., Chung, H. and Whiteman, J. (2020) *Managing employees during the COVID-19 pandemic: Flexible working and the future of work*. Available at: Equal Parenting Project, United Kingdom: https://www.birmingham. ac.uk/schools/business/research/research-projects/ equal-parenting/research.aspx (Accessed 17 November 2022).

Fuller, K., Cliffe, J. and Moorosi, P. (2015) Women's leadership preparation within the senior leadership team. *Planning and Changing*, 46 (3/4), pp. 388–415. Available at: https://search.proquest.com/docview/1917699804?accountid=13827

Gatrell, C. (2005) *Hard labour; The sociology of parenthood*. Maidenhead: Open University Press.

Goodson, I. (2008) *Investigating the teacher's life and work*. Rotterdam: Sense.

Gov.uk. (2014) *Flexible working*. Available at: https://www.gov.uk/flexible-working/types-of-flexible-working (Accessed 17 November 2022).

Gov.uk. (2017) *National statistics school workforce in England: November 2017*. Available at: https://www.gov.uk/government/statistics/school-workforce-in-england-november-2017

Hakim, C. (2000) *Work-lifestyle preferences in the 21st century*. Oxford: Oxford University Press.

Hakim, C. (2006) 'Women, careers and work-life preferences'. *British Journal of Guidance and Counselling*, 34 (3), pp. 45–61. Available at: https://doi.org/10.1080/03069880600769118 (Accessed 18 November 2022).

Hughes, C. (2002) *Key concepts in feminist theory and research*. London: SAGE.

Jacobsen, D.I. (2000) Managing increased part-time: Does part-time work imply part-time commitment? *Managing Service Quality*, 10 (3), pp. 187–201. Available at: https://doi.org/10.1108/09604520010336713 (Accessed 18 November 2022).

Jerrim, J. and Sims, S. (2019) *The teaching and learning international survey (TALIS) 2018-A Research report*. Available at: https://assets.publishing.service.gov.uk/government/uploads/system/uploads/attachment_data/file/919064/TALIS_2018_research.pdf (Accessed March 29 2022).

Legislation.gov.uk (2014) Children and Families Act. Available at: http://www.legislation.gov.uk/ukpga/2014/6/contents/enacted- (Accessed 18 November 2022).

Long, R. and Donechi, S. (2022) *Teacher recruitment and retention in England: September 2022*. Available at: https://researchbriefings.files.parliament.uk/documents/CBP-7222/CBP-7222.pdf

Longhurst, R. (2008) *Maternities: Gender, bodies and space*. New York: Routledge.

Measor, L. (1985) Critical incidents in the classroom: Identities, choices and careers, in S.J. Ball and I.V. Goodson (eds.), *Teachers' lives and careers*. London: Falmer Press. pp. 61–77.

Measor, L and Sikes, P. (1992) Visiting lives, ethics and methodology in life history, in I. Goodson (ed.) *Studying teachers' lives*. London: Routledge. pp. 209–233.

Miller T. (2017) Doing narrative research? Thinking through the narrative, in J. Woodiwiss, K. Smith and K. Lockwood (eds.), *Feminist narrative research*. London: Palgrave Macmillan. pp. 39–63.

Modestino, A.S., Lincoln, A. and Ladge, J. (2020) *The importance of childcare in reopening the economy*. Available at: https://econofact.org/the-importance-of-childcare-in-reopening-the-economy (Accessed 17 November 2022).

Moreau, M. (2018) A matter of time? Gender equality in the teaching profession through a cross national comparative lens. *Gender and Education*. doi: 10.1080/09540253.2018.1533918 (Accessed 31 July 2023).

Moreau, M., Osgood, J. and Halsall, A. (2005) *The career progression of women teachers in England: A study of barriers to promotion and career development*. Available at: http://www.londonmet.ac.uk/londonmet/library/c51886_3pdf

Moreau, M., Osgood, J. and Halsall, A.(2007) 'Making sense of the glass ceiling in schools: An exploration of women teachers' discourses'. *Gender and Education*, 19 (2), pp. 237–253. Available at: https://doi.org/10.1080/09540250601166092 (Accessed 17 November 2022)

NASUWT. (2016) *Flexible working: The experience of teachers*. Available at: https://www.nasuwt.org.uk/uploads/assets/uploaded/6fd07ce3-6400-4cb2-a8a87b736d-c95b3b.pdf (Accessed 17 November 2022).

National Education Union. (2018) Paying the price. *Report*, May. pp. 10–11.

Negrey, C. (1993) *Gender, time and reduced work*. New York: Albany.

See, B.H., Morris, R., Gorard, S., Kokssaki, D. and Abdi, S. (2020) 'Teacher recruitment and retention'. *Education Sciences*, 10, p. 262.

Sharp, C., Smith, R., Worth, J. and Van den Brande, J. (2019) Part-time working and flexible working in secondary schools. *National Foundation for Educational Research*. Available at: https://www.nfer.ac.uk/part-time-teaching-and-flexible-working-in-secondary-schools (Accessed 17 November 2022).

Smith, J.M. (2012) Reflections on using life history to investigate women teachers' aspirations and career decisions. *Qualitative Research*, 12 (4), pp. 486–503. Available at: https://doi.org/10.1177/1468794111433090 (Accessed 17 November 2022).

Smith, J.M. (2016) Motherhood and women teachers' career decisions: A constant battle, in K. Fuller and J. Harford (eds.), *Gender and leadership in Education. Women achieving against the odds*. Bern: Peter Lang AG. pp. 83–114.

Soraya, S. and Rondon, M. (2021) 'Women's wellbeing and the burden of unpaid work'. *The BMJ*. Available at: https://doi.org/10.1136/bmj.n1972 (Accessed 17 November 2022).

Stanley, L. and Wise, S. (2002) *Breaking out again: Feminist ontology and epistemology*. London: Routledge.

Teachers' Pensions (2020) *When can you retire?* Available at: https://www.teacherspensions.co.uk/members/planning-retirement/when-can-you-retire.aspx#:~:text=What%20is%20my%20Normal%20Pension,when%20you%20entered (Accessed 17 November 2022).

Tronto, J. (1993) *Moral boundaries: A political argument for an ethic of care*. London: Routledge.

Vyas, L. (2022) '"New normal" at work in a post-COVID-19 world: Work–life balance and labor markets'. *Policy and Society*, 41 (1), pp. 155–167. Available at: https://doi.org/10.1093/polsoc/puab011 (Accessed 17 November 2022).

Walker, M., Worth, J. and Van den Brande, J. (2019) *Teacher workload survey 2019* [online]. Available at: https://assets.publishing.service.gov.uk/government/uploads/system/uploads/attachment data/file/855933/teacher_workload_survey_2019_main_report_ amended.pdf (Accessed 27 May 2020).

Walker, M., Sharp, C. and Sims, D. (2020) 'Schools' responses to Covid-19. Job satisfaction and workload of teachers and senior leaders'. *National Foundation for Educational Research*. Available at: https://www.nfer.ac.uk/media/4074/schools_responses_to_Covid-19_job_satisfaction_and_workload_of_teacher_and_senior_leaders.pdf (Accessed 17 November 2022).

Worth, J. and Faulkner-Ellis, H. (2022) Teacher labour market in England: Annual Report 2022. *National Foundation for Educational Research*. Available at: https://www.nfer.ac.uk/teacher-labour-market-in-england-annual-report-2022/ (Accessed 17 November 2022).

3
EXPERIENCES OF STUDENT-TEACHER MOTHERS BEFORE AND DURING COVID-19

Lessons in flexibility

Joan Woodhouse

Introduction

This chapter draws on an investigation into the experiences of student-teachers who were mothers (STMs). The women were following a one-year, full-time, initial teacher education (ITE) programme in an English university from September 2019 to June 2020. The participants were therefore a part of the first COVID-19 cohort, ideally and uniquely placed to provide a view of the challenges they had faced in combining motherhood with ITE both before and during the pandemic, as COVID-19 restrictions started in March 2020 in England.

From March 2020, with the exception of key workers, adults in England were required to work from home. Schools were closed. Teachers devised online learning resources, with which pupils engaged remotely, supervised as required by their parents/carers. Student-teachers, who would normally have completed a second school placement in spring-summer 2020, were required to complete online tasks in order to evidence that they had met the professional standards for teachers. The STMs in this study therefore completed the first half of their training at university and/or in school and the second half from home, whilst caring for and home-schooling their own children.

I wanted to gather insights into the particular challenges faced by this cohort of STMs. These insights are important because student-mothers are a largely overlooked, invisible group in higher education (HE) (see Woodhouse and Guihen, 2022). It seems that, despite discourses of inclusivity, equality and widening participation, universities continue to organise and operate largely on the basis of a set of assumptions about the average student, who is white, male, middle class, single, solvent, mobile and child-free. Like other groups of students who do not fit this ideal model, student-mothers are othered by their institutions, at best viewed as 'non-traditional'. In order to investigate the perspectives of this non-traditional group, I sought first-hand, qualitative accounts of their experiences. In this chapter, I present some of the key findings from the study and consider the implications for long-term change, if we are to work towards meaningful, family-friendly flexibility in ITE provision post-COVID.

Literature review

The difficulties associated with combining motherhood and a teaching career are well documented. There is evidence, for example, that women teachers' career progression is affected by the challenges they face in managing family and professional work (see, for instance, Bradbury and Gunter, 2006; Coleman, 2002; Moreau, Osgood and Halsall, 2007; McNamara et al., 2010; Smith, 2011; Smith, 2016). There is some evidence, too, from the pre-COVID-19 era, of the particular challenges STMs face in trying to meet academic deadlines, undertake school placements and successfully complete the ITE programme (for example, Murtagh, 2017, 2019; NUS, 2009). The challenges include financial and practical difficulties in completing ITE whilst managing family routines and domestic commitments (Griffiths, 2002; Woodhouse and Guihen, 2022), as well as emotional conflicts implicit in trying to balance professional and domestic lives (Woodhouse and Guihen, 2022). Such conflicts arise, Griffiths (2002) argues, out of the distinct tension between maternal responsibilities and the demands of ITE and reflect the reality for STMs of studying in the exclusive, largely family-unfriendly institution (Woodhouse, Guihen and Scalise, 2022).

The reality of women's struggles and conflicts in managing domestic and professional responsibilities is well evidenced, yet it seems that ITE providers do not routinely build into their policies and practices any consideration of STMs' need to plan ahead for childcare and other practical and logistical matters (Woodhouse and Guihen, 2022). Neither do ITE providers gather data about students who are parents. Consequently, ITE tutors do not necessarily know which of their students have children, and this may only become apparent when problems arise (Moreau, 2016). In the event, the nature of the STM's experience may well be determined by the extent to which the individual staff members she encounters are able to offer empathy and benevolent support (Lynch, 2008; Murtagh, 2017, 2019). In some cases, it seems, tutors even equate students' parental responsibility with a lack of academic commitment (Moreau and Kerner, 2015: 227). If support for student-parents is dependent on the empathy of individual tutors, rather than any institution-wide policy, it brings into question the commitment of higher education institutions (HEIs) to inclusivity and widening participation. It appears that institutions are not yet acknowledging student-parents as a group who face particular challenges. Aside from individual tutors who may well do what they can, within a set of constraints, to support the students they know, it seems ITE providers are not yet able to pre-empt and cater for STMs' support needs in any systemic or sustained way. Consequently, STMs have to be particularly well organised, resilient, agentic and determined if they are to complete their ITE programme successfully and enter their chosen profession (Woodhouse, Guihen and Scalise, 2022).

The successful completion of the ITE year as an STM was already challenging pre-pandemic (Griffiths, 2002; Woodhouse and Guihen, 2022; NUS, 2009; Murtagh, 2017, 2019; Woodhouse, Guihen and Scalise, 2022). It seems reasonable therefore to consider how COVID-19 restrictions may have impacted the lives and experiences of STMs undertaking their training during lockdown. The picture emerging from the developing body of research in this area is both complex and contradictory. Research into the impact of enforced working at home during the pandemic suggests that across the board, women were more adversely affected than men by lockdown restrictions. The burden was stressful: most of the women surveyed (73%) in Lacey et al.'s (2020) study, for example, reported that they found working at home difficult, as their job limited time for family or their family limited time for their job (Chung et al., 2020; Lacey et al., 2020). The women felt rushed, stressed and under time pressure, struggling to find the time and space to undertake their paid work at home (Chung et al., 2020). Where heterosexual couples needed to prioritise time, space and equipment to work from home, men's working needs tended to be accommodated as a priority, to the detriment of the women's home working arrangements (Lacey et al., 2020).

On the other hand, there were also indications that men's enforced time at home resulted in many fathers in heterosexual relationships becoming more 'hands-on' with children and home-schooling, with men reportedly doing more unpaid household work and childcare than before, at least at the start of the pandemic (Andrew et al., 2020; ONS, 2021). It has been argued (for example by Andrew et al., 2020 and Chung et al., 2020) that this initial, increased involvement of fathers with children could have positive, longer-term impacts on how heterosexual couples share childcare responsibilities: there may be a shift in culture in terms of the long-established gender divide in domestic responsibilities and childcare. It seems, however, that even if fathers spent more time than previously with their children during lockdown, women still spend more time overall on childcare than do men (ONS, 2020). Most (72%) of the mothers in Lacey et al.'s (2020: 1) study of gender and family adjustments during the pandemic describe themselves as the 'default' parent for most or all of the time, with primary responsibility for 'all child related tasks'. This default responsibility remains stable, irrespective of the women's work commitments (Lacey et al., 2020). When working at home, women tend to take on the bulk of the housework and extra childcare, including home-schooling, even when both men and women are working at home (Andrew et al., 2020; Chung et al., 2020; Lacey et al., 2020; ONS, 2021). Unsurprisingly, working mothers report that they have experienced 'very high levels of work-family conflict' during the pandemic (Chung et al., 2020: 7), which impact negatively on their mental health and well-being (ONS, 2021).

The small body of research into the experiences of working mothers during lockdown is drawn from a range of women across the employment spectrum. At the time of writing, there is no evidence drawn specifically from the experiences of STMs. The study on which I report in this chapter sought to address this gap. The women who took part in the study had started their ITE year pre-pandemic and so completed the first half of the year under 'normal' circumstances. This involved a full-time school-based placement, with, for some, some lengthy commutes, plus face-to-face, taught sessions at the university and the completion of academic work, as well as lesson planning and evaluations. As the lockdown started towards the end of March 2020, the second part of their course took place in unprecedented circumstances, the taught part of their programme being made available online via a combination of synchronous and asynchronous modes of provision. Student-teachers had to negotiate with schools and tutors to find ways to evidence that they were meeting the professional standards through the completion of tasks online, some of which included teaching and tutoring pupils remotely.

I was interested in how women with children experienced combining ITE and parenting pre- and during COVID-19 restrictions. The investigation was guided by the following research question:

> How do STMs describe their experiences of combining the ITE year and motherhood (i) pre-COVID-19 and (ii) during the COVID-19 restrictions?

I turn below to the process I followed in gathering and making sense of data to answer this question.

Research design

Participants and recruitment

In order to recruit participants, I emailed information about the study to the directors of the primary and secondary ITE courses at the case study university, which is located in England. I asked tutors to share this with their students, inviting students to respond if they met the criteria for inclusion, that is, they were mothers and current ITE students at the university. Twelve participants responded. Nine agreed to be interviewed.

Participants were asked to complete a short, factual, pre-interview questionnaire in order to provide brief biographical details. The questionnaire contained short questions relating to participants' financial status (specifically, whether or not they were in receipt of a training bursary or salary), their ethnicity, relational status, sexuality, number and ages of children and the type of course they were following. Whilst the students were all following one-year programmes leading to the main teaching qualification in the UK, the PGCE (Postgraduate/Professional Certificate of Education), they were following a variety of routes. Options included primary or secondary, university-led, school-led or school-based training. School-led routes were offered through School Direct, and school-based possibilities through School Centred Initial Teacher Training (SCITT). SCITT providers are government-approved centres able to run their own teacher training courses and award Qualified Teacher Status. SCITT students therefore undertake most of their training and teaching practice in their allocated school, with quality assurance provided by a university for master's level work. School Direct students are equally based between the university and a school partnership group.

Responses to the questionnaire are summarised in Table 3.1, below, which includes the following information:

- Financial situation, that is, whether or not the student was in receipt of a bursary. This is included because an earlier study suggested that financial difficulties could be considerable for some students (see Woodhouse and Guihen, 2022);
- Ethnicity, as this was a diverse group:
- Relationship status, which might be relevant in understanding the extent to which individual women were supported or otherwise in bringing up children;
- Number of children: as this varied from one to five children, this has been included as an indication of the likely demands on individual women.

The age of the children has also been included because, as some of the women commented, as children grow up and become more independent there may be greater scope for women to fit in professional work and studies than when children are pre-school age and more dependant.

As all of the participants described themselves as heterosexual, sexuality has not been included in the detail of Table 3.1. Pseudonyms are used in this table and throughout the chapter.

TABLE 3.1 Biographical details of the participants in the study

Pseudonym and Financial Status	Ethnicity	Relationship Status	Number of Children	ITE Programme/Phase/Subject
Jawaria Self-funding; no bursary	Indian	Married and living with husband	3 (aged 19, 14 and 12)	University-led Primary
Rosalie Bursary	White European	Divorced Single parent	5 (aged 20, 18-year-old twins, 12 and 9)	School Direct Secondary Modern Foreign Languages
Monika Self-funding; no bursary	White British	Married and living with husband	2 (aged 5 and 2)	University-led Primary
Mary Self-funding; No bursary	White British	Living with partner	2 (aged 3 and 9)	University-led Lower Primary
Faiza Bursary	Arab	Married and living with husband	2 (aged 6 and 4)	University-led Secondary Modern Foreign Languages
Hua Bursary	Chinese	Living with partner	1 (aged 6)	SCITT Secondary Mathematics
Elena Bursary	White British	Married and living with husband	2 (aged 4 and 7)	SCITT Secondary Science
Olivia Financial status not disclosed	Black British	Married and living with husband	5 (aged 24, 21, 19, and 17-year-old twins)	SCITT Secondary Social Sciences
Sonia Financial status not disclosed	Ethnicity not disclosed	Married and living with husband	Number of children not disclosed	Programme not disclosed

Data collection

A research assistant carried out the nine semi-structured interviews online via Zoom or Teams or via telephone, during the period May–July 2020. The interview schedule included a number of core questions, with probing questions asked as appropriate. Topics included motivation to teach, childcare arrangements, the challenges they faced as a student-teacher and a mother, coping strategies and sources of support, and aspirations for the future.

Participants were asked to comment on their experiences before as well as during COVID-19. The interviews were recorded and transcribed in full, and thematic analysis was undertaken, as I explain below.

Data analysis

An inductive, phased approach to thematic analysis was used to examine the STMs' experiences of ITE before and during COVID-19 restrictions (Braun and Clarke, 2006; Terry, Hayfield, Clarke and Braun, 2017). I began my analysis of the STMs' accounts by familiarising myself with the dataset. This involved reading and re-reading each of the nine transcripts and noting down features of interest. Next, I systematically and inclusively generated initial codes related to the women's experience. Once all of the transcripts were thoroughly coded, I set about developing themes. It is important to note that themes did not 'emerge' from the dataset during this phase. They were actively constructed and, in acknowledging this, I emphasise my own agency as the researcher and the active choices made during the analytic process (Terry et al., 2017: 27). Once codes were grouped into potential themes, I reviewed, defined and named the themes. This was a lengthy process, and I found that greater clarity regarding theme names and definitions was achieved through writing about the project. I constructed five themes that were common across the student-mothers' accounts, which were labelled as follows:

- Advantages of being an STM (in terms of combining teaching and parenting)
- Challenges of being an STM pre-COVID-19
- Advantages of being an STM during COVID-19
- Challenges of being an STM during COVID-19
- STMs' views on improving provision for STMs in future/advice for other STMs.

The themes identified above have been incorporated into the report of the findings, presented in the next section, below.

Findings

The interviews focused on the women's experiences of ITE both before and during what became known as 'lockdown'. Whilst the nine interviewees reported unique, idiosyncratic experiences, there was a degree of commonality in their perspectives, and I report here on the themes that appeared in the transcripts of four or more participants. As a reminder, the research question guiding the study was:

How do STMs describe their experiences of combining the ITE year and motherhood (i) pre-COVID-19 and (ii) during the COVID-19 restrictions?

Findings are presented under the sub-headings:

- Experiences pre-COVID-19
- Experiences during COVID-19

In each section, consideration is given to the women's perceptions of the challenges they faced and the factors that sustained them.

Experiences pre-COVID-19

The major challenges identified in the women's accounts of their pre-COVID-19 experiences ranged from the practical to the affective and included (i) managing the multiple workload; (ii) logistical difficulties associated with travel to and from school placements; and (iii) feelings of guilt. I present examples of each of these challenges below and then discuss the sources of support on which the women drew and the coping strategies that helped them.

Most of the women (6 of 9) commented that they had found the combined workload intense and, at times, overwhelming during the first part of the year, before COVID-19. They talked about the difficulty of having to juggle academic and domestic work, teaching and parenting. For example:

> The most stressful part was doing all the teaching and trying to juggle that with [...] childcare, and housework chores, and the assignment [...] The hours of teaching I was having to do [...], having to plan four or five lessons a day - it was getting a bit too much [...] trying to get everything done [...], making sure the school uniform was washed and ironed and ready to go for Monday [...] That was difficult [...] The whole PGCE thing [was difficult], making sure that I had lesson plans ready for the next day. What I tried to do was to stay at school and make sure I did everything there, so by the time I got home I'd done everything I needed to do [...] but that meant that I would have to stay at school until 7 or 8 o'clock at night, which was silly. It was unrealistic. I'd come back, my child would have been fed and he was in bed. I didn't see him some nights. So it kind of didn't work (Hua).

> The workload, the amount of paperwork and the number of hours I was having to put in have been extortionate, much more than I expected [...] I didn't think it would be like this. [...] So that's challenging [...] But I think most challenging is getting my kids to school in the morning and trying to go into school with a clear head so you can start your day. So

stressful! I've got two boys. They're close in age. Just getting them out of the house in the morning, getting their clothes on, then having all the lessons […] prepped, I think that's challenging with children […] I'm probably doing a 70 hour week a lot of the time (Elena).

Associated with the multiple workload were the logistical difficulties many of the women faced, travel arrangements being a significant challenge for some. Two-thirds of the participants talked about difficulties associated with travelling to and from school placements during the programme:

> [My school] wasn't really far, but I had to take public transport [and] drop my daughter [at her school]. My husband took the little one to the nursery, and then I got my daughter after school, and then I would take the bus to the secondary school where my placement was, and the same thing on the way back […] Sometimes it takes so much time too for the bus to come! […] It was just a vicious circle (Faiza).
>
> I don't drive, so I get the train to the university and back. When I'm on placement, I've been quite lucky where my placements have been. They've both been in the city on main transport links, but I think my third placement for the summer term would have been a bit more out in the sticks. […] I think I probably would have struggled to get to one of those schools at a reasonable time (Monika).

Practical difficulties in managing the competing workloads led most of the women to feel they were not fulfilling their role as a parent particularly well. Two-thirds of the women talked about the guilt they had felt, particularly during the first term of the ITE year (pre-COVID-19), when they were struggling to juggle professional and personal lives, feeling at times that they were neglecting their children in some way. For example:

> I had my children go to a breakfast club, and an after-school club, and then onto another after school club. So, sadly, with a heavy heart, putting them into these settings meant changing twice in a day: the breakfast club is at school, and then after school they're ferried across to somewhere else. That makes you feel terrible really (Elena).
>
> Marking and planning lessons at home [takes] up a lot of my time, which I should really be giving to my children, some of it anyway […] [and] as a single mum I don't have a partner who can take [the children] out and do some activities with them, help them with homework […] Certainly the workload is an issue but there is no other way around it, as I have to take [work] home. I have to be home. I'm here physically but not giving [my children] attention (Rosalie).

Pragmatically, the women drew on a range of sources of support pre-COVID-19 to help them manage their domestic, academic and professional work. Husbands or partners, immediate and extended family members were cited as key sources of help and support by seven of the nine participants. For example:

> My husband has been very supportive. His role since January changed and he had some flexibility to be able to take the children to school in the mornings for a few months, so he's very supportive to me in that way. On days where I had to be at a different school, he would take the children in the morning (Elena).
>
> I had to organise it so that each person in the family was taking turns cooking and taking responsibility for their own washing and own ironing, doing a rota where we would divide the chores up (Sonia).
>
> My sister lives quite close […] so we had an arrangement that she would come over to the house and take [my son] to school and she'd pick him up as well, and […] she'd sort him out and look after him in the afternoon until I got back […] That was always a big help, so sometimes if I didn't get back until after tea, at least I'd know that he'd been fed because she'd feed him, because she was cooking anyway […] I'd come back, my child would have been fed. He was in bed (Hua).
>
> My mother-in-law lives just a few doors down from me, so if ever one of [my children] is not well, or if I feel like I don't want to leave them alone, she's never said no to me. They can always go sit at hers, and she'll keep an eye on them […] My mum and my mother-in-law […] are the two that are always available when I need them […] Not having my mum and mother-in-law would cause considerable problems for us (Jawaria).

Organised childcare, such as pre- and post-school clubs, was also found to be very helpful:

> I was fortunate [that] the school my kids are at [has] after school care club. So, I just paid for that, and that was so cheap rather than taking them to a child minder. So, they are just in school. I pick them up. I paid up to 5:45pm. It works well (Olivia).
>
> I had to arrange childcare for my 9 year old, but my other children are older, the 12 year old could take the bus and come back on his own. The 9 year old, I had to drop off at breakfast club 7.30 in the morning. She then had to be picked up by a minibus to be taken to another school club on the other side of town, where I had to pick her up at 5.30 in the evening (Rosalie).

Reflecting on their own experiences and coping strategies, the women offered advice for other student-teacher mothers. In particular, emphasis was placed on:

i   making sure reliable, flexible childcare arrangements are in place, with contingency plans to cope with illness. Hua advised, 'Make sure you have some decent childcare arrangements definitely, you know, and that you have back up';
ii being very well organised and planning your time well. In Jawaria's words, 'Go into it with your eyes open and just be organised, really organised';
iii asking for and accepting help from others, professionally and personally. Rosalie reflected, 'It has been really, really hard and challenging, so what I would say is be prepared, it's going to be really, really hard, hang in there. Don't hesitate to ask for help ever, from anybody. The only thing you can get is a no, and that's not going to kill you';
iv and ensuring you really want to teach before you start the programme: 'I think that my advice would be that [you] really look into it, make sure it's something [you] really want to do, maybe get some experience, if [you've] not had experience in a school or anything, go and do that first because it is a lot of commitment' (Mary).

These comments were borne out of the participants' own experiences of coping with the combined pressures of home and ITE, especially during the first half of the year. The women's daily lives continued to be challenging during the COVID-19 restrictions, yet the nature of the challenges they described, their feelings about them and the factors that sustained them shifted, as I discuss below.

Experiences during COVID-19

The interviews, which were carried out during the first few months of the UK COVID-19 restrictions, provide a snapshot of how participants were experiencing lockdown at that point (spring/summer 2020). Had I revisited the women 6, 12 or 18 months later, the stresses and pressures on them might have been different. However, at the time of the interviews, the interviewees reported relatively few additional challenges as compared to their pre-COVID-19 recollections. Indeed, their accounts suggested that they were experiencing fewer challenges than before. The pressures of combining school placement, university assignments, domestic and familial responsibilities had been intense for most participants pre-COVID-19. Now based at home, their daily lives had become more manageable, For example, Faiza commented:

> It [was] very intense [before lockdown], […] very difficult to have a balance between work and family life, and also some time for myself […] The

work-life balance, I found it difficult to manage that, because it's quite demanding to do the lesson plans, teaching and reflecting [....] I don't see, actually, any challenges about COVID-19. COVID-19 hasn't [presented] any challenges for me. I think I'm OK. I'm still doing work to meet the standards and so on. It's just, you do it at your own pace [...] The only thing that has changed is just the pace. It's not just the pace, I mean we are together. I'm with my children as well. I think we have more quality time. [My husband is] working as well, so [I have] time to do my work when he's working. We see each other, we talk to each other a little bit better than before. I think even my children - I mean, the lifestyle that we had because of my training, and I had to drop my daughter at 7:30am and pick her up around 5:30pm or sometimes 6pm when I was at the university, I think it had an impact on [my children]. They lost a little bit of weight, [they were] tired, you know? My son is 4 and he had to spend the whole day at nursery (Faiza).

The women identified a combination of factors that had eased the pressure on them, diminishing the multi-layered burden of lesson planning and teaching, childcare, academic work and housework. Firstly, they were no longer under pressure to plan lessons and teach on a daily basis:

With the lockdown, and the closures of the schools, the teaching was taken away, so the planning was taken away (Hua)

The school that I'm currently on placement at isn't doing all that much in terms of online lessons. It's fairly light touch. There are presentations and links to videos, materials like that being sent out to the children, and fortunately, though I offered, they haven't needed my assistance, and because I've got two children at home I haven't been required to go in and help with the keyworker children, which has been very kind and understanding [...] After having done the last six months training in schools and working late at night to lesson prep, I felt now during this closure period, I didn't want to keep working late nights if I didn't have to. I'm now trying to fit a bit of knowledge enhancement in between teaching my [own] kids. So yeah, pretty fine at the moment really, much less stress than when I was in the school (Elena).

Second, the hectic commutes between home, childcare providers and school/university were no longer a daily pressure:

[Before I was] juggling everything. The most challenging thing was dropping off in the morning, and going to the other side of town to pick up in the evening. That was a killer basically, because I had to travel across town to pick [my daughter] up at 5.30 and on occasions the traffic was so bad it would take me a good hour to go and pick her up, then coming back preparing dinner, getting uniforms ready and so on, putting everyone to bed early enough. [Now the children] are all at home with me (Rosalie).

Third, being at home with their children during the COVID-19 restrictions meant the women did not now have to organise childcare:

[Before COVID my sister] would come over to the house and take [my son] to school and she'd pick him up as well, and because she [lives] so close, she'd sort him out and look after him in the afternoon until I got back [...] [My sister] doesn't have to do anything now [and my husband is] working from home, whereas before he had to go into work, which has helped, as he can help more with the childcare as well. I am [coping] OK now, because the most stressful part was doing all the teaching, and trying to juggle that with doing some childcare and housework chores and also doing the assignment (Hua).

Although the women now had the additional responsibility of having to home-school their own children, the flexibility offered by the online provision of their ITE programme allowed them to fit their own work around home-schooling activities. For example, Monika explained:

I've got both of the children at home with me [...] My daughter is 5 so she's in foundation stage. The [teachers] are sending through her learning, so I'm doing that with her, and our [ITE] course is also running remotely still, but the workload isn't too heavy. I just work in the evenings on what I've got to do [...] I am at home, and because I'm still studying, and because [the university has] been very flexible about the learning that they're sending us, I can be flexible (Monika).

I consider below how the insights gleaned in this study might begin to inform post-COVID-19 ITE practical arrangements, pedagogies and programme design, as well as provide some insights for forthcoming STMs regarding what to expect and how they might cope with the multiple demands of combining motherhood and ITE.

Discussion

I have reported here on the experiences of women combining motherhood and ITE during the academic year 2019–2020. I base my observations on the snapshot I gained of their experiences at the time of the interviews, whilst conceding that as the COVID-19 restrictions continued, participants' lives may have changed, becoming more, or less, challenging.

The women's accounts suggest that, in terms of managing their multiple workload, living under UK COVID-19 restrictions was less stressful in some ways than their pre-COVID-19 lives had been. In this, they were different from the women in other COVID-19 studies (see Lacey et al., 2020; Chung et al., 2020), who struggled to undertake their paid work at home. The STMs in this study drew to some extent on the support of their husbands or partners with childcare and some aspects of domestic work, which is consistent with the findings of Andrew et al. (2020) and ONS (2021). The removal of logistical difficulties, such as commuting and delivering children to childcare providers, lightened their load somewhat, and, although they were home-schooling their children, this did not seem to be perceived as particularly challenging. Perhaps as student-teachers, they were equipped with the skills and knowledge to undertake home-based tutoring in ways that other parents may not have been.

Overall, their combined workload was perceived to have been alleviated when compared with their pre-COVID-19 experience. Importantly, a contributory factor in their sense of relief was the shift in the mode of delivery of their training programme, from face-to-face to online. Student-teachers were now to engage with synchronous and asynchronous tasks and activities to complete their academic and teaching-related work. This shift afforded the STMs greater flexibility, thus empowering them to make their own decisions about what to study, when, where and how. Faiza, for example, commented that the more flexible online provision offered scope to do the course 'at your own pace', and Monika explained, 'I just work in the evenings on what I've got to do […] because [the university has] been very flexible about the learning that they're sending us, I can be flexible'. This flexibility allowed the STMs to fit their training around the demands of childcare, home-schooling and domestic responsibilities.

Flexibility in the way students can access provision would seem to be, potentially, a key factor in ensuring inclusivity for non-traditional students in HE, such as student-parents or those with caring responsibilities. It seems reasonable that ITE providers might henceforth consider which elements of the programme lend themselves to asynchronous, online activities that can be accessed flexibly and independently at students' convenience, allowing students with caring responsibilities greater scope to fit vocational training around their home circumstances.

At the same time, it is worth noting that the development of effective, asynchronous, online activities for independent study requires that course designers and developers are trained not only in using the different available technologies but in understanding online pedagogy. Online instruction, as Poe (2020: 211) comments, 'is not a hobby'. Flexibility of provision does not in itself ensure learning, nor does it guarantee that student-teachers will be able to evidence that they have met the standards for Qualified Teacher

Status. ITE providers need therefore to provide time and resources for collaborative staff reflection on course design and pedagogy in order to pilot and develop coherent, effective, online provision.

Evidently, there is a place for flexible, independent study in ITE. That said, the social and relational aspects of collaborative learning and face-to-face engagement should not be underestimated (Dewey, 1938; Vygotsky, 1978). Technology, Poe (2020: 211) argues, 'cannot, and certainly must not, replace social interaction'. Whilst it is relatively easy to convert a teacher-centred talk or lecture to an online video or narration, important opportunities for more student-centred, experiential forms of learning are rather more challenging to simulate online. It is very difficult to create an online environment conducive to meaningful collaboration, with students fully engaged in working together to solve problems, discuss issues and produce solutions. Most of us now have the experience of setting up breakout rooms on platforms such as Microsoft Teams or trying to lead a group discussion on Zoom, with varying degrees of success (or failure). This was difficult, though not impossible in 2019–2020, when the students had formed friendships and working relationships during the first half of the academic year. Without the opportunity for students to meet face-to-face and bond as colleagues on the same programme during the first part of the course, efforts to engage trainees in online discussions can be still more difficult. I would recommend therefore that some thought be given to which aspects of the ITE programme are best offered face-to-face in order to be effective and to build a programme that combines timetabled, face-to-face, whole-group sessions with flexible, asynchronous elements for individual access.

Even if we are able to move to a more flexible provision, incorporating some face-to-face and some online resources, this does not guarantee equal access to all. Whilst there are advantages in terms of the potential offered for flexibility and asynchronous study, there are also inequalities and challenges associated with online pedagogies. Students are likely to experience their programmes differently, depending on their home and personal circumstances. Poe (2020: 212) observes that 'some students' life situations [are] exponentially more complicated than others'. Single parent Rosalie, for example, in this study, may have experienced greater limitations in combining caring responsibilities with study than some of her peers. It seems clear therefore that ITE providers need to know more about their students if they are to attempt to address some of these inequalities. At present, in HE, whilst we collect data about our students' gender, ethnicity and disability, we do not know which of our students are parents or carers. Thus, STMs remain, as I have argued elsewhere, the 'missing statistic' in ITE (Woodhouse and Guihen, 2022: 291). This omission leads me to recommend that ITE providers begin to collect such data when students register (although students must also retain the right to withhold personal and family details should they wish to). By acknowledging this group of students, we can begin to monitor their progress and experiences and put tailored support in place. It is only by knowing which of our students face particular challenges that we can hope to develop more inclusive practices.

It is interesting to reflect that working remotely and connecting with colleagues and students via Zoom, Teams or other platforms during the COVID-19 restrictions gave us a window into each other's home lives. Comic moments of cats walking across laptops, toddlers stealing the show and husbands bringing in tea and toast offered moments of levity, but also added a sense of the previously hidden nature of colleagues' and students' other lives beyond the classroom walls. Poe (2020: 212) notes that we have undergone a 'cataclysmic shift': not only are we learning new educational and people skills, we are also realising that:

> faculty and students are not just the people we see in class, but they have lives outside of class that affect their work. We must be cognizant of these outside factors to fully understand our colleagues and our students […] If we approach each other [post-COVID-19] with these newly learned realizations, it could enrich the learning environment.

Knowing more about students before they arrive might help ITE providers to find ways in which they could ensure the logistical challenges for STMs and other carers are minimised. For example, informing STMs of their schools and timetables as early as possible would allow them to arrange childcare and plan ahead for travel and commuting arrangements prior to the start of the programme, removing a layer of anxiety and stress for many students in this position. It might be helpful too to allocate school placements to students with parental or caring responsibilities before allocating placements to single and care-free students. That said, this is not something ITE providers can ensure without the co-operation and support of policymakers and school-based colleagues. Even twenty years ago when I was an initial teacher educator in the South of England, finding school placements for students was an immense challenge. The number of offers of school placements is still very limited. This situation has more recently been exacerbated with the roll-out of the Early Career Framework in the UK, which requires mentors for newly qualified teachers for the first two years of teaching, thus limiting schools' and teachers' capacity to support student-teachers. Needless to say, further difficulties have resulted from the pressures generated by COVID-19 in schools.

To conclude, the COVID-19 experience of teaching and preparing teachers has been challenging. Yet, it has opened up new possibilities, as we have become more aware of alternative ways of working that offer the potential to enrich students' experiences in lasting and meaningful ways. In the context of

ITE, this enrichment might helpfully start with a recognition that the student body is rather more diverse than the traditional view of the 'ideal' or 'normal' student as white, male, single, child-free and mobile. We might begin to take notice of the ways in which lives outside the university impact on our students' experiences of HE. This would provide us with a base on which to build a more inclusive culture in ITE. In the appendix to this chapter, I include a set of prompt questions that may be useful as a toolkit for reassessing the nature of institutional ITE provision and the scope for developing a more inclusive model. Yet this is not simply within the gift of ITE providers and tutors to offer: the scope for them to make decisions and imagine new possibilities is heavily constrained by reforms from the Department for Education (DfE: the government body responsible for children's services and education in the UK) and the requirements of Ofsted (Office for Standards in Education, Children's Services and Skills: the government body responsible for inspecting a range of educational institutions, including schools). Moreover, at the time of writing, ITE providers are also bound by the imperative to prepare for courses that incorporate the new quality requirements that will be a part of the ITE criteria from September 2024. Policymakers and educational leaders are key to making it possible for ITE providers to ensure inclusivity.

Acknowledgements

I am grateful to the University of Leicester School of Education for funding this study. I am indebted to Laura Guihen and Maria Scalise for their help with data collection and analysis, to Farhat Syyeda and Fay Baldry for comments on earlier drafts of the chapter and to the nine women who gave generously of their time to be interviewed for this study.

References

Andrew, A., Cattan, S., Costa Dias, M., Farquharson, C., Kraftman, L., Krutikova, S., Phimister, A. and Sevilla, A. (2020) *How are mothers and fathers balancing work and family under lockdown? Institute for Fiscal Studies Report.* Available at: https://www.ifs.org.uk/publications/14860 (Accessed: 19 May 2021).

Bradbury, L. and Gunter, H. (2006) 'Dialogic identities: the experiences of women who are headteachers and mothers in English primary schools', *School Leadership and Management*, 26 (5), pp. 489–504.

Braun, V. and Clarke, V. (2006) 'Using thematic analysis in psychology', *Qualitative Research in Psychology*, 3 (2), pp. 77–101.

Chung, H., Seo, H., Forbes, S. and Birkett, H. (2020) *Working from home during the Covid-19 lockdown: changing preferences and the future of work. Universities of Birmingham and Kent.* Available at: Working from home during the COVID-19 lockdown: changing preferences and the future of work - Kent Academic Repository (Accessed: 19 May 2021).

Coleman, M. (2002) *Women as headteachers: striking the balance*. Stoke on Trent: Trentham Books.

Dewey, J. (1938) *Experience and education*. New York: Collier Books.

Griffiths, V. (2002) 'Crossing boundaries: the experiences of mature student mothers in Initial Teacher Education', *International Journal of Inclusive Education*, 6 (3), pp. 267–285.

Lacey, A., Cartwright-Hatton, S., Colling, L.J., Banerjee, R. and Lester, K.J. (2020) *Covid-19: relationships, emotional well-being, and family adjustment study. Gender and equalities preliminary report: 10th June 2020.* Available at: Gender+and+Equals_report_final.pdf (squarespace.com) (Accessed: 19 May 2021).

Lynch, K. (2008) 'Gender roles and the American academe: a case study of graduate student mothers', *Gender and Education*, 20 (6), pp. 585–605.

McNamara, O., Howson, J., Gunter, H. and Fryers, A. (2010) *No job for a woman? The impact of gender in school leadership*. Birmingham: NASUWT.

Moreau, M.P. (2016) 'Regulating the student body/ies: university policies and student parents', *British Educational Research Journal*, 42 (5), pp. 906–925.

Moreau, M.P. and Kerner, C. (2015) 'Care in academia: an exploration of student parents' experiences', *British Journal of Sociology of Education*, 36 (2), pp. 215–233.

Moreau, M., Osgood, J. and Halsall, A. (2007) 'Making sense of the glass ceiling in schools: an exploration of women teachers' discourses', *Gender and Education*, 19 (2), pp. 237–253.

Murtagh, L. (2017) 'Invisible perceptions: understanding the perceptions of university tutors towards trainee teachers with parental responsibilities', *Asia-Pacific Journal of Teacher Education*, 45 (4), pp. 383–398.

Murtagh, L. (2019) 'Others and othering: the lived experiences of trainee teachers with parental responsibilities', *Journal of Further and Higher Education*, 43 (6), pp. 788–800.

National Union of Students (2009) *Meet the parents. The experience of students with children in Further and Higher Education. National Union of Students*. Available at: Meet the Parents: the experience of students with children in further and higher education (2009) @ NUS Connect (Accessed: 31 March 2022).

Office for National Statistics (2020) *Parenting in lockdown: coronavirus and the effects on work-life balance*. Available at: https://www.ons.gov.uk/peoplepopulationandcommunity/healthandsocialcare/conditionsanddiseases/articles/parentinginlockdowncoronavirusandtheeffectsonworklifebalance/2020-07-22 (Accessed: 18 May 2021).

Office for National Statistics (2021) *Coronavirus (Covid-19) and the different effects on men and women in the UK, March 2020 to February 2021*. Available at: https://www.ons.gov.uk/peoplepopulationandcommunity/healthandsocialcare/conditionsanddiseases/articles/coronaviruscovid19andthedifferenteffectsonmenandwomenintheukmarch2020tofebruary2021/2021-03-10 (Accessed: 19 May 2021).

Poe, C.P. (2020) 'Pedagogy in the time of COVID-19', *Croatian Medical Journal*, 61, pp. 211–212.

Smith, J. (2016) 'Motherhood and women teachers' career decisions: a constant battle', in Fuller, K. and Harford, J. (eds.) *Gender and leadership in education: women achieving against the odds*. Bern: Peter Lang, pp. 83–114.

Smith, J.M. (2011) 'Agency and female teachers' career decisions: a life history study of forty women', *Educational Management Administration and Leadership*, 39 (1), pp. 7–24.

Terry, G., Hayfield, N., Clarke, V. and Braun, V. (2017) 'Thematic analysis', in Willig, C. and Stainton Rogers, W. (eds.) *The Sage handbook of qualitative research in psychology* (2nd Ed.). London: Sage. pp. 17–37.

Vygotsky, LS. (1978) *Mind in society: the development of higher psychological processes*. Cambridge, MA: Harvard University Press.

Woodhouse, J. and Guihen, L. (2022) 'The missing statistic in initial teacher education: experiences and support needs of student teachers who are mothers', in Showunmi, V., Moorosi, P., Shakeshaft, C. and Oplatka, I. (eds.) *The Bloomsbury handbook of gender and educational leadership and management*. London: Bloomsbury, pp. 291–304.

Woodhouse, J., Guihen, L. and Scalise, M. (2022) "I've just got to get through It!' Student teacher mothers negotiating the challenges of the initial teacher education year', *Teacher Education Advancement Network Journal*, 14 (1), pp. 46–60.

APPENDIX

Toolkit for re-thinking ITE provision post-COVID-19: key points and prompt questions for leaders, policymakers and ITE providers

1. Acknowledge student carers in the equity monitoring statistics
   - How and when can data about students with caring responsibilities be gathered?
   - What might be the concerns of potential students about providing such information?
   - How might student anxieties about providing such data be alleviated?
   - How will this data be shared, and with whom?
   - How can it be used to inform decisions, e.g. about school placements?
   - Is it possible to gather data in order to monitor the progress of students with caring responsibilities?

2. Develop a blended learning model
   - Which elements of the programme lend themselves to asynchronous, online, flexible provision for independent access?
   - Is there scope to streamline face-to-face, taught content in order to optimise online provision?
   - Which elements of the programme are more effectively taught face-to-face?

3. Practicalities
   - Are there elements of the ITE programme that could be omitted, and/or left for schools to provide when novice teachers join the profession? Can the DfE take the lead in making this possible?
   - Is there scope for greater flexibility on assignment deadlines? And/or could more part-time courses be offered?

- Is there scope for a wider range of modes of assignment (e.g. presentations/videos rather than written assignments? Other modes?)
- Are there ways in which calendar dates, timings of days etc can be more family-friendly?
- Is it possible that handbooks, course information and guidance can be made available earlier to assist with planning for those with caring responsibilities?
- Can school placements be allocated to student-parents/carers as a priority?

4

TEACHING THROUGH THE MENOPAUSE

A flexible work paradox

Belinda Steffan and Kristina Potočnik

Introduction

Teacher retention is becoming a crisis in the UK and is often associated with high levels of emotional exhaustion as a key reason for an early exit from the profession (Van Eycken et al., 2022). Job demands are high for teachers; characteristics of their job, such as high workload, the fast pace of work, and high levels of job insecurity, are among the main reasons why teachers leave the profession (Amitai & Van Houtte, 2022; Evers et al., 2016). Teaching is associated with a high risk of burnout, and teachers who experience burnout are more likely to report lower job commitment (Hakenen, Bakker, & Shaufeli, 2006). Further, work pressure and emotional demands of the job itself can evoke negative psychological states (Evers et al., 2016).

There is an expectation that teachers are experts in their field and can cope with a changing landscape of professional requirements and student diversity, meeting societal expectations of what it means to be a teacher (Organization for Economic Cooperation and Development, 2009). Teachers are expected to be flexible employees with flexible competences, defined as 'employees' capacity to function both effectively and efficiently in their profession' (i.e. being competent or an expert) (Evers et al., 2016, p. 228). The work of teachers reflects a range of technical capacities, but also foregrounds an emphasis on care (Beauchamp et al., 2021). Further, a higher teaching commitment is associated with high job efficacy or being able to maintain performance at work (Van Eycken et al., 2022; citing Coladarci, 1992). Taken together, the teaching profession is one of high personal and professional standards but also one that is susceptible to burnout-related factors, which threaten the profession itself.

As the COVID-19 pandemic swept through the UK, the majority of workers who could work from home were obligated to do so. This included teachers due to the closure of schools to limit the spread of the virus, resulting in the majority of children being educated from home. For teachers, this created a significant challenge of recreating the classroom situation from home (Kim & Asbury, 2020), something they were never expected to do before the pandemic. More details on the breadth of this challenge are covered in other chapters of this book, suffice to say that COVID-19 created a challenge to well-being and the ability to teach in line with personal and professional standards.

The evidence above suggests that the teaching profession, while rewarding, can be stressful and demanding. There is an additional burden for the vast majority of teachers of menopausal age who identify as women, due to the potentially disruptive effects of menopause transition on their health and other work-related outcomes and attitudes. Menopause also affects individuals who identify as trans and non-binary (Steffan & Potočnik, 2022). Menopause is particularly relevant to this occupational group as the teaching workforce is predominately composed of women.[1] Specifically, 75.5% of teachers in England are women (UK Government, 2021). Further, until 2017, the teaching profession was becoming younger; however, since then, the age groups between 40 and 59 years have been increasing, with the over-60 age group remaining constant (UK Government, 2021). While there is a lack of published research on how teachers in the UK experience menopause at work, one recent qualitative study found that teachers had specific challenges in coping with their menopause symptoms due to performance pressures of the job and a lack of flexible work options (Steffan, 2021).

Taken together, this raises the question of how teachers cope with menopause at work and how this was affected by work-related changes during the pandemic. We explored this question in our research on menopause and flexible working during the pandemic, finding that while COVID-19 presented a stressor to teaching (from home), working from home provided an ease to managing menopause. We discuss these findings in more depth in this chapter.

We proceed as follows. First, we review the literature and research evidence on individual and organisational mechanisms of managing menopause at work. We then explain the mixed-methods methodology we used in our research and present our quantitative and qualitative findings. We start by comparing how teachers experienced menopause at work compared with employees from other occupations in a range of different workplace indicators. We then draw on participant narratives to report how specific symptoms affected teachers at work. We conclude the chapter with a discussion of these findings and provide nuanced practical recommendations around flexible work arrangements that could be implemented to help teachers manage their menopause at work.

Individual and organisational mechanisms of managing menopause at work

The current wave of menopause awareness is directly translating to increased menopause awareness at work, which is a positive development as more women than ever before are working throughout their entire menopause cycle (Hardy et al., 2018). Menopause is the end of a reproductive cycle, being that point where an individual has not had a period for 12 months, which usually happens between the ages of 45 and 55. Prior to this point is the peri-menopause phase, which lasts on average four years and can include an experience of around 34 symptoms, including reduced energy, increased anxiety, hot flushes, irregular periods, and night sweats (National Health Service, 2022). While there are many symptoms ranging in severity, the experience of medical, social, and organisational support is variable depending on where a woman lives and works. To this end, the current wave of awareness around menopause is encouraging.

Recent research on menopause and work has focused on individual and organisational levels of how menopause is experienced at work. Individually, women manage their symptoms at work by drawing on social and psychological coping mechanisms (Griffiths et al., 2013), hiding and denying symptoms (Brewis et al., 2017), and using menopause as a point of work identity distinction (Butler, 2020). Organisationally, increasing awareness and creating an environment where menopause can be openly discussed can normalise and destigmatise menopause (Atkinson et al., 2021; Grandey et al., 2020). Steffan and Potočnik (2022) revealed that participants were struggling to cope with menopause symptoms at work and very few sought assistance from external sources. There was a sense that women wanted to discuss how menopause symptoms impact their work ability within their organisations, although very few felt that they had supervisory or social support networks to facilitate this discussion. Further, there was a clear acknowledgement from women in this study of a detrimental impact on work performance owing to a range of physical and psychological menopause symptoms, which is significant for this chapter as recent research on teaching has suggested that the work of teachers 'does not include physical labour' (Evers et al., 2016). This is at odds with teacher participants in our broader research on menopause, who generally discuss their jobs as both emotional and physical (e.g. Steffan, 2021).

Flexible work has gained attention during the pandemic as a mechanism through which workers in mid-to-later life can manage their health and how organisations can entice workers to stay at work for longer (Centre for Ageing

Better, 2021). Menopausal employees are also encouraged to engage in flexible hours and flexible workspaces in order to manage menopause symptoms more effectively (UK Government, 2022; Verdonk et al., 2022). However, this presents a problem for those with limited access to flexible work. While some studies have demonstrated that teachers' engagement in flexible work has the potential to support job satisfaction through the mediation of work–life balance (Gudep, 2019; Rahman, 2019), arguably the teaching profession has limited access to flexible work arrangements. Indeed, Suzanne Brown's findings in her chapter within this book reveal a failure of flexible work options to achieve desired outcomes for female teachers working part-time.

To better understand how teachers cope with menopause at work, our chapter focuses on both individual and organisational mechanisms of support. First, we examine how women use personal adaptive behavioural strategies to cope with menopause symptoms at work. Second, we draw on the concept of psychological safety, which can help us explain how organisational and team contexts contribute to how individuals respond and adapt to change and stress (Edmondson, 2012). This dual focus on individual and organisational support mechanisms highlights the importance of the person–context interaction in promoting adaptive responses at work (Edmondson et al., 2016).

Personal adaptive behavioural strategies can be used as a 'buffer against the demands of work that helps employees to remain healthy and to maintain performance levels even when resources become scarce' (Philipp & Kunter, 2013, p. 3). One often used theory to discuss personal behavioural strategies is selection, optimisation, and compensation (SOC) (Baltes, 1997). This lifespan development model is based on the principle that age-related changes in individual potential can be mitigated by maximising gains and minimising losses (Baltes, 1997). Selection is about prioritising one's goals, optimisation is about improving the use of existing resources, and compensation is based on alternative or external resources to work towards this balance of offsetting gains and losses in individual potential. Steffan and Potočnik (2022), drawing on SOC, found that adaptive behavioural strategies alongside supervisory and female peer support ameliorated the negative impact of physical menopause symptoms on work performance. In terms of how teachers use adaptive behavioural strategies, Philipp and Kunter (2013) found age-related differences whereby teachers over 50 years of age engaged in fewer non-teaching tasks and were more likely to invest time in less-demanding tasks. Crucially, older teachers' effective use of time resources acted as a buffer against the high demands of teaching. Moghimi et al. (2019) reported that increasing teachers' awareness of adaptive behavioural strategies and how to use them could increase job performance and employee well-being. Therefore, this chapter explores how managing menopause symptoms, as an important health-related indicator, is supported by teachers' use of adaptive behavioural strategies.

Psychological safety is relevant to the study of teachers' interaction with work as teaching is 'enveloped by high-stakes accountability systems, professional norms, organisational structures and local markets' (Edmondson et al., 2016, p. 66). Psychological safety occurs when employees and employers can engage in respectful and constructive conversations and where employees have a voice in how continuous improvements can be made at work. Due to the dynamic nature of teaching, where the need for creativity and continuously high-performing attention for students can be effortful, psychological safety may be beneficial to cope with the uncertainty of work (Edmondson, 2012). As psychological safety requires mutual accountability, we are reminded that teachers are expected to be flexible employees (Evers et al., 2016), raising the question of a mutual expectation of education providers to be flexible employers. Professional norms can act as a barrier to 'speaking up' within the education sector (Edmondson et al., 2016). As such, what is 'reasonable' to ask for in terms of workplace adjustment might be made in relation to what is best for the student and not the teachers themselves. There is little evidence on how psychological safety influences teachers' experience of menopause at work. However, we do know that women's menopause symptoms improve when they feel psychologically safe to 'speak up' or ask for support at work, either from their line managers or other female colleagues (Atkinson et al., 2021; Steffan & Potočnik, 2022).

Education providers should be mindful that emotional exhaustion and work pressures are often cited as contributing factors to teachers' intention to quit their job or indeed the teaching profession entirely (Amitai & Van Houtte, 2022; Van Eycken et al., 2022). Specifically in relation to psychological safety, we must consider the role of school management in a post-COVID-19 teaching climate (Boin et al., 2020), reinforcing an expectation of mutual accountability, whereby teachers should feel empowered to ask for specific sources of support and employers should do all they can to accommodate teachers' preferences (Evers et al., 2016).

In sum, the aim of this chapter is to explore how teachers manage their menopause symptoms and whether there are lessons to be learned from ways of working throughout the pandemic in how education providers can support teachers experiencing menopause. As teachers return to pre-COVID-19 work climates, with potentially limited options for flexible work, we look to individual adaptive behavioural strategies and organisational and team psychological safety to explore how teachers manage their experience of menopause at work.

Discussion of methodological approaches

This chapter is underpinned by two studies that were conducted within a broader mixed-methods longitudinal project on menopause and flexible work. The first study draws on quantitative survey data, and the second draws on qualitative interview data. Specifically, we collected our data from UK-based participants across three waves. Wave 1 took place in June 2021, when 976 participants, all identifying as women, retrospectively reflected on their experience of flexible work arrangements before and since COVID-19 started along with other strategies for managing their menopause symptoms by completing an online survey. Wave 2 survey was completed in December 2021, when 687 participants from Wave 1 responded about their experience of flexible work and other strategies for managing menopause in the post-COVID-19 context. In Wave 3 (June 2022), we interviewed 53 participants, all of whom were respondents in the online survey at Waves 1 and 2, to gain a deeper understanding of how different symptoms affect workplace outcomes and the usefulness of flexible work arrangements. Our first study is based on the quantitative analysis of Wave 1 and Wave 2 survey data to explore any differences between teachers and participants from other occupations in terms of different work-related attitudes and outcomes. Our second study draws from Wave 3 interview data, with qualitative analysis conducted both inductively to identify emerging themes and deductively to provide further insights into the quantitative findings and to present the experience of teachers themselves.

Study 1: Quantitative analyses

Survey participants were asked to indicate the category of their job type from the following options: administration and clerical, teaching, research, professional, management, manual job, and other. At Wave 1, out of 976 respondents, 154 (15.8%) selected 'teaching' as their job type. Participants were also asked to indicate their industry, with 250 (25.6%) selecting 'teaching and education'. We report Wave 1 quantitative findings based on data from 154 participants who described their job as a 'teacher' rather than those who indicated 'teaching and education' as their industry. This is because teaching and education as an industry covers job types that do not necessarily include student-facing jobs.

We conducted a number of different quantitative analyses to better understand how teachers experienced menopause at work compared with employees from other occupations. We compared teachers' perceptions on the severity of menopause symptoms, adaptive behavioural strategies (measured using the SOC framework), psychological safety, flexible work options, outcomes of job performance, burnout (exhaustion and disengagement), and retention with the perceptions of employees from other occupations by means of a series of independent samples t-tests and one-way analysis of variance. We also explored any differences in the use of flexible work arrangements between teachers and other jobholders by means of chi-square tests.

Quantitative findings

Using Wave 1 data, we found the following differences between teachers and other occupational groups combined: teachers reported significantly lower use of the SOC framework compared to all other occupations combined. They also reported that flexible work arrangements both pre- and post-COVID-19 were significantly less helpful to manage their symptoms compared to all other jobholders. Finally, teachers also experienced significantly higher exhaustion compared to all other occupations.

When comparing the results of teachers against each of the specific occupations, we found that teachers perceived significantly lower levels of psychological safety in their organisations compared to managers. Teachers also reported that flexible work arrangements before COVID-19 were significantly less helpful to manage their menopause compared to those in professional and managerial jobs. In terms of flexible work arrangements since COVID-19 started, teachers reported that such arrangements were significantly less helpful compared to those in administrative, professional, and managerial jobs. On a more positive note, teachers showed significantly lower disengagement – i.e. the extent to which employees psychologically distance themselves from everything related to work – than those holding manual jobs. Although we were not specifically analysing resilience, we observed that teachers were significantly less resilient than managers.

In Wave 2, 109 teachers (out of 154 who participated in Wave 1) completed the survey. These results showed that teachers found flexible work arrangements since COVID-19 started significantly less helpful compared to all other jobholders. We also observed that teachers exhibited significantly higher exhaustion and significantly lower retention compared to participants from other occupations. In terms of differences between specific occupations, the results showed significant differences only in terms of flexible work arrangements since COVID-19 started. We found that teachers were less likely to find these arrangements helpful compared to those in administrative and clerical positions. Also in Wave 2, teachers were significantly less resilient than managers.

Teachers and flexible work

Flexible work is one of the most desirable ways to manage menopause at work (e.g. Trade Union Congress, 2021). The COVID-19 pandemic has forced a large number of occupations to work remotely and/or flexibly for some period of time during lockdown, including teachers. Our surveys at both waves asked respondents to tell us about their experience of flexible work arrangements (see Table 4.1 for a summary of each type of arrangement).

Teaching through the menopause: A flexible work paradox 71

TABLE 4.1 The percentage of teachers highlighting the availability and usefulness of different flexible work adjustments

Flexible Work Arrangement	This Would Be Helpful W1	This Would Be Helpful W2	This Would Not Be Helpful W1	This Would Not Be Helpful W2	This Is Already Helpful W1	This Is Already Helpful W2	This Is Available and Is Not Helpful W1	This Is Available and Is Not Helpful W2	Not Available to Me W1	Not Available to Me W2
Ability to work from home	25.30%	18.50%	3.90%	6.50%	14.30%	20.40%	2.60%	/	53.90%	54.60%
Advice from employer about coping with menopause at work	36.20%	47.40%	13.80%	12.60%	8.50%	8.40%	3.10%	3.20%	38.50%	28.40%
Flexible uniform or dress code	16.80%	17.30%	10.70%	4.80%	48.30%	63.50%	4.00%	1.90%	20.10%	12.50%
Ability to work flexibly	28.80%	26.90%	3.30%	1.90%	21.60%	26.90%	0.70%	/	45.80%	44.40%
Move from full-time to part-time work	20.30%	22.40%	6.50%	5.10%	37.70%	39.80%	6.50%	3.10%	29.00%	29.60%
Access to informal support at work	41.90%	44.80%	6.60%	4.20%	25.70%	25.00%	5.10%	4.20%	20.60%	21.90%
Provision of a rest area	31.00%	35.60%	6.20%	4.80%	35.90%	28.80%	4.80%	4.80%	22.10%	26.00%
Supporting a reduction in workload	46.80%	51.50%	7.20%	4.00%	9.40%	12.90%	1.40%	2.00%	35.30%	29.70%
Better ventilation, air conditioning, and temperature control	52.40%	46.00%	4.80%	4.00%	21.80%	30.00%	2.70%	4.00%	18.40%	16.00%
Regular/predictable working hours	22.80%	21.90%	2.00%	/	60.40%	66.70%	5.40%	5.70%	9.40%	5.70%
Supporting a reduction in responsibilities	36.70%	40.40%	10.80%	10.10%	13.70%	16.20%	5.00%	2.00%	33.80%	31.30%
Readily available cold drinking water	21.60%	16.30%	0.70%	3.80%	67.30%	73.10%	3.30%	1.90%	7.20%	4.80%
Occupational health campaigns in workplaces to increase staff awareness of the difficulties women might face during the transition	53.50%	61.30%	9.40%	5.40%	9.40%	11.80%	3.10%	2.20%	24.40%	19.40%

(Continued)

TABLE 4.1 (Continued)

Flexible Work Arrangement	This Would Be Helpful W1	This Would Be Helpful W2	This Would Not Be Helpful W1	This Would Not Be Helpful W2	This Is Already Helpful W1	This Is Already Helpful W2	This Is Available and Is Not Helpful W1	This Is Available and Is Not Helpful W2	Not Available to Me W1	Not Available to Me W2
Adequate access to clean, well-equipped toilets	24.30%	26.60%	0.70%	/	69.70%	72.50%	1.30%	0.90%	3.90%	/
Mandatory equality and diversity training covering gender and age, and menopause specifically	50.40%	62.80%	9.90%	9.30%	18.30%	12.80%	4.60%	2.30%	16.80%	12.80%
Management awareness of the menopause	63.40%	65.30%	4.50%	4.20%	16.40%	16.80%	2.20%	2.10%	13.40%	11.60%
Paid leave for treatment, advice, and/or medical appointments	53.20%	65.30%	2.10%	2.10%	32.60%	26.30%	1.40%	1.10%	10.60%	5.30%
Ability to take breaks when needed	54.10%	50.50%	2.00%	3.90%	13.50%	20.40%	0.70%	/	29.70%	25.20%
A policy or guidance on the menopause	73.40%	68.60%	7.00%	9.30%	4.70%	9.30%	1.60%	/	13.30%	12.80%

Note. W1 – Wave 1; W2 – Wave 2. The sample size at Wave 1 was N =154 teachers and at Wave 2 it was N = 109 teachers.

In comparison with other job types, a set of chi-square comparison tests noted significant differences at Wave 1 (i.e. when we were well into the first year of the COVID-19 pandemic) between teachers and other jobholders in terms of the ability to work from home, ability to work flexibly, availability of occupational health campaigns and policy or guidance on menopause, respectively, and ability to take breaks when needed. Compared with other jobholders, teachers were more likely to respond that the ability to work from home and work flexibly were not available to them. Other jobholders were more likely to report that these two arrangements were already helpful compared with teachers. Regarding the ability to take breaks when needed, teachers were slightly more likely to report that this would be helpful compared with other jobholders, yet other jobholders were much more likely to report that this is already helpful compared with teachers. In terms of policy or guidance on menopause, teachers were more likely, compared with other jobholders, to report that this arrangement would be helpful, yet other jobholders were more likely to state that this arrangement was already helpful. Similar results were observed on a Wave 2 sample – i.e. at the time we thought the UK was coming out of the pandemic, only to be hit by the Omicron wave.

Finally, we were also interested in how teachers felt about working flexibly compared with other jobholders (see Table 4.2). In both waves, we found that teachers were significantly more likely to find flexible work arrangements unsuitable since they made them feel disconnected from the workplace. Teachers were also more likely to report that their supervisors, as well as other people in their workplace, would react more negatively if they used flexible work arrangements compared with other jobholders.

To summarise, our quantitative results show that teachers were more likely to suffer from higher emotional exhaustion than other jobholders and they were also less likely to find flexible work arrangements helpful. There is also some support that teachers use adaptive behavioural strategies to a lesser extent than other occupations and they are also prone to suffer from poorer retention than other occupations. Teachers also noted that certain widely used flexible work arrangements were less likely available to them compared to other jobholders. We also found that flexible work arrangements were less helpful for teachers compared with other jobholders, and this is likely due to fear of feeling disconnected from the workplace as well as assuming that their supervisors or other peers would not agree with teachers using flexible work arrangements.

Study 2: Qualitative analysis

Of the 53 interviews conducted at Wave 3, 17 women, from all over the UK, worked in the 'teaching and education' sector: 12 teachers, 3 university

TABLE 4.2 Comparisons between teachers and other jobholders on four specific questions around flexible work

Flexible Working (Albion, 2004)	Teachers W1	Teachers W2	Other Job Types W1	Other Job Types W2
I cannot afford the loss of pay associated with flexible work options that involve reduced hours.	3.67 (1.23)	3.72 (1.22)	3.49 (1.33)	3.74 (1.25)
Flexible work options do not suit me because they tend to make me feel disconnected from the workplace.	3.08 (1.24)*	2.73 (1.16)*	2.42 (1.27)	2.43 (1.23)
Supervisors at my workplace react negatively to people using flexible work arrangements.	2.76 (1.22)*	2.99 (1.31)*	2.50 (1.26)	2.70 (1.32)
Other people at my workplace react negatively to people using flexible work arrangements.	2.73 (1.18)*	3.02 (1.25)*	2.52 (1.26)	2.72 (1.29)

Note. W1 – Wave 1; W2 – Wave 2. We report *M* and *SDs* (in brackets) for each question. The sample size at Wave 1 was *N* =154 teachers and at Wave 2 it was *N* = 109 teachers.
* Significant differences between teachers and other jobholders.

lecturers, and 2 in other educational support roles. The age range of these 17 interview participants was from 43 to 56 years, 13 of them had a female line manager, and 5 worked part-time hours (Table 4.3).

Interviews were recorded via Microsoft Teams, and informed written consent was obtained prior to the interview in line with the University of Edinburgh's research ethics protocol. Interviews were professionally transcribed and thematically coded (Braun & Clarke, 2006), using an inductive codebook that was developed in NVivo throughout the coding process. Interviews were completely coded to allow for reflexive coding within a latent approach to enable underlying patterns to become apparent (Braun & Clarke, 2006, 2021) and to identify relationships between key factors that affect the experience of menopause at work. We acknowledge that any qualitative work is an interpretive process (Braun & Clarke, 2006); nevertheless, to promote rigour throughout the inductive analysis of this study, the authors engaged in inter-rater reliability coding. Final themes were reviewed, discussed between

TABLE 4.3 Overview of our sample in qualitative analyses

Pseudonym	Age	Job Title	Tenure at Current Org (Years)	Self-Rated Health 1-5 (1 = Excellent)	Hot Flushes, Sweating (Episodes of Sweating)	Sleep Problems	Depressive Mood	Irritability (Feeling Nervous, Inner Tension, Feeling Aggressive)	Anxiety (Inner Restlessness, Feeling Panicky)	Mental Exhaustion (Decrease in Performance, Memory, Concentration)	Reduced Confidence	Bladder Problems (Increased Urination, Incontinence)	Lowered Resilience (e.g. Increased Vulnerability)	Joint and Muscular Discomfort (Joint Pain)	Fatigue, Tiredness, Decrease in Energy	Menstrual Flooding
Bronwyn	43	Teacher – Special Needs (adults)	13	3	Mild	Moderate	Moderate	Moderate	Moderate	Moderate	Mild	Mild	Mild	Mild	Moderate	Moderate
Kelly	43	Teacher	7	2	Mild	Severe	Moderate	Moderate	Moderate	Moderate	Moderate	Mild	Severe	Moderate	Moderate	Mild
Olivia	43	Teacher	22	2	Moderate	Severe	Severe	Severe	Severe	Severe	Severe	Severe	Severe	Severe	Severe	None
Alice	46	Teacher/ Self-emp. consultant	5	2	Mild	Moderate	Mild	Moderate	None	Mild	Moderate	Mild	Moderate	Mild	Moderate	Mild
Rita	46	Teacher	3	3	Mild	Moderate	Moderate	Moderate	Moderate	Mild	Moderate	None	Moderate	None	Severe	Mild
Fiona	48	Teacher	18	2	None	Moderate	Moderate	Moderate	Moderate	Mild	Moderate	Moderate	Mild	Mild	Mild	None
Pat	48	Research Associate	12	2	Mild	Moderate	Moderate	Moderate	Mild	Mild	Moderate	Moderate	Mild	None	Moderate	None
June	49	Teacher	28	2	Severe	Severe	Very severe	Very severe	Very severe	Severe	Severe	Severe	Moderate	Mild	Moderate	Severe
Diana	50	University Notetaker	18	3	Mild	Severe	Moderate	Moderate	Severe	Moderate	Severe	None	Severe	None	Moderate	None
Elspeth	50	Teacher (Head of Dept)	25	3	Moderate	Mild	Severe	Severe	Severe	Very severe	Severe	Severe	Severe	Very severe	Very severe	None
Greta	51	Teacher	5	3	Severe	Severe	Moderate	Moderate	Severe	Severe	Moderate	Moderate	Severe	Moderate	Severe	Moderate

(*Continued*)

TABLE 4.3 (Continued)

Pseudonym	Age	Job Title	Tenure at Current Org (Years)	Self-Rated Health 1–5 (1 = Excellent)	Hot Flushes, Sweating (Episodes of Sweating)	Sleep Problems	Depressive Mood	Irritability (Feeling Nervous, Inner Tension, Feeling Aggressive)	Anxiety (Inner Restlessness, Feeling Panicky)	Mental Exhaustion (Decrease in Performance, Memory, Concentration)	Reduced Confidence	Bladder Problems (Increased Urination, Incontinence)	Lowered Resilience (e.g. Increased Vulnerability)	Joint and Muscular Discomfort (Joint Pain)	Fatigue, Tiredness, Decrease in Energy	Menstrual Flooding
Holly	51	Support – Special Needs	8	3	Mild	Moderate	Moderate	Moderate	Moderate	Mild	Moderate	Severe	None	None	Moderate	Mild
Mandy	52	Lecturer	10	2	Mild	None	Moderate	Mild	Mild	Severe	Mild	Severe	Mild	Moderate	Severe	Severe
Shirley	53	Lecturer	2.5	1	Mild	Mild	Severe	Severe	Severe	Severe	Moderate	None	Mild	Mild	Severe	None
Lara	54	Lecturer (Senior)	14	3	Mild	None	None	Mild	None	Moderate	None	Mild	None	Mild	Moderate	None
Natalie	54	Teaching Asst (specialist)	7	3	Very severe	Moderate	Mild	Moderate	Moderate	Severe	Severe	Mild	None	Moderate	Severe	None
Catherine	56	Teacher	30	4	Mild	Mild	Mild	Mild	Mild	Mild	Moderate	Moderate	Mild	Mild	Mild	None

the authors, and applied to subsequent deductive analyses in response to the quantitative findings.

Teaching through the menopause

Teachers' experience of menopause covered a range of psychological and physical symptoms. Frequency analysis of the interview data found that the most common symptoms to significantly impact teachers at work were as follows: heat and sweats; fatigue, exhaustion, and low energy; anxiety, stress, and emotional changes; brain fog, cognition, and memory changes; and flooding. Teachers spoke about their job as an emotional job, requiring a balance of mood in order to maintain job performance, and as a physical job, not allowing for reduced energy levels.

The findings provided are those that specifically relate to teachers and the context of teaching and are presented in the first section by symptom type, demonstrating individual adaptive behavioural strategies and suggestions for organisational support. The following section provides findings around flexible work during and post-COVID-19. We conclude with a finding on how a culture of gendered ageism within the teaching profession hinders psychological safety and reinforces the taboo of menopause at work.

Heat and sweats

Women who were affected by heat and sweats coped by wearing clothing in layers so that they could adjust their body heat to suit the combination of their symptom and the room temperature. Some teachers had to change rooms throughout the day, which was problematic as their rooms could vary in temperature and required a walk (sometimes a run) between classes. Teachers coped by opening windows to let in fresh air and adjust the temperature of the space; however, sometimes this was met with complaints from students. The return to classrooms post-COVID-19 encouraged the opening of windows, which provided a form of excuse for teachers to open the windows in their teaching spaces. Some teachers used fans and others tried to stay hydrated by drinking enough water throughout the day; however, this resulted in the need to urinate more frequently, which was problematic if there was no access to a toilet or the time to use it. Toilets were also used as a space to breathe and cool down in private away from students and other colleagues. Beyond personal adaptive behaviours of clothing and hydration, teachers would generally like to be able to control the temperature in their teaching spaces, for example:

> Just really simple things like if you were too warm, to be able to open the window and it not cause problems... or being able to use the bathroom

whenever you want which also sounds a bit insane, but if you're a teacher and you teach all day, finding time to get to the bathroom is not always the easiest thing.

(Alice, 46, Teacher)

Flooding

Women who experienced flooding, or excessive menstruation, felt reassured by being close to accessible toilets when the need arose. For example, a participant gained access to the key to the disabled toilet, which was closer to her classroom and was private. Clothing again was a personal adaptive strategy of coping with blood leaking through clothes, for example by only wearing black trousers to work or keeping a spare change of clothes at work, just in case. One participant, whose teaching activities required driving around on a school bus with her students (as a special needs teacher), requested a protective sheet for the bus seats to avoid leaking on to the seat fabric, demonstrating psychological safety in that she felt able to ask for help in this way. The nature of periods throughout menopause is that they are often irregular, even for women who have experienced regular periods throughout their entire life. As such, it is difficult to plan for the timing of a workplace adjustment. For example, one teacher asked to leave her class to go home as she had leaked through her clothes and had no change of clothes at work. She described the embarrassment of having to ask for this accommodation and the shame she felt when she arrived home, showered, changed, and had to return to school. Flooding appears to be a symptom that women unequivocally connect to menopause. For example:

> I'm much more aware of just how it's potentially affecting me in so many different ways and a couple of weeks ago when I got my period and I had to come home I've never had to do that ever in my life so it was like, oh dear, okay, this really needs me to start taking it a bit more seriously and seeing if there's other ways that I could maybe just manage it.
>
> *(Bronwyn, 43, Teacher)*

Teachers can be better supported through awareness of menopause, access to toilets, and urgent and reflexive cover for class if needed.

Tired/energy/exhaustion

Women overworked (i.e. worked a higher number of hours) to compensate for feeling tired and working more slowly, which arguably contributed to feelings of fatigue as home was less a place for rest and increasingly a place for catching up on work. Many women coped by going to bed much earlier than they would have done normally. Some drank coffee and energy drinks, and others improved nutrition. Several participants spoke about setting goals for the day or for the week and working towards more manageable goals, prioritising work, and no longer achieving what they referred to as 'over and above'. This prioritisation of time was also evidenced through a focus on doing existing work, relying on experience, and not taking on new work. Some teachers spoke about engaging in less effortful activities with students, a reminder of the physical nature of the majority of teaching work and extra-curricular activities. Teachers inferred that their fatigue-related symptoms might be better supported by flexible hours, where starting later was an option and where they might have input into their timetable. For example:

> ...some days I can laugh it off, but other days you just think, What is happening to me?... strategies in work? [pause] there's not too many strategies; it's trying to keep cool, I can do nothing about the classes I teach, I can do nothing about my timetable, I can't change the working day at all, if I'm tired I could potentially try and do something a little less effortful with the children, but that's hard as well because sometimes it's easier to teach them, to do a poster, because then there's just behaviour issues, so my job isn't very flexible in that respect.
> *(Elspeth, 50, Teacher and Head of Department)*

Brain fog

Brain fog, or mental exhaustion, was expressly reported as one of the most significant symptoms affecting the ability to work, resulting in the job taking longer. Women generally coped with the effects of brain fog by overworking (longer hours). An example of this was writing more lists and notes or going over work more than was previously necessary. A change to memory recall was also coped with by list-making, not only about the work itself but also about general day-to-day tasks like putting fuel in the car on the way home from work. Some women felt that staying hydrated helped with mental exhaustion, but again this was done with caution where there were inadequate toilet facilities available. One teacher moved to a condensed working day (Monday to Thursday), which did help manage her overall energy levels as Friday was a day to recharge. However, while this was agreed with her employer as a workplace adjustment for menopause, she often worked on a Friday to catch up with her high workload. As with fatigue and tiredness, teachers felt that a more flexible timetable would help them with mental exhaustion symptoms such as brain fog. For example:

> I get in at 07:15 and I generally don't leave until about 17:30, 18:00 at night. Because I just need to now have everything planned and in place so

that I know when I come in the next day everything is there and sorted... working crazy long hours... Yes, yes and it's [since menopause] because I've certainly become more aware of my limitations. So, it's taking me longer to do things because I'm having to do the written back up that goes alongside it as opposed to just being able to just fly away with it.

(June, 49, Teacher)

Anxiety/emotional fluctuation

Anxiety and emotional fluctuation appeared to be the most challenging to cope with using individual adaptive behaviours. Women 'coped' by taking time off work and 'suffering in silence', demonstrating a lack of psychological safety. Again, women spoke about coping by overworking due to their perceived need for repetition of work or checking over what had been done previously to maintain job performance. Women prioritised working in their 'comfort zones' and declined new tasks (as with physical fatigue symptoms).

Flexible work – lessons to be learned from COVID-19

An overarching finding from the interview data was that menopause symptoms present a challenge to teachers largely due to the lack of flexible work options in their work in pre- and post-COVID-19 contexts. Women spoke about work pressures, workload, and expectations as a normal part of the job, but these were exacerbated by menopause symptoms. The majority of teachers reported a 'return to normal' in ways of working, reflecting a lack of post-COVID-19 change to work from the pre-COVID-19 context, despite almost all teachers reporting that managing their menopause symptoms during COVID-19, i.e. from home, was 'easier'. This experience provides a valuable insight to both individuals and education providers and managers as it demonstrates what works for women in terms of better managing their symptoms. As mentioned in the previous section, the most commonly reported benefits of home working were access to a toilet (and time to use it), being able to control ambient temperature, and being able to sleep in slightly later due to lack of commute, thus having some control over their time. Many teachers spoke about time and timetabling as a way to help them with menopause symptoms. Specifically, participants expressed a desire to be able to start later due to the common inter-related symptoms of sleep disturbance and night sweats. Teachers who asked for a timetable adjustment upon returning to work post-COVID-19 were rejected. For example:

It would be really nice if we had flexibility about start time because if I haven't slept a lot during the night ... an extra half an hour's sleep would make a massive difference to my day just if I'd managed to get that bit of extra sleep.... I don't feel that's the way the real world works in terms of there is this expectation that you are there at 08.30.... I wish it could be flexible.

(Rita, 46, Teacher)

The inflexibility of (pre and post-COVID-19) teaching presents a barrier to women accessing reasonable workplace adjustments to manage their menopause symptoms. The majority of teachers spoke about such constraints through a narrative of personal responsibility of health in conjunction with low expectations in gaining support from the organisation. However, some participants reported that they had or were planning to challenge their employer for menopause-related workplace adjustments based on their experience of managing menopause symptoms during COVID-19. It should be noted that women who felt that they had this agency were university lecturers suggesting a higher potential for job autonomy:

It really was great in COVID because I could do it all. And our institution has gone back to, "No, everything pretty much apart from staff meetings has to be face-to-face." And I'm like why have you destroyed all of that, why have you gone backwards?

(Lara, 54, Senior Lecturer)

While some schools have implemented menopause policies, simply providing access to a helpline has actually highlighted the lack of flexible work and time constraints inherent in the job. This finding is exemplified by Elspeth, who phoned a helpline provided by her school:

I did phone up [a menopause] helpline and they said, "Can you ask for flexible working? Can you ask for a room with a fan and air-conditioning to go and sit in when you're hot, can you ask for water so that you can get a drink whenever you want? Can you ask for cover so you can go to the toilet when you want? Can you ask for reduction in your timetable?" and I did go to see the HR lady in school about this, and she just, didn't laugh at me but she said, "Well how are we going to do that? There's nobody else who can teach [subject], we can't change your timetable."

(Elspeth, 50, Teacher and Head of Department)

A culture of gendered ageism in teaching

As indicated above, women who felt able to ask for workplace adjustments to help them manage their symptoms tended to fare better, i.e. they perceived higher psychological safety which appeared to support them with managing their symptoms. Seeking micro-adjustments was made easier by an inclusive, open, and supportive school or team culture. However, many women expressed a challenge around being able to ask for help from their colleagues or their managers (e.g. department heads). While the majority of teachers spoke about the intensity of workloads and a 'fear of scrutiny' that accompanies regular performance evaluation, the most common reason given was a culture of gendered ageism within their school. Gendered ageism is the intersection of discrimination or bias relating to gender and age and can work to reduce psychological safety or asking for help at work. Gendered ageism manifested as participants not speaking about their menopause through fear of it being associated with being older at work and how that might be judged by younger and/or male colleagues. There was a sense from participants that older women hold a precarious position in the teaching profession due to a relatively high, tenure-related labour cost and a perceived lack of value of experience. For example

> I think with the menopause because you don't feel like you're functioning and being looked upon as a pre-menopausal woman... You don't look to the outside world as if you'll be as flexible, as capable. A lot of things you just sort of subconsciously pick up about expectations I think...
> *(Diana, 50, University Notetaker)*

> ... I think as with most schools our Head Teacher seems to be on this warpath of getting rid of older teachers and replacing them with newly qualified teachers. Because for the cost of me you could get two newly qualified teachers in. ... And I just worry that if I start saying anything that I need any help in any way, shape or form that will put me next on the hit-list. And I can't afford not to have a job to be quite frank.
> *(June, 49, has been a teacher for 28 years)*

Discussion and conclusion

This chapter presents much-needed empirical data on teachers' experience of managing their menopause symptoms at work. Our findings show that an increase in flexible work during COVID-19 restrictions enabled women to better manage their menopause symptoms. While teachers as a professional group were at a higher risk of burnout through the pandemic (Kim & Asbury, 2020), working from home presented a way in which well-being was improved for menopausal women. However, returning to work was aligned with the pre-COVID-19 workplace, with little or no change to accessing flexible work. This finding highlights that broader government and research initiatives encouraging flexible work for menopause management and overall work retention (Centre for Ageing Better, 2021; UK Government, 2022; Verdonk et al., 2022) are unlikely to have a meaningful impact on the teaching profession.

The aim of this chapter was to explore how teachers manage their menopause symptoms and whether there are lessons to be learned from COVID-19 in how education providers can support teachers experiencing menopause. We did this by asking how teachers cope with menopause at work and how this was affected by work-related changes during the pandemic. Evidence from this study strongly supported previous findings that teaching is a profession of high expectations and high workload pressures, associated with a high risk of burnout (Amitai & Van Houtte, 2022; Hakenen, Bakker & Shaufeli, 2006; Van Eycken et al., 2022).

As with previous menopause research (e.g. Brewis et al., 2017), teachers in this study reported hiding and denying symptoms at work, and very few sought assistance from external sources (Steffan & Potočnik, 2022). We know that increasing awareness and creating an environment where menopause can be openly discussed can normalise and destigmatise menopause at work (Atkinson et al., 2021; Grandey et al., 2020), however, teaching appears to be an environment where the taboo of menopause persists and where teachers do not perceive enough psychological safety to ask for flexible work arrangements or adjustments. This chapter contributes knowledge about how teachers experience menopause and how they would like to be better supported at work by individualised workplace adjustments around temperature, toilets, and time. Specifically, women asked for the ability to control temperature and access to fresh air, often simply by being able to open a window; having access and time to use a toilet; alleviating time pressure within the working day by providing options for later start times; or a flexible timetabling, or at least the ability to have input into the timetabling process. Time was also important in relation to alleviating high workloads (Philipp & Kunter, 2013).

Adaptive behavioural strategies and how to use them can increase job performance and well-being (e.g. Moghimi et al., 2019), which is particularly salient as teachers reported significantly lower use of adaptive behavioural strategies compared with other jobholders. Anxiety and emotional fluctuation appeared to be the most challenging to cope with using adaptive behaviours, which supports previous findings that agentic behaviours are useful to protect performance when suffering from physical, but not psychological, symptoms (Steffan & Potočnik, 2022). This is also important as participants referred to teaching as both a physically and mentally exhausting job, as such, both groups of symptoms should be considered in supporting menopause at work.

Speaking up and asking for help can initiate the individualised support that the majority of menopausal women need (Atkinson et al., 2021; Grandey et al., 2020; Steffan & Potočnik, 2022); however, teachers appear to have low psychological safety in being able to do so, which was evident from both quantitative and qualitative results in this study. Much of the language used by teachers referred to a culture within teaching of gendered ageism, a judgemental work climate, which appeared to adversely impact their sense of psychological safety. It appeared that gendered ageism around a preference for youth and a judgement against being an older woman at work acted as a barrier to 'speaking up' within the education sector (Edmondson et al., 2016). Providing an environment of supporting menopause at work requires a climate of mutual accountability (Evers et al., 2016); findings in this study suggest a lack of reciprocity of flexibility, communication, and support around menopause symptoms.

This study has shown that the organisation can play a crucial role in teacher support (Evers et al., 2016), specifically around the management of menopause symptoms at work. The challenge for education providers is that menopausal women have glimpsed an alternative way of managing their symptoms at work during the pandemic and might be somewhat reluctant to return to a lack of flexible work, which might in turn influence their attitudes to their future of work. School management is encouraged to learn from positive influences brought about by the stressful time of working through the pandemic. School management should embrace mutual accountability (Evers et al., 2016) in supporting menopause symptoms at work by providing a climate of psychological safety where women can ask for help and can engage in their personal adaptive behaviours more effectively. Evidence here suggests that addressing gendered ageism might be a crucial first step for many schools. Mutual accountability does not place the emphasis of support entirely on the organisation or the individual; it encourages and supports reasonable challenge to the current ways of teaching with the ambition of improving people management within the teaching profession.

Funding

This research received no specific grant from any funding agency in the public, commercial, or not-for-profit sectors. There are no conflicts of interest to declare.

Acknowledgements

We would like to thank our participants for their valuable time given to this study. We would also like to thank Katy Marsh-Davies for the invitation to write a chapter on teachers and their experience of menopause. We would also like to acknowledge the University of Edinburgh Business School for providing funding for data collection and transcription.

Note

1 Menopause can be experienced by diverse gender groups, but official statistics only report data from cis-women and cis-men.

References

Albion, M. J. (2004) A measure of attitudes towards flexible work options. *Australian Journal of Management*, 29(2), pp. 275–294.

Amitai, A., and Van Houtte, M. (2022) Being pushed out of the career: Former teachers' reasons for leaving the profession. *Teaching and Teacher Education*, 110, table 103540.

Atkinson, C., Beck, V., Brewis, J., Davies, A., and Duberley, J. (2021) Menopause and the workplace: New directions in HRM research and HR practice. *Human Resource Management Journal*, 31(1), pp. 49–64.

Baltes, P.B. (1997) On the incomplete architecture of human ontogeny: Selection, optimization, and compensation as foundation of developmental theory. *American Psychologist*, 52(4), pp. 366.

Beauchamp, G., Hulme, M., Clarke, L., Hamilton, L., and Harvey, J.A. (2021) 'People miss people': A study of school leadership and management in the four nations of the United Kingdom in the early stage of the COVID-19 pandemic. *Educational Management Administration & Leadership*, 49(3), pp. 375–392.

Boin, A., Lodge, M., and Luesink, M. (2020) Learning from the COVID-19 crisis: An initial analysis of national responses. *Policy Design and Practice*, 3(3), pp. 189–204.

Braun, V., and Clarke, V. (2006) Using thematic analysis in psychology. *Qualitative Research in Psychology*, 3(2), pp. 77–101.

Braun, V., and Clarke, V. (2021) Can I use TA? Should I use TA? Should I not use TA? Comparing reflexive thematic analysis and other pattern-based qualitative analytic approaches. *Counselling and Psychotherapy Research*, 21(1), pp. 37–47.

Brewis, J., Beck, V., Davies, A., and Matheson, J. (2017) *The effects of menopause transition on women's economic participation in the UK. Research report*. London: Department for Education.

Butler, C. (2020) Managing the menopause through 'abjection work': When boobs can become embarrassingly useful, again. *Work, Employment and Society*, 34(4), pp. 696–712.

Centre for Ageing Better (2021) *Flexible working for older workers*. [Tavistock Institute].

Edmondson, A.C. (2012) *Teaming: How organizations learn, innovate and compete in the knowledge economy*. San Francisco: Jossey-Bass.

Edmondson, A.C., Higgins, M., Singer, S., and Weiner, J. (2016) Understanding psychological safety in health care and education organizations: A comparative perspective. *Research in Human Development*, 13(1), pp. 65–83.

Evers, A.T., van der Heijden, B.I., Kreijns, K., and Vermeulen, M. (2016) Job demands, job resources, and flexible competence: The mediating role of teachers' professional development at work. *Journal of Career Development*, 43(3), pp. 227–243.

Grandey, A.A., Gabriel, A.S., and King, E.B. (2020) Tackling taboo topics: A review of the three M's in working women's lives. *Journal of Management*, 46(1), pp. 7–35.

Griffiths, A., MacLennan, S.J., and Hassard, J. (2013) Menopause and work: An electronic survey of employees' attitudes in the UK. *Mauritas*, 76(2), pp. 155–159.

Gudep, V.K. (2019) An empirical study of the relationships between the flexible work systems (fws), organizational commitment (oc), work life balance (wlb) and job satisfaction (js) for the teaching staff in the united arab emirates (uae). *International Journal of Management*, 10(5), pp. 11–27.

Hakanen, J.J., Bakker, A.B., and Schaufeli, W.B. (2006) Burnout and work engagement among teachers. *Journal of School Psychology*, 43(6), pp. 495–513.

Hardy, C., Griffiths, A., Thorne, E., and Hunter, M. (2018) Tackling the taboo: Talking menopause-related problems at work. *International Journal of Workplace Health Management*, 12(1), pp. 28–38.

Kim, L.E., and Asbury, K. (2020) 'Like a rug had been pulled from under you': The impact of COVID-19 on teachers in England during the first six weeks of the UK lockdown. *British Journal of Educational Psychology*, 90(4), pp. 1062–1083.

Moghimi, D., Scheibe, S., and Freund, A.M. (2019) The model of selection, optimization, compensation. In Baltes, B., Rudolph, C., and Zacher, H. (Eds.), *Work across the lifespan*, pp. 81–110. London: Academic Press.

National Health Service (NHS). (2022) *Menopause*. Available at: https://www.nhs.uk/conditions/menopause/ (Accessed on 19/12/22).

Organization for Economic Cooperation and Development. (2009) *Creating effective teaching and learning environments*. First results from Talis. Paris, France: Organization for Economic Cooperation and Development.

Philipp, A., and Kunter, M. (2013) How do teachers spend their time? A study on teachers' strategies of selection, optimisation, and compensation over their career cycle. *Teaching and teacher education*, 35, pp. 1–12.

Rahman, M.F. (2019) Impact of flexible work arrangements on job satisfaction among the female teachers in the higher education sector. *Work*, 11(18), p. 97.

Steffan, B. (2021) Managing menopause at work: The contradictory nature of identity talk. *Gender, Work & Organization*, 28(1), pp. 195–214.

Steffan, B., and Potočnik, K. (2022) Thinking outside Pandora's Box: Revealing differential effects of coping with physical and psychological menopause symptoms at work. *Human Relations*, 00187267221089469.

Trade Union Congress (TUC). (December 2021) *Menopause and the Workplace*. Available at: https://www.tuc.org.uk/research-analysis/reports/menopause-and-workplace (Accessed on 19/12/22).

UK Government. (2021) *School workforce in England*. Available at: https://explore-education-statistics.service.gov.uk/find-statistics/school-workforce-in-england (Accessed on 19/12/22).

UK Government. (2022) *Menopause and the Workplace*. Available at: https://www.gov.uk/government/publications/menopause-and-the-workplace-how-to-enable-fulfilling-working-lives-government-response?utm_medium=email&utm_campaign=govuk-notifications-topic&utm_source=8f3d1f2a-1e9f-4f94-9f25-bf11c4a562f6&utm_content=immediately (Accessed on 25/7/22).

Van Eycken, L., Amitai, A., and Van Houtte, M. (2022) Be true to your school? Teachers' turnover intentions: The role of socioeconomic composition, teachability perceptions, emotional exhaustion and teacher efficacy. *Research Papers in Education*, pp. 1–26. https://doi.org/10.1080/02671522.2022.2089208.

Verdonk, P., Bendien, E., and Appelman, Y. (2022) Menopause and work: A narrative literature review about menopause, work and health. *Work*, (Preprint), pp. 1–14.

5
TEACHER WELL-BEING IN TIMES OF COVID

Chris Forde, Judith Hanks, and Rachel Mathieson

Introduction

Prior to the COVID-19 pandemic, a number of reports had already identified the retention crisis in teaching, identifying poor well-being as a key factor contributing to teachers leaving the profession (Education Support, 2019; OFSTED, 2019). In this chapter, we examine the effects of the COVID-19 pandemic on the well-being of teachers in England. What do the experiences of teachers before, during and after COVID-19 tell us about the causes and consequences of poor well-being, and how it might be improved?

Poor well-being in teaching has been attributed to a number of causes, including high workload levels, stress, accountability and performance management systems, and an erosion in autonomy (see, for example, Department for Education, 2017; Perryman and Calvert, 2020; Teacher Workload Advisory Group; TES, 2022). Some of these factors are causes of poor well-being in other sectors (see Jeffrey et al., 2014; CIPD, 2021), whilst others may be more prominent in teaching.

We begin the chapter by considering the wider literature on the drivers and causes of well-being, and the impact on teachers and the teaching profession. Taking an exploratory practice (Allwright and Hanks, 2009; Hanks, 2017) approach, we examine practitioners' accounts of the effects of the pandemic on teaching practice. We draw on qualitative evidence from more than 50 interviews and focus groups with teachers, senior leaders, union representatives and human resource professionals, gathered during a project[1] conducted in partnership with the two largest teaching unions in England[2] between 2019 and 2021. Structural and institutional factors, notably high workloads, performance management systems, poorly designed or implemented human resource management practices and poor leadership, exerted a significant negative influence on teacher well-being during the pandemic. Teachers had to adapt their practice fundamentally, working remotely and digitally, as well as face-to-face, and often reactively and independently, all of which affected their well-being. Teachers were more likely to thrive in environments where they could build good relationships and exercise their professional judgement, within a positive school culture, with supportive leaders.

We conclude that teaching, like so many professions, has been undergoing profound changes as a result of the COVID-19 pandemic. Issues such as poor management, heavy or misaligned workloads, which were already stretching teachers to breaking point, were, in some cases, exacerbated. Conversely, some aspects of work during the crisis enabled teachers to reinvigorate their sense of professionalism, allowing them to work according to the values which brought them into teaching. As norms and working patterns fell away, the focus shifted to the nurturing, caring and pastoral aspects of teachers' professional identity. This return for some, but not all, teachers, to the core principles of teaching, contributed, in these cases, to enhanced teacher well-being and may hold the key to retaining teachers in the profession.

The importance of well-being at work

Well-being at work has long aroused considerable interest, with debates around its causes and consequences. Widespread evidence demonstrates that happy, satisfied workers are more likely to be effective and productive and to have higher levels of overall well-being (Jeffrey et al., 2014). Poor well-being at work has been estimated to cost the UK economy around £99 billion per annum, £42 billion of which is borne by employers because of lower worker productivity, higher staff absences, and increased levels of employee turnover (Stevenson and Farmer, 2017). Well-being has come to feature prominently in policy and strategy statements of Conservative governments over the last decade, including, previously, the Industrial Strategy (Department of Business, Energy and Industrial Strategy, 2017) and the subsequent policy proposal, *Levelling up the UK* which states (Department of Levelling Up, Housing and Communities, 2022, p. 186):

> Well-being captures the extent to which people across the UK lead happy and fulfilling lives – the very essence of levelling up.

Within organisations, employee health and well-being has gradually assumed greater importance, increasing yet further during the COVID-19 pandemic (CIPD, 2021). For individual industries, organisations and occupations, changes in people management and human resource practices may have followed, focusing specifically on issues such as mental health, flexible working and work–life balance. However, considerable debate remains around the definition of well-being, the factors that matter to employees in terms of happiness and satisfaction at work, and the causes of good and/or poor well-being.

Models and theories highlight a range of elements contributing to well-being at work (see Jeffrey et al., 2014; Thompson and Marks, 2008; Warr, 2012). Bryson et al. (2017) argue that two broad approaches dominate: hedonic and eudemonic. Hedonic approaches explore the types of feelings which people experience in their job and the extent to which people are satisfied with certain aspects of their job, such as pay and job security. Eudemonic approaches examine the extent to which people experience feelings that are considered to demonstrate good mental health. Bryson et al. (2017) give the example of someone feeling a sense of purpose in their job. Many models identify and organise factors which shape well-being at work, often called 'drivers' of well-being. Jeffrey et al. (2014) and Warr (2012) have pinpointed three sets of factors worthy of particular attention. First, personal resources, which are health and vitality, resilience, general happiness, and self-confidence that individuals bring to work, and the work–life balance that they experience. Second is the organisational system, meaning the way in which jobs are designed, how the organisation is managed, the quality of the work environment and how employees assess the social value of their work (Brown et al., 2008, 2012). Third, Jeffrey et al. (2014: 33) highlight functioning at work, which is defined as "whether the things that employees do in their day-to-day work create positive interactions within their surroundings and help them to meet their basic psychological needs". This includes whether employees feel they can express themselves, use their strengths and have a sense of control over their work.

Notably, many of the factors above relate to human resource and people management. There is increasing recognition within the field of human resource management (HRM) that well-being impacts crucially individual and organisational performance. Indeed, a number of commentators have argued that the management of well-being needs to be more central to HRM theory and practice (Guest, 2017; Kowalski and Loretto, 2017). Individual HRM practices, such as pay and reward systems, training and development, and performance management, can have a significant positive or negative impact on individual employee well-being. The changing economic and institutional environment (e.g. globalisation, increased competition, digitalisation, economic crises, changing regulations around work and employment) can all also impact approaches to HRM and well-being. However, the nature of the relationship between practices, individual well-being and performance is recognised to vary across sectors. There is no 'one size fits all' approach to managing well-being at work (Kowalski and Loretto, 2017; Peccei et al.,

2013), and a greater understanding of employee well-being within specific sectors, occupations and contexts, such as teaching, is needed.

Causes and consequences of poor well-being in teaching

Occupational well-being within teaching has been described as "worryingly low" (Ofsted, 2019: 16) even where perceptions towards teaching as a vocation are positive. Quantitative work has identified the extent of well-being and mental health problems in teaching, highlighting that teachers are exiting the profession due to factors including excessive workload, bureaucratic burdens, de-professionalisation and toxic management styles (see Brown, Daly, and Liou, 2016; Green, 2021; Grenville-Cleave and Boniwell, 2012; Hobson and Maxwell, 2017; Skinner et al., 2019). Teachers are twice as likely as the average worker to suffer work-related stress (Health and Safety Executive, 2021). In a study conducted just prior to the pandemic by Education Support (2019), 78% of teachers and 84% of senior leaders in education reported feeling stressed, and over a quarter of the teaching workforce reported experiencing behavioural, psychological or physical symptoms such as insomnia, mood swings, tearfulness and panic attacks. One in three teachers said they had experienced a mental health issue in the preceding year, and the well-being of education professionals was found to be markedly lower than the general population.

Alongside this, notions of professionalism, sense of identity and autonomy associated with teaching have also undergone significant changes over the years, and research suggests that these changes are important to understanding the problems of well-being, retention or burnout for teachers (see below for further discussion). For example, many have suggested that the identity of teachers has been destabilised through cultures of assessment and monitoring where primacy is given to performance and compliance with accountability regimes.

Many teachers also point to poor relationships with senior managers. They cite a growing culture of managerialism, with pressures of excessive scrutiny stemming from performance management systems (Perryman and Calvert, 2020). Here, teachers are redefined as 'producers' or 'educational entrepreneurs' (Ball, 2003; Day and Smethem, 2009) rather than as competent, caring, responsive and reflective professionals.

The imposition of business management practices in schools has, for many teachers, eroded the autonomy and expertise traditionally respected as a mark of the profession. High workloads caused largely by the necessity to track and monitor performance impact directly upon levels of stress and teachers' abilities to do their jobs, thus leading to poor well-being, as the integrity of teachers' identities as professionals is challenged by exhaustion (see Worth and Faulkner-Ellis, 2021).

Research has consistently found that pay is not the most important motivator for teachers and is not the main factor driving decisions to leave (e.g. Worth et al., 2018). Having left the profession, teachers often take lower-paid jobs, including staying within schools and working as teaching assistants, but report a healthier work–life balance and regained job satisfaction (NFER, 2017).

Although there have been some strategic policy responses to poor well-being levels, including the Workload Reduction Toolkit (Department for Education, 2018), the Teacher Recruitment and Retention Strategy (Department for Education, 2019) and the Framework for Ethical Leadership (Ethical Leadership Commission, 2017), there is no evidence that these have had much impact. Well-being levels in the teaching profession continue to be a cause for concern.

The long-term decline in teachers' quality of life, caused by increased workload, increased stress and diminished autonomy, has resulted in high rates of turnover. The National Foundation for Educational Research (2017, 2022) finds that the proportion of teachers leaving the profession or moving school has been increasing for at least the last decade. Notably, one-third of teachers are leaving the profession within five years of starting their career (Department for Education, 2021; Worth et al., 2018; Walker, 2023). The relationships between teacher well-being, turnover and socio-economic deprivation are of particular concern. In the context of a national teacher recruitment and retention challenge, schools in disadvantaged and deprived areas struggle to recruit (Allen and Sims, 2018). Arguably, teacher quality and continuity of teaching are the most important determinants of children's progress, and the absence of these inevitably has a detrimental effect on pupils' educational outcomes and life chances. Pupils already disadvantaged by their socio-economic circumstances suffer a second blow because of inconsistency in the teaching they receive: for example, Jerrim et al. (2018) found more than twice as many unqualified or temporary teachers in schools with the highest proportion of children from families receiving state benefits, as those in schools with the lowest proportion.

The relationships between teacher well-being and turnover and the educational performance of children have been increasingly recognised by policy-makers and the government. The Northern Powerhouse Schools Strategy, for example, was developed in response to educational underperformance in the North of England and includes the view that "the most important step we can take to address educational underperformance in the North is to meet the challenge of teacher supply" (Weller, 2016: 18).

To sum up, some aspects of the conditions under which so many teachers are leaving their jobs are widely recognised, whilst others merit much closer scrutiny and analysis.

The impact of the COVID-19 pandemic on teacher well-being: early studies

The pandemic was experienced as a series of phases (Mathieson and Walker, forthcoming), and reports must reflect this. Indeed, the pandemic and its effects continue to bear on the life and work of educators (see Hanks et al., 2021), and research is ongoing.

Early research into teachers' experiences of the COVID-19 pandemic highlighted a range of impacts. In a climate of fear and bewilderment, teachers had to adapt their roles and activities overnight. Importantly, the role of teachers developed significantly to prioritise a wide range of health, safety, and social welfare functions (see Mathieson et al., 2021; Moss et al., 2020). Teachers had to plan, implement and undertake remote, hybrid and in-person teaching. Classified as essential or 'key' workers, many teachers remained on the 'front line' and continued to provide face-to-face teaching in schools during the various lockdowns. In a study of the early days of the COVID-19 pandemic, Allen et al. (2020) found that anxiety levels rose immediately before the first lockdown began in March 2020 and rose again when schools in England reopened briefly at the end of the summer term 2020. They reported that some aspects of their measures of anxiety, such as having energy to spare and being able to think clearly, improved, whilst other aspects (e.g. feeling useful, feeling optimistic) declined during the first lockdown. This mixed picture was also reflected elsewhere, with Kim et al. (2022) reporting mostly negative impacts, stemming from increased job demands, increased workload and higher levels of uncertainty. Moss et al. (2020) and Harmey and Moss (2021) noted the effects of negative perceptions of the profession and health struggles. Whilst individual and organisational resources such as social support, work autonomy and coping strategies may have reduced some of the negative effects, teachers reported overall declines in well-being and mental health. Further research is needed, however, to understand the contexts and experiences of individual teachers within specific school settings.

Findings from the Leeds teacher well-being and burnout study

In the remainder of this chapter, we consider detailed examples of the varied effects of the COVID-19 pandemic on teacher well-being, derived from the findings of a small-scale, qualitative study into well-being and burnout, conducted from Summer 2018 through to Summer 2021 by the authors, in partnership with the Leeds offices of the National Education Union (NEU) and the National Association of Schoolmasters and Women Teachers (NASUWT).

This co-produced work involved teachers of children of all ages, at different career stages and in different settings, from schools in Leeds and the wider West Yorkshire region, together with union representatives, HRM professionals, and senior leaders and managers. The project aim was to give voice to those in the teaching profession, through meetings, roundtables, workshops and one-to-one conversations, where they could discuss what they viewed as the causes of poor well-being and burnout amongst teachers, and also identify where, and how, positive well-being can be promoted and sustained.

The project had already generated important findings prior to the emergence of COVID-19, but in March 2020, it took an unexpected turn with the national lockdown interrupting normal activities. At first, we (the authors) feared that the pandemic would call a halt to our study; on the contrary, it pointed up some important aspects of working practices, as described below. We were tentative about taking up the time of our participants, who were already extremely busy and subject to instability and pressure from changing expectations and requirements in their workplaces. However, these professionals remained interested in the project, continuing to volunteer to join workshops and roundtables after school hours. As in most exploratory practice work around the world, this project was explicitly designed to prioritise teachers' accounts of their experiences. Consequently, they were keen for their work, their struggles, their highs and lows during the pandemic, and their recommendations for improved practice, to be recognised. From the in-person events of the period before COVID-19, we moved to online meetings and interviews, in which teachers willingly participated, despite the long hours of screen time they were already undertaking.

As data collection proceeded, thematic analysis of transcripts was undertaken following each phase of the project, and a series of publications and resources were developed on the project website (https://leedsteacherwellbeing.leeds.ac.uk/). Drafts were shared with the teachers from the beginning, and their comments/responses were incorporated into the analysis, ensuring a sense of agency. This chapter presents findings relevant to how COVID-19 affected teacher well-being and practice. Key findings are presented in five sections below, examining workload, performance management and workplace culture, external pressures, recruitment and the need to support newly qualified teachers, and the role of teachers in the community during the pandemic.

Workload

Participants in our project repeatedly raised workload as an issue which impacted their well-being. Working late in the evening and often at weekends was described as necessary for them to complete essential tasks, something highlighted by teachers before the pandemic in our interviews and meetings in the summer and autumn of 2019.

Poor management practices had a significant effect on workload. Teachers reported that very short turnaround time was often allocated to requests for additional work to be done, with extra tasks compounding an already heavy workload. In many cases, workload impact assessments in schools were not completed:

> The Head says 'You have to drop something', and I say 'tell me what you want me not to do. Here's my list of deadlines'.
>
> NQT, Primary

All was not negative, though. Some teachers described examples of good practice, with leaders discussing workloads with staff, proactively engaging with unions and attempting to ensure reasonable, well-managed timeframes were attached to requests to take on extra work. Teachers, senior leaders and unions all highlighted how the effective management of workload in schools depended on the capabilities, skills and attitudes of individual leaders and school heads. One headteacher encapsulated this as follows:

> What [teachers] really do respond to is a workplace where they feel supported. Where professional learning is intrinsic and built into what they do. Then they are prepared to work hard, and they see that meaningful work is well worth putting the hours in for. So, when we see that going askew, we see high stress rates.
>
> Chief Executive Officer, Multi-Academy Trust

As the pandemic took hold, the UK entered its first lockdown in March 2020. During this time, high workloads intensified further, with teachers required to change their practice, and often their curriculum and foci, when most children were learning from home. Teachers, now working from home, suddenly had to convert their working practices, in order to provide remote teaching to the majority of their pupils who were now learning at home. Some schools were better placed than others to support teachers in this endeavour; this depended on the extent to which schools already used an established IT system and/or online platform, the extent to which staff were familiar with these and how much support was available. Our participating teachers described a variety of approaches to remote provision. Some schools decided not to offer any synchronous lessons during the first lockdown for safeguarding reasons. In other cases, typically in private (fee-paying) schools, teachers reported that the school expected every lesson to be delivered synchronously online, to the same timetable as if everyone were still in school. In yet other schools, teachers said the timetable was simplified, but there was still an expectation that online lessons would be delivered synchronously.

In autumn 2020, schools were officially open to all pupils. Government guidelines introduced a system of 'bubbles' in schools, whereby children and teachers would – as far as possible – remain grouped with the same individuals each day to minimise their number of contacts and limit the risk of infection transmission (see Quinn, 2020a). If one person, whether a teacher or pupil, became infected, the whole 'bubble' had to be sent home. Teaching would then move online. As 'bubbles' were 'bursting' often and repeatedly, it became increasingly difficult to manage continuity and planning, resulting in teachers in the project recounting how they were working even harder than usual. The lockdown of January to March 2021 saw teachers maintaining on-site teaching for children of key workers and vulnerable children whilst also managing newly developed ways of offering online education for children at home. For periods of the academic year 2020–2021, teachers would repeatedly find themselves simultaneously teaching pupils who were present in the classroom and others who were isolating or in lockdown at home:

> … we're almost double-planning. So we plan for our in-class lessons, and then, as a team… we are then having to plan online lessons that can be uploaded as a PowerPoint that the students can then access and work through by themselves at home. And then you've got kids in and out, isolating, not isolating, so they've missed this lesson but not that lesson…
>
> Secondary School Teacher

Teachers in the project repeatedly told us that they were focusing, to an even greater extent than before the pandemic, on pastoral care for their pupils and also managing rapidly changing government guidance around teaching and assessments (see also Moss et al., 2020; Harmey and Moss, 2021). Although teachers were accommodating of these various demands, they reported feelings of constant and increasing exhaustion. They noted that 'this situation cannot go on' and 'something has to give', as their already high workloads became unsustainable.

Performance management and workplace culture

Prior to the pandemic, our participant teachers echoed academic research (e.g. Ball, 2003; Reeves, 2018) which found that well-being was adversely affected by performance management and accountability systems detached from the most important elements of teaching: learning, building relationships with pupils, and ongoing, formative assessment of progress. As one secondary teacher who had recently left a role in a school after suffering panic attacks told us in 2019:

> That sense of accountability… You're trying to do your best for the children all the time, and you've got two customers: the children who are in

front of you and want interesting, engaging lessons, and to be enthralled, but you've got management breathing down your neck saying 'you must make sure you do tests to make sure they have learnt things'

Secondary Teacher

Performance management was described by many as a mechanism of control, a means through which teachers' autonomy was reduced and their activities closely monitored, with a focus on ensuring behaviours assisted with the achievement of externally required targets. For teachers, this was seen as having little or no impact on the quality of the teaching they delivered:

> They hide behind tick-boxes. It's all about monitoring. No people management. They monitor, not manage, in the vast majority of schools.
>
> Supply Teacher, Primary

Much depended on the behaviours and values of individual leaders and on relationships between teaching staff, departmental heads and senior management teams. Well-being was better – heads reported fewer instances of stress-related illness – in working environments where they believed strong, supportive relationships were fostered and participatory practices were valued. There was a sense that when teaching teams and leaders were able to work together to implement developmental approaches to supervision, mentoring and performance management, more positive well-being was the result.

In 2020, as the first lockdown took place, it was noted by some of our participants that their schools stepped back from regular performance management activities such as classroom observations, walk-throughs, goal-setting and monitoring.

> I have to be absolutely honest with you, I loved the first bit of lockdown, and that's a terrible thing to say, because there was so much misery and suffering and terrible things… because what was missing was… I didn't have link meetings, I didn't have to produce data, and the management attitude was, they were in, sort of like, panic, firefighting mode of like just, just get it done, do your best. And we did… So the removal of all of that was the most enormous relief…
>
> Secondary School Teacher

This was, of course, as most teachers were working from home, teaching their classes online. However, as the pandemic persisted into the new academic year from September 2020, many schools appeared to adopt a 'business as usual' approach to gathering data and managing staff performance:

> … we had performance management last half-term as, sort of as normal really… which I was a bit surprised about… but there you go. I can't even

remember what my objectives are now. And we've got reports to write for December... we used to do them this time of year and in May, but to get it flung on you at the moment just seems... a bit weird, you know, especially at the moment when everybody is, we are feeling that, people are feeling under pressure.

Early Years Leader

Teacher participants were often scathing about senior leadership teams' reported attitudes to health and safety in these new conditions. One participant discussed these issues extensively in interviews, and we include a number of quotes below highlighting how health and safety was managed (or mismanaged) over the months:

... it was very stressful just coming back to work, especially this surreal situation of pretending there's a lockdown like the first lockdown, and yet you're being told specifically, pretend there is no lockdown and carry on... students don't have to wear masks because the government has stuck to that line. And again, the contradiction with the rest of society...

... I was talking to one of my classes at the end of the lesson today, because one of them had had COVID, and we were having this conversation where we were saying, it's really weird that more of us haven't had COVID, because the kids were saying like this is, this is so obviously unsafe, what we're doing....

...The risk assessment isn't done properly. They don't take crowding seriously. But the other thing they then do is they pretend that everything's alright. So we are told that we can stay two metres away from all the students. And that is a line that the Principal doggedly sticks to. It is simply impossible. You cannot sit or stand in a box, and teach, for a whole term...early on it was kind of like, well it's your fault, if you get COVID, because we've made you safe, when they clearly haven't.

All quotes from Head of Subject, Sixth Form College

External pressures

Even prior to the pandemic, existing pressures stemming from the national context were key factors contributing to low well-being and burnout. The effects of a decade of austerity and consequent budgetary constraints were seen in the lack of accessible training and professional development and the lack of cover for colleagues off sick or on a training course, and teachers reported feeling unable to take time off:

There's a pressure to come in when you're ill, cover for colleagues et cetera... They shouldn't ask... [but] what teacher in the current climate feels able to say 'I'm not coming in to my class tomorrow'?

Retired PE Teacher/SENCO

These stresses became more acute during the pandemic. Teachers and school leaders reported facing unclear and rapidly changing guidance from the government around safety, PPE, social distancing, mask-wearing and ventilation in schools. Many participants took the view that guidance and policies from the government were problematic or even unhelpful. Fundamental decisions about the closure or reopening of schools were made with little or no consultation with heads, teachers and unions, and the guidance was often vague, leaving school leaders to interpret and manage policies at a local level.

> I don't think there has been a bigger gap between senior team and teaching staff as there is now. And that's not to say that they're not trying, 'cause I recognise that they are working really hard. They're in an impossible situation. I do get that. But I think, for a lot of the senior team, 'cause they don't teach as much, the recognition and the understanding of the impact that this is having on a day-to-day basis, I don't think that is there.
>
> Secondary School Teacher

Government guidelines and decisions around General Certificate of Secondary Education (GCSE)[3] and A-level[4] assessment in 2020 were a recognised debacle, which led to vociferous calls for the government's Secretary of State for Education to quit (see Quinn, 2020b). The government's vacillation around public examinations and assessment persisted into 2021, as teachers told us of the uncertainty they felt they were experiencing. Teachers felt very strongly that they were being unfairly blamed by the media, by parents and even by government spokespeople, for pupil grades that were only partially their responsibility:

> … in the media, they are still using that term 'teacher assessment'. And yes, teacher assessment is part of it, but they are centre assessed grades… not all the grades that the teacher put in were the grades that the students ended up with… The teacher puts it in and it's then moderated by the management at college, to make sure it's in line with three years' worth of data. And then it goes off to the exam board and they moderate it again. So when the government did its U-turn [allowing pupils to be given their centre assessed grades instead of the Ofqual-moderated grades which had been standardised by algorithm], it said it was going back to the teacher assessed grades, but they weren't, and that's what caused a lot of students to be angry with a lot of teachers. They didn't go back to the teacher assessed grades - they went back to the centre assessed grades, which had almost wholly been moved down.
>
> Head of Subject, Sixth Form College

Whilst some school leaders did consult with staff and unions as best they could about health and safety best practice, some teachers felt particularly stressed because they were themselves vulnerable or living with family members who were shielding due to health concerns:

> We felt a little pressurised into coming back in June… We were, I'm not saying pushed, but we were 'encouraged', shall I say, to come back, to teach another year group. And that was quite stressful, coming in to children that, OK you knew them because you've taught them in the past, but you were coming in to teach them two to three times a week, when you were still vulnerable yourself…
>
> Primary Teacher

Recruitment and the need to support newly qualified teachers (NQTs)

By 2019, recruitment and retention challenges in the sector were already being reported (see NFER, 2017; Ofsted, 2019). National initiatives to attract new teachers were seen by many as problematic because they set unrealistic expectations on NQTs, who were often unprepared for the realities of teaching:

> Through no fault of yours, five of your teachers leave, you know, in summer, and you've got to replace them, and there's a recruitment problem. You'll probably get more NQTs than you would've planned for. You've already got, because of that departure, a middle leadership that's stretched to capacity. You've got to find some of them to mentor these NQTs. You can see it's a systemic thing…
>
> NEU Official

Many participant teachers reported feeling even more isolated than usual because of rules around social distancing, mask-wearing, not mixing with other bubbles and not congregating in staff or workrooms. This was particularly difficult for newly qualified teachers or those beginning a job in a new school:

> … the other thing is, everybody's very isolated. … we pretty much hunker down in our Department. I've been to the staff room about three times…
>
> Teacher, Sixth Form College

For NQTs who started a job, or trained, during the pandemic, there were problems with incomplete placements, interruptions and disruption to their all-important first steps in teaching. Many were still trying to learn how to work out their style of teaching, yet were unable to get the support they needed from colleagues. The consequence of this has been that NQTs are even less likely to continue beyond their first year, adding to acute shortages in the profession.

Teachers, caring and the community during the pandemic

The pandemic shed light on the crucial role of schools in providing pastoral care and practical support, not only to pupils but also to the wider community. Throughout the pandemic, the community and welfare functions of schools came to the fore, enhancing the sense of purpose and strengthening the identities of teachers and teaching.

Form teachers reported that they phoned family homes regularly to check on pupil progress. Concerns about a child were followed up by teachers, leaders or welfare teams. Members of staff went out to visit pupils' houses, delivering packs of work and food parcels, but equally importantly to make contact. Headteachers and school leadership teams were closely involved in this activity.

> What became obvious as the weeks rolled by was… that half the students were struggling and a small group of the students were completely disengaged. And we were trying really, really hard to catch up with them. It was a very depressing eye-opener to begin to, you know, dig down into the lives of those students.
>
> Head of Subject, Sixth Form College

Despite the government introducing a voucher system to replace free school meals during the lockdowns of spring/summer 2020, many schools chose to persist with providing food bags or parcels, in order to keep an eye on their families:

> We've found that our families really appreciate having the face-to-face contact, having the food parcels, the welfare. We've put parents in touch with mental health workers… we've contacted the local [supermarket]… so there are parents now that can go to the front of the queue and just walk in… so communication with parents has gone through the roof.
>
> Senior leader, Special Provision School

Some teacher participants reported that, in their areas, hubs formed, even joining together local authorities and academy trust schools, in order to pool resources and share the responsibility for providing education and support. This prioritising of pastoral and social care over curriculum provision, which broke out of the usual system boundaries, and the enveloping of whole families into the care of the school was a development which teachers told us seemed the right thing to do, as it reflected their values and purpose in looking after well-being and welfare first, before any continuation of learning was possible. This focus on activities that allowed them to demonstrate and practise values that were core to their sense of professionalism and identity, were factors that, in some cases, positively impacted teacher well-being, as well as on the well-being and welfare of pupils and the wider community.

Conclusion

Carr (2004) noted the negative effect of 'technologisation' and 'bureaucratisation' on education, and, like many others, Hobson and Maxwell (2017) have highlighted the need to support the well-being of teachers. As Hanks (2017: 101) argues, "quality of life does not mean that all things are good and/or easy; rather it may include working very hard, but on something that is interesting, rewarding, and relevant to those working on it". The experiences of the teachers, senior leaders, heads and union representatives revealed through our project and presented in this chapter provide a more nuanced understanding of well-being than has typically been reported.

It is often overlooked that schools remained open throughout the lockdowns. Teachers performed essential front-line roles, adapting rapidly to new pedagogies and technologies, providing hybrid teaching, managing safety in schools and monitoring pupil well-being and welfare. Our meetings with teachers revealed the anxiety caused by pressure to adapt to remote teaching, through the use of new technologies and preparation of different kinds of lessons and activities to deliver the curriculum. With unstable and often unpredictable government requirements, and teachers' own health concerns, during the pandemic, it is unsurprising that studies found average stress levels amongst teachers increased (Education Support, 2020).

Whilst there was little let-up in workload, the first lockdown in particular provided some respite from particular sources of stress associated with school workplaces, such as the tyranny of being observed and monitored. Some teachers in our study reported feeling a greater sense of autonomy. With rules, regulations and guidance constantly evolving, teachers were often left to make their own judgements, which was a source of improved well-being: almost a relief. Teachers enjoyed and valued the opportunity to use their professional knowledge and expertise and to draw on their creativity to (re-)construct curriculum and pedagogy in emergency teaching settings. Being trusted to exercise professional judgement without constant (negative) scrutiny was valued highly and contributed to their sense of well-being.

As the pandemic passed through its various phases, these changes were often revealed to be temporary. Teachers, like others, have faced constant uncertainty in the workplace and ongoing changes to their professional practices. Flexible working may become more acceptable post-COVID-19 (see Marsh-Davies, 2021), but many teachers have faced continuing and mounting pressures. From the dramatically altered demands of curriculum delivery and assessment, whether online or face-to-face, along with health and safety concerns about virus transmission for those working in-person in schools, teachers have been working long hours under stressful conditions, balancing work with family needs and health considerations.

In conclusion, we highlight some surprisingly positive elements from teachers' accounts of their kaleidoscope of experiences during the early stages of the COVID-19 pandemic. Many expressed a renewed pleasure in returning to the essentials of teaching: caring for the educational, social and pastoral development of the young people in their classes. Teachers noted that school rankings, academic exam results and inspections faded away, as the crucial elements of education came into focus. This, in many cases, involved a return to some of the central principles of what it means to be an educator, and for many, this renewed their determination to stay in the profession. Unfortunately, for others, the continuing issues of poor management, overwork, incongruity of values or lack of recognition meant that the only option was to leave.

The experiences of teachers during COVID-19 highlight important issues about the nature of teaching, the factors that impact teacher well-being and the structural and institutional factors that shape teacher well-being during a period of profound crisis and change. Many of the challenges and issues covered here remain important post-COVID-19: there continue to be acute shortages and retention issues. In teaching, stress levels remain high, and workload pressures and performance management systems continue to exert a negative impact on teacher well-being beyond the pandemic. The government has not systematically tackled or addressed these issues since COVID-19, focusing instead on the development of voluntary codes and charters to tackle some of the systemic pressures in teaching. This includes the Education Staff Wellbeing Charter launched in 2021, a voluntary initiative which school leaders are encouraged to sign up to, which highlights a number of principles and commitments around well-being (Department for Education, 2022). However, the most recent evidence suggests that in 2022, record numbers of teachers considered quitting the profession due to poor well-being or mental health (Education Support, 2022). If teachers are to be encouraged to enter, and remain in, the profession, then the issues highlighted in this chapter need urgent attention.

Notes

1 https://leedsteacherwellbeing.leeds.ac.uk/about/
2 NEU and NASUWT

3 National public examinations taken by the majority of pupils in England, usually at the age of 16.
4 National public examinations of a predominantly academic nature, taken in England by pupils as school-leaving qualifications, usually at the age of 18, and typically leading to university entry.

References

Allen, R. and Sims, S. (2018). Do pupils from low-income families get low-quality teachers? Indirect evidence from English schools. *Oxford Review of Education*, 44(4), pp. 441–458.

Allen, R., Jerrim, J. and Sims, S. (2020). How did the early stages of the COVID-19 pandemic affect teacher wellbeing. *Centre for Education Policy and Equalising Opportunities (CEPEO) Working Paper*, 1, No. 20-15.

Allwright, D. and Hanks, J. (2009). *The Developing Language Learner: An Introduction to Exploratory Practice*. Palgrave Macmillan.

Ball, S. J. (2003). The teacher's soul and the terrors of performativity. *Journal of Education Policy*, 18(2), pp. 215–228.

Brown, A., Forde, C., Spencer, D. and Charlwood, A. (2008). Changes in HRM and job satisfaction, 1998–2004: Evidence from the Workplace Employment Relations Survey. *Human Resource Management Journal*, 18(3), pp. 237–256.

Brown, A., Charlwood, A. and Spencer, D.A. (2012). Not all that it might seem: Why job satisfaction is worth studying despite it being a poor summary measure of job quality. *Work, Employment and Society*, 26(6), pp. 1007–1018.

Brown, C., Daly, A. and Liou, Y.H. (2016). Improving trust, improving schools: Findings from a social network analysis of 43 primary schools in England. *Journal of Professional Capital and Community*, 1(1), pp. 69–91.

Bryson, A., Forth, J. and Stokes, L. (2017). Does employees' subjective well-being affect workplace performance? *Human Relations*, 70(8), pp. 1017–1037.

Carr, W. (2004). Philosophy and education. *Journal of Philosophy of Education*, 21(2), pp. 163–175.

Chartered Institute of Personnel and Development (2021). *Health and Well-Being at Work, Report 2021*. London: CIPD.

Day, C. and Smethem, L. (2009). The effects of reform: Have teachers really lost their sense of professionalism? *Journal of Educational Change*, 10(2), pp. 141–157.

Department of Business, Energy and Industrial Strategy (2017). *Industrial Strategy: Building a Britain Fit for the Future*, Cm 9528. London: HM Government.

Department for Education (2017). *Teacher Workload Survey 2016: Research report*. London: Department for Education.

Department for Education (2018). *School Workload Reduction Toolkit*. London: Department for Education.

Department for Education (2019). *Teacher Recruitment and Retention Strategy*. London: Department for Education.

Department for Education (2021). *School Workforce in England*. London: Department for Education.

Department for Education (2022). *Education Staff Well Being Charter*. London: Department for Education.

Department of Levelling Up, Housing and Communities (2022). *Levelling Up the UK*, CP604. London: HM Government.

Education Support (2019). *Teacher Well-Being Index*. London: Education Support.
Education Support (2022). *Teacher Well-Being Index*. London: Education Support.
Ethical Leadership Commission (2017). *Framework for Ethical Leadership*. London: Association of School and College Leaders.
Green, F. (2021). British teachers' declining job quality: Evidence from the skills and employment survey. *Oxford Review of Education*, 47(3), pp. 386–403.
Grenville-Cleave, B. and Boniwell, I. (2012). Surviving or thriving? Do teachers have lower perceived control and well-being than other professions?. *Management in Education*, 26(1), pp. 3–5.
Guest, D.E. (2017). Human resource management and employee well-being: Towards a new analytic framework. *Human Resource Management Journal*, 27(1), pp. 22–38.
Hanks, J. (2017). *Exploratory Practice in Language Teaching: Puzzling about Principles and Practices*. London: Palgrave Macmillan.
Hanks, J., Bewick, B., Dixon, H., Farnsworth, V., Forde, C., Jackson, E., Ledger, A. and Mathieson, R. (2021). Educator wellbeing: Quality of life, inclusion and belonging in/after the COVID-19 pandemic. *BERA Research Intelligence: 'The state of the discipline'*, 149, pp. 22–23.
Harmey, S. and Moss, G. (2021). Learning disruption or learning loss: Using evidence from unplanned closures to inform returning to school after COVID-19. *Educational Review*, pp. 1–20. doi: 10.1080/00131911.2021.1966389.
Health and Safety Executive (2021). *Work Related Stress, Anxiety or Depression in Great Britain: Statistics 2021*, HSE.
Hobson, A.J. and Maxwell, B. (2017). Supporting and inhibiting the well-being of early career secondary school teachers: Extending self-determination theory. *British Educational Research Journal*, 43(1), pp. 168–191.
Jeffrey, K., Mahony, S., Michaelson, J. and Abdallah, S. (2014). *Well-Being at Work: A Review of Literature*. London: New Economics Foundation.
Jerrim, J., Greany, T. and Perera, N. (2018). *Educational Disadvantage: How Does England Compare?* London: Educational Policy Institute.
Kim, L. E., Oxley, L. and Asbury, K. (2022). "My brain feels like a browser with 100 tabs open": A longitudinal study of teachers' mental health and well-being during the COVID-19 pandemic. *British Journal of Educational Psychology*, 92(1), pp. 299–318.
Kowalski, T.H. and Loretto, W. (2017). Well-being and HRM in the changing workplace. The *International Journal of Human Resource Management*, 28(16), pp. 2229–2255.
Marsh-Davies, K. (2021). Can COVID-19 break the rigid opposition to teachers working flexibly? Available at: https://womened.org/blog/can-covid-19-break-the-rigid-opposition-to-teachers-working-flexibly (Accessed 20 December 2022).
Mathieson, R., Forde, C. and Hanks, J. (2021). *Well-Being and Burnout in Teaching: Final Report from the Leeds Teacher Well-Being Project*. Report. University of Leeds.
Mathieson, R. and Walker, M. (Forthcoming). How primary schools experienced the Covid-19 pandemic as a series of distinct phases. *Working Paper, Hillary Place Papers*, School of Education, University of Leeds.
Moss, G., Allen, R., Bradbury, A., Duncan, S., Harmey, S. and Levy, R. (2020). *Primary teachers' experience of the COVID-19 lockdown–Eight key messages for policymakers going forward*. Available at: https://discovery.ucl.ac.uk/id/

eprint/10103669/1/Moss_DCDT%20Report%201%20Final.pdf (Accessed 20 December 2022).
National Foundation for Educational Research (2017). *Teacher Retention and Turnover by Subject*. Slough: NFER.
National Foundation for Educational Research (2022). *Teacher Labour Market in England*. Slough: NFER.
Office for Standards in Education (OFSTED) (2019). *Teacher Well-Being at Work in Schools and Further Education Providers*. Available at: https://assets.publishing.service.gov.uk/government/uploads/system/uploads/attachment_data/file/936253/Teacher_well-being_report_110719F.pdf (Accessed 20 December 2022).
Peccei, R.E., Van de Voorde, K.C. and Van Veldhoven, M. (2013). HRM, wellbeing and performance: A theoretical and empirical review. In J. Paauwe, D.E. Guest, and P.M. Wright (eds.), *Human Resource Management and Performance* (pp. 15–46). Chichester: Wiley.
Perryman, J. and Calvert, G. (2020). What motivates people to teach, and why do they leave? Accountability, performativity and teacher retention. *British Journal of Educational Studies*, 68(1), pp. 3–23.
Quinn, B. (2020a). Back to school in Covid times: What can pupils in England expect? Available at: https://www.theguardian.com/world/2020/aug/28/back-to-school-in-covid-times-what-can-pupils-in-england-expect- (Accessed 22 December 2022).
Quinn, B. (2020b). UK exams debacle: How did this year's results end up in chaos? Available at https://www.theguardian.com/education/2020/aug/17/uk-exams-debacle-how-did-results-end-up-chaos (Accessed 23 December 2022).
Reeves, J. (2018). Teacher identity work in neoliberal schooling spaces. *Teaching and Teacher Education*, 72, 98–106.
Skinner, B., Leavey, G., & Rothi, D. (2021). Managerialism and teacher professional identity: Impact on well-being among teachers in the UK. *Educational Review*, 73(1), 1–16.
Stevenson, D. and Farmer, P. (2017). *Thriving at Work: The Independent Review of Mental Health and Employers*. Available at: https://www.gov.uk/government/publications/thriving-at-work-a-review-of-mental-health-and-employers (Accessed 20 December 2022).
TES (2022). *Wellbeing Report 2022: UK*. London: TES.
Thompson, S. and Marks, N. (2008). Measuring well-being in policy: issues and applications. *Report commissioned by the Foresight Project on Mental Capital and Well-being, Government Office for Science*. Government Office for Science.
Walker, P. (2023). Third of England's teachers who qualified in last decade 'have left profession'. *The Guardian*. Available at: Third of England's teachers who qualified in last decade 'have left profession' | Teaching | The Guardian (Accessed: 9 January 2023).
Warr, P. (2012). How to think about and measure psychological well-being. In M. Wang, R. R. Sinclair and L. E. Tetrick (eds.), *Research Methods in Occupational Health Psychology* (pp. 100–114). London: Routledge.
Weller, N. (2016). *A Northern Powerhouse Schools Strategy*. London: Department for Education.
Worth, J. and Faulkner-Ellis, H. (2021). *Teacher Labour Market in England: Annual Report 2021*. Slough: NFER.
Worth, J., Lynch, S., Hillary, J., Rennie, C. and Andrade, J. (2018). *Teacher Workforce Dynamics in England*. Slough: NFER.

6
STORIES FOUND WITHIN HIGHER EDUCATION

Shifting professional identities of academics

Kathryn Coleman, Melissa Cain, and Chris Campbell

Introduction

This storied chapter has been written collaboratively across digital platforms (Campbell & Coleman, 2020) that allow the co-authors Kate, Melissa and Chris to co-story the stories found within the data of academic teachers in higher education during the pandemic, collected as part of the 'Teaching & Learning in COVID-19 Times' (2020) study (Phillips et al., 2021) that explored innovations, novel partnerships, and enhanced questions of access in teaching and learning practices across sectors due to COVID-19 precautionary measures (see OMEKA https://omeka.cloud.unimelb.edu.au/teaching-and-learning-in-a-pandemic/). We are humanities, arts, and social sciences academics in three eastern state Australian universities from a team of nine collaborators from four countries (Australia, New Zealand, Singapore, and the USA) who co-investigated the impact of COVID-19 on learning and teaching in 2020. We began this scholarship of teaching and learning collaboration when Associate Professor Louise Phillips put out a call on Facebook asking if any connected colleagues were interested in capturing and archiving the many stories of educators across the world during this unique time. This began a chain of digital events as we replied with a 'yes'. The research team consisted of Louise Phillips with co-investigators Dr Kathryn Coleman, Esther Joosa, Dr Susan Davis, Associate Professor Chris Campbell, Dr Melissa Cain, Dr Geraldine Burke, Dr Jenny Ritchie, and Dr Cynthia Brock.

During 2020, and the ongoing pandemic (post-2020), Australian higher education saw many changes. Educators across all sectors responded to these changes with resilience. Some thrived, and others survived (Phillips & Cain,

DOI: 10.4324/9781003352129-8

2020; Cain & Phillips, 2021; Phillips et al., 2021) as they learned to learn and teach online while at home. To capture the seismic changes that were occurring in education internationally and locally, the research team created a twenty-two-question qualitative survey that was distributed to colleagues in communities of practice globally and across social media sites in the midst of the global lockdown in early 2020. We chose to begin working with the data of the higher education academics because we related strongly to the responses, as we too were experiencing the pivot online and race to get students and faculty ready for learning to learn in a health crisis all while in a global lockdown. We resonated with the responses which were strikingly similar to those we were hearing our colleagues discuss. As such, this chapter is focused on data that highlighted academic 'matters of concern' specific to the one hundred and five stories of academic teachers across nineteen countries including Australia. To ensure that we held the data with care, the team chose to work with data that resonated with their roles or interests. We chose to analyse data using a story-making approach (Bunda et al., 2019) or an arts-based methodology (Leavy, 2009) that allowed us to story the data and connect the responses to each other through a narrative form. This iterative narrative writing as the method of analysis is a creative data analysis process and, when complete, invites readers to consider their own stories as they encounter the stories that we have created through interactions with the data. As Rice and Mündel (2018) attest, "this methodology… contributes to the existing qualitative lexicon by providing innovative new approaches not only for chronicling marginalized/misrepresented experiences and critically researching selves, but also for scaffolding intersectional alliances and for imagining more just futures" (p. 211).

Background and context

In March 2020, the World Health Organization declared COVID-19 a pandemic. In turn, we witnessed and felt the immediate impact as teachers across the world went home to work and teach. To limit the spread of the virus, many Australian universities began teaching using online communications applications such as Zoom or MS Teams. Our learning management system spaces, which were previously just collections of uploads, became a hive of activity and pandemic-related communication. Many academic teachers quickly pivoted to this new way of working, sometimes haphazardly, designing living classrooms of activity and innovative experience in a time of unknowns. As university educators teaching the so-called millennial generation who have only known a digital world, we knew that many of our students were tech-savvy in their social lives living post-Facebook digital communities, yet often standardized by brick-and-mortar education that had yet to really embrace digital learning opportunities. Remote emergency university teaching online was a daunting experience that colleagues took on with flair, yet we knew that this cohort of students, a generation of myths and legends where 'learning styles' and 'digital natives' tropes linger on were already living and learning across multiple digital places and desired more. The impact of these unprecedented times for this cohort of pandemic university students born after the advent of the internet into a globalized world led by edu-capitalism and continuing shifting political ideologies now living and learning in a pandemic was and will remain unprecedented. But what about the educators?

The 'Teaching & Learning in COVID-19 Times' study (Phillips et al., 2021) significantly captures the pressures, stress, and self-efficacy of academic teachers as they managed the multiplicities of difficulties and differences confronting them daily. The survey was co-designed to capture the shifts educators across all education sectors felt, as they needed to significantly reconfigure their teaching at very short notice. The biggest change was that teaching and learning were now largely contained to the domain of people's homes, so families needed to become much more involved in facilitating education programs, especially for early childhood and primary-aged children. Academic teachers were also key communicators about how the virus spreads and how to keep safe and support their students, their families, and flatmates. These changes in education were global, urgent, and life-changing for many. It was and continues to be a time of rapid innovation, novel partnerships, and enhanced questions of access, belonging, and care.

As educational researchers, the co-authors were focused on academic concerns during 2020, and quickly began to work within this important data set of one hundred and five stories of academic teachers across nineteen countries including Australia, the USA, Singapore, and Japan. Of the one hundred and five participants, 85% had over a decade of teaching experience. Within this educational expertise, our first important story to emerge was that only 10% of these higher education faculty were teaching online before COVID-19. This is striking, as we had expected this to be proportionately higher considering the digital transformation that had occurred for over a decade in our own educational research (Campbell, 2009; Rourke & Coleman, 2010). What we saw occurring in the data was that many of the academic teachers felt fragmented. As their roles shifted, previous confidence in professional identities was destabilized. Some of our participants found the sudden pivot to remote online learning challenging and stressful; they encountered many technological and pedagogical obstacles, yet told us about their agility to remain flexible, adaptable, and resilient in their situated stories.

In our roles across education, we know that many educators in universities are passionate about teaching, but few have formal academic teaching qualifications, and even if they do, it might only be K-12 teaching experience. Many have completed professional learning and development opportunities such as a graduate certificate in higher education to develop innovative learning and teaching and new assessment knowledge. Many work hard to learn about learning and pedagogies and practices; they sustain scholarship of teaching and learning (SoTL) inquiries to learn new educational technologies for assessment and content delivery in lecture halls, tutorials, or workshops. Many develop these skills throughout their doctoral studies as they learn to teach other adults or learn through peer networks and communities of practice. The higher education data were showing us that this did not prepare them for teaching and learning during COVID-19 times.

Discussion of methodological approaches

As a digital ethnography (Pink et al., 2015), we have used digital principles, methods, and practices (Campbell & Coleman, 2020) to recruit, collect, curate, and publish the data in the 'Teaching & Learning in COVID-19 Times' study. As a cross-sectoral research design across social and cultural educational spaces, we began collecting data in mid-2020, the first year of the COVID-19 pandemic. The survey was hosted on Qualtrics, an online platform. We chose a digital qualitative survey-based methodology to enable widespread access during restrictions. The survey included several questions to gather demographic data, as well as 16 open-ended questions which invited in-depth responses about how teachers were making sense of the pandemic and the disruptive impacts upon their teaching and learning practices and how this might be influencing or changing these practices (Phillips et al., 2021). This large and effective data set holds six hundred and thirty-five educator responses collated between May 2020 when most countries had instituted remote learning, until the end of November 2020. Forty-two participants were from the USA, 40 from Australia, with three each from Singapore and Canada, two from Japan and Fiji, and one respondent from 13 other countries. The responses came from educators across sectors and included early childhood to higher education contexts. The co-designed survey captured demographic data, as well as the impact of COVID-19 on teaching and learning (see Table 6.1), through questions that invited storying the impact of teacher's COVID-19 encounters, and to do this with a pandemic perspective was an imperative of the team.

From the survey that collected our written responses and long-form stories, we quickly began curating into our OMEKA teaching-and-learning-in-a-pandemic data gallery. Provided and supported through a university platform: omeka.cloud.unimelb.edu.au, we began curating all the online archives and exhibits we could find. The OMEKA cloud site served as an outward-facing publication of the data archive collection of teaching and learning artefacts from our COVID-19 investigation. We were committed to building a digital project for online communities to recognize what was being

TABLE 6.1 Teaching and learning in COVID-19 times survey questions 7–22 (Questions addressing the impact of COVID-19)

7. How has COVID-19 impacted your teaching & learning?
8. What is different about your delivery?
9. How has the children's/students' learning been affected?
10. How are you addressing diverse learning needs and approaches, cultural relevance and cultural responsiveness in the altered practices to teaching and learning?
11. What are children/students' questions and concerns and how do you address them?
12. What are the issues you are struggling with and need support with?
13. If you have moved your teaching online what platform/s are you using?
14. If you are teaching online what have you changed in regard to your teaching to support students?
15. What are the strategies that your students are using to study online?
16. Who and what are your key knowledge sources for teaching remotely?
17. What new partnerships have you formed to deliver teaching and learning?
18. What innovations have you forged or experimented with?
19. Please share a story of a successful teaching & learning encounter. Include a unique url (e.g., dropbox page, Instagram page) with max. of 5 images of artefacts as relevant. Please make sure images have no identifying features (e.g., no people, no local signs)
20. What have you learnt about yourself and your teaching?
21. What helps you get through each day?
22. What do you think your students have learnt broadly about these changes (such as about humanity, about themselves as learners)?

achieved by our colleagues and were interested in capturing and archiving items of data that told us about COVID-19 in and across education. The team collected resources or articles as evidence of the pandemic in education so that we could story a digital narrative about what was happening in the world, for the time the survey was open and for the future. Using OMEKA allowed us to curate a digital data warehouse, filled with all of the things that people in the team found useful to the project; had found useful to their own practices; and thought might be useful for other people in the future. OMEKA was selected as a living data space, and instead of designing a website that would need its own archiving and upkeep, we selected a university-supported platform that would be persistent and stable post-pandemic. The OMEKA site, supported by the University of Melbourne is already a valuable tool for educational researchers and teachers in future.

Storying as method

Storytelling opens a path for others to follow in, see themselves and their experience with, and offers space to feel the effect of the encounters we find ourselves in, especially during COVID-19. Stories are rich in their location of time and effect, and the research team knew that at this moment in time across the world, capturing the stories and feltness of learning and teaching during COVID-19 was important. The co-authors were committed to this method of creative data analysis because "stories are both history and prophecy, stories for a time yet to come" (Kimmerer, 2013, p. 207). Many educational researchers use storying, creative writing, and narrative analysis to come to know the research participants' stories and narratives from their own ways of being, doing, and knowing. As Flood (2009) reminds us, "throughout the study it was important to remember that when investigating narratives it is not the story itself, but what the story tells us that is relevant" (p. 64). As researchers, we sit in contiguity with the participants and read and write as an interactive process of data analysis. Storying the data along with our own stories allow for openings in the data. There is a duality of interpretation in the method, as the researcher and the participant both interpret their lives through narrative. In this case, the co-authors interpreted the construction of the narrative as a triadic, sharing their stories of the data in conversation with each other. Narrative inquiry is a creative, complex, and innovative methodology. As Chakraborty (2017) attests, "carrying out narrative research requires researcher's reflexivity as it brings the personal dimension into the research" (p. 2964). In many cases of narrative inquiry, the researcher and the participant constantly negotiate the meaning of the stories through sense-making and check-in points as the data are collected and analysed. In our research, the co-authors did this sense-making through their triadic storying relationship. Our first readings of participants' stories left us captivated. The co-authors felt their emotional responses precipitated by the immediate shift to remote teaching and learning, underscored by confusion and unknowing. We read and now re-story these stories, two years later, with illuminating hindsight. This process allowed for check-in points as data analysis, and to ensure that stories we were writing with the data created opportunities to make the implicit explicit for others inside and outside of the academy.

The uncertainties we found ourselves in captured through the story, and re-storying was an important aspect of our data collection and method. Other narrative collections emerged during the pandemic such as the Corona Chronicles (2021) and The Pandemic Reader (2021), both edited collections published by DIO Press in the USA that sought to capture the stories of educators in the rapidly changing landscape. Pre-COVID-19, it was suggested that "precarity is the condition of our time" and that "our time is ripe for sensing precarity" (Tsing, 2015, p. 20). The precarity of the pandemic shifted all aspects of our lives as educators, as we were forced to professionally develop ourselves in the midst of a global and economic crisis. This precarity has affected academic teachers post-2020; through the shifts required for remote emergency teaching, learning, and assessment, but also through policy reform and job insecurities as higher education continues to feel the impact of this unfolding crisis (Molla & Cuthbert, 2022). The precarity of teaching across higher education has been felt for some time as the casualization of the workforce (Blackmore, 2020) becomes more apparent and research funding dries up. But this rapid and immediate in many cases unsupported shift and move to online many academic teachers had not encountered before. In this assemblage of precarity, the methods of storying data through the collection of told stories allowed us to capture these times for future generations of educators. The research design was developed to be transformative for the participant, the research team, and the audience to offer some respite and care for us all.

We invite readers to three stories here that the co-authors have developed through digital narrative inquiry. These stories are representative of the stories we encountered and written with care to ensure that names, places, and identifying information are removed or disguised. To open these stories up for resonance, you will note there is no gender, job title, or country, rather three stories that explore the consequence of the pandemic to contribute to SoTL and offer insight for future generations of educators. The stories are written ethically and use a storied narrative. While narrating these stories, the co-authors have become entangled in the stories and pieced "together fragments from their working lives to add sense to their stories and thus provide scope to widen the researcher's interpretation of the creative process" (Chakraborty, 2017, p. 2965). When the co-authors use inverted commas as punctuation marks or text shifts into italics or these indicate words captured within the data to quote or block quote the participants' own words.

Story 1

I'm "talking to an empty computer screen, as the students do not turn on their camera[s], while reading chat messages" states an older person who has now "shifted from face-to-face teaching in the middle of the trimester". I work in Humanities, Arts and Social Sciences, and have been "PLANNING, planning, planning...". This is something many of those teaching in higher education will relate to, as we shifted our teaching from face-to-face to fully online.

I have been conducting discussions online as well as organized experiential exercises online and assessed online via open book exams and take-home exams. One of the things that has changed for me is that I now have "too much writing" because I "must prepare slides for every step of an experiential process". I have felt that the need to assist students in negotiating and "managing competition and cooperation concurrently". This is because I believe in context:

an online environment supports competitive behaviour but does not support cooperative behaviour in a mix-motive situation, as trust and open communication are fundamental to cooperation in a mix-motive situation, and this is more difficult to achieve online. The online experience diminishes learning about strategy and strategic actions.

Pre-COVID-19, my "students always ask about assessment but in an online world they [ask] about technology". They have told me that the "internet connectivity is critical for experiential learning". Most days I find myself worried about online learning:

A group of four engaged in an exercise and one of the four has a flawed microphone - So [they] can use the chat function but clearly cannot participate fully. The learning of all four students is diminished by technology problems. Poor internet connectivity is a more serious problem, as student[s] cannot even get online or if they get online and then are assigned to an experiential group they drift in-and-out and again it diminishes the learning for all members of that group.

My "university offers a lot of support but in the end the lecturer has to deliver on their own". It means staff need to be comfortable solving any problems they have while teaching and with some technologies this can be challenging. I have been able to solve most technical problems in a unique way because I "actually used my own external research funding (that allowed teaching buy-out) to hire a sessional staff not to teach but to provide technical support".

The biggest surprise is that "students still value my teaching although online". The "student summary evaluation of my course in an online environment was 4.5/5 in an undergraduate course (36% response) and 4.8/5 in a graduate course (61% response)".

Story 2

I'm an Australian post-grad educator in Humanities, Arts and Social Sciences and I've been in higher education for a decade. I think I'm doing some things well and I'm really worried about others. The thing that concerns me most is engagement, and what that now means.

Everything is now online, and I really miss the interaction with students. I feel like I am less motivated and enjoy my teaching less. I have become a curator and creator of learning resources rather than an educator.

I think what I have felt through this process is a change in who I am as an educator, and what my role is in the subject and in the sector. I've really tried to change a lot about what I do as an educator. The biggest takeaway for me is that binge watching has become a learning strategy for students. For me, my teaching strategies are now trial and error.

My professional learning community and Twitter have been important to my easing off a little bit on myself and what I'm learning how to do. I can see on Twitter, that there are colleagues across higher education also encountering similar issues, and I feel less alone, and less exposed by reading these short little stories from my colleagues.

I feel like I've been able to innovate and experiment with new ideas, thinking with new strategies that include embedding surveys and online assessment, particularly thinking about ways that I can extend and expand on learning activities, and learning experiences in lieu of formal lectures. I don't have any evidence or data to say that what I have done is working. I really hope what I'm doing is working for my students, but I just really don't know.

I am proud of some of the learning resources and opportunities I have created but fear that many students don't have the time or capacity to engage with them, and only have the bandwidth to focus on bare minimum for assessment. The focus is less on learning and more on getting through so, I guess if most can get over that line this will be a successful outcome.

I've learned a lot about myself and about teaching. My teaching practice relies heavily on spontaneous storytelling, and I link this to critical discussion. But I am very aware that I am being recorded. And, I'm being careful about not wasting time in my video lectures, this is a shift in my teaching. I hope that students have learnt about these changes that help us understand education differently particularly. I hope they now see their lecturers and tutors as people who experience similar problems to them. I hope they can now recognize what good practice is; hopefully, the good intent of practice. What it looks like, feels like, and how they come to know the experience of that practice.

Story 3

I pride myself on teaching excellence and have been awarded a Distinguished Faculty Teaching Award. I have a lot of experience in language and literacy particularly focused on teaching emerging bilinguals and multilingual students. The greatest impact on me has been leaving the profession because of COVID-19.

With COVID-19, we moved to teaching remoting [sic] for the second half of the Spring, 2020 semester. I sadly and reluctantly resigned at the end of the semester because I found my online teaching to be artificial, ineffective, and very unsatisfying.

Everything about my teaching has been different, especially the delivery. My teaching style that was incredibly active because I don't really lecture, and I pride myself on a student-centred, highly interactive experiential classroom. I found it difficult to engage my students during Zoom and Moodle classes. It was as if something changed in them overnight. Their enthusiasm and preparedness changed into a disengaged sadness. Some of them seemed bored and tired, many disinterested.

> *It was very sad and disheartening to see, despite my best efforts to engage them. And my confidence was shaken as never before when we had to go online with a week's preparation.* I tried to teach online as I'd always taught, and it just didn't work. It was frustrating for the students and demoralizing for me.

To ensure that I continued to be inclusive and attentive to diverse learning needs and approaches, cultural relevance and cultural responsiveness in my classroom, I set up individual conferencing with Zoom. I ensured that students could contact me via phone or email. I've even had international students contact me because I wanted to provide individual help that I couldn't over Zoom. I just really couldn't ensure they were getting it. *I could barely see one (sat in dark room; far from screen), and none participated as they had before quarantine, even in the frequent break-out room activities.*

I have struggled because we were provided with very little training and within one week I had to prepare for the change and how to use Zoom. "I've taught for 50+ years but had no idea how to make online teaching as effective as my face-to-face teaching. For this fall, if I had continued, I would have really liked some help with how to effectively engage students in interacting with each other. I would have made more use of Padlet. But it's not about computer programs as much as it is about how to provide interaction and collaboration opportunities within online teaching".

Discussion

What emerges from these stories is a focus on learning and teaching, but more importantly the impact on the people, that is our academic teachers and students in higher education. We position the data, and data work through storying methods before discussing what emerges in these stories to invite the reader into our experience of 'living' with this data during the pandemic. As many SoTL literature reviews do, this discussion draws from a breadth of bodies of knowledge that we found emerging in the data and stories data. Because of this, post-pandemic SoTL inquiries like this one often take scholars into unfamiliar and new territory. Like other COVID-19 studies (Ferdig et al., 2020; Naylor & Nyanjom, 2021; Baumgartner et al., 2022), we have stories of academic teachers thriving in various and unique ways during remote teaching. Many learning a lot about themselves and about teaching and for some who have just survived struggling with little training and time to prepare for both the change and educational technology integrations such as Zoom. What we found as co-investigators in the 'Teaching & Learning in COVID-19 Times' study is that educators often view themselves as proficient in either face-to-face or online delivery as a component of their professional identities (Cain et al., 2022) and feel personal and professional disequilibrium when this is disrupted or challenged. Our own beliefs about learning and teaching were being affected through remote emergency teaching as we held our students tight in a global health crisis.

The three stories we have chosen to share we resonate strongly with, feeling their joy, their frustrations, and concern for student well-being, the worry about equity, access, and safety for themselves, their colleagues, and their students. The lessons we have learned from storying these data make important contributions to professional learning for academic teachers in the future and post-pandemic SoTL. Knowing that a teacher's epistemic beliefs and values are intertwined with relationships to pedagogies, people, places, and practices, we located four themes that emerge from within our creative data analysis and sense-making discussions: shifting professional identities; epistemic beliefs; pressures, stress and self-efficacy; and agility, risk, and creativity. To further dialogue and discussion, we explore these emergent themes to create new opportunities and generate post-pandemic SoTL imaginaries through a discussion with the literature.

1. Shifting professional identities

Found across all of the 'Teaching & Learning in COVID-19 Times' data was how a teacher's relationship with their profession "evolves with reference to the educational contexts that academic teachers find themselves in, their personal agency in these contexts, and changing professional experiences" (Cain et al., 2022, p. 2). Within the higher education data, the co-authors found that academic teachers moved smoothly from pre-pandemic 'education-as-usual' to teaching solely via Zoom and other video conferencing technologies, it was clear for most of our participants in this study that their sense of professional identity had been shaken, and for some, irrevocably broken as storied.

While the initial anxiety around the impacts of COVID-19 on health and freedom of movement has now eased, these continue to be unsettling times for academic teachers. Significant global shifts in methods of delivery and ways of engaging with students have continued to impact academic teachers' resilience. Tomej and colleagues (2022) note that "while the long-term effects and consequences of this disruption in higher education are yet to be seen, some are already obvious" (p. 1). This may be so, but COVID-19 has already proven to be "monumentally disruptive" to education (Frank, 2022). Recent research from Kulikowski and colleagues has documented three significant impacts on higher education academic teachers' professional identities and associated job motivation. Firstly, a forced engagement with digital technologies as the primary source of connecting with students during the pandemic has permeated into current practice and will continue to expand. Secondly, academic teachers continue to have greater responsibility for student care and counselling caused by COVID-19-induced anxiety and students' declining self-efficacy. Finally, the realization that higher education will not return to the pre-pandemic status quo. Uncertainty in job security, job expectations, and job workload continues to cloud past confidence and assurance (Kulikowski et al., 2022) and causes academic teachers to question what matters in education, and their role within higher education. Indian novelist Arundhati Roy suggests that this is good and necessary and despite longing for a return to what was "nothing could be worse than a return to normality" (2020).

Shift 1: Digital delivery

Globally, steady growth in online delivery in higher education was underway prior to COVID-19 restrictions (Means et al., 2014; Shankar et al., 2021). This has been in part due to a desire to increase accessibility and flexibility for potential students who may face barriers to on-campus learning due to work or family commitments, disability, or geographic location. Some academic teachers with online experience have favoured this mode of delivery, while others have chosen to prefer face-to-face engagement and the on-campus experience. Academic teachers may view themselves as proficient in either in-person or online delivery and see this preference as an important component of their professional identities; inextricably connected to their epistemic beliefs and values about teaching (Cain et al., 2022). A sudden change in mode of delivery notes Naylor and Nyanjom (2021) can "disrupt these deep and personal connections giving rise to an emotional response" (p. 1) and has the potential to cause experienced educators to feel deskilled, vulnerable, or isolated (Downing & Dyment, 2013). Due to the rapid pace of technological initiatives, previously confident academic teachers felt like novices, with this new deficiency challenging their role identity (El-Soussi, 2022). While in many cases the forced move to online learning resulted in an increase in skills and skill variety for academic teachers, DeCoito & Estaiteyeh (2022) noted that for many, this was accompanied by lower job motivation, lower instructional self-efficacy, reduced sense of agency, and higher emotional exhaustion.

Shift 2: Care and concern

The second unexpected shift in academic teachers' professional identities was prompted by greater care and counselling expectations during COVID-19 restrictions. Teaching, notes Cain et al. (2022) "is inherently a social practice, and care is integral to successful teaching" (p. 4). Post-COVID-19 restrictions, higher education academic teachers continued their pastoral role but in very different ways, and in response to previously unexperienced catalysts. Many found challenges in connecting emotionally with their students at a distance and expressing empathy and compassion was found to be more difficult in the online space (Casacchia et al., 2021). Academic teacher data showed that our participants worried about how to support those with mental health concerns, those who experienced increased anxiety from a lack of social connection, and those whose families had lost employment or indeed lost loved ones to COVID-19. Our higher education participant data showed that they worried about how to help students who did not have reliable internet, digital devices, or a place to study at home. Academic teachers' greatest concern was for the most vulnerable students, recognizing that the impacts of COVID-19 served to highlight the existing challenges and issues of inequity. Kim and Asbury (2020) suggest that this high level of anxiety about disadvantaged and vulnerable students was due to a strong sense that the pandemic highlights "broader problems that were always there, just hidden" (p. 12). Academic teachers worried about their own families as the blurring of their professional and personal lives eroded any work–life balance. If time permitted, they worried about their own emotional self-care. Rawle (2021) insists that a pedagogy of kindness was the cornerstone for students' learning and wellness during this pandemic.

Shift 3: Questioning

Positive coping strategies and feelings of control and optimism contribute to teacher resilience but erode during times of crisis (Sharma et al., 2022). Wright and colleagues (2021) highlight that crises are "destabilizing to one's ontological security" (that is, individual agency derived from being 'a whole and continuous self') and that post-pandemic times have created "an existential anxiety that has developed around the purpose of the university" (p. 164). Roy asserts that pandemics across history have "forced humans to break with the past and imagine their world anew" (2020, npn). This is ideal, suggests Frank (2022), as post the disruption, "it would be a loss if we were to just fall back into old routines" (p. 7). The impacts of COVID-19 on teaching and learning have indeed prompted many academic teachers in higher education to question what they thought they always knew about themselves as educators, their role within their university, and indeed, what really matters in and as education. For those who subscribe to or aim for the ideals of 'slow scholarship' (Berg & Seeber, 2016), a "thoughtful and deliberate approach to contemporary academic practice" (Mahon, 2021, p. 457) this was not possible during the initial months of remote teaching and learning. The race to 'get learning online' and to satisfy the 'new normal' of large-scale migration to online learning "is radically impactful on the speed or slowness of any student experience" (Mahon, 2021, p. 455). In mourning what was lost during COVID-19, and to be lost, is a reason to "rethink the purposes of schooling and the potentials for education in our time" (Frank, 2022, p. 8).

2. Epistemic beliefs

Knowing that a teacher's epistemic beliefs (personal theories of knowledge and knowing) and values are intertwined with relationships to pedagogies, people, places, and practices during the pandemic, they became reified as the three teacher stories demonstrate. Our system of beliefs was affected on many fronts during the pandemic as certainty, structure, and sources of knowledge were slippery and often unable to be captured. Epistemic beliefs are about knowledge and the acquisition of knowledge, and these are integral to change. The pandemic disrupted so much of what we do and know about education: what we value, recognize, and strive to create as a transformative experience for students. Lammassaari et al. (2022) suggest that

> adopting pedagogical ideas that are not based on traditional subject-matter teaching and schooling practices and bringing them into the classroom may fundamentally challenge academic teachers' intuitive epistemic theories, as they need to rethink the basis of their ideas about what learning is and how it should be promoted.
>
> *(p. 2)*

Our research has shown us that through the pandemic, academic teachers have been challenged in every way to rethink the basis of their ideas about what learning is as digital reforms and educational technology-enabled learning changed their practice. For academic teachers who believe that knowledge is relational and can change over time and see themselves as changemakers, the pandemic offered a space to grow professionally as they were willing to learn and adapt their practice with agility. However, many academic teachers who see knowing as certain and unchangeable were resistant to the change being forced upon them. We understand epistemologies in terms of how they are done rather than something an individual has – making them contingent, relational, and contextual. Epistemic change requires dynamic pedagogical leadership to develop academic teachers' critical awareness of their beliefs.

As academic teachers negotiated new epistemic cultures (Knorr Cetina, 2007) and ways of knowing at the boundaries of disciplinary curriculum, novel ways of knowing (epistemologies) were ruptured as many colleagues clung tight to traditional pedagogies and practices that did not easily transfer online. What we have learned through the pandemic about lectures, exams, delivery, content, and assessment types is that teaching and learning can be interdisciplinary, hybrid, flexible, and digital, but this is hard when done overnight and without much reflection or time for slow scholarship.

3. Pressures, stress, and self-efficacy

Much has been written on the pressures and stress academics felt with the rapid remote shift to online learning during the pandemic (Houlden & Veletsianos, 2020; Kupe & Wangenge-Ouma, 2020). Many of us experienced higher levels of occupational stress, mental health issues, and work-related pressures, with many still recovering from burnout in the first two years of COVID-19. As new constraints in the understanding of what was needed for the new 'COVID-19-normal' physically distanced classroom emerged, much of the discussion was still focused on content and delivery, rather than on creative and critical learning and how the learner would engage, participate, and attend during a global health crisis.

There were new affordances that required new metaphors for 'knowing' and 'being' pedagogies and new experiences built out of trauma, sickness, and for many, fears as educators shifted their labour. As the university pivoted, many academic teachers turned to colleagues for support and new ways of knowing because "co-constructing ontological meaning requires taking time to slow down and engage in deep social experiences that build strong bonds through speculating, theorizing and philosophising about ourselves, others, our world(s), our Future(s)" (Wright & Coleman, 2019, p. 328). However, there was little time for slow and collaborative scholarship and considered observation to support academic teachers to be agile, creative, and innovative educators. The self-efficacy of the teaching staff was a necessary resilience factor against perceiving high levels of stress. "The university is ontologically secure when knowledge production is possible in a safe environment, wherein 'creative performance' (generating research ideas) and 'innovative performance' (turning these ideas into published manuscripts) are within grasp" (Da Silva & Davis, 2011, p. 373). The opposite, however, appears to be the default.

4. Agility, risk, and creativity

There was much risk to creativity in moving teaching and learning online during the COVID-19 pandemic as many academic teachers quickly attempted to shift what they did one week on campus and the next online while learning more about the virus and dealing with an emerging pandemic. There was little time to reflect on what might be needed, as academic teachers discovered whole new ways of working and living alongside students from their living rooms. Many academic teachers quickly developed video recording skills while uplifting their knowledge of video conferencing and learning to be creative inside their learning management systems. Pre-pandemic, many academic teachers were just learning how to engage in flipped learning pedagogies, using digital ways of knowing to invite multi-modalities and new digital literacies into their flexible and accessible classrooms. During the pandemic, there was a felt expectation to be agile, risky, and creative in approaches to remote emergency teaching for students to continue in their studies and keep them 'entertained' during long bouts of lockdown. Facebook groups popped up across the world as academics shared their tips and tricks, and newfound practices and experiences with each other. For many, there was little time for slowness and reflection on what was happening as the world seemed to shift and notions of time changed. As Mahon (2021) suggests, "'slowness' involves questioning the value of productivity and reinstating the value of the local; 'slowness' champions the ability to create in the present and to sidestep the endless pressure to produce for the future" (p. 457).

Conclusion

The co-authors have listened carefully to the digital stories gifted during trying times that told us something about the moment in time that highlighted the complexity of teaching, learning, and researching while living during a global pandemic. These times have been difficult for many of us, possibly the most difficult times in our lives as educators, as well as being parents, children, friends, and caregivers. We were privileged through this research to be the recipients of stories about the public and private lives of teachers and use re-storying as a method to ensure ethics of care in sharing their identity stories as we speculate on how teachers might view themselves now. Our re-storying allows for a deep dive into the teachers' pandemic responses and the important implications of being a teacher post-COVID-19.

Since our data collection in 2020, education has seen many of these academic teachers leave the profession, making these data more important than we thought it might be. These stories witnessed how academic teachers view themselves and create their identities, seeing their epistemic beliefs and values intertwined with relationships to pedagogies, people, places, and practices. They relate the public and private lives of academics who generously shared their stories of shifting professional identities, pressures, stress and self-efficacy, agility, risk, and creativity stories for future generations to read. When we tell our stories of the times, we open ourselves to scrutiny, we open ourselves to judgment, but we do so in service to our field in these moments when education and educators have much to learn from the generative nature of our stories of hope and despair.

We have learned much from these storied gifts. Despite the initial feelings of frustration and anxiety accompanied by a lack of efficacy in online teaching techniques and facility with digital technologies, academic teachers demonstrated resilience as they worked to find ways of connecting personally with their students, keeping them engaged, and making learning meaningful. They felt the anxiety of separating from their well-honed professional identities, using trial and error to craft new confidence and agility in the online space. As they negotiated blurred personal and professional lives, they worried about their students, particularly those most vulnerable, knowing they had limited ability to assist with financial, medical, and relational problems these students experienced during COVID-19 restrictions. Most importantly, academic teachers in our study lamented the breadth and depth of research and preparedness they would normally engage in before embarking on a new teaching experience.

After three years of the impact of COVID-19 on teaching and learning, it is evident that future sudden shifts to online instruction are a certainty. For academic teachers in the future to learn from our experiences, we need to reflect on the practicalities and emotions experienced during this time. Higher education institutions must endeavour to provide frequent opportunities for academics to learn from professionals and from each other about the most recent advances in online pedagogies and applications. They must have communications and procedures ready to execute at a moment's notice and ensure that stakeholders' questions are answered. They must recognize the considerable increase in workload that a change of pedagogy brings and honour the emotional and social impacts on their teachers and their families. Academic teachers should acknowledge that they have the creativity and resilience to take on new ways of working and that they can maintain quality teaching through varied means. They should appreciate that relationships are essential for learning. Taking time to 'check in' with their students' welfare is not time wasted.

Acknowledgement

We acknowledge that we live and work in many countries and lands of First Nations' people who have been custodians of these lands for thousands of years. We acknowledge and pay our respects to their elders past, present, and emerging. The digital ethnographic study is approved by the James Cook University Human Research Ethics Committee (H8090) and led by an Associate Professor in Education at James Cook University, Singapore, Dr Louise Phillips. We are a team of nine collaborators from four countries: Australia, New Zealand, Singapore, and the USA, and are also facing similar shifts in our own practice/s. We are co-investigating the impact of COVID-19 on learning and teaching and building an OMEKA gallery of related digital data at https://omeka.cloud.unimelb.edu.au/teaching-and-learning-in-a-pandemic/

References

Baumgartner, E., Kaplan-Rakowski, R., Ferdig, R. E., Hartshorne, R., & Mouza, C. (Eds). (2022). A retrospective of teaching, technology, and teacher education during the COVID-19 pandemic. *Association for the Advancement of Computing in Education* (AACE). https://www.learntechlib.org/p/######/

Berg, M., & Seeber, B. (2016). *The slow professor: Challenging the culture of speed in the academy*. University of Toronto Press.

Blackmore, J. (2020). The carelessness of entrepreneurial universities in a world risk society: A feminist reflection on the impact of Covid-19 in Australia. *Higher Education Research & Development*, 39(7), 1332–1336.

Bunda, T., Heckenberg, R., Snepvangers, K., Phillips, L., Lasczik, A., & Black, A. (2019). Storymaking belonging. *Art/Research International: A Transdisciplinary Journal*, 4(1), 153–176. https://doi.org/10.18432/ari29429

Casacchia, M., Grazia Cifone, M., Giusti, L., Fabiani, L., Gatto, R., Lancia, L., Cinque, B., Petrucci, C. Giannoni, M., Ippoliti, R., Frattaroli, A. R., Macchiarelli, G., & Roncone, R. (2021). Distance education during COVID 19: An Italian survey on the university academic teachers' perspectives and their emotional conditions. *BMC Medical Education*, 21, 1017. https://doi.org/10.1186/s12909-021-02780-y

Cain, M., & Phillips, L. (2021). Found poems and imagery of physical and social dis/connections in inclusive education during a pandemic. The kaleidoscope of lived curricula: Learning through a confluence of crises (pp. 109–125). 13th Annual Curriculum and Pedagogy Group 2021. Edited Collection.

Cain, M., Campbell, C., & Coleman, K. (2022). 'Kindness and empathy beyond all else'. Challenges to professional identities of Higher Education academic teachers during COVID-19 times. *Australian Educational Researcher*, 1–19. https://doi.org/10.1007/s13384-022-00552-1

Campbell, C. (2009). Learning in a different life: Pre-service education students using an online virtual world. *Journal of Virtual worlds Research*, 2(1), 1–15.

Campbell, C., & Coleman, K. (2020). Connecting the dots: Digital tools for doing educational research on COVID-19 during a pandemic. *ASCILITE Technology Enhanced Learning Blog*, 10 July 2020. https://blog.ascilite.org/connecting-the-dots-digital-tools-for-doing-educational-research-on-COVID-19-during-a-pandemic/

Chakraborty, S. (2017). Using narratives in creativity research: Handling the subjective nature of creative process. *Qualitative Report*, 22, 2959–2973. https://doi.org/10.46743/2160-3715/2017.3176

Da Silva, N., & Davis, A. R. (2011). Absorptive capacity at the individual level: Linking creativity to innovation in academia. *The Review of Higher Education*, 34(3), 355–379. https://doi.org/10.1353/rhe.2011.0007

DeCoito, I., & Estaiteyeh, M. (2022). Transitioning to online teaching during the COVID-19 pandemic: An exploration of STEM academic teachers' views, successes, and challenges. *Journal of Science Education Technology, 31*(3), 340–356. https://doi.org/10.1007/s10956-022-09958-z

Downing, J., & Dyment, J. (2013). Teacher educators' readiness, preparation, and perceptions of preparing preservice academic teachers in a fully online environment: An exploratory study. *The Teacher Educator, 48,* 96–109. https://doi.org/10.1080/08878730.2012.760023

El-Soussi, A. (2022). The shift from face-to-face to online teaching due to COVID-19: Its impact on higher education faculty's professional identity. *International Journal of Educational Research Open.* https://doi.org/10.1016/j.ijedro.2022.100139

Ferdig, R. E., Baumgartner, E., Hartshorne, R., Kaplan-Rakowski, R., & Mouza, C. (Eds). (2020). Teaching, technology, and teacher education during the COVID-19 Pandemic: Stories from the field. *Association for the Advancement of Computing in Education* (AACE). https://www.learntechlib.org/p/216903/

Flood, A. (2009). Finding new landscapes of a creative identity. *ACCESS: Critical Perspectives on Communication, Cultural & Policy Studies, 28*(1), 55–71.

Frank, J. (2022). Rethinking the purposes of schooling in a global pandemic: From learning loss to a renewed appreciation for mourning and human excellence. *Studies in Philosophy and Education* (online). https://doi.org/10.1007/s11217-022-09850-8

Houlden, S., & Veletsianos, S. (2020, March 12). Coronavirus pushes universities to switch to online classes-but are they ready? *The Conversation.* https://theconversation.com/coronavirus-pushes-universities-to-switch-to-online-classes-but-are-they-ready-132728

Kim, L. E., & Asbury, K. (2020). 'Like a rug had been pulled from under you': The impact of COVID-19 on academic teachers in England during the first six weeks of the UK Lockdown. *British Journal of Educational Psychology, 90,* 1062–1083. https://doi.org/10.1111/bjep.12381

Kimmerer, R. W. (2013). *Braiding sweetgrass: Indigenous wisdom, scientific knowledge and the teachings of plants* (First edition.). Milkweed Editions.

Knorr Cetina, K. (2007). Culture in global knowledge societies: Knowledge cultures and epistemic cultures. *Interdisciplinary Science Reviews, 32*(4), 361–375.

Kulikowski, K., Przytuła, S., & Sułkowski, Ł. (2022). E-learning? Never again! On the unintended consequences of COVID-19 forced e-learning on academic teacher motivational job characteristics. *Higher Education Quarterly, 76*(1), 174–189. https://doi.org/10.1111/hequ.12314

Kupe, T., & Wangenge-Ouma, G. (2020, November 15). Post COVID-19: Opportunity for universities to have a rethink. *The Conversation.* https://theconversation.com/post-COVID-19-opportunity-for-universities-to-have-a-rethink-149474

Lammassaari, H., Hietajärvi, L., Salmela-Aro, K., Hakkarainen, K., & Lonka, K. (2022). Exploring the relations among academic teachers' epistemic theories, Work engagement, burnout and the contemporary challenges of the teacher profession. *Frontiers in Psychology, 13,* 861437. https://doi.org/10.3389/fpsyg.2022.861437

Leavy, P. (2009). *Method meets art: Arts-based research practice.* New York: Guildford.

Mahon, A. (2021). Towards a higher education: Contemplation, compassion, and the ethics of slowing down. *Educational Philosophy and Theory, 53*(5), 448–458. https://doi.org/10.1080/00131857.2019.1683826

Means, B., Bakia, M., & Murphy, R. (2014). *Learning online: What research tells us about whether, when and how*. New York: Routledge.

Molla, T., & Cuthbert, D. (2022). Crisis and policy imaginaries: Higher education reform during a pandemic. *Higher Education*. https://doi.org/10.1007/s10734-022-00899-5

Naylor, D., & Nyanjom, J. (2021). Educators' emotions involved in the transition to online teaching in higher education. *Higher Education Research and Development*, 40(6), 1236–1250. https://doi.org/10.1080/07294360.2020.1811645

Phillips, L., & Cain, M. (2020). 'Exhausted beyond measure': What academic teachers are saying about COVID-19 and the disruption to education. *The Conversation*, August 4. https://theconversation.com/exhausted-beyond-measure-what-academic-teachers-are-saying-about-COVID-19-and-the-disruption-to-education-143601

Phillips, L. G., Cain, M., Ritchie, J., Campbell, C., Davis, S., Brock, C., Burke, G., Coleman, K., & Joosa, E. (2021). Surveying and resonating with teacher concerns during COVID-19 pandemic. *Academic teachers and Teaching, Theory and Practice*, 1–18. https://doi.org/10.1080/13540602.2021.1982691

Pink, S., Horst, H., Postill, J., Hjorth, L., Lewis, T., & Tacchi, J. (2015). *Digital ethnography: Principles and practice*. Los Angeles: Sage Publications.

Rawle, F. (2021). A pedagogy of kindness: The cornerstone for student learning and wellness. *Times Higher Education*. https://www.timeshighereducation.com/campus/pedagogy-kindness-cornerstone-student-learning-and-wellness

Rice, C., & Mündel, I. (2018), Story-making as methodology: Disrupting dominant stories through multimedia storytelling. *Canadian Review of Sociology/Revue canadienne de Sociologie*, 55, 211–231. https://doi.org/10.1111/cars.12190

Rourke, A. J., & Coleman, K. S. (2010). Knowledge building in 21st century: Learners, learning and educational practice. In C. H. Steel, M. J. Keppell, P. Gerbic & S. Housego (Eds.), *Curriculum, technology & transformation for an unknown future*. Proceedings Sydney 2010 (pp. 821–828). http://ascilite.org.au/conferences/sydney10/procs/Rourke-concise.pdf

Roy, A. (2020). The pandemic is a portal. *The Financial Times*. https://www.ft.com/content/10d8f5e874eb 11ea 95fe fcd274e920ca/

Shankar, K., Arora, P., & Binz-Scharf, M. C. (2021). Evidence on online higher education: The promise of COVID-19 pandemic data. *Management and Labour Studies*. https://doi.org/10.1177/0258042X211064783

Sharma, U., Laletas, S., May, F., & Groves, C. (2022). 'In any crisis there is an opportunity for us to learn something new': Australian teacher experiences during COVID-19-19. *The Australian Educational Researcher* (online). https://doi.org/10.1007/s13384-022-00556-x

Teaching & Learning in COVID-19 Times Study (2020). *Teaching & Learning in COVID-19 Times Study Online collection*. Omeka. https://omeka.cloud.unimelb.edu.au/teaching-and-learning-in-a-pandemic/

Tomej, K., Liburd, J., Blichfeldt, B. S., & Hjalager, A.-M. (2022). Blended and (not so) splendid teaching and learning: Higher education insights from university academic teachers during the COVID-19 pandemic. *International Journal of Educational Research Open*, 3, 100144. https://doi.org/10.1016/j.ijedro.2022.100144

Tsing, A. L. (2015). *The mushroom at the end of the world: On the possibility of life in capitalist ruins*. Princeton University Press.

Wright, S., & Coleman, K. (2019). studioFive—A site for teaching, research and engagement in Australian arts education. In C. H. Lum & E. Wagner (Eds.), *Arts education and cultural diversity. Yearbook of arts education research for cultural diversity and sustainable development*, vol 1. Springer, Singapore. https://doi.org/10.1007/978-981-13-8004-4_11

Wright, K., Haastrup, T., & Guerrina, R. (2021). Equalities in freefall? Ontological insecurity and the long-term impact of COVID-19 in the academy. *Gender, Work, and Organization, 28*(1), 163–167. https://doi.org/10.1111/gwao.12518

7
CLAIMING PROFESSIONALISATION

Supporting Caribbean early childhood teachers' professional identities post-COVID-19

Zoyah Kinkead-Clark and Sabeerah Abdul-Majied

Introduction

As in other jurisdictions, the COVID-19 pandemic has had a significant impact on Caribbean education systems. Unlike other tiers of the education system which more readily received government support, the lack of prioritisation of early education forced teachers of young children to become more creative, innovative and resilient in order to maintain and deliver required teaching practices. While much has been documented about practices in primary and secondary classrooms since the pandemic, very little is known about the unique practices teachers had to employ to reach children at the early childhood level. These changes have had ripple effects, not only on pedagogical practices but more so, by shifting teachers' professional identities. Although strides had been made towards professionalising the sector by governments across the region, gains in this direction were threatened by mandated pandemic health and safety measures such as those which increased teachers' workload or reduced remuneration. What needs to be determined is whether resulting changes also highlight additional shortcomings to be overcome for advancing the early childhood sector, into the mainstream teaching service. This chapter details changes to the Caribbean early childhood teachers' professional identities post-COVID-19. It also highlights areas where change is needed and reasons for the changes. This shift is necessary for sustaining advances in the sector and ultimately meeting the diverse needs of all young learners in the region.

Two primary questions guided this chapter (what were some of the changes to Caribbean Early Childhood Care and Education (ECCE) teachers' professional identities during the COVID-19 pandemic and what were some of the factors which accounted for these changes during the COVID-19 pandemic?). In order to answer these questions, we used document analysis of extant literature including newspaper articles, policy documents and journal articles. We also conducted unstructured interviews with key stakeholders in ECCE in the Caribbean.

The context

The countries which comprise the Caribbean are described as Small Island Developing States (SIDS). According to Bates and Angeon (2015), this classification inherently describes the vulnerability of the region's "environment and development" which tremendously impacts its ability to advance sustainably (p.16). Though Caribbean countries have had frequent encounters with natural and man-made disasters over several centuries, they have always had to demonstrate a high level of resilience and agility to overcome the effects, in spite of the financial and human resource limitations which overwhelmingly prevail.

It has been unquestionably the case, however, that no other disaster has created more seismic shifts (affecting all states of the Caribbean simultaneously) than the COVID-19 pandemic. More importantly, while the effects of the pandemic are notable on all facets of Caribbean societies, as suggested by Abdul-Majied, Kinkead-Clark and Burns (2022), it is clear that the region's education systems were more greatly affected than other sectors of society with the exception of the health care sector.

Though geographically limited when compared to other territories especially in Europe and North America, attempts have been made in the media, published research and other extant sources to quantify and qualify some of the effects the COVID-19 pandemic has had on Caribbean education systems. For example, reports have highlighted: lost teaching and learning hours and their effects on student achievement (Blackman, 2021; Saavedra & Di Gropello, 2021), the struggles of parents and teachers in navigating the COVID-19 pandemic (Abdul-Majied, Kinkead-Clark & Burns, 2022; Leacock & Warrican, 2020), and the challenges children with special needs faced as they navigated the pandemic (Parker & Alfaro, 2021).

What we have found is that while most of the existing research has centred on COVID-19's effects on primary and secondary school students, there is a gap relative to its effects on learners at the early childhood level. Further, while there is a growing number of studies which investigate teachers working at the primary and secondary levels, there is a dearth on the effects of the COVID-19 pandemic on early years teachers. This gap is particularly striking because, across the Caribbean, early childhood teachers were already in a professionally vulnerable position largely due to the failure of legislation and professional systems to acknowledge and advance their professional well-being (Abdul-Majied, Kinkead-Clark & Burns, 2022). Professional well-beingis important because it addresses teachers' confidence in the systems which affect their practice. Additionally, it is impacted by teachers' comfort with the available resources, which allow them to practice autonomously.

Theoretical framing of the chapter

In order to describe and explore the COVID-19-related factors which have shaped Caribbean teachers' professional identities, we draw on the framework for vulnerability analysis (FVA) suggested by Turner et al. (2003). The overarching premise of the FVA is to understand the inexorable links between human and environmental factors and to assess their impact on the sustainability of humans and/or the environment. According to Turner et al. (2003, p. 8075), "[t]he Vulnerability Analysis illustrates the complexity and interactions involved in vulnerability analysis, drawing attention to the array of factors and linkages that potentially affect the vulnerability of the coupled human–environment system in a place".

Turner et al note that FVA provides an opportunity to look at critical issues which affect both humans and the environment because it provides one the opportunity to answer questions such as:

> Who and what are vulnerable to the multiple environmental and human changes underway, and where? How are these changes and their consequences attenuated or amplified by different human and environmental conditions? What can be done to reduce vulnerability to change? How may more resilient and adaptive communities and societies be built?
> *(p.8074)*

To justify the selection of this framework, we position the COVID-19 pandemic as one of the most impactful environmental factors which has shaped Caribbean nations in the 21st century. We also proffer that the effects of COVID-19 on Caribbean education systems were far-reaching and multifaceted in that not only did it affect schools and the teaching/learning process in more obvious ways, but, in less overt ways as well. In this chapter, we argue that Caribbean early childhood teachers' professional identity was also impacted. Understandings derived from a study of these effects are applicable not only to the pandemic period but post-COVID-19 as well.

What shapes teachers' professional identity?

While there are diverse interpretations and conceptualisations of the definition of the term professional identity, according to Beijaard, Meijer and Verloop (2004) a teacher's professional identity is not innate but rather develops over time as the teacher interacts with the environment. Changes in the teaching and learning environment will therefore result in changes to one's professional identity. Beijaard, Meijer and Verloop (2004) proposed that in order to understand teachers' professional identities one has to consider the range of personal and professional factors which impact how teachers view themselves and their practices both in and outside the classroom.

Similar to the perspective of Beijaard, Meijer and Verloop (2004) is the suggestion that the lived experiences of teachers create the lens through which they view themselves and how they formulate their identity (Day, Sammons & Stobart, 2007). This therefore provides the basis upon which, according to Lasky, teachers "define themselves to themselves" (2005, p. 901). Additionally, how teachers define themselves is not static. Rather, it varies and corresponds to plethoric factors including those within their personal and professional space which they have to navigate on a frequent basis. Some of these factors include for example: experience, qualifications, value of self, social acceptance, working conditions, professionalising practices (autonomy, responsibility, accountability, remuneration) and agency (Fuller, Goodwyn & Francis-Brophy, 2013; Hsieh, 2010; Voinea & Pălășan, 2014).

The interplay of the aforementioned factors on teachers' professional identity is particularly impactful because, as Zhao (2022) explained, how teachers view themselves also determines how teachers identify themselves in their professional practice. In essence, as Zhao describes; "[e]ducators' professional identity frames educators' explanation of their functions, academic changes, and alterations in syllabi, class exercises, utilization of approaches and strategies, and their connection to other problems in the academic setting" (p.1, 2022).

The literature cited provides support for the importance of studying teachers' professional identity in so far as it ultimately impacts teaching and learning. There is however very little literature which speaks to how Caribbean early childhood teachers see themselves and limited documentation of government response to those challenges. However, the challenges teachers encounter which could affect their professional identities could be deduced, or assumed, based on the many difficulties they face almost on a daily basis (Kinkead-Clark, 2021).

Assessing factors at play in the formation of Caribbean early childhood teachers' professional identity

Although the negative effects of COVID-19 on education have been well documented in the international literature, studies of COVID-19's effects on ECCE in the Caribbean, though increasing, remain limited. Nevertheless, both UNESCO (2020) and UNICEF (2020) have highlighted the devastating effects of the pandemic on the sector. They note that ECCE has been more greatly impacted than other levels of education across the region. Further, the issue of preserving gains made over the last 30 years and maintaining efforts to advance the early childhood sector regionally remains critical. In the wake of challenges exacerbated by the COVID-19 pandemic, research-based efforts to identify teachers' professional identity status aimed at ensuring that the educational needs of the region's children are met seem important.

In order to identify changes to teachers' professional identity, it seems important to contextualise ECCE in the Caribbean by providing background information on progress leading to the status of ECCE pre-COVID-19. Early childhood covers the period of birth to eight years across the Anglophone Caribbean Community (CARICOM), which comprises 15 member states and five associate members. A significant contributor to the current status of ECCE in this region is embedded in landmark initiatives by governments (who are minority employers along with private employers) towards improving ECCE practices within their respective countries. One noteworthy action involved the ratification of the Convention on the Rights of the Child (CRC), by individual CARICOM member states following its 1989 adoption by the United Nations (UN). Later, member countries that ratified the CRC such as Jamaica and Trinidad and Tobago also signed the Education for All (EFA) initiative launched in Jomtien, Thailand, which required signatories to provide quality education for all citizens (UNESCO, 1990). The Dakar Framework followed, which directed attention towards improving all aspects of education quality so that recognised and measurable learning outcomes could be achieved by all (UNESCO, 2000). Subsequent improvements include increased teacher training, improved teacher qualifications and the construction of high-quality ECCE centres. (These improvements will be discussed further in the chapter.)

These initiatives led to notable improvements in the ECCE sector across the Caribbean. Governments invested in ECCE because they understood that the early years are critical for children's physical, social, emotional and intellectual development. Consequently, they acknowledge that returns on investment in ECCE are high since it can increase children's potential earnings as adults and decrease social dysfunction and gender inequality (Charles & Williams, 2008). Although the time period for investment as well as the quality and quantity of investment vary among Caribbean countries, there is a similarity in structure between the CRC and early childhood policies and programme development across the region (Kinkead-Clark, Burns & Abdul-Majied, 2020). There is also alignment with other even more recent global targets such as the Sustainable Development Goals (SDGs) and Vision 2030. To this end, support is provided by legislative acts like the Child Care and Protection Act, 2005 (Jamaica), the Early Childhood Act 2005 (Jamaica) and the Children Act, 2012 (Trinidad) and government policies (like the National

Child Policy of Trinidad and Tobago 2020–2030) aimed at developing the sector for sustainability and to meet the needs of young children.

Having provided a summary of regional governments' initiatives for developing the ECCE sector, we will now focus on how the professional identities of ECCE educators have been affected in the process. Although the sector includes learners 0–3, 3–4 years and 5–8 years, this chapter will be limited to teachers of 3–5-year-old learners at the preschool level. It is also important to note that data are mainly derived from the authors' home countries of Jamaica and Trinidad and Tobago. Beijaard, Meijer and Verloop's (2004) view, that in order to understand teachers' professional identities we need to consider the variety of personal and professional factors which impact how they view themselves and their practices, will guide the analysis.

To source data, the researchers extensively read and reviewed mainly online documents and texts related to the research topic and questions. Data from 27 documents were then selected and used for this study. Thirty-three percent of these data were derived from credible international and regional agency reports, prepared by UNICEF, UNESCO, The World Bank, CARICOM and Ministries of Education. Additionally, 25% of the data were sourced from regional early childhood reports on teaching and good practice. Data on teacher professional identity and effectiveness included were derived from texts and journal articles, while data on COVID-19 teaching experiences from international publications were also included. Finally, unstructured interviews with key stakeholders from the ECCE sector including teachers and administrators were done. The interviews centred around the status of their professional identities before, during and after COVID-19 lockdown measures.

The issue of changes to qualifications required for the job of ECCE teacher was a significant factor which would have influenced teachers' professional views of themselves. Table 7.1 highlights the status of ECCE teachers' qualifications in Jamaica.

TABLE 7.1 Table showing ECCE teachers' qualifications in Jamaica

Level of Education	Count	%
Primary	620	7.89
Secondary	320	4.07
Tertiary – Bachelor's Degree	1,016	12.9
Tertiary – Education Diploma	1,607	20.5
Tertiary – Master's Degree	124	1.57
Vocational training – Levels 1, 2 & 3		
NCTVET Level 1	1,192	15.17
NCTVET Level 2	2,703	34.4
NCTVET Level 3	275	3.5
Total	7,857	100

Note. Table derived from Early Childhood Commission

Approximately 34% of the teachers at the early childhood level have tertiary level training at the bachelor's, master's or teachers diploma level. The majority of the teachers, however, 52%, have attained up to TVET level training. Further, there is still another 12% of the workforce who have only achieved only primary or secondary school education. This indicates that while teacher training has improved over the last 30 years, the percentage of qualified teachers serving young children remains inadequate.

Data available on the status of teacher qualifications in Trinidad and Tobago show that ECCE teachers who previously worked as village/community teacher/caregiver without professional qualifications steadily improved their qualifications. Thornhill (2014) noted that entry requirements for teaching young children increased from one academic subject prior to the 1970s to three academic subjects and some working experience in the 1970s. Thereafter, a certificate in early childhood was needed. From approximately 2005, the entry requirement became a B.Ed. degree to teach.

Table 7.2 represents Trinidad and Tobago data for teachers' qualifications as reported by Thornhill (2014). It shows that 85%–90% of teachers at private ECCE centres have professional training up to the certificate level. With the government's expansion of the ECCE sector, the entry requirement for the upgraded position of ECCE teacher became a Bachelor of Education Degree (B.Ed). The government introduced contract teaching positions for ECCE. The positions are ECCE Teacher, ECCE Teacher Assistants and ECCE Auxiliary (Cabinet Minute No 105, 2007, in Thornhill, 2014, p. 28). All teacher assistants at ECCE centres have the entry-level qualification of five academic subjects and professional ECCE certification (Ministry of Education, 2011).

Similar to what was obtained in Jamaica, the Government of Trinidad and Tobago also provided incentives for teachers to improve their credentials via the Government Assistance Tuition Expenses (GATE) Programme, which fully funds tuition at universities and other tertiary institutions for undergraduate programmes and provides 50% of the tuition for postgraduate

TABLE 7.2 Table showing ECCE teachers' qualifications in Trinidad and Tobago

Highest Level of Education/Qualification	Teaching Position	ECCE Sector	%
Certificate in ECCE	ECCE teacher	Private	85–90
Bachelor of Education Degree in ECCE	ECCE teacher (on contract)	Government	100
Certificate in ECCE	ECCE teacher assistant (on contract)	Government	100

programmes. The incentivisation of professional development is very attractive for early childhood teachers, and therefore unlike in other Caribbean countries, many teachers in Trinidad and Tobago continue to seize the opportunity to enrol in professional development courses to upgrade their qualifications, which also makes them eligible for promotions. The data indicate that although in some countries early childhood teachers are very well trained, in many other Caribbean countries, teachers at the early childhood level are predominantly untrained and minimally trained.

Pre-COVID-19 teachers' professional identity

Prior to the COVID-19 pandemic, there were rapid changes to ECCE teachers' professional practice across the Caribbean. In a system overwhelmingly dominated by females, the increased focus and investments by regional governments resulted in sweeping changes which resulted in many positive developments for ECCE. In countries like Trinidad and Tobago, Belize, St. Vincent and the Grenadines and Jamaica, teachers' entry-level qualifications and working conditions changed. The professional identity of early childhood teachers also started to transform. Teachers developed professional identities based on how they viewed themselves in relation to their job requirements and work conditions. A significant factor was that teachers had to be more qualified in some Caribbean countries. They needed to receive or actively seek to achieve university degrees to become competent early childhood professionals. Teachers felt that the value of their work, as highly trained professionals with a new professional identity, should be reflected in their terms and conditions of employment. They should, for example, receive adequate remuneration; have improved working benefits; and have reasonable working hours and clear job descriptions. However, this did not happen to the extent which teachers had been asking for or in some cases expected.

On the one hand, they had to have professional qualifications which made them view themselves as professionals. However, on the other hand, ECCE teachers have longer working hours, fewer holidays and lower wages than primary and secondary school teachers. Also, in Trinidad and Tobago for example, they became contract employees even though primary school teachers with similar qualifications, are permanent employees with more attractive terms and conditions of work and salaries (Thornhill, 2014, p. 2). They also belong to a non-formal education sector since the legislative framework for governing the sector has not yet been proclaimed.

In Jamaica, teachers' who actively sought and worked to improve their academic qualifications quickly realised that very little would change for them. The government's decision to pay the salary of one trained teacher (at schools with one hundred or more children enrolled) meant that if two or more teachers completed their studies, only one would be able to benefit from increased salaries while others would not. This issue remains and continues to be a controversial and demoralising practice in ECCE institutions across the island. More so because the matter relative to choosing which teacher will be paid by the government has in some schools been implemented in a punitive way. Because the member of staff has to be selected by each school administrator, there have been instances where teachers believe that the process for selection lacked clarity.

The disparity in pay as well as differences in the terms and conditions of employment between teachers in the ECCE and primary sector are two major issues affecting teachers' identity. Beijaard, Meijer and Verloop (2004) view that in order to understand teachers' professional identities, the personal and professional factors which impact how they view themselves and their practices have to be considered, seems applicable here. ECCE teachers feel undervalued by their employers who are mainly from the private sector and the government (the minority employer). These factors have contributed to ECCE teachers' identity even before the pandemic.

COVID-19 shaped teachers' professional identity

According to UNESCO (2020), it was quite clear that across the globe, minimal government responses and support of ECCE during the COVID-19 pandemic warranted the need to ensure that early childhood systems around the world be protected. This vulnerability occurred because in the vast majority of countries, evidence suggested that even before the COVID-19 pandemic, ECCE had always been put on the periphery to make way for what was perceived to be "other important areas" of education (Kinkead-Clark & Escayg, 2019). In the Caribbean, this issue was further exacerbated in that while ECCE was already in a state of vulnerability, what COVID-19 brought to the fore was the heightened vulnerability of the teachers working in the ECCE sector. In the Caribbean, while the permanent closure of schools was most frequently highlighted as one of the major consequences of COVID-19 on Caribbean early childhood systems (over 400 ECCE institutions closed in Jamaica alone), there were more impactful reverberations, though less known effects that occurred across the region.

Considering that most Caribbean early childhood institutions (that cater to children five years and under) are privately owned (though some are state-owned), the effects of mandated school closures were immediate due to the fact that schools were unable to collect school fees, which is a major source of income. The loss of this much-needed source of revenue had numerous consequences on Caribbean early childhood institutions. Many teachers were furloughed and/or made redundant, some schools were permanently shuttered, and some teachers had cuts in their salaries. Several studies also point to a large number of teachers who experienced mental and physical health challenges as a result of the stress brought on by navigating the COVID-19 pandemic (Abdul-Majied et al., 2022; Parker & Alfaro, 2021). Though limited data exist relative to the number of early childhood teachers who lost their jobs, estimates from the Jamaican Early Childhood Commission indicate that almost 450 early childhood centres closed and the majority of the teachers employed by these institutions lost their jobs.

What was also clear is that the teachers and children who faced greater financial needs were more greatly affected by the pandemic. In many disenfranchised communities, children at a disadvantage had little access to technology, for example, to benefit from continuity in learning. These communities needed support systems to be put in place to assist teachers and families to better meet the needs of young learners. This practice goes against many of the agreements regional governments are signatories to. For example, Caribbean leaders have signed on to agreements such as UNESCO's SDGs, The Salamanca Convention (1994) and Vision 2030. To meet their commitments, all countries need to make sure that they put support systems in place to ensure that children do not make retrograde steps in terms of their learning outcomes.

Following media coverage of the crisis many early childhood institutions and other private schools faced as they struggled to survive, in Jamaica, the government attempted to tangentially intervene through the provision of a minimal one-off grant to address this issue. In Trinidad and Tobago, there was no stimulus support for ECCE. With no union to bargain and advocate for early childhood teachers (and by extension the children they serve), they had no bargaining power. The government's interventions to buttress small businesses throughout the economic crises brought on by COVID-19 did not extend to the small, privately owned early childhood institutions. Therefore, unlike bars, community shops and stores which received stimulus support, the early education system was not as fortunate. Though many teachers and administrators appealed to the government to reconsider such a decision, the teachers' efforts proved futile as they were told to apply for grants like other small businesses. Needless to say, the conditions for accessing grants were deterrents, especially to smaller private schools. Consequently, for many teachers, the effects were immediate and continue to have consequences, as identified below, which impact working conditions and therefore teachers' professional identities.

Consequences included teachers having limited or no sources of income. Many teachers were therefore forced to find alternative employment. Some found jobs in the education system (for example as private tutors for young children). Many others, however, had to secure employment outside of the teaching profession (such as at fast food outlets). In cases where teachers were experiencing physical and mental health challenges, teachers had to pay out of pocket for health treatment if they had lost health insurance coverage. Additionally, due to the worsened working conditions and limited financial remuneration, some teachers made the decision to exit the early childhood teaching profession to survive.

Next steps: addressing early childhood teachers' professional identify post-COVID-19

While the lessons learned from the COVID-19 pandemic are numerous, what the pandemic has done is that it has starkly illuminated some of the working conditions of Caribbean early childhood teachers. Further, it has highlighted the level of professional and personal vulnerability many of these teachers experience as a result of their unstable and poor working conditions. Essentially, and perhaps more importantly, the COVID-19 pandemic has brought to the public's awareness many of the systemic issues which create fertile breeding grounds for many of the crippling issues affecting teachers' ability to sustain their personal and working lives. Consequently, ECCE teachers are recognising that in spite of the proclamations and increased spotlight on ECCE on the part of the region's governments, efforts to advance the system and their working conditions will have to come through self–advocacy and lobbying. Any meaningful attempt to improve teachers' working conditions, it seems, will only be achieved through relentless work to advance the professionalisation of the sector.

The evidence clearly indicates that the factors which impact teachers' professional identity include new issues which arose as a result of the pandemic alongside others which have evolved over time. Some of these include compensatory funding for private ECCE centres to cover increases in operating costs and meeting other expenses to ensure the effective functioning of the facilities. Teachers also need salary increases to meet personal expenses such as increased food prices, securing health and safety needs and meeting the rising cost of living. To address the problems in the ECCE sector and in the process improve teachers' professional identities, both pre-existing problems and the new ones which resulted from the pandemic have to be addressed.

A new problem to be addressed is the increased attrition of qualified and experienced teachers. This is an issue of tremendous concern across the region. Though some leave early childhood institutions and take up employment in government-funded infant and primary schools, in recent years many teachers in Jamaica for example are leaving to find jobs in countries that offer better remuneration and working benefits. Mass teacher migration has now been highlighted to be a critical issue which has the potential to bring Jamaica's education to its knees. When experienced and qualified teachers choose to leave schools in some of the island's most needy communities, this has a tremendous impact on schools' ability to meet the diverse needs of young children. This impact is immediate as it has implications for school and programme quality.

Another critical issue is that in Caribbean countries, ECCE does not operate within the legislative framework guiding other tiers of education. Working conditions are more susceptible to the fluidity of economic stability and social change. In both Jamaica and Trinidad and Tobago, teachers' susceptibility to these shifts is even more heightened because they are not unionised and therefore do not have the collective bargaining power to advocate for better working conditions, protection from job losses and improved remuneration.

In Jamaica and Trinidad and Tobago, the teachers' herculean efforts to reach children and their families during the pandemic have not had any significant impact on the respect due to them in the long run. While their efforts were lauded during the height of the pandemic, it is clear that very little has changed on the part of the government's management of the sector, the government's prioritisation of the sector, their views of ECCE teachers and the financial support given to the sector. It is in fact for these reasons that teachers continue to struggle for visibility and improved working conditions.

In spite of the many challenges early childhood teachers faced (and which therefore impacted their professional identity), they should be recognised for their resilience, hard work and commitment to the region's children. Numerous reports in media across the Caribbean highlighted instances of early childhood teachers (some of which were furloughed and made redundant) and administrators establishing learning spaces in communities to reach young children who would otherwise have remained unreached. Many of these teachers were lauded in the media during the pandemic. In fact, if not for their efforts, many children at the early childhood level would not have had the chance to advance developmentally during the pandemic.

Changes to teacher education and professional development

Considering that many of the personal and professional experiences of teachers have an impact on their professional identity, our charge to regional governments is to improve the working conditions for teachers in the ECCE sector. Not only is this necessary for improving how teachers view themselves, but more importantly it is necessary to improve their facilitation of young children's learning. Governments need to support the professionalising of the sector. An important aspect is the development of a legislative framework to ensure that teachers' benefits and working conditions are at least the same as primary school teachers. Since teachers understand their issues, the voices of teachers should be included when decisions are being made about their work. Meaningful community and parental involvement and also increased private sector involvement is needed. Further gains in teacher credentialing and professional development need to be maintained and increased, especially in territories where teachers are professionally underqualified. All Caribbean teachers in the ECCE sector need to have access to professional development to meet the SDGs.

Teacher professional development programmes and policies can assist in meeting these needs if they focus on:

- Governments addressing legislative gaps as a matter of urgency to provide a legal framework upon which to develop policies and advance the sector
- Governments providing solutions to the existing poor working conditions in the sector
- Addressing poor remuneration and job insecurity
- Meeting standards for class sizes, learning environments, equipment and resources
- Ensuring systems are put in place for professional development opportunities which are affordable for all teachers
- Addressing the lack of prioritisation of ECCE such that there is no difference between ECCE and the primary sector
- Providing more visible support for the government's advancement of ECCE in Caribbean territories.

Conclusion

In this chapter, we detailed issues and changes to Caribbean early childhood teachers' professional identities post-COVID-19. Lingering issues which affected teachers' professional identities pre-COVID-19 were analysed in conjunction with new ones. It is important to recognise that teachers are ready for change. A paradigm shift is therefore needed to advance the programmes, policies and processes which impact teachers' professional identities and ultimately teaching quality. This shift is necessary for sustaining many of the otherwise short-lived developments which ECCE professionals fought long and hard to achieve. Such a feat will provide a solid basis that will allow Caribbean teachers to feel empowered and secure in their profession.

To reiterate, the evidence presented indicates that effort must be made to improve the working conditions of ECCE teachers. What is clear is that the current conditions under which many ECCE teachers work can be considered demoralising (Abdul-Majied, Kinkead-Clark & Burns, 2022). Though we acknowledge this does not reflect the reality for all teachers, in many circumstances, where teachers' working conditions are below standard, staff morale is impacted. Working conditions thus need to be elevated to the required status for the profession if we expect early childhood teachers to perform optimally. Elevation of the profession and teachers' identity would therefore be achieved by ensuring that teachers have the necessary support, remuneration commensurate with their qualifications and improved working conditions.

This study maintains that reform of the support system in place for the professionals who teach at ECCE centres is necessary. Not only would this steer efforts back on course to sustain advances made in the Caribbean ECCE sector, but it would allow the sector to progress towards meeting its mandate towards providing high-quality care and education for all three- to five-year-old children in the Caribbean.

References

Abdul-Majied, S., Kinkead-Clark, Z., & Burns, S. C. (2022). Understanding Caribbean early childhood teachers' professional experiences during the COVID-19 school disruption. *Early Childhood Education Journal*, 51(3), 1–11.

Bates, S., & Angeon, V. (2015). Promoting the sustainable development of small island developing states: Insights from vulnerability and resilience analysis. *Région et Développement*, 42, 16–29.

Beijaard, D., Meijer, P. C., & Verloop, N. (2004). Reconsidering research on teachers' professional identity. *Teaching and Teacher Education*, 20, 107–128. Retrieved fromhttps://hdl.handle.net/1887/11190

Blackman, S. N. (2021). The impact of Covid-19 on education equity: A view from Barbados and Jamaica. *Prospects*, 51(4), 611–625.

Charles, L. & Williams, S. (2008). Caribbean early childhood development good practice guide. UNUICEF. Retrieved from Caribbean Early Childhood Development Good PracticeGuide.pdf

Day, C., Sammons, P., & Stobart, G. (2007). *Teachers matter: Connecting work, lives and effectiveness*. McGraw-Hill Education.

Fuller, C., Goodwyn, A., & Francis-Brophy, E. (2013). Advanced skills teachers: Professional identity and status. *Teachers and Teaching*, 19(4), 463–474.

Hsieh, B. (2010). Exploring the Complexity of Teacher Professional Identity. *UC Berkeley*. ProQuest ID: Hsieh_berkeley_0028E_10768. Merritt ID: ark:/13030/m5x63rzm. Retrieved from https://escholarship.org/uc/item/9406p4sb

Kinkead-Clark, Z. (2021). Teachers' tensions and children's readiness. Taking a discursive approach to understanding readiness for primary school. *Early Years*, 41(2–3), 262–274.

Kinkead-Clark, Z., & Escayg, K. A. (2019). Getting it right from the start: A retrospective and current examination of infant-toddler care in Jamaica. *Occasional Paper Series*, 2019(42), 9.

Kinkead-Clark, Z., Burns, S., & Abdul-Majied, S. (2020). Actualizing children's rights through early childhood care and education: A focus on the Caribbean. *Journal of Early Childhood Research*, 18(1), 58–72. Retrieved fromhttps://doi.org/10.1177/1476718X19875765

Lasky, S. (2005). A sociocultural approach to understanding teacher identity, agency and professional vulnerability in a context of secondary school reform. *Teaching and Teacher Education*, 21(8), 899916.

Leacock, C. J., & Warrican, S. J. (2020). Helping teachers to respond to COVID-19 in the Eastern Caribbean: Issues of readiness, equity and care. *Journal of Education for Teaching*, 46(4), 576–585.

Ministry of Education (2011). Statistical Data for a Comprehensive Analysis of the ECCE Sub Sector –Trinidad and Tobago. Port of Spain:Ministry of Education ECCE Division.

Parker, M., & Alfaro, P. (2021). Education during the Covid-19 pandemic: Access, inclusion and psychosocial support leaving no Caribbean child behind. Retrieved from https://www.cepal.org/sites/default/files/events/files/education_during_the_Covid-19_pandemic.pdf

Saavedra, J., & Di Gropello, E. (2021). COVID-19 and the learning crisis in Latin America and the Caribbean: How can we prevent a tragedy. *World Bank Blogs*. https://blogs. worldbank. org/education/Covid-19-and-learning-crisis-latin-america-and-caribbean-how-can-we-prevent-tragedy.

Thornhill, A. (2014). National report on teachers for early childhood education: Trinidad and Tobago. Santiago: UNESCO. Retrieved fromhttp://ceppe.uc.cl/images/contenido/publicaciones/proyecto-estrategico-regional/2012/Informe-Primera-Infancia-TRINIDAD-and-TOBAGO.pdf

Turner, B. L., Kasperson, R. E., Matson, P. A., McCarthy, J. J., Corell, R. W., Christensen, L.,… & Schiller, A. (2003). A framework for vulnerability analysis in sustainability science. *Proceedings of the National Academy of Sciences*, 100(14), 8074–8079.

UNESCO (1990). Education for all: Status and trends. Report published by UNESCO for the International Consultative Forum on Education for All, a global mechanism established to promote and monitor progress towards Education for All goals. Jomtien: Thailand.

UNESCO (2020, July 17). New drive to protect early childhood education in the context of the COVID-19 crisis. Retrieved from https://en.unesco.org/news/new-drive-protect-early-childhoodeducation-context-Covid-19-crisis

UNESCO (2000). The dakarframework for action: Education for all: Meeting our collective commitments. Adopted by the World Education Forum, 2000. Dakar: Senegal.

UNICEF (2020). UNICEF study reveals the impact of Covid-19 challenges on children and families in Jamaica. Retrieved from https://www.unicef.org/jamaica/press-releases/unicef-study-reveals-impact-Covid-19-challenges-children-and-families-jamaica

Voinea, M., & Pălăşan, T. (2014). Teachers' professional identity in 21st century Romania. *Procedia-Social and Behavioral Sciences*, 128, 361–365.

Zhao, Q. (2022). On the role of teachers' professional identity and well-being in their professional development. *Frontiers in Psychology*, 13, 913708.

Alliances

Relationships, Connections, and Community

8
"WE'RE STILL TRYING TO FIGURE OUT EVERY SINGLE DAY"

Teaching since COVID-19

Maxine Cameron and Sandra Schamroth Abrams

Introduction

"Pandemic pedagogy" (Milman, 2020), or patchwork instruction that resembles triage-style teaching, became an educational approach swiftly adopted when the COVID-19 outbreak forced schools in New York City (NYC) and surrounding areas to move suddenly to remote instruction in March 2020 (Schaefer et al., 2020, 2021). After all, NYC was an "epicenter of the coronavirus disease (COVID-19) outbreak in the United States during spring 2020" (Thompson et al., 2020), and "the rate at which disaster ensued was in every sense of the word breathtaking. A mighty city silenced. Thousands dying alone. Bodies stacked in freezer trucks. Half a million people out of work" (Ferguson et al., 2022). Education shifted in unprecedented ways, with sickness and uncertainty looming in every corner. The NYC school system, which is the largest in the United States, encountered "a series of abrupt changes that disrupted and reshaped the lives of about 1 million children and 1,800 schools" (Heyward, 2021). When classes resumed in person in fall 2021, 18 months after the lockdown and the shift to online learning (Heyward, 2021), teaching continued to evolve and questions remained, including: To what extent have teachers modified their practices given shifts in teaching modalities and spaces? How, if at all, are teachers attending to their students' needs and supporting student meaning making? And how, if at all, are shifts in practices reflective of meeting teachers' needs as well? Although these questions are not simple to answer, explorations of teaching since the COVID-19 pandemic can provide insight into educational turns that very well might transform practice and pedagogy.

DOI: 10.4324/9781003352129-11

This chapter draws on the experiences of four NYC charter school educators—three elementary school teachers and their principal—as they transitioned online in March 2020 and then to in-person instruction in fall 2021. More specifically, this study addresses the 18-month period wherein the educators needed to adjust continuously their instructional practices to meet the needs of all learners. By focusing on the practices that these elementary school educators have adopted, maintained, and/or refined since the COVID-19 pandemic, we explore the construction and reconstruction of educational practices, which include assessment and professional learning.

Teaching since COVID-19

Educational research since the COVID-19 pandemic began has called attention to "children struggling with an ever-growing list of needs—for food, housing, medical care, physical safety, emotional support, mental health services, tutoring, and much more" (Berry, 2020, p. 15). Additionally, COVID-19 has had a riveting effect on teaching and learning, and there has been much discussion about "stymied learning" (Angrist et al., 2021) and "academic declines" (Mervosh, 2022, para 7). Although such effects have been addressed as "learning loss" (Beteille et al., 2020; Horowitz, 2020; Kuhfeld et al., 2020; Mervosh, 2022), that term is complex and has been contested (see Harmey and Moss, 2021). Nonetheless, there is no question that there have been considerable disruptions to learning due to COVID-19 protocols, illness, and overall stress, all which have affected the learning landscape.

These disruptions occurred despite best efforts. Without training or warning, teachers-as-first-responders joined the ranks of essential workers: "schools were positioned, along with school counselors, as de facto first responders for student well-being" (Beard et al., 2021, p. 1). Furthermore, teachers had additional responsibilities when pedagogy and practice primarily focused on shifts to online learning (McQuirter, 2020). As a result, teachers became "uncertain about their role, unable to use technology effectively to communicate and teach" (Beteille et al., 2020), and the importance of teacher well-being also had come to the fore (Beard et al., 2021; Ceglie, Black, and Saunders, 2022). Pressley (2021) argued, "Teachers are facing new demands and showing high levels of stress with the new instructional requirements and the anxieties due to the current state of education and the pandemic" (p. 5). Unsurprisingly, research investigating teacher experiences has focused on a range of issues, including, but not limited to, shifts in instructional time and interactions (Arnove, 2020; Jones et al., 2022), teacher burnout (Pressley, 2021) and exhaustion (Kim et al., 2021), and teacher stress and anxiety (Pressley, Ha, and Learn, 2021; Pressley and Ha, 2022). And a recent study (Kush et al., 2022) indicated that "teachers showed a significantly higher prevalence of negative mental health outcomes during the pandemic when compared to healthcare and office workers" (p. 596).

In light of these data, a keen focus must be placed on teachers' well-being. Beteille et al. (2020) suggested that professional learning can "support [teacher] effectiveness through coping, managing continuity, and improvement and acceleration" (Beteille et al., 2020), and Angrist et al. (2021) noted that "ongoing expert coaching and peer monitoring [can help teachers] to develop the skills to follow and embed the practices within their repertoire" (Angrist et al., 2021). Thus, in addition to offering insight into teachers' experience since COVID-19, this study considers teachers' well-being and how professional learning supported educators' needs.

Exploring practices through social constructivism and care

Although often associated with ways that learners build upon previous experiences, as well as the connection between students and their teacher (Carlson, 1999), social constructivism (Vygotsky, 1986/1934) also informs ways that educators develop and refine their practice and pedagogy, especially via conversation and collaboration (Hollingsworth, Dybdahl, and Minarik, 1993; Shabani, 2016). For this study, in which we examine educators' individual and collective practices and needs, we look to social constructivism to identify areas of consonance (e.g., how educators built upon their prior knowledge of practice and pedagogy) and dissonance (e.g., how the COVID-19 pandemic disrupted norms and practices) to understand better how the four elementary school educators (i.e., three teachers and one principal) (re)negotiated teaching since the pandemic and to identify how teachers' needs also came to the fore as the educators engaged in triage-like pedagogy.

Additionally, similar to Hollingsworth, Dybdahl, and Minarik (1993), who focused on "teachers' learning as a personal and relational process… socially constructed through shared understandings" (p. 8), we explore teachers' (re)development of pedagogy in light of pandemic-related shifts. In order to do so, we draw upon features of a "careful and committed teacher" (Hollingsworth, Dybdahl, and Minarik, 1993), which are informed by Noddings and Shore's (1984) intuitive modes: "involvement of the senses, commitment and receptivity, a quest for understanding or empathy, and a productive tension between subjective certainty and objective uncertainty" (Hollingsworth, Dybdahl, and Minarik, 1993, p. 10). Due to space limitations, we focus on "commitment and receptivity" and "the quest for understanding or empathy" in particular as we explore teaching since COVID-19. Through these intuitive modes, Noddings and Shore (1984) offered a process-based approach to understanding meaning making, explaining "Success in an analytic mode is realized in an answer: a proof, a numerical result, a sustained hypothesis, a finished poem. Success in an intuitive mode is realized in seeing, creating a picture in our minds, understanding" (p. 81). Although the educators in our study had years of experience to inform their practice, they also rather suddenly faced unprecedented circumstances that required the teachers to move to a solely online teaching modality, to create new materials beyond their grade band, and to shift assessments away from output and on to student well-being. There was a movement away from product and on to process. In this way, Noddings and Shore's concept of intuition and receptivity, which "requires a letting go of…attempts to control…[as well as] a deliberate giving-over of subjectiveness" (p. 74), also helps us to discuss the educators' negotiation of practice, pedagogy, and care. Thus, when we consider a constructivist lens, we do so with the aspect of intuition—process-related receptivity and understanding—to help to identify and to discuss the ways in which the educators in our study modified their practices since the COVID-19 pandemic to meet their students' needs and, eventually, their own needs.

Furthermore, we look to Noddings's (1984/2013, 2019) concept of care, which hinges on aspects of human relations and the "caring relation, one to which both carer and cared-for contribute" (2019, p. 2). Noddings's emphasis on the role of reflexivity and receptivity enables us to identify and to explore how such reflexivity and receptivity might inform the pedagogical shifts associated with (post) pandemic pedagogy. After all, Noddings (2019) argued that teachers must pay attention to students' needs, and we examine how the teachers and the principal worked to meet students' shifting needs since the COVID-19 pandemic began.

Because the intersection of social constructivism and care acknowledges teachers' experiences, we consider the ways both concepts cohere to help us

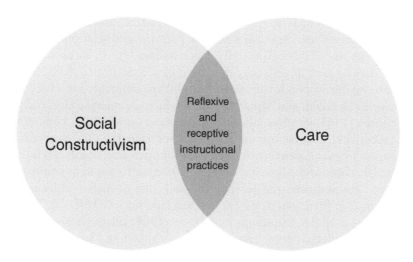

FIGURE 8.1 Conceptualizing teaching post-COVID.

understand how, if at all, the teachers in our study built upon these ways of being to reimagine educational practices that are sustainable and meaningful. Thus, drawing on our data, we conceptualize teaching since COVID-19 as reflexive and receptive not only to students' needs, but also to teachers' needs (see Figure 8.1).

As we go on to explore, social constructivism and care both include reflexive and receptive practices that are process-based *and* reciprocal: There is an ongoing effort to reassess how to build upon what one already knows (e.g., about pedagogy and practice), as well as how to support and enhance the meaning-making experiences of students, of self, and of fellow teachers.

Discussion of methodological approaches

This qualitative multi-case study includes the voices of three NYC charter school teachers and their principal as they recounted their experiences of teaching online and then in person since COVID-19 reshaped how, when, and where they have taught their elementary school students. As a principal of a NYC public elementary school engaging in research on teacher recruitment and retention (Cameron, 2022), Maxine had met Marcia (all names are pseudonyms), an elementary charter school principal, in 2020. Initially, for a related research study, Marcia introduced Maxine to three educators who teach at her school—Anjaynee (a kindergarten teacher), Rosalina (a third- and fourth-grade teacher), and Jackie (a fourth-grade teacher)—who had been teaching at the same NYC charter school for more than six years. For this current study, Marcia, Anjaynee, Rosalina, and Jackie agreed to share their experiences teaching prior to and during the COVID-19 pandemic as well as after they returned to the classroom in person 18 months later in fall 2021.

More specifically, this seven-month study began with recruitment in December 2021, followed by data collection from January 2022, when we sent all four educators an initial 10-question survey, through June 2022, during which we engaged in two iterations of Zoom-based interviews. Prior to interviewing each educator (three teachers and one administrator), we asked each participant to complete a survey, understanding well that we were not looking for generalizable data; rather, we were hoping to get a an initial sense of the educators' experiences prior to and since the COVID-19 pandemic. We then used these preliminary data to inform the interviews. Over the course of five months, we conducted individual interviews with each participant (i.e., four interviews), as well as a final focus group interview that, in a member-checking fashion (Yin, 2017), helped us to confirm and clarify understandings of the educators' experiences.

Initially, data were coded inductively so as to avoid *a priori* assumptions. The first round of data analysis included only the survey responses, and the emergent themes—technology use, cooperative learning, preparation and planning, strengths and challenges—informed the development of individual interview questions. Relatedly, our review of the individual interview data yielded questions about how the educators developed their professional learning since COVID-19, a topic that informed the focus group interview that included questions about resources and supports, which helped to clarify, challenge, and/or confirm the educators' post-COVID-19 needs.

Subsequent rounds of coding occurred both inductively and deductively. Inductively, we recorded *in vivo* codes, such as "just trying to survive on a daily basis" or "grind hard," as well as emergent codes like teaching practices, exhaustion, mindset, and culture. Deductively, and, in particular, looking for instances of professional learning and instantiations of assessment, we used those codes (e.g., professional learning, assessment) as we examined and categorized the data corpus. This "second cycle coding" included such pattern codes, "lay[ing] the groundwork for cross-case analysis by surfacing common themes and directional processes" (Miles, Huberman, and Saldaña, 2019, p. 79). Furthermore, we engaged in coding together synchronously to establish intercoder agreement and support the reliability of our data analysis (Creswell and Poth, 2018).

Our cross-case analysis, which included data from the survey, individual interviews, and focus group interview, helped to bring to the fore how the educators acknowledged the shift in their preparation, the mismatch between pre-COVID-19 assessments and post-COVID-19 achievement levels, and the need to create space for care not only for students, but also for teachers.

Findings

Prior to the pandemic, it was common for one teacher to specialize in and prepare lessons for a particular subject area. However, given that pre-COVID instruction primarily was non-digital with the use of technology as a supplemental tool, the shift to teaching online during the pandemic—first suddenly from March through June 2020 and then again during the 2020–2021 academic year—translated into an entire overhaul of practices. Fourth-grade teacher, Jackie, lamented, "I only taught science, that was the only subject that I prepped to teach. [Since COVID] everything is a big learning curve for us as teachers to do…I need to learn the math standards, the standards for guided reading." This is one of the reasons the survey responses (see Table 8.1) included some educators noting that they teach across different grades and subjects. It also is a reason why every facet of teaching—from instructional planning to student assessment—shifted in the face of the unanticipated disruption to educational practice and to everyday life.

Embracing Herculean efforts to adjust continually to different permutations of remote learning, the teachers "had to think outside the box when it came

"We're still trying to figure out every single day" 151

TABLE 8.1 Initial survey questions

CRITERIA	PARTICIPANTS			
	Teacher #1	Teacher #2	Teacher #3	Principal
SUBJECT				
Mathematics	X	X	X	
Science	X	X		
Guided Reading				
Literacy		X	X	
GRADE				
Kindergarten		X		
First				
Second				
Third			X	
Fourth	X		X	
Fifth				
INQUIRY				
Social distancing has impacted students' engagement in cooperative learning. (1) Strongly Disagree, (2) Disagree, (3) Neither Agree or Disagree, (4) Agree, (5) Strongly Agree	4	5	3	3
The integration of technology tools in all subjects has increased students' achievement. (1) Strongly Disagree, (2) Disagree, (3) Neither Agree or Disagree, (4) Agree, (5) Strongly Agree	3	5	3	4
Please briefly describe what it was like to prepare to teach prior to the COVID-19 pandemic. More specifically, please not what you did and how you did it.				
Since the pandemic started until now, how, if at all, has planning and preparation changed while teaching during COVID-19?				
Since the pandemic started until present day, what, if any, new tools have you integrated while teaching during COVID-19?				
What are your thoughts about "learning loss" due to COVID 19?				
Have you worn a mask while teaching?				
If you have worn a mask, what has it been like to teach while wearing a mask?				

to delivering and executing lessons, meaning differently than we have ever taught before, and have had to incorporate more technology." Fourth-grade teacher, Jackie, continued, "When the pandemic started, we had no idea what to expect and we're just going day by day," and the teachers incorporated the use of familiar and unfamiliar technological platforms, such as Google Classroom, Zoom, Hapara, Nearpod, Pear Deck, Parent Square, and Kami.

After the initial shock of quarantine and the constant rearrangement of practices in a triage-like style, the teachers had time to regroup during the summer of 2020 to prepare for the following year, which, given the state of COVID-19 infections in the NYC area at that time, meant that teaching and learning remained remote. Teachers still "worked around the clock to create content (GoogleSlide decks) and collaborate with co-teachers to adjust content to meet students' needs."

Fast forward to fall 2021, and the teachers continued to engage in pandemic pedagogy, but with greater facility. According to Rosalina, once the educators developed their remote learning repertoires for the 2020–2021 academic year, the educators were able to build upon them for the 2021–2022 school year, which included a combination of in-person and remote scheduling. Although Jackie agreed that it was beneficial to adjust lessons "rather than creating everything from scratch," she still said that her colleagues and she "are surviving one lesson, one day at a time…the back and forth to remote has been tough emotionally." The constant adjustments did not happen in a vacuum; the culture of the school also shifted to create space for students' new emotional and academic needs. Amidst all the change, the teachers' sense of dedication to their students never seemed to wane.

"We grind hard": turning the wheel of assessment prior to the pandemic

It is common practice for educators to prepare in advance for the classes they will teach. However, at the charter school, according to kindergarten teacher Anjaynee, prior to COVID-19, teachers needed to "have lesson plans done at least 2wks in advance." Such preparation also was ongoing, as the teachers used student work and real-time data to create and revise lessons. Jackie explained that she was part of a team of teachers who would stay at school until "6, 7, 8 o'clock every night…[to] take a look [at the data and to prepare] the best lesson plans for tomorrow…planning and preparation, it was truly never ending." This data-informed preparation had been part of the school's culture, which included "a constant assessment of looking at our data, looking at our kids' needs, looking at where they're pulling groups, addressing it, responding to the data, and so it's just like a constant wheel."

Since COVID-19, this rhythm changed dramatically. Jackie captured the minute-by-minute pivots when she spoke about daily survival: "What am I doing tomorrow? It is incredibly overwhelming to think about what we are doing next week, what are our targets for next month, when we are truly, truly just trying to survive on a daily basis." When the school day ended, the teachers had a diminished ability to give. "Pre-COVID was very, very much data driven. Our team stayed late every day until 8 o'clock. We looked for gaps and how we can address and challenge students. Post-COVID planning is day by day…hour by hour and minute by minute—not for the lack of desire or lack of passion, or lack of dedication; it is really burn out."

These educators' sentiments also were shared by their principal, Marcia, who spoke about juggling contact tracing, last-minute bussing changes, and sudden teacher absences that required her to step away from administrative duties to teach. She attested that, before COVID-19, her focus involved reviewing teacher plans, observing classes, and offering educators feedback, and, since the pandemic, "I try to plan and then it gets blown up in my face every day. You know, it's like I have a plan. I know what my schedule is supposed to [be]. And then, I mean, 90% of the time, it wasn't."

"Learning loss is real" (Jackie)

When students returned to the classroom in September 2021, they were a year below reading level, and the teachers needed to rethink how they would move forward because of the great disparities in student abilities and readiness. Marcia put it simply: "Our third graders were in first grade when they were last in school," and all that time without being in person had a tremendous effect on students' social skills and their ability to "sit and open a book and start reading" because they needed to learn what it meant to do school.

Jackie stressed how the learning "curve that we're seeing is nothing that was ever seen or experienced before." Thus, it is understandable that teachers struggled to meet students' needs. Marcia acknowledged, "we're trying to teach multiplication but my third graders can't add and subtract anymore." She also explained that, despite being "so lucky to have such wonderful teachers," those teachers are "struggling" to teach the content given the chasms of differentiation: "the curriculum calls for this chapter, but it's five levels above the average reader in my class."

The educators questioned how to modify instruction best, and what materialized was a shift away from the set curriculum and a rethinking of assessment. After all, the assessments and benchmarks of years past seemed inappropriate, and teachers, like Rosalina, wondered, "How do I support them to fill that gap? I don't know, and that's something we're still trying to figure out every single day."

Although Anjaynee felt that the pandemic "intensified" learning loss, Rosalina offered another perspective, one that included issues of access: "access and/ or ability to use the remote online platforms have impeded [student] learning…for reading and math." Yet, when students returned to school, there were challenges with the transition back to in-person instruction. Marcia explained, "In person and remote school are very different and we have seen [students] really struggling as they returned from remote." During the interviews, Jackie revealed that, on the most recent math exam, students' grades had an unusually dramatic range from "19% to 91%."

Thus, it is not surprising that Marcia explained that such performance disparities translated into educators "teaching content two or three years behind where they have been trained to teach" because of "profound" gaps in learning.

Given this context, we turn to explore the changes in practice that stemmed from shifts in thinking and the imperative to meet students' new needs, especially given that, as Jackie said, "If COVID taught us anything, it's that there is so much more happening in people's lives than we realize."

At a loss: how to support students despite the vast challenges

Facing unprecedented student learning disparities, the teachers maintained a focus on differentiating instruction as best as possible: "how are we going to keep things moving, challenge students who need that extra push on, and help close that gap for students that haven't yet mastered certain concepts? Yet, as Rosalina explained, it was not as simple as modifying instruction because student attendance constantly shifted: "Take this kid who missed out on certain days because they weren't here due to their COVID reasons. What's fair, what's right, what's the best decision and that's the part that's like, what are we going to do?".

Teachers also felt that they were unable to engage in and fully support the cooperative learning that had been in place prior to COVID-19. Mask mandates and social distancing protocols not only precluded the students' and teachers' ability to communicate, but also increased feelings of anxiety because there was a lack of connection to each other. All the teachers acknowledged that they wore masks and that staying safe was a group effort; in her survey response, Anjaynee explained that "when someone, whether a student or teacher, is not wearing their mask correctly, we hold one another accountable and kindly remind them to adjust or to fix it. This is to keep everyone in our school safe." Although Marcia, the principal, responded to the survey questions about masks with "We are getting used to it :)", the reality for the teachers was the fact that masks were painful to wear and they obstructed communication. Anjaynee said that "since wearing a mask I have had consistent laryngitis and earaches," and Rosalina explained that it was difficult to hear and communicate effectively with students. Furthermore, as Rosalina noted, the specter of infection loomed, shifting instructional needs to include sanitation and distance protocols:

> beginning instruction is checking the masks, sanitizing the kids, making sure that their space is clean...What I find is that I want to get so close to the kids [so] that I can hear them when I'm conferencing or...give them some quick feedback...That's when I'm like, I'm too close...remember we have to be about three feet away...my mask is up and then also the

windows have to be open. That was a struggle…I'll tell the kids, bring your coat because the room was cold.

The teachers worked to keep the physical space sterile, which also impacted instruction. Rosalina was limited in what she could do: "I can't give the feedback one on one because I can't get so close to them." Additionally, the shifts in instructional time to include COVID-19 precautions and support students' academic growth and well-being were taxing. As Jackie recalls, between last year and this year, "I am doing what I can when I can…we're all feeling the effects and we're all playing catch up. We're in person and this is great, but we're *dead* every single day so just like one day at a time."

A culture of caring not scoring

COVID-19 might have led to sterilized spaces, but the culture was anything but sterile. Although the charter school had a pre-COVID emphasis on benchmarks in reading and math, there was a dramatic shift. Marcia noted that her school was "Not this strict regimented environment…[If] you're having a hard time, we're gonna talk about it—you're in your feelings." In other words, student well-being became the forefront of instruction, and that included a receptivity and understanding of each student's needs. Jackie clarified:

> We used to have a behavior tracker. We used to be very regimented, super strict and that…was in service of holding a high bar…but at the end of the day, we prioritized in this pandemic: Are our kids safe? Are they happy? Are they healthy? Do they know that they're loved?…As awful as so many moments have been [due to COVID-19], there's been so much beauty and grace that has come out of it, that we can now just talk to our kids. There doesn't need to be a consequence for everything. It's "Hey you look like you're having a hard day. Do you need a breather? Do you need a walk? Do you need a hug? Not like, "Just grit through it. Keep going.' It's hard to keep going sometimes. You take a minute. You let me know.

The teachers and principal emphasized this acknowledgement of care, and Jackie even saw "beauty and grace" despite the "awful" circumstances. Anjaynee also saw care in the ways achievement became fluid. Since COVID-19, she adopted a new understanding for her kindergarteners: "Math or reading may not be your strongest subject. But if you try your best, then you can leave with your head high and say, 'Hey, I did what I can.'" In other words, a process-based, rather than a product-based, assessment had become part of Anjaynee's teaching. Relatedly, Jackie explained that "right now I'm defining achievement as 'you are trying,'" lamenting "We need to rethink the bar and just meet kids where they're at… we cannot continue to operate as business as usual when thinking about kids' learning, the bar, and where they should be." Shifting the narrative to this understanding of achievement is a defining feature of one of the changes in and *challenges to* the charter school's culture. The space that once included behavior tracking and preset benchmarks changed to honor the students *where they were*.

Teachers' needs seem related to students' needs (e.g., addressing student well-being also includes their own realizations and well-being), and the role of professional learning at the charter school is important to consider, especially with regard to the development of reflexivity and the inclusion of debriefing to meet teacher needs and support a stance of gratitude.

Not just a pause: teacher needs, professional learning, and care

The shift in school-wide culture from rigidity to flexibility stemmed from the receptiveness of administrators and teachers to the experiences of students *and* teachers. What was once an extensive planning session that would include week- or month-long trajectories became focused on minute-by-minute needs. Nonetheless, professional development remained a pillar of continued learning even in the face of uncertainty. Marcia acknowledged, "Am I able to get through my checklist? Definitely not. But I'm prioritizing how people feel supported."

Even after returning to in-person teaching in fall 2021, every week, an instructional coach visited each teacher's classroom to observe practice and provide explicit feedback. Marcia shared, "As an organization, we are committed to teacher development, specifically teacher feedback." This included three levels of interaction and support: (1) All staff members, including the principal, had a coach with whom they met every week for observation and one-on-one debriefing, and teacher coaching and development were frequent intentional practices. (2) Weekly, grade-wide teams engaged in lesson studies to discuss content, standards, and student outcomes. (3) Trends observed throughout the school week informed the professional learning sessions that occurred for 150 minutes every Friday afternoon. Marcia noted, "We meet as a leadership team twice a week and one of those meetings is around how to spend our time during the weekly professional development." These professional learning sessions that drew on teacher reflexivity inherently were responsive to student and teacher needs.

Rosalina, acknowledging the range of students' needs in her class, explained that professional learning involves "developing myself and my skills…[so] that [I] can access the learning for each student." Rosalina appreciated "the space for teachers to come together and collaborate with one another and identify…the needs of our classrooms…the needs of our school… to feel that ownership…to reflect, share." Marcia also touted the inclusion of activity-based professional learning that "create[d] space for gratitude" and included the teachers as co-facilitators of a game or activity as a team builder and, at times, content-based professional learning.

Discussion

COVID-19 caused a dramatic shift in the charter school's culture and how the educators perceived instructional practice. Through the lenses of social constructivism and care, which include reflexive and receptive practices that are process-based and reciprocal, we discuss the educators' modifications of practice—returning to in-person schooling, focusing more on well-being, and drawing on professional learning—and how these shifts were related to a reflexivity and receptiveness. More specifically, educators had to reassess their conceptions of pedagogy and practice and slow down their pace of instruction to greater support student and teacher meaning-making experiences *and* well-being.

Modified practice: being in-person

When returning to the classroom, the teachers continued to feel supported by their colleagues and their principal, and the shift in school-wide culture from rigidity to flexibility indicated the receptiveness that administrators and teachers had to the experiences of students *and* teachers.

All the educators spoke about a shift away from technology integration practices and on to the details to support physical presence: sanitizing hands and workspaces, creating and maintaining social distancing among the children, policing the use of masks, and mitigating related issues of obfuscated communication. Although Anjaynee and Jackie spoke most about the issues related to hygiene and safety protocols, all four educators acknowledged that COVID-19-related health concerns continuously informed—and interfered with—their planning. Additionally, contact tracing measures, along with the sudden discontinuation of buses and classroom closures, required immediate pivoting for transportation, instruction, and oversight.

Relatedly, the teachers' planning changed dramatically from long-term forecasting to day-by-day, hour-by-hour, minute-by-minute responses to students' and teachers' needs. This was seemingly radical. The educators, who used to stay at school until late at night, left immediately after school ended because they simply did not have the bandwidth to do more. And that was okay, especially because the space enabled the teachers to become mentally ready for their students the following day. In other words, the teachers realized that they needed to engage in self-care in order to successfully provide care for their students. Relatedly, in the classroom, what comes to the fore is that teaching in-person post-quarantine required flexibility and receptiveness to unanticipated changes to the educational environment and to the children's needs. Although helping students recover from learning loss was a priority, the educators emphasized well-being.

Modified practice: focus on well-being

Prior to COVID-19, the charter school's focus was on preparing students to meet and exceed academic benchmarks (e.g., the "grind"). Since the pandemic, the educators all noted a cultural shift that privileged student and teacher well-being over meeting pre-COVID-19 benchmarks. Although the educators did not adopt a particular measurement for assessing student well-being, there was a shift to evaluate continuously students' behavior, be it checking in when a student had a head down on a desk or pausing instruction to cater to students' emotions. Even the principal, Marcia, spoke about student well-being when she suddenly taught a class needing coverage. What once included heavy content-based instruction that stemmed from an ongoing "grind," turned to a focus on students' mental and physical health.

More specifically, educators created reflexive and receptive instructional practices that not only helped the educators to have an ongoing sense of their students' well-being, but also stressed the importance of accepting one's individual abilities in the moment. This repositioning of instruction is not to discredit pre-COVID-19 interests in helping students succeed. Rather, the revised approach underscores the educators' intentional and ongoing recognition that their students' success started with their overall well-being, and such a revised instructional approach hinged on flexibility and care. Such modified practice also was supported by professional learning that met the teachers where they were at that moment.

Modified practice: professional learning

Across the educators' feedback, there was an acknowledgement of their own exhaustion and burnout, and the principal highlighted the needs of the staff to ensure their wellness. As a result, the principal initiated a "touchpoint" once each week to engage educators in team-building activities. Although some of these approaches and concerns existed before COVID-19, what changed was a greater emphasis on educator reflexivity and receptivity, which was evident in the flexible instruction and ongoing support that continued to take shape depending on the immediate and long-term needs of the students and the teachers.

For example, Marcia's pre-COVID-19 responsibilities primarily centered on instructional support, and that did not waiver; rather, it shifted. Although instructional planning and feedback remained a cornerstone of the educators' professional learning, since COVID-19, there has been an emphasis on camaraderie and educator well-being, especially given that Marcia prioritized the support of her faculty. Holding on to prior practices, the educators continued to receive weekly classroom visits and related feedback, support from instructional coaches, and weekly debrief sessions wherein the teachers contemplated the appropriate strategies to leverage to support student *and* teacher growth.

Additionally, the weekly 150-minute professional learning sessions were not designed as a top-down staff development event. Rather, Marcia worked with the educators to focus on what they needed, such as troubleshooting differentiation, parent support, and student readiness. But at the heart of the professional learning sessions was the intent "to just come together as a staff, to build camaraderie, and to also develop whatever skills need to be." Rosalina's points about self- and collaborative-care (e.g., "ownership," "reflect, share") underscore how the educators' needs—also grounded in their support of the students' needs—were part of the educational shift that emphasized well-being. This radical cultural change from grit and grind to flexibility and care occurred because the educators perceived and responded to the immediate needs of their students and were receptive to changing their practice—even in professional learning—to support and enhance the meaning-making experiences and the well-being of students and faculty.

Limitations

We acknowledge that, despite focusing on a NYC charter school, we did not adopt a culturally responsive pedagogy lens to explore the needs of the teachers or the students. Ladson-Billings (2021) contended that there needs to be a hard reset in schools during COVID-19, so "teachers will need to build their pedagogical repertoires to ensure they are reaching all students" (p. 74). Although this is an implication for future research, we also see it as a limitation because the majority of the charter school's students are underserved children, and our findings do not extend beyond the teachers' perceptions of what meeting the needs of underserved children might look like, and that is something needing greater attention.

Additionally, although interviews took place at mutually agreeable times, the educators seemed to fit our Zoom meetings into the moments they had available. The principal wore a mask while videoconferencing from school. Two educators Zoomed from their homes. And one connected with us outside a grocery store. We wonder to what extent these moments contributed to feelings of being overwhelmed and might have affected how the educators spoke about their exhaustion. Furthermore, although our study took place over the course of seven months, we wonder what cultural shifts exist today, when COVID-19 variants, coupled with respiratory syncytial virus (RSV) and the flu, have created a trifecta of infections during winter 2023.

Conclusions and implications

This study contributes to the "limited empirical research on the impact of the COVID-19 pandemic on teachers" (Pressley, Ha, and Learn, 2021, p. 367). The integration of reflexivity and receptivity, spurred by teachers' outcry for continued strength and wellness, pervaded the educators' modified practices. There was a seismic shift in cultural practices away from the charter's protocol to use benchmark-based assessments to embrace in-the-moment intuitive assessments and acceptance of well-being.

Furthermore, despite the administration's intentional focus on teacher collaboration and feelings of unity, more attention to and intentional support of teachers (i.e., care) is needed. Are all the teachers equipped to be responsive to students' needs? If not, why not? If so, how so? Is the focus on camaraderie the same as care? Overall, the data revealed a concerted effort by the educators to shift the narrative to one of support, but there also is a need for a shift in thinking: recovery. Beteille et al. (2020) argued that "fostering teacher resilience will be essential for recovery" (p. 2). The students need help, but their educators should not be forgotten as they continue to face myriad COVID-19-related challenges. Although camaraderie is important, during this tumultuous time, for students *and* for teachers "education must be seen as a pathway to attaining lifelong learning, satisfaction, happiness, wellbeing, opportunity and contribution to humanity" (Zhao and Watterston, 2021, p. 5). The data from our study suggest that such a pathway is not simple nor is it paved. The latter, however, can offer educators and students opportunities to resurface the educational landscape.

References

Angrist, N., de Barros, A., Bhula, R., Chakera, S., Cummiskey, C., DeStefano, J., … & Stern, J. (2021). 'Building back better to avert a learning catastrophe: Estimating learning loss from COVID-19 school shutdowns in Africa and facilitating short-term and long-term learning recovery', *International Journal of Educational Development*, 84, https://doi.org/10.1016/j.ijedudev.2021.102397

Arnove, R. F. (2020). 'Imagining what education can be post-COVID-19', *Prospects*, 49(1), pp. 43–46.

Beard, K. S., Vakil, J. B., Chao, T., & Hilty, C. (2021). 'Time for change: Understanding teacher social-emotional learning supports for anti-racism and student well-being during COVID-19, and beyond', *Education and Urban Society*. https://doi.org/10.1177/00131245211062527

Berry, B. (2020). 'Teaching, learning, and caring in the post-COVID era', *Kappan*, 102(1), pp. 14–17. https://doi.org/10.1177/0031721720956840

Beteille, T., Ding, E., Molina, E., Pushparatnam, A., & Wilichowski, T. (2020). 'Three principles to support teacher effectiveness during COVID-19', *World Bank*. Available at: http://hdl.handle.net/10986/33775

Cameron, M. (2022). 'Recruitment and retention of highly qualified teachers in marginalized school communities', *Eastern Educational Research Association Conference*, 3–4 February. Clearwater, Florida.

Carlson, H. L. (1999). 'From practice to theory: A social constructivist approach to teacher Education', *Teachers and Teaching*, 5(2), pp. 203–218. https://doi.org/10.1080/1354060990050205

Ceglie, R. J., Black, G., & Saunders, S. (2022). 'COVID-19's impact on teachers and the teaching profession', in Cegile, R. J., Abernathy, D. F., and Thornburg, A. W. (eds.) *Schoolchildren of the COVID-19 pandemic: Impact and opportunities*. Bingley: Emerald Publishing Limited, pp. 59–81.

Creswell, J. W., & Poth, C. N. (2018). *Qualitative inquiry & research design: Choosing among five approaches* (4th ed.). Thousand Oaks: SAGE.

Ferguson, W., Furticella, J., Hinderaker, A., Howard, H., Newman, A., & Rogers, K. (2022). 'Two years of the pandemic in New York, step by awful step', *The New York Times*, 15 March. https://www.nytimes.com/interactive/2022/nyregion/nyc-covid-timeline.html

Harmey, S., & Moss, G. (2021). 'Learning disruption or learning loss: Using evidence from unplanned closures to inform returning to school after COVID-19', *Educational Review*, pp. 1–20. https://doi.org/10.1080/00131911.2021.1966389

Heyward, G. (2021, Sept. 13). 'From shutdown to reopening: Here's a look at N.Y.C. schools' trek through the pandemic', *The New York Times*, 13 September. https://www.nytimes.com/2021/09/13/world/reopening-timeline-nyc-schools.html

Hollingsworth, S., Dybdahl, M., & Minarik, L. T. (1993). 'By chart and chance and passion: The importance of relational knowing in learning to teach', *Curriculum Inquiry*, 23(1), pp. 5–35.

Horowitz, J. M. (2020). 'Lower-income parents most concerned about their children falling behind amid COVID-19 school closures', *Pew Research Center*. https://www.pewresearch.org/fact-tank/2020/04/15/lower-income-parents-most-concerned-about-their-children-falling-behind-amid-covid-19-school-closures/

Jones, N. D., Camburn, E. M., Kelcey, B., & Quintero, E. (2022). 'Teachers' time use and affect before and after COVID-19 school closures, *AERA Open*, 8(1), pp. 1–14. https://doi.org/10.1177/23328584211068068

Kim, L. E., Oxley, L., & Asbury, K. (2021). 'My brain feels like a browser with 100 tabs open': A longitudinal study of teachers' mental health and wellbeing during the COVID-19 pandemic in 2020', *British Journal of Educational Psychology*, 92(1), pp. 299–318. https://doi.org/10.1111/bjep.12450

Kuhfeld, M., Soland, J., Tarasawa, B., Johnson, A., Ruzek, E., & Liu, J. (2020). 'Projecting the potential impact of COVID-19 school closures on academic achievement', *Educational Researcher*, 49(8), pp. 549–565.

Kush, J. M., Badillo-Goicoechea, E., Musci, R. J., & Stuart, E. A. (2022). 'Teachers' mental health during the COVID-19 pandemic', *Educational Researcher*, 51(9), pp. 593–597. https://doi.org/10.3102/0013189X221134281

Ladson-Billings, G. (2021). 'I'm here for the hard re-set: Post pandemic pedagogy to preserve our culture', *Equity & Excellence in Education*, 54(1), pp. 68–78.

McQuirter, R. (2020). 'Lessons on change: Shifting to online learning during COVID-19', *Brock Education*, 29(2), pp. 47–51. https://journals.library.brocku.ca/brocked

Mervosh, S. (2022). 'Pandemic learning loss', *The New York Times*, 28 November. https://www.nytimes.com/2022/11/28/briefing/pandemic-learning-loss.html

Miles, M. B., Huberman, A. M., & Saldaña, J. (2019). *Qualitative data analysis: A methods sourcebook* (4th ed.). Thousand Oaks: SAGE.

Milman, N. B. (2020, March 30). 'This is emergency remote teaching, not just online teaching', *Education Week*. https://www.edweek.org/leadership/opinion-this-is-emergency-remote-teaching-not-just-online-teaching/2020/03

Noddings, N. (2013). *Caring: A relational approach to ethics and moral education* (2nd ed.). University of California Press. (Original work published 1984.)

Noddings, N. (2019). 'Concepts of care in education', *Oxford Research Encyclopedia*, pp. 1–13.

Noddings, N., & Shore, P. J. (1984). *Awakening the inner eye: Intuition in education*. New York: Teachers College Press.

Pressley, T. (2021). 'Factors contributing to teacher burnout during COVID-19', *Educational Researcher*, 50(5), pp. 325–327.

Pressley, T., & Ha, C. (2022). 'Teacher exhaustion during COVID-19: Exploring the role of administrators, self-efficacy, and anxiety', *The Teacher Educator*, 57(1), pp. 61–78. https://doi.org/10.1080/08878730.2021.1995094

Pressley, T., Ha, C., & Learn, E. (2021). 'Teacher stress and anxiety during COVID-19: An empirical study', *School Psychology*, 36(5), pp. 367–376. https://doi.org/10.1037/spq0000468

Schaefer, M. B., Abrams, S. S., Kurpis, M., Abrams, M., & Abrams, C. (2020). '"Making the unusual usual": Students' perspectives and experiences of learning at home during the COVID-19 pandemic', *Middle Grades Review*, 6(2). https://scholarworks.uvm.edu/mgreview/vol6/iss2/8

Schaefer, M. B., Abrams, S. S., Kurpis, M., Abrams, C., & Abrams, M. (2021). 'Pandemic meaning making: Messing toward motet', *English Teaching: Practice & Critique*, 20(2), 261–274. https://doi.org/10.1108/ETPC-07-2020-0073

Shabani, K. (2016). 'Applications of Vygotsky's sociocultural approach for teachers' professional development', *Cogent Education*, 3(1), 1–10. http://doi.org/10.1080/2331186X.2016.1252177

Thompson, C. N., Baumgartner, J., Pichardo, C., Toro, B., ... Fine, A. (2020). 'COVID-19 outbreak—New York City, February 29-June 1, 2020', *Morbidity and Mortality Weekly Report*, 69(46), 1725–1729. http://dx.doi.org/10.15585/mmwr.mm6946a2external icon

Vygotsky, L. (1986/1934). *Thought and language*. Cambridge: MIT Press.

Yin, R. K. (2017). *Case study research and applications: Design and methods*. Thousand Oaks: SAGE.

Zhao, Y., & Watterston, J. (2021). 'The changes we need: Education post COVID-19', *Journal of Educational Change*, 22(1), pp. 3–12.

9

NEW WAYS OF WORKING AND NEW OPPORTUNITIES

Early childhood leaders' professional practice post-COVID

Wendy Boyd, Marg Rogers, and Margaret Sims

Background

When the COVID-19 pandemic was announced and lockdowns were introduced in Australia in mid-March 2020, EC education leaders (EC leaders[1]) were obligated to respond immediately to implement changes. The Australian Government required the EC sector to remain open for children of 'essential workers'. Essential workers were classified as people who needed to leave their home to work on the frontline, such as doctors and nurses, and emergency service personnel. Despite having to work onsite, EC educators were not recognised as 'essential', a contradiction that impacted their eligibility for government support. While all of Australia was put into lockdown in March 2020, as the pandemic entered its second year, different states and territories in Australia controlled their own responses resulting in different periods of local lockdowns with different rules around quarantines, contacts outside the home, and access to public spaces. For example, the states of Western Australia and Queensland managed the climax of the COVID-19 pandemic during 2020–2021 by locking out the rest of Australia. Other states such as New South Wales had hotspot lockdowns where a region would be locked down and the rest of the state remained open. Indeed, Australia became one of the most locked down countries in the world because the government chose to purchase and roll out the vaccination programme much later than comparable countries.

The impact of COVID-19 has been found to have had a significant impact on the wellbeing of EC educators who were required to apply the health and safety guidelines to keep the children, their families, and themselves

DOI: 10.4324/9781003352129-12

safe and free from COVID-19 (Logan et al., 2021). Being excluded from the official definition of essential workers resulted in a lack of policy support for the EC sector, leading to an ongoing need to support EC educators in policy solutions for the EC workforce (Hanno et al., 2022). This is complicated by the governmental positioning of the EC sector as a workforce issue rather than an educational one. An analysis of ten countries' government policies related to the EC sector's experience of COVID-19 (Rothe et al., 2022) found that in all ten countries (including Australia) the governments, overall, did not view EC as part of the educational continuum. Rather EC was viewed as a system that provided care for children so that families could work (Rothe et al., 2022). Neuman (2022) questioned the lack of priority given to EC in four countries and identified that the COVID-19 pandemic put EC at a further disadvantage with less support from society and governments post-COVID-19 to elevate the status of EC in society.

Zhao (2020) warned that changes in education arising from the pandemic would only be temporary if the global pandemic was treated as a short-term crisis. Rather, fragilities exposed in the EC sector and more widely across society during the lockdowns, and subsequent reopening of society, need to be the basis of transformative changes (Popa, 2022). In particular, the positioning of the EC sector made evident in government responses to the pandemic creates an opportunity for the EC sector to drive changes in how the sector is perceived and how it develops in the future (Sims et al., 2022). In Australia, as in a number of other nations, the EC sector suffers from low status (Arndt et al., 2021; Boyd, 2020; Rogers et al., 2023). For example, Australian EC teachers are paid approximately 20% less than their primary school teacher counterparts, even though they may have studied a four-year degree and have fewer holidays and longer hours of work per week.

While the United Nations asserted that the world was in a childcare crisis prior to the pandemic (Gromada et al., 2020), recommendations for change in EC services continue to be made following the pandemic. Jalongo (2021) identified that when families were forced to spend more time with their children, as a result of lockdowns during the pandemic, they developed a deeper gratitude for the role of EC teachers. As a result, recommendations have been made that teachers' capacity to deliver online education is addressed and that children's resilience, creativity, and problem solving are encouraged (Noble et al., in Jalongo, 2021). As EC is ultimately essential work, even though it was not categorised as such by the Australian government during the pandemic, EC services were necessary to enable society to continue to provide essential services. Unfortunately, while schools were supported during the pandemic to maintain their educational role, the EC sector was only considered important in providing non-parental care for the children of essential workers, that is, the sector was identified as important as a support for the essential workforce (Barnes et al., 2021; Sims et al., 2022).

Despite this positioning, the EC sector continued to operate with an educational focus with EC leaders required to not only maintain quality environments for children's learning but also to establish directions for ongoing quality improvement (ACECQA, 2020). The ongoing improvement involves evaluation, reflection, and review of the centre's philosophy, policies, and procedures that includes risk management to ensure a safe learning environment (ACECQA, 2020). Simultaneously, EC leaders are required to support educators to reflect on their teaching and professional knowledge and establish strong relationships with children and families (ACECQA, 2020). While these requirements are part of 'normal' practice, the impact of the COVID-19 pandemic meant that EC leaders needed to work in different ways and to reconceptualise the way they worked in order to achieve these outcomes. The provision of quality was found to be supported during the pandemic by EC leaders by having a strong cohesive philosophical approach and prioritising relationships (Neilsen-Hewett et al., 2022). Cultivating leadership is impacted by the complexities of the EC environments (Gibbs, 2021); however, the complexities that came with the pandemic challenged EC leaders even further (Gibbs, 2021).

It is within this complex context of the EC sector experiencing the COVID-19 pandemic, and during the second year of the pandemic, the data for this chapter were collected asking what new ways of working and new opportunities were implemented by EC leaders for re-imagining EC. This study asked how COVID-19 could provide a portal (Arnove, 2020) for opportunities for transformation in education. Data were collected within two regional areas in the state of New South Wales, during a time when there had recently been a lockdown.

Discussion of methodological approaches

The study applied an interpretive ontology grounded in the understanding that reality is created independently by each person. We used a social constructionist epistemology that aligned with this ontology, where truth was positioned as constructed by humans in their social world and open to individual interpretation of each person's experience. The social world of each person impacts how truth is constructed (Alvesson & Sköldberg, 2018; Denzin, 2017; Denzin & Lincoln, 2017). In this way, we came to a shared understanding with each participant of their perspectives during the interviews. The participants in this study were EC leaders: directors of community preschools and long day care services, and one business leader in family daycare. These different contexts provided nuances in their experiences; however, there were many common themes that emerged. Our participants were selected using the following criteria:

1 The six participants were the EC leaders of an ACECQA-accredited New South Wales EC service that operated during the lockdown periods and continued to operate from March 2020 to September 2021.
2 The participants were willing to spend time with one research team member to undertake the interview.

To develop the interview questions for this study, a theoretical framework was applied that aligned with the literature identifying what we believed to be the ways in which the pandemic impacted the work of EC professionals and our own experiences (see Appendix 1). This framework was used to guide the development of the semi-structured interview questions and the analysis.

The social world used in this study aligns with the ecological systems theory explained by Bronfenbrenner and Morris (2006). The participant is situated in the microsystem bringing EC leader characteristics that influence, and are influenced by, the surrounding exosystem, the macrosystem, and the chronosystem. The exosystem is the context of the EC setting, including the educators, children, and families. The exosystem and the microsystem interact in a system termed the mesosystem. In this case, the mesosystem was the interactions and relationships between and within the microsystem and the exosystem participants. The macrosystem includes the government laws and societal customs, which in this study included the health departments in each jurisdiction who mandated the lockdowns and enforced the essential services' actions in providing care for essential workers' children. The lockdowns occurred across the period 2020 and 2021, a period that required a new way of working in response to the global pandemic and is represented by the chronosystem.

In order to understand our participants' truth, data collection was conducted individually through in-person interviews with six EC leaders from their services via video conferencing due to the pandemic. The open-ended questions included questions about the EC service, impact of lockdowns on stakeholders, children's experiences during transitions, impact on self as a leader, and future changes.

Human research ethics approval was gained from Southern Cross University. Participants could withdraw from the study at any time, and they were informed that their identity would be protected. Permission was gained from the participants to record the interviews, and transcription of the interviews occurred. Pseudonyms were used to name the six interviewees.

To analyse the data for meaning-making, each researcher obtained a sense of the data as a 'whole', so that initial ideas were obtained. Of importance is for the researchers to take notes about the key themes emerging from areas to best address the research questions. The researchers met to discuss the emerging themes. From the broad themes that emerged, coding was then undertaken and allocated to each theme enabling interpretation for analysis (Braun & Clarke, 2022). A second analysis involved scrutiny by the third researcher to find themes not identified in this initial analysis, a process required for research rigour (Lincoln & Guba, 1985). Given the rich data from the interviews, the researchers decided to write two separate papers (Rogers et al., 2023; Sims et al., Under review) plus this chapter to highlight different major themes within the analysis. Additionally, three research-based news media articles were published (see Rogers, 2021; Rogers et al., 2022a, 2022b). The findings from the analysis of the data for this chapter are now reported.

Findings

The findings highlight that the EC leaders held a powerful role as they learned to work differently during the COVID-19 pandemic. The EC leaders developed new ways of working as they implemented significant changes in the operation of their EC service, all the while being responsive and mindful of the health and wellbeing of all stakeholders: children, families, staff, and the EC service's community. Their characteristics as leaders during a time of significant disruption are illuminated as they took action to keep people safe.

The EC leaders' responses to working during the COVID-19 pandemic revealed that they were flexible with work arrangements, organised, effective communicators, compliant to requirements, innovative, and strategic. The data revealed that these ways of working were possible owing to the contexts of the EC setting. Having a cohesive team of educators enabled new ways of working that were responsive to the changing pandemic environments, and the staff were aligned in their philosophy and goals. A supportive management committee enabled the EC leader to carry out actions necessary to work differently and keep stakeholders safe. However, EC leaders experienced tensions as they tried to be available for families but also the need to be mindful of their own needs and comply with health and safety requirements. The following section presents the key ways that EC leaders worked responsively and differently during the COVID-19 pandemic, creating new opportunities for ongoing improvement in EC delivery.

Working in new ways as EC leaders

The EC leaders' characteristics placed them in good stead to take responsibility to manage the EC service to keep staff, families, and children safe and, in doing so, created new ways of working. While the EC services were not classified as 'essential', the services were required to be open for the children of essential workers, suggesting that the role of the service was associated with caring for children rather than providing education and care. Indeed, the EC leaders identified that all people felt vulnerable amidst the pandemic, not only the essential workers, as Evie stated:

This whole period has seen a new definition of vulnerable. In terms of families and the Community ... I don't believe that anyone is in a position to be able to say who does or does not need care – it's not only the doctors and nurses. If somebody says I want to put my child in after school care, even if they hadn't been at school, I'm happy to give them those three hours to give them that precious time for themselves.

To enact this caring role, the EC leaders exemplified their flexibility in the management of the EC service. The EC leaders developed staff rosters that demonstrated how EC leaders assisted their community, even though they were not recognised as being essential. For example, Cassie stated:

There was a real connection over that time, and an empathy for each other that was hard and times when staff are feeling quite stressed and making sure that we're all here for each other because, just that, insecurity and not knowing, how bad is this going to get...that was quite challenging being told you're an essential worker, but the way that early childhood educators are valued and the conditions of early childhood in Australia was (a) real contradiction that staff were trying to grapple with.

The EC leaders were responsive and felt that they were constantly called on and were always available, highlighting their professional approach to being a leader of an EC service. This is highlighted by EC leaders' actions during the pandemic, as Alice stated:

I think having a good sense of yourself as a professional and being in the profession, but also being able to stand up when these things come up, offer support, but also look after yourselves. I think it's really important and think this has highlighted that we have to do that as a field, as a profession. We have to stand up and really shout out to the policymakers and the government that it's fine to call on us, great, and we keep answering, but you'd better show us some respect.

The EC leaders reported that their role involved sourcing necessary information, designing appropriate ways to enforce new requirements (for example new hygiene requirements and new attendance eligibility requirements), and communicating with staff and families. During the pandemic, the constantly changing health requirements increased the time spent on this role significantly. Cassie stated

> *I found that I was in more sort of an administrative role because we had to have policies, we had to look at what changes we needed to implement in our service, and why we were doing it. I suppose there was fear that one of us could get sick and what happens if we did have COVID in here? And I suppose my way of coping ... we would follow procedures, we would follow what we needed to know, there were people out there. We knew that the New South Wales Health Department, the Education Department would give us the advice of what to do.*

Cassie shared how complex this sourcing of information was:

> *There was huge amounts of information to try and get your head around, to understand the implications and the changes in our practises....But to do it in a way that's respectful of children and families and to find out- and - make sure it came from recognised authorities...it came from New South Wales Health, came from (auspicing agency) or it came from the Department of Education*

The EC leaders took responsibility for managing staff including recruitment, approving leave, and the staff's roster during the lockdowns of the pandemic. While these duties are a normal part of the responsibility of the EC leader, the EC leaders worked differently enabling recruitment of staff directly associated with the COVID-19 health and hygiene situation, enabling staff to take leave or work from home if they had primary school-aged children to care for at home, so each staff's situation needed to be planned for. Because there were fewer children attending the EC services, fewer staff were required at the service, so some staff were able to take annual leave, or leave without pay, during the lockdowns. As Cassie stated:

> *To start with it was quite challenging for some of our educators because they actually had preschool age children, so they found it quite difficult to say that we are frontline workers because we have to come to work but we have to then go and put our children into care to do this work....we didn't want our educators to burn out... we offered our educators paid stand down time too, so we're still looking at their wellbeing at that particular time.*

Staffing arrangements were often complicated by the attendance of new children: some EC services closed at times, which meant that children of essential workers needed to attend an available EC service, as Cassie shared:

So there was this whole group of new children, from other services in town and then writing the rosters for staff and then writing work plans every week, and keeping abreast and up-to-date with changes in requirements; where are hotspots; with families that have been to visit the hotspots; just all of that extra communication, the extra paperwork ... Funding was increasingly challenging. We lost parent fees, we lost childcare subsidy, our staff- because (the auspicing agency) wasn't eligible for JobKeeper, we didn't get JobKeeper.

The EC leaders created ways of working to ensure educators' wellbeing was provided for and understood the need to keep educators safe and feeling secure. While this kept staff feeling safe, it contributed to the staff feeling isolated, along with not being respected by the government for the role they were playing as Franky stated:

Child care is, you know, one of the front-line areas, but I don't think we were acknowledged and respected for what we were doing..... Some of them (staff) are way out of their comfort zone but, in the spirit of helping families they've actually all come to the fore really well.

In some EC services, new staff were employed to assist in undertaking the additional cleaning required as a result of the pandemic health requirements. Schools in the same state were given an extra 2 hours of cleaning a week to cope with the additional burden, but ECEs were expected to pick up the work, often unpaid. However, some services were able to afford extra hours for educators as Franky said:

We needed to have extra staffing to do it, and so we were able to employ somebody, to start earlier ... to be able to go around wipe surfaces off, and document all of that.

Thus, the data showed that EC leaders needed to work in different ways to not only achieve the outcomes they would have expected of themselves prior to the pandemic but to achieve new outcomes arising from the pandemic. New ways of supporting staff, juggling rosters to meet different (and new) staff needs, sourcing the latest information on constantly changing requirements, sharing this information, developing the necessary policies and procedures to ensure compliance, and supporting staff to undertake new and additional work requirements were all necessary. It is important to recognise that this work was taking place in a context where the EC sector was not identified as essential yet was required to continue to offer onsite services.

Working in new ways with families

Being an effective communicator was a necessity during the COVID-19 pandemic to ensure that staff, families, and children knew what was happening. The EC leaders talked about how they worked hard to ensure that parents knew about the EC service's state of operation. Some children were allowed to attend as their parents fitted the description of being an 'essential worker', but other children were not allowed to attend and the EC leaders had to communicate the health policies clearly with families. They were able to be flexible and respond according to the changes required by the Government. As Franky stated:

> *When our numbers were low my educators took on that role (communicating) because I was constantly trying to find out what was happening, what we needed to do, what policies we needed, how we had to communicate with families, the board of management, all of those sorts of things. I suppose it was a very fluid time, that things could change quickly, and we kept that message going to families too.*

As a result of the information provided by the Department of Health, the EC leaders reported that they developed strengths in forcing compliance with families. Prior to the COVID-19 pandemic, EC educators had reported difficulty enforcing compliance to families if they brought their children to the EC service with signs of ill health which could lead to further infections among staff and children as parents had to engage in paid work (Roman, 2017). This could create a situation where the educator felt uncomfortable about rejecting a child from attending as it would stop the parent from going to work in order to care for the child. The orders from the Health Department assisted educators to become more assertive to enforce compliance, and an example cited by the EC leaders of enforcing compliance came from Bev who said:

> *We tightened up our infection control policy. Really if I was going to say one good thing that's come out of it is the ability to, say, be very clear about children who can come and can't come when you're sick or not sick. I think that was good for staff. Just referencing Department of Health, Department of Education, and being quite clear. I'm not the police, I'm not the person who is making these rules, the government is. They're asking us to enact them. I am passing this on to you, this is what we're expecting.*

Similarly, Franky stated that she worked to ensure that parents complied with the health orders:

We were insistent that if one parent's at home, then leave them home with that parent rather than bring them into the service. The Health Minister kept saying, please keep your children at home, I think that's validated what we're trying to do.

Bev summarised this when she said:

I'm not the police, I'm not the person who is making these rules, the government is. They're asking us to enact them. I am passing this on to you, this is what we're expecting. Just reiterating that.

Sharing learning experiences via videos, emails, and social media became the normal way of communicating with children and families. Bev reported that because they wanted to find out what the families wanted, they did a survey:

We did a survey of our families sent via monkey survey. The responses identified what the families wanted from us because a lot of families were saying "We've got three children at home. We are also working at home we do not want to have much- have Zoom sessions with the children." So we really listened to what our families wanted. We were using an App called Seesaw, and so that became invaluable because we took turns of uploading stories and songs.

During the lockdown period, children were required to stay at home with their parents if their parents were not essential workers working away from home. As a result, while parents were working on their own job, the children required care and education. The EC educators were innovative in creating many educational resources to share with the children and their parents. For example, Franky said:

We would send videos and stories via email and Facebook so that either way they could get the information...and we sent out packs with some tomato seeds to grow, (and) science experiments like the yeast and balloons to go with that, so that they didn't have to go to the shops. It's been beautiful because we've asked for feedback from families, and we are getting videos of children doing the experiments, and we're getting photos of families at home doing what they're doing at home.

The educators shared these home videos with the children who were attending the EC service. In this way, connections between children were maintained to a certain extent. Stronger family relationships had developed as a result of these new ways of working with the educators learning more about the children's capabilities. Franky highlighted this when she said:

The relationship with families… is just getting stronger and stronger, and I think a lot of that's because of our communication with them on a daily basis…

We had one family that sent us (a video of) a nature hunt, the children (were) actually doing the nature hunt - you know feeling the grass under their feet and describing it was prickly it was soft. I didn't know they had all those words.

EC leaders shared their perspective that parents who kept their children at home during this period developed a deeper respect for the role of the EC educators' work. As Franky stated:

We are making a big effort to communicate with our families and get to know them. I think … there's a lot more, I suppose respect and understanding of what we do now, because they're realising that the children are at home with them. 'Oh, my goodness how do you do that?'

Dana shared:

…they could see, I think from what some of the comments from our families, they could see how play was so important for their children and actually see the value of play and see the learning that was occurring.

Thus, the data show that the pandemic created a context where communication with families, always identified as an important element of a quality service, became even more important. EC leaders needed to share constantly changing requirements with parents and enforce government rules around eligibility to attend. Having government mandate these requirements made it easier for EC leaders to enforce compliance, even when they felt empathy for the impossible situation parents found themselves in, having to simultaneously work from home and care for (and educate) their children. Finding ways to share educational activities with parents also developed as a new strategy in parental communication. EC leaders shared their belief that parents developed a better understanding of the work they do and thus a better appreciation of the importance of the EC sector, an appreciation that might, in the future, leverage change in societal perceptions and ultimately in government support for the sector.

Working in new ways with children

COVID-19 created new opportunities and different ways of working with children in the EC sector. The EC leaders reported that these different ways of working could be finessed to improve service delivery in the future. One key element of this arose from the ways in which learning activities were shared with parents whose children remained at home. The process of identifying learning activities and communicating them with parents helped EC educators remember the value of the work they were doing, to articulate important elements of learning. As Bev stated: 'It's given more clarity around, and guidance I think to what we do and how we do it'.

Franky shared how her service used a Facebook page to share learning activities with parents and how this experience increased the confidence of her staff:

> *Last week, everyone had to do a science provision that they could put up and do a story. So this week, everyone will be doing a story again so. And plus another activity, so their choice, whatever whether it's cooking or whatever. So everyone's being involved and the ones that are a little bit shy about being on the, on the video screen we're recording their voice reading a story ... some of them are way out of their comfort zone but, in the spirit of helping families they've actually all come to the fore really well.*

To re-establish relationships between children who had been absent during the lockdown, the EC leaders reflected on how to welcome back children who had been away. The re-socialising of the children back into the EC service was a new challenge for the educators. As Dana said:

> *I think the educators worked really hard in that area of saying "Oh look here's your friend, so and so," ...you know actually engaging them in the conversation and bringing them back in. They're interested in this so once we got that engagement and routines back in the children sort of settled. It was that initial coming back that we just thought this was like so weird they were like, you know, 40 individual children.*

Alice explained that this transition process for the children from home back to the EC setting was complex for the educators, children, and families. She commented that relationships helped children smoothly return to the EC services:

> *It depends on a whole range things, and obviously depending on the children themselves, and their home environment, and what sort of disposition they have and what [support] they've got. We quite often see*

children - some children that are fine and cruise back into it but might pop up with the odd little statement or question occasionally that makes you realise that there's probably some underlying things that they're thinking about that maybe they don't show you so much.

Once the children returned to the EC services, the EC leaders noticed that the children were including social distancing rules in their play as noted by Evie:

What we did find was even in home corner children were saying "Oh you have to stand back here." or "You can't stand here." or "This is what my sign says." or they're actually role-playing things that were happening in their world and their lives, that was interesting.

Some children presented challenging behaviours which required staff to be innovative in supporting these children and guiding their behaviour. As Evie stated

Children that had been waited on hand and foot, for babies that had been carried around by my mum or dad, or not had to settle to sleep on a mat, eating when they wanted to, have everything that they wanted to, and then they go back into care ... and had incredible meltdowns. The first day or two when the parents would leave the child with the educators, that was fine, as it was a nice break from mum and dad but then, by the end of day five (the child was thinking) "Hang on this is going (to) keep going - I prefer the way of was".

Thus, the data suggest that new ways of working with children benefited both the children and the EC educators. A focus on relationships (always an element of quality EC practice) helped maintain contact with children at home and helped them in the transition back into the service post-pandemic. Sharing learning opportunities with parents who were at home with their children helped EC educators articulate what they did and built their confidence in their professionalism.

This section has presented the ways of working that the EC leaders adopted in order to ensure that they were continuing to provide education and care for the children who attended their service. In the next section, we draw across these findings to consider new ways of working as EC leaders amidst the COVID-19 pandemic.

Discussion

This chapter has explored the new ways of working that EC leaders have developed as a result of the COVID-19 pandemic in EC services. The key findings highlight EC leaders' characteristics of flexibility, efficient management, care for their staff, effective communication, professionalism, and their work in developing innovative approaches to introduce new practices to support children, families, and colleagues. Using the Bronfenbrenner ecological systems model to analyse the way the EC leaders worked, it is clear that the qualities of the EC leaders, which is in the microsystem, strongly impacted the fellow staff, the families, and the children's experiences during the COVID-19 lockdowns and beyond. While these qualities may be expected in the role of the leader, the EC leaders were able to pivot their practices to ensure their services remained responsive and provided the necessary education and care for children who attended, or who were at home during lockdowns. Gibbs (2021) identified that the quality of the EC service is linked to the EC leaders' approach, and the six leaders interviewed in this study were highly aware of the complexities of their role in supporting staff, children, and families. The context of each EC service, that is the mesosystem, interacted with the EC leaders' characteristics to provide safe learning experiences for children both in the EC service and in the home. The degree of congruence between the flexibility of the EC leaders, the EC service, and the home learning environment was key in supporting children's learning needs during lockdowns.

A key concern that needs new ways of working and addressing urgently is that the EC sector was not viewed as being essential, yet the Australian Government, whose work could be seen as part of the macrosystem, insisted that the EC services remain open, putting the EC leaders and their staff, and by default the educators' families, on the 'frontline' to being exposed to COVID-19. Similar to findings by other researchers (Neuman, 2022; Rothe et al., 2022; Sims et al., 2022), this action by the government highlights that the EC sector was viewed as providing 'care', not necessarily education. In light of this, we argue that the status of EC needs to improve so that EC workers are respected, acknowledged, and thanked for the complex job that they do to support children's learning and development. Not only does the low status of the EC impact the attraction and retention of staff in the EC sector, there is also a view that anyone can care for children (Boyd, 2020), which demonstrates a lack of understanding of the complexity of the work involved as an EC educator. In their systematic review of the determinants of educator burnout, Ng, Rogers, and McNamara (2023) found educators' perceptions of low job status were exacerbated during the pandemic. As illustrated through the data explored above, work in the EC sector involves managing multiple and complex demands. The EC field is at a disadvantage as anyone is perceived as able to produce and rear children and caring for children can be done by 16-year-olds, as babysitters. Despite considerable effort, it would appear that the EC sector has not successfully explained their work to society regarding how they enact their roles of educating and caring for children in a stimulating, safe, and secure learning environment. Additionally, there is a lack of community and government understanding of the emotional cost of caring (Jena-Crottet, 2017). However, this research found that parents developed a deeper appreciation for the role of the EC educators during lockdowns as the parents found caring for their children quite challenging. EC educators themselves developed more confidence in articulating the work they do. EC educators were not just carers but provided important early learning experiences for children and shared these experiences with families in an environment that was safe and hygienic.

To support colleagues, the EC leaders were responsive to their needs and effectively communicated with all stakeholders. Some staff required staying at home to keep safe, while others were willing to attend the EC service. Those at home were able to take leave of some description or develop learning programmes for the children illustrating the flexibility of the workforce. The staff created educational online resources for children and families, and families deeply appreciated being connected in this way. Online resourcing was innovative as educators created videos of themselves telling stories. They also shared the stories of children who were at home with children in the centre, thereby keeping children's peer relationships active. This demonstrates an innovative way of working in the future.

Following the onset of the COVID-19 pandemic, recommendations for change have been highlighted by Gromada et al. (2020) and Jalongo (2021). The strong resilience of EC leaders to continue to provide quality essential services, in spite of not being acknowledged for this, shows the capacity of the EC leaders for new ways of working as their focus is to do what is best for children and their families. The professionalism the EC leaders brought to their work is outstanding. The leaders were mindful that while care was viewed as of prime importance by outside agencies including the government, the EC leaders in this study were dedicated to providing educational learning experiences for the children both in the EC service and in the home for those children unable to attend the EC service during lockdowns. Beyond the provision of quality care and education for the children, the EC leaders practised professionalism in the extraordinary times thrust upon them. Their professional practices included supporting their staff, the families, the communities, and themselves and their own families, to ensure their needs were met under the circumstances. They demonstrated commitment to their role as EC leaders and loyalty to their services. While being mindful that this is a small sample of six EC leaders, the findings signify the deeply held beliefs and philosophical approaches to the new ways of working under such circumstances. The transformative changes (Zhao, 2020) the EC leaders undertook during the COVID-19 pandemic are lessons that can be shared across the educational sector: including innovating communication modes of learning to support children and families, being flexible and adapting quickly to changing requirements for practices, and ensuring self-care so that the high level of professionalism required to manage the EC service was possible.

Note

1 EC leaders in this chapter are directors/managers of EC services who may not necessarily be the nominated educational leader in their service.

References

Alvesson, M., & Sköldberg, K. (2018). *Reflexive methodology. New vistas for qualitative research* (3rd Ed.). London: Sage.

Arndt, S., Smith, K., Urban, M., Ellegaard, T., Swadener, B.B., & Murray, C. (2021) Reconceptualising and (re) forming early childhood professional identities: Ongoing transnational policy discussions. *Policy Futures in Education*, 19(4), 406–423. DOI: 10.1177/1478210320976015

Arnove, R. (2020). Imagining what education can be post COVID-19. *Prospects*, 49, 43–46.

Australian Children's Early Childhood Quality Authority (ACECQA) (2020). Guide to the national quality standard. https://www.acecqa.gov.au/sites/default/files/acecqa/files/National-Quality-Framework-Resources-Kit/NQF-Resource-03-Guide-to-NQS.pdf

Barnes, B., Quiñones, G., & Berger, E. (2021). Constructions of quality: Australian Childhood Education and Care (EC) services during COVID-19. *Teachers and Teaching*. DOI: 10.1080/13540602.2021.1979510

Boyd, W. (2020). *Australian early childhood teaching programs: Perspectives and comparisons with Finland, Norway and Sweden*. Singapore: Springer.

Braun, V., & Clarke, V. (2022). *Thematic analysis. A practical guide*. London: Sage.

Bronfenbrenner, U., & Morris, P. A. (2006). The bioecological model of human development. In W. Damon & R. M. Lerner (Eds.), *Handbook of child psychology: Theoretical models of human development* (Vol. 1, pp. 793–828). Chichester: Wiley.

Denzin, N. (2017). Critical qualitative inquiry. *Qualitative Inquiry*, 23(1), 8–16. DOI: 10.1177/1077800416681864

Denzin, N., & Lincoln, Y. (Eds.). (2017). *The SAGE handbook of qualitative research* (5 ed.). London: SAGE Publishing.

Gibbs, L. (2021). Leading through complexity in early childhood education and care. *Australasian Journal of Early Childhood*, 7(46), 335–341.

Gromada, A., Richardson, D., & Rees. G (2020). Childcare in a Global Crisis: The Impact of COVID-19 on work and family life. Florence: UNICEF Office of Research Innocenti. https://www.unicef-irc.org/publications/pdf/IRB-2020-18-childcare-in-a-global-crisis-the-impact-of-covid-19-on-work-and-family-life.pdf.

Hanno, E., Gardner, M., Jones, S. M., & Lesaux, K. (2022). An ecological perspective on early educator well-being at the start of the COVID-19 pandemic. *Early Childhood Research Quarterly*. DOI:10.1016/j.ecresq.2022.02.002

Jalongo, M. (2021). The effects of COVID-19 on early childhood education and care: Research and resources for children, families, teachers, and teacher educators. *Early Childhood Education Journal*, 49, 763–774. DOI: 10.1007/s10643-021-01208-y

Jena-Crottet, A. (2017). Early childhood teachers' emotional labour. *New Zealand International Research in Early Childhood Education*, 20(2), 19–33.

Lincoln, Y., & Guba, E. (1985). *Naturalistic inquiry*. London: Sage.

Logan, H., McFarland, L., & Cumming, T. (2021). Supporting educator well-being during the COVID-19 pandemic: A case study of leadership in early childhood education and care organisations. *Australasian Journal of Early Childhood*, 46(4), 309–321. DOI: 10.1177/18369391211040940

Neilsen-Hewett, C., Linsay, G., Warren, J., Tonge, K., & Cronin, L. (2022). Early childhood leadership: Risk and protective factors during the COVID-19 pandemic. *Australasian Journal of Early Childhood*, 0(0), 1–14, DOI: 10.1177/18369391221103286

Neuman, M. (2022). Political prioritization of Early Childhood Education during the COVID-19 pandemic: A comparative policy analysis of low- and middle-income countries. *Early Childhood Research Quarterly*. DOI: 10.1016/j.ecresq.2022.01.006

Ng, J., Rogers, M., & McNamara, C. (2023). A systematic review of burnout and quality of life of early childhood educators. *Issues in Educational Research*, 33(1), 173–206. http://www.iier.org.au/iier33/ng.pdf

Popa, S. (2022). Taking stock: Impacts of the Covid-19 pandemic on curriculum, education and learning. *Prospects*. DOI: 10.1007/s11125-022-09616-7

Rogers, M. (2021). Early childhood directors are carrying an exhausting load during COVID-19, even beyond major outbreaks: Research. Women's Agenda. https://womensagenda.com.au/latest/early-childhood-directors-are-carrying-an-exhausting-load-during-covid-19-even-beyond-major-outbreaks-research/

Rogers, M., Boyd, W., & Sims, M. (2022a). Smile and wave ladies: The attempts to silence Grace Tame mirrors the plight of early childhood educators. Women's Agenda. https://womensagenda.com.au/latest/smile-and-wave-ladies-the-attempts-to-silence-grace-tame-mirrors-the-plight-of-early-childhood-educators/

Rogers, M., Boyd, W., & Sims, M. (2022b). The top four ways COVID placed harsher burdens on educators. There's an urgent need for change. *EduResearch Matters*. https://www.aare.edu.au/blog/?p=12455

Rogers, M., Boyd, W., & Sims, M. (2023). "Burnout central": Australian early childhood educational leaders' experiences during the Covid-19 pandemic. *Issues in Educational Research*, 33(1), pp. 284–306.

Roman, C. (2017). Between money and love: Work-family conflict among Swedish low-income single mothers. *Nordic Journal of Working Life Studies*, 7(3). DOI: 10.18291/njwls.v7i3.97093

Rothe, A., Moloney, M., Boyd, W., Dovigo, F., Rogers, M., O'Síoráin, C. A., Mellon, C., Calder, P., Blyth, D., Silberfeld, C., Girlich, S., Sims, M., Kakana, D., Opazo, M.-J., & Tadeu, B. (2022). Lessons from the COVID-19 Pandemic: A qualitative study of government policies relating to the early childhood sector across ten countries. In M. Jalongo (Ed.), *Educating the young child* (pp. 67–88). New York: Springer.

Sims, M., Calder, P., Moloney, M., Rothe, A., Rogers, M., Doan, L., Kakana, D.-M., & Georgiadou, S. (2022). Neoliberalism and government responses to Covid-19:

Ramifications for early childhood education and care. *Issues in Educational Research*, 32(3), 1174–1195.

Sims, M., Rogers, M., & Boyd, W. (Under review). The more things change the more they stay the same: Early childhood professionalism in COVID-19 times. *Australian Journal of Teacher Education*.

Zhao, Y. (2020). COVID-19 as a catalyst for educational change. *Prospects*, 49, 29–33.

10
PANDEMIC PARENTING – BALANCING CHANGE, CAPABILITIES, AND CULTURE

Kadia Hylton-Fraser and Kamilah Hylton

Introduction

Homeostasis refers to biological balance. When small changes occur in the human body, activities counter to restore balance. This is possible, however, only when changes occur within certain defined normal ranges. During significant disruptions, on the other hand, counterbalance measures are unable to keep pace with the level of disruption in progress and so imbalance persists. This imbalance typically requires a complex interplay of numerous variables such as intrinsic characteristics and the nature of the external environment to reset the system or facilitate adaptations. The achievement of equilibrium therefore is a constant manipulation of and manoeuvring between opposing forces. Balance is critical if the organism is to function optimally in the changed environment.

Up to early 2020, educational ecosystems consisting of parents, teachers, students, and policymakers seemingly existed with their own defined equilibria. As educational professionals, the struggle to align theory and practice became even more salient and was complicated by the different synergies arising from simultaneous changes at work and home during the pandemic and the perceived capabilities to manage those changes. Formal education, as it has been imagined and enacted for the last century, conceived parents as primarily playing a supporting role (Cooper, 1989; Roderique et al., 1994). In this supporting role, parental functions typically included assistance with homework and consultations with teachers regarding their child's progress and perhaps extended to participation in parent/teacher associations (Dauber and Epstein, 1993). The reinforcing tasks of the parent in their child's education have been shown to enhance positive outcomes (Ceka and Murati, 2016;

Eccles and Harold, 1993). Additionally, research indicates that the nature of parental involvement is predicated on the parent's perception of their ability to provide support (Hoover-Dempsey and Sandler, 1997) to their child.

Further research shows that how parents perceive their children's academic and cognitive abilities also determines the level and type of support that they provide (Hoover-Dempsey and Sandler, 1997). Another set of studies indicates that parents' own experiences and expectations of their role as parents (role construction) influence their involvement in their child's education (Hoover-Dempsey and Sandler, 1997; Walker et al., 2005). Moreover, the literature suggests that the level of parental involvement is also influenced by several factors such as socioeconomic status (Brown and Beckett, 2007), beliefs about social networks (Sheldon, 2002), levels of formal education (Lareau, 1987), linguistic diversity (Delgado-Gaitan, 1991), and cultural capital (Lareau and Horvat, 1999). On the other hand, researchers indicate that when parents do not know how to help their children due to a lack of understanding of their own role as parents or the school's expectations, this can negatively impact their involvement (Barton et al., 2004; Lareau and Horvat, 1999). Additionally, the number of children at home also impacted the amount of time a parent could spend helping their child/ren (Ribeiro et al., 2021). Consequently, there are several factors which influence how parents support their children's education.

Sudden change across education systems

The monumental and sudden shock of COVID-19 was arguably a significant challenge which resulted in severe disruption, not only across education systems, but within the medical, business, and political spheres, which swiftly shifted previously established equilibria. UNESCO (2020) reported that approximately 1.5 billion students worldwide were impacted by the sudden and complete cessation of the traditional classroom experience. UNESCO's Director-General Audrey Azoulay, at the onset of the pandemic, made reference to the need for countries to collaborate because there now existed one similar force impacting nations with varying capacities to counteract that force (UNESCO, 2020). There was also the suggestion made for widening communities of practice and providing support to students and parents alike to help them to adjust to the quickly changing environment. With the immediate and wide-scale quarantines implemented in many countries, many people were now isolated from extended circles of support and had to navigate new routines in isolation.

A study of Italian households revealed that parents who felt most competent had children who were best able to emotionally navigate the change (Morelli et al., 2020). Moreover, a study in Portugal found that parents invested a significantly greater amount of time in school-related activities for their children, making it difficult for them to manage their own work responsibilities (Ribeiro *et al.*, 2021). Other studies suggest that a parent's influence on their child's education became more significant during COVID-19 because parents were now expected to play larger roles in the formal education system (Ribeiro *et al.*, 2021). Furthermore, the attendant challenges that came with the onset of the pandemic created greater levels of stress for children and their families (Wajdi *et al.*, 2020).

However, considering the number of adjustments parents had to make, much consideration must be given to the context within which those adjustments occurred in addition to parents' deeply held beliefs and assumptions about education. The circumstances within which this instability happened are also unique, since COVID-19 precipitated a change initiative that had several drivers. As parents tried to manage their children, they also had to manage their professional and personal lives, and teachers had to do the same, as did school leaders.

This chapter interrogates how the authors as Jamaican educators managed their role as parents as their equilibrium was set off kilter. The authors' experiences are further buttressed by other parents' accounts shared in national news media. These accounts represent perspectives from different spheres of the Jamaican society and include parents who are also teachers. Further, this interrogation examines how a significant change in the Jamaican education system was further hampered by culturally embedded attitudes towards education. To foreground the discussion, however, a brief context is given on the Jamaican education system.

The Jamaican education system

Jamaica can be described as a developing island nation with a population of approximately 2.97 million people (European Union, 2022) and a poverty rate of about 12.3% (World Bank, 2023). Despite these factors, Jamaica has been able to achieve high enrolment rates up to the secondary education level and good completion rates up to the primary level. Enrolment rates average 90%, while completion rates up to the primary level average 96% (European Union, 2022). Jamaica, a former British colony, has significant European, Asian, and African influences, and the culture therefore is an amalgamation of these various ethnic groups. Education, though, was birthed from a plantocracy wanting to educate the poor, former enslaved people (Altink, 2019), and thus, education was a privilege. This initial focus on education has resulted in a legacy of stratification in the sector such that early post-independent Jamaica saw better schools largely populated by those in the higher socioeconomic strata (Hylton and Hylton-Fraser, 2022).

This stratification is reflected in how schools are divided into "high-tier or prestige 'grammar' style, middle-tier comprehensive or technical, and low-tier elementary or 'all-age'" (Hickling-Hudson, 2015, p. 5). There is also evidence that this stratification across schools still exists and is demonstrated by the inequitable distribution of resources and the recognition that top student performances reside in approximately 10% of institutions (JETC Report, 2021). Children are typically introduced to formal education at age three and transition from early childhood institutions to primary school (ages six to 12) and then to secondary schools (ages 12–18). Jamaicans, on average, complete close to 12 years in the formal education system. When compared to high-performing education systems, this, however, equates to approximately seven years (TES: Commitment Statement 2022). This means there is an average of a five-year learning deficit for Jamaican students when compared to their counterparts in top-performing countries. Jamaican children up to the secondary level are in school from 7:30 am to 2:30 pm, while the average student–teacher ratio is 35:1 (MoEY, 2019).

In recent years, teachers have indicated that these hours are becoming increasingly painful due to factors such as a significant decline in parental involvement (Murphy, 2022). Many teachers cite denial and lack of capacity for the waning parental support. Consequently, many teachers in the classroom feel overwhelmed and are left to deal with some students' maladjusted behaviour, for which they feel ill-prepared.

Jamaican parents, culture, and education

The role of parents in education has long been considered crucial to the success of children (Bertheelsen and Walker, 2008; Reynolds and Clements, 2005). Consequently, many schools have parent–teacher or home–school associations as a formal structure to facilitate collaborative efforts. In 2006, the National Parent-Teacher Association of Jamaica was established as a key component of the Education System Transformation Programme. The primary aim was to engage parents in a strategic manner in the operation of schools (JIS, 2016). Additionally, to build parenting capacity, the World Bank financed a US$15 million project called the Early Childhood Development Project for Jamaica in 2008 (World Bank, 2020). A key component of this project was the strengthening of the Early Childhood Commission's parenting subcommittee and the development and implementation of national Early Childhood Development parenting education. The project also included the development of substrategies for parenting of children up to age six.

In recent years, there has been a decline in the supportive role of parents and the collaborative practices normally facilitated through the school. The current Minister of Education believes this decline is evidenced by the significant display of maladaptive behaviour of children in schools and the blatant attacks on teachers by both parents and students (Radio Jamaica, 2022). Additionally, this breakdown has been attributed to the absence of parents in the education process and the general culture of violence in the Jamaican society. According to Samms-Vaughn (2006), the Jamaican parenting style has been depicted as one in which children are required to follow rules with harsh punishments doled out for noncompliance. This is accompanied by low levels of affection and acknowledgement of the child's feelings. This manifests itself as behavioural problems and poor performance in school.

The education minister, Fayval Williams, has further indicated that the prevalence of violence in schools is due in part to Jamaica's prevailing culture that perceives corporal punishment of children as par for the course (Williams, 2021). In 2016, the Jamaican government acknowledged the severity of the problem of violence in schools and committed to decreasing such incidences by launching the "Global Partnership to End Violence against Children" campaign in Kingston. Additionally, in 2020, the European Union–United Nations' Spotlight Initiative (SI) was launched to target family violence. This initiative seeks to broaden the School-Wide Positive Behaviour Intervention and Support (SWPBIS) framework. The SWPBIS resulted from a UNICEF/Ministry of Education and Youth partnership geared at reversing the proliferation of violence in schools.

According to the last census done in Jamaica, approximately 42.4% of households are headed by females (STATIN, 2013). Consequently, a significant number of households are dependent on single-parent income and so space to work is critical. It should also be noted that Jamaica has one of the highest costs of living in the region, and so even in two-parent households, typically both parents require full-time jobs in order to support their families (Murphy 2022).

Parents are generally balancing work and home responsibilities, and pre-COVID-19 data suggest that the parent stress index for Jamaican parents was high. Additionally, Samms-Vaughn (2005) suggests that those in the lower socioeconomic brackets experience higher levels of stress. The average Jamaican situation, prior to COVID-19, therefore, is one in which parents send children to school, go to work, and see children in the afternoon or late evening, in some cases. In many instances, teachers are forced to shoulder parental roles.

Recently celebrating 60 years of independence would place Jamaica as a young sovereign nation. Specifically, Jamaican culture is an amalgamation of experiences and cultures which are influenced by aspects of both traditional and modern life. Seaga (2005) posits that "Jamaica is a well-defined model of a dual society: two Jamaicas blending at points of contact" (p. 79). This duality also manifests in how the current education system is structured and the prevailing societal attitudes. These societal attitudes, beliefs, and practices concerning non-traditional versus traditional schools have been more difficult to change considering the continued disparities in support, infrastructure, and resources between the two categories of schools (Jennings, 2020).

Jamaican parents, particularly those from the lower class, primarily have been interested in having their children attend traditional schools as they recognize that this can significantly improve their status in the community (Altink, 2019).

Additionally, students must sit high-stakes examinations at the primary level to gain access to these "traditional" secondary institutions. These examinations, traditionally, act as a sorting tool for students between primary and secondary schools. Most notably, the examination is used to assess student academic performance and "determine their suitability for traditional or non-traditional high school placement" (Bourne *et al.*, 2015, p. 1). Moreover, the test culture within Jamaica at the primary level has created additional psychological stress for students who feel pressured to perform to be perceived as intelligent, or desirous of accessing tertiary education and obtaining professional employment (Bourne *et al.*, 2015). Parents' ability to manage these myriad issues within this cultural context is therefore invariably exacerbated by the instability wrought by the global pandemic.

Purpose

According to the American Psychological Association (2022), parenting should be focused on ensuring the general well-being of a child and equipping them with the tools to become positive contributors to society. Parents, however, know they are not equipped to cover all aspects of their child's growth and development, and so various experts are inserted at the relevant points. Children will spend approximately 40% of their waking hours at school, and so parents are accustomed to being engaged in a manner that supports the teaching and learning process. Parenting through difficult situations, particularly in a crisis, presents its own unique set of challenges.

Research has concluded that the stressors brought on by the pandemic have had what they term a "bidirectional" influence on individuals and their environment (Menter *et al.*, 2022). Specifically, they note, "the increased stressors and demands on caregivers posed by the COVID-19 pandemic have the potential to influence…. parent–child interactions by disrupting the way that family members relate to one another" (Menter *et al.*, 2022, p. 133).

Pandemic parenting, in this chapter, refers to the fact that there was no longer any discrete separation between the spaces of work and home. This chapter interrogates the parenting experience during COVID-19 through the lens of change management, specifically regarding parents' response to change within the context of a drastic change event. Further, it explores cultural nuances regarding education and parents' role in the process, which may or may not be impacted by parents' ability to not only cope with drastic change but also the significance of that in terms of their own changing role in the education of their children. Also, the chapter discusses the implication of parents' change response in terms of their overall health and well-being and makes recommendations for educators and school leaders going forward.

Discussion of methodological approaches

This chapter is bound up in the personal narratives of the authors' experiences during the pandemic as they straddled dual roles as educators and parents. Specifically, it adopts a quasi-narrative inquiry approach as it seeks to make sense of the authors' lived experiences (Connelly and Clandinin, 1990; Merriam and Tisdell, 2016) as parent-educators. According to Merriam and Tisdell (2016), these stories are central "as a source of understanding the meaning of human experience" (p. 34). Strauss (1987) similarly opines that "these experiential data should not be ignored....there is potential gold there!" (p. 11).

The authors depend on their stories and those of other Jamaican parents as data sources to make connections with their experiences (Merriam and Tisdell, 2016) throughout the pandemic as parents or parent-educators. While it is a limited perspective, the authors draw on media accounts to relate the stories of other parents' experiences, interwoven with their own. Moreover, as the authors provide the cultural context within which the stories unfold, they seek to centre authentic Jamaican experiences, "concerns and worldviews.... for our own purposes" (Tuhiwai Smith, 2022, p. 43). Additionally, these stories are examined through a conceptual framework that explores the balance between culture, capabilities, and change. This will be discussed in the next section.

Conceptual framework

Grounded in the concepts of the Awareness, Desire, Knowledge, Ability, Reinforcement (ADKAR) model of change management, this chapter seeks to underscore the fact that change in society, though inevitable, forms part of the fabric of human response to change. As seen in Figure 10.1, one's response to change highlights two fundamental realities – the ability to adapt quickly to change and the culture within which that change is embedded. As

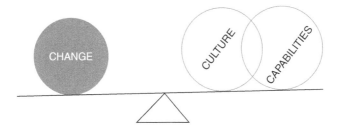

FIGURE 10.1 Conceptual framework for pandemic parenting.

argued earlier, the ability to respond effectively to drastic change has implications for either creating or destabilizing equilibrium. More importantly, as the figure also highlights, one's ability to manage change (capability) and its attendant challenges within the cultural milieu acts as a counterbalance in the midst of change. First, however, the change model is discussed.

ADKAR change model

The ADKAR model was originally developed by Jeff Hiatt in 2003 after he had conducted research with more than 700 companies which were undergoing major change projects. Hyatt's conclusion was that for any change initiative to be effective, it was important to understand the human element involved in the process. Similar change theorists underscore that change occurs at the individual level and must be managed skilfully (Kotter, 1995; Lewin, 1943). The ADKAR model, then, was integral in understanding and managing change at the individual level. Each model component highlights the expected outcomes based on specific change management activities and processes.

Awareness is the first step that indicates the individual's recognition of the reason for a change. This awareness typically occurs when there is early communication surrounding an impending change. *Desire* is the individual's desire to be part of the impending change process, which is dependent on how change is supported and resistance is managed within the organization. The next step is *Knowledge* about what is involved in the change process. Importantly, this knowledge is facilitated through coaching and training. The next step in the model is *Ability*, which is indicative of a recognition that a certain level of skill is required to implement the necessary changes. An individual's ability to respond effectively to change processes is developed through training, coaching, and opportunities to practice. Another important element in developing this ability is time.

Finally, there is *Reinforcement*. This step is critical to sustaining change initiatives. At this stage, enough accountability mechanisms have been implemented to ensure that individuals do not revert to former practices. Undergirding the ADKAR model is the fact that the steps are linear and must be considered in that order if the change is to be effective, much less sustained. The model also demonstrates how people will respond to change at different points and the kind of support that is required to get them to the next level.

Although the circumstances of the pandemic that are highlighted do not surround an organized change management project, the nature of the change in the education system prompted by the pandemic was seismic in its impact. Policymakers, school leaders, educators, and parents had no choice but to respond quickly if they were to keep the business of educating the nation's children at the forefront. However, as this chapter examines more closely the elements of the ADKAR model, it begins to unpack where the gaps were as parents responded/reacted to the change, the response of the system in terms of providing support, coaching, or training, and the opportunities for improving education as countries approach a post-COVID era. Additionally, the chapter demonstrates how the authors and other parent-educators were duly impacted by this unprecedented change process.

Findings

Jamaican pandemic perspectives

In this section, accounts from national newspaper outlets, government websites and the authors' personal narratives coalesce with the experiences of other parent-educators to represent a snapshot of what occurred in the Jamaican education sector during the COVID-19 pandemic. The overarching change that every household had to confront across the world was the introduction of a disease that spread rapidly, caused large numbers of deaths, and forced countries to close borders, pause daily routines, and be in quarantine. Additionally, some households encountered reductions in income due to job losses or reduced engagement at work, food shortages, uncertainty, children being out of school and simultaneously working while caring for children (Cluver *et al.*, 2020).

Research has also shown that mental health issues have seen a significant increase, and children may be more prone to abuse or mistreatment (Chung *et al.*, 2022; Huang and Zhao, 2020; Pierce *et al.*, 2020). Other changes stemming from the emergence of COVID-19 included:

1. coping with overeating (children and parents alike)
2. lack of physical activity and general social engagement of children
3. spending more time than usual with children (which some parents countered by allowing more screen time)
4. assuming a greater role in the child's teaching and learning process

These changes have significant implications for Jamaican parents as approximately 80% of families experienced a loss of income with this more disproportionately occurring in lower-income-bracket households. Parents indicated they had to grapple with fear of COVID-19 and increased levels of stress, exhaustion, and frustration. Even parents in nuclear families complained of feeling overwhelmed. Other parents also struggled with keeping their children focused during school hours, as children felt they were on vacation. Many parents had difficulty adjusting to the marked difference in scheduling a child for 24 hours, seven days a week as opposed to just on weekends (Lyew, 2020). In some instances, the combination of cascading changes coupled with stress, fear, and frustration resulted in parents expressing their irritation with their children.

Some Jamaican parents indicated that while they did not hit their children, they found themselves shouting more (Ross Shiel, 2020). Without the support of their village, parents found themselves struggling to ensure their children remained engaged in school via distance learning. Additionally, parents were now forced to confront mental health issues in their children, anxiety and fear while simultaneously dealing with their own (UNICEF, 2020).

Teaching challenges

The changes brought on by COVID-19 were even more severe for those in rural areas and those on the lower level of the socioeconomic strata. Scarce resources in these circumstances meant parents had little or no access to electricity, internet, or devices. The issue of access meant students in these areas had limited or no engagement with their schools. There were examples of teachers in rural areas riding into communities to deliver education packets to students or converting community notice boards into a blackboard so students could access some amount of learning.

Teachers were also experiencing high levels of anxiety as they had to adjust to a modality with which some were not familiar or comfortable while dealing with their own children at home. For some teachers, this led to feelings of depression and burnout (Hibbert, 2020). Since the pandemic, the Ministry of Education and Youth (MoEY) has implemented programmes to offer more psychosocial support but that has targeted students, and to a lesser extent teachers. Since May 2022, several Jamaican educators (teachers, vice-principals, and principals) have died suddenly, precipitating a clarion call for more efforts to support educators whose job is already a difficult and burdened one (Jamaica Observer, 2022b).

Despite coping with fear and feeling overwhelmed and anxious, there were parents who maintained job security, had family support, and so found they were able to spend more time with their children and engage in more meaningful family activities. However, Haynes-Brown, Hordatt-Gentles, and Brown (2021) surmise that the pandemic has made teaching for Jamaican teachers even more stressful as they grappled with their own issues of access, an inability to facilitate remote teaching using new online modalities, and balancing teaching with the work of parenting. In recognition of the significant support parents required under these conditions, international organizations such as United States Agency for International Development (USAID), Centers for Disease Control and Prevention (CDC), UNICEF, World Health Organization, Parenting for Lifelong Health, and others partnered to provide parenting resources (Cluver, 2020).

Parenting and teaching

To understand the impact of COVID-19 and the magnitude of change parent-educators experienced, it is necessary to summarize the modus operandi prior to March 2020. Work is full time. Children are at school between the hours of 7:30 am and 2:30 pm. Therefore, formal education of the children occurred in a separate space and was overseen by other teachers. Hence, during these hours, parents have the time and ability to fully concentrate on their own work either as teachers or other professionals. Many children are also involved in extracurricular activities, and so there is an additional opportunity for parents to focus on professional or personal activities. As a parent-educator that may mean additional time to grade assignments, complete lesson planning, or collaborate with other colleagues. Further, being an educator requires specific skills like classroom management, subject content expertise, and dealing with the demands from the administration.

Once the parent is at home, the focus is on homework and providing support. Additionally, there may be help at home for domestic activities. In April 2020, however, the discrete spaces disappeared. The formal education of children shifted as they were no longer fully under the influence of the teacher in their physical classrooms. Moreover, the social learning that happened from interaction with their peers was removed. Children were technically at school but so were the parents as they juggled connectivity/device issues, ambient noise over which they had no control, learning challenges via a new modality, for which little training was provided and adjusting to numerous requirements from each teacher.

The natural lunch period that would allow teachers a break was now disrupted, and lines were blurred. The parent-teacher must interrupt their work project or their own classes to prepare a meal. The child's routine was also disrupted as they no longer had the option to play or socialize with friends. The choice was now sustained time in front of a device. Unfortunately, this has had negative impacts for families as the obesity rates among children and adults have become a growing cause for concern (Storz, 2020). Additionally, some teachers have reported the need for prescription glasses, where there was none previously and a kind of "double work" balancing home and school responsibilities (Jamaica Gleaner, 2021).

In the initial phases of the pandemic, the choices that had to be made and decisions taken were seen to be temporary and so appeared manageable. In fact, while schools struggled to re-tool and re-imagine how they would operate, the education system was in flux and so there was mounting uncertainty about the time to be spent at home. There was not much consideration given to the situation being an extended one. One could not have imagined that Jamaican students would have remained out of the physical school environment for two years. As one month extended to a year, it prompted consideration about how parents who are themselves educators were navigating the space and how their various contexts influenced the pathways taken.

Jamaican parenting

The changes being experienced during the pandemic have been significant. These are particularly significant in the Jamaican context where many households are single parent, led primarily by mothers (Samms-Vaughn, 2008). Moreover, as a developing country with a culture of violence, many of Jamaica's citizens traditionally have negative attitudes towards mental health care (Jackson and Heatherington, 2006; Jackson Williams, 2012).

Another component that created additional stress for parents was the management and support of children with behavioural, mental, or special learning needs. Schools indicated that under normal circumstances, the wait time for support personnel can range anywhere between one and six months, and so parents often must undertake great costs to ensure their children are properly supported. During the pandemic, many parents did not have the capacity to cope with their children with these various needs. Eventually, various institutions like The Sam Sharpe Teachers' College in conjunction with the Kiwanis Club facilitated training for parents and caregivers supporting children with special needs (Jamaica Observer, 2022a).

Given these changing dynamics between the expectations of the former role of parents in education, it is not surprising that the "pandemic may serve as a tipping point" (Davidson and Hylton-Fraser, 2021, p. 15) wherein more is required from the parent just as it is required from the teacher. For some level of balance to be restored, however, management of change in crisis situations needs to be countered with enabling capacity to confront the nuances related to the cultural realities embedded within the context within which the change is occurring.

Discussion

In this section, the chapter returns to the conceptual framework to discuss the implications of the experience of Jamaican parent-educators who had to make sudden changes, whether or not they were prepared or equipped to change.

Managing change

Change is important because it opens new pathways to learning and creates different and improved ways of completing tasks, thus making life easier and more beneficial. Change also provides individuals with an opportunity to gain more education about how things function, which facilitates a greater level of adaptability in changing environments. As Lewin (1948) purports, "to bring about any change, the balance between the forces which maintain the social self-regulation at a given level has to be upset" (p. 47). As the chapter has articulated, COVID-19 upset the equilibrium which previously existed. Parent-educators, who were previously accustomed to a sort of separate existence from their children for several hours a day, no longer enjoyed that "luxury".

Although change is a gradual process, in many ways, the pandemic did not afford individuals an opportunity to take gradual steps towards changing either their attitudes towards education or the use of technology, for that matter. Neither did it allow parents the chance to gradually adjust to a 24-hour, seven-day-a-week existence with their children while also balancing the demands of their teaching role. As Kotter (1995) notes, "the change process goes through a series of phases that.... usually require a considerable length of time" (p. 59).

Unlike the linearity espoused in the ADKAR model, there was no time to communicate messages around an impending change which would segue to people having the desire to change. The pandemic, after all, was a crisis event. However, perhaps because of the abrupt nature of the change, individuals' level of awareness and desire for doing education differently was enhanced. Therefore, it is not surprising that changes were made. Simultaneously, though, there was resistance as parents and educators were forced to confront new ways of existing in their homes while managing their professional and personal responsibilities. They wrestled with new technologies and their own personal philosophy surrounding education.

Additionally, the nature of the change caused parents and educators to quickly recognize the kinds of adjustments that had to be made – they had little choice in the matter, especially after Jamaican schools were closed after March 13, 2020. The type, frequency, and quality of communication which ensued in the coming days and weeks left much to be desired, however. A critical part of reducing the negative impact of change is ensuring effective communication systems are in place. In fact, the ADKAR model asserts that communication is essential in creating awareness around change processes. Understandably, therefore, the system experienced even more instability.

Not surprisingly, better-resourced schools and households were able to make the required adjustments – a critical component of the ADKAR model which highlights the importance of supporting systems. Such schools already had learning management systems in place and established methods of communicating with their stakeholders. Those better-resourced homes had devices, reliable internet access, and parents (and even children) who were technologically savvy. Accordingly, parents' capacity to adjust and provide support for their child/ren was a more seamless process.

Capability

The pandemic created changes that were multidimensional and which required far more than designing procedures and planning steps (Purcell, 2002). Rather, it required the engagement of all stakeholders since inevitably they were affected most by the seeming instability. There was evidence that the MoEY and other public and private entities intervened to provide support through training for educators upon the realization that though parents and educators *desired* to do all they could for their students and children, their *knowledge* about how to help and their *ability* to do what was necessary, in some cases, was lacking.

Consequently, this lack of knowledge impacted their ability to make some of the required changes to facilitate effective online teaching and learning. Navigating *Google Classroom* or other online learning tools was challenging, monitoring class schedules while also teaching class was a struggle, as was reducing screen time, especially for younger children.

Parenting during the pandemic, particularly as an educator, was also against the background of a stratified Jamaican education system. Those parents in lower-income households had the added burden of low to no internet penetration, devices being shared among family members, and dealing with a loss of boundaries regarding communication from parents and administrators. These factors may have influenced their ability to engage with their children and render assistance with schoolwork.

Evidently, with more creative solutions from school leaders and the MoEY, the 2021 academic year reinforced the changes that had been made in the previous year. There was acceptance across the sector that schooling would continue remotely, and both parents and educators seemed to be more adept at implementing the strategies they had gained in the previous year. Seemingly, the invisible but far-reaching influence of deeply embedded cultural beliefs and practices was hard to break, and as all schools returned to face to face in September 2022, many Jamaican schools have reverted to pre-pandemic attitudes and practices.

A fundamental part of the ADKAR model is the implementation of accountability mechanisms that create sustained change. Sadly, those schools that can maintain hybrid learning systems may continue to surpass their counterparts. Ultimately, educators must take a proactive stance and accept the fact that they can no longer be passive in their approach to education; rather, they must seek ways in which to disrupt the status quo and contribute to the creation of schools in which all students have a chance at a quality education.

Moreover, there must be a conscious effort to recognize the strengths of individual students and create an environment in which each student is valued for their uniqueness and the contribution they can make to society.

In an increasingly complex, competitive, and challenging environment, the teacher must uphold core principles of social justice and equity and demonstrate a capacity for vision, entrepreneurial skills, instructional design, and crisis management (Scott and Webber, 2008). The pandemic has brought into sharper focus the need for parents and teachers to be greater collaborators in their children's learning process. Simultaneously, because of the work overload, there needs to be sustained effort at mental health support for educators, students, and families.

Cultural influences

Undoubtably, Jamaica's historical background, cultural, social, and political milieu are critical factors that have shaped its education system and its resulting practice. Therefore, how educators work towards a social model of learning that reduces barriers for students, creates multiple formats for learning material, and facilitates multiple ways of engagement must be prioritized. The pandemic highlighted a broken education system, which created a situation in which educators were converted into pawns rather than agents of change. This is problematic since the school *should* act as a bridge between home and society so that students are able to reap some level of success regardless of their background. Even more problematic were the blurred lines between roles for parent-educators and outmoded ways of "doing" education.

Furthermore, approaches to school leadership are constantly changing, particularly as global shifts occur which demand a new breed of leaders to respond effectively to those shifts. According to Sergiovanni (1984) "the net effect of the cultural force of leadership is to bond together students, teachers and others as believers in the work of the school" (p. 9).

Additionally, Theoharis and Causton-Theoharis (2008) note that a change in mindset can challenge the positionality of administrators as emancipators rather than oppressors so that schools become places in which *all* students succeed. This is more potent in a two-tiered education system such as Jamaica, which has traditionally benefitted some students over others. Consequently, this chapter makes recommendations aimed at creating the necessary structures within education systems that can help to improve quality and delivery for *all* persons, even in the face of instability.

Moreover, the authors recognize that such changes cannot be divorced from Jamaican cultural nuances regarding parenting and education. Culture impacts one's worldview and how knowledge is constructed. It will therefore influence one's practice and approaches to solving problems. Consequently, the interaction between culture and capabilities will determine how we respond to changes and are able to achieve homeostasis and restore some semblance of equilibrium to the education system.

Recommendations

The role of leadership

At the school level, principals are critical in ensuring that there is school reform and system transformation. As instructional leaders, they must focus on curriculum development and delivery, continuous staff development, and improvement of student outcomes; lend support for new policies within the education system; and liaise with parents and community members as a means of engaging them in any change process. Perhaps more critical is the need for social justice leadership across education systems. The pandemic highlighted the disparities between students, schools, and school systems. However, as Jamaica contemplates what is required to shift thinking and transform systems in a way that does not serve to further marginalize, leaders at all levels of the system must contemplate issues of equity. However, social justice leadership is inherently complex as it involves the consideration of multiple elements, so leaders are challenged to "engage in continuous praxis to keep these complex relationships in mind" (Lewis, 2016, p. 326).

Additionally, if schools are to remain relevant, leaders must ensure that they are adaptable to internal and external changes. Principals and teachers are change agents and can lead the transformation of the education system through the adjustment and improvement of curriculum and pedagogy, "aimed at promoting a democratic society and teaching the 'other'" (Ladson-Billings, 2001, p. 60). There is an urgent need to challenge the status quo, for leaders at the local level to be advocates for change and facilitators who confront the values and actions of their students, for continuous professional development aimed at increasing teacher readiness in inclusive and demanding settings, and for government not only to provide the requisite support but also to mobilize all stakeholders regarding the role of education in promoting social justice and teaching to the whole child.

Parent engagement and support

Research has already shown that parental involvement in a child's education is crucial to their academic outcomes. Regardless of the motivating factors which propel parents to be involved, the pandemic has forced us to think differently about how school systems engage parents and other stakeholders. Simultaneously, parents must be cognizant of old attitudes towards learning which they possess and find ways to either release or transform them to the benefit of their children. The pandemic taught many parents some hard lessons, but evidently, those who felt more capable were able to pivot more easily. The efforts at providing support for parents and teachers should be ongoing, as the recent exodus of teachers from the system signals that things cannot return to pre-pandemic realities. This approach could go a long way in ensuring sustained change, which would augur well for the entire Jamaican education system.

Conclusion

COVID-19 has arguably wrought a devastating blow on systems across the world, forcing people to make changes and respond quickly, even if they did not feel equipped to do so. This chapter has argued that parenting during the pandemic while balancing teaching/work responsibilities within the Jamaican context created a level of disequilibrium. However, it is critical that the COVID-19 crisis is perceived as an opportunity for radical change in values, attitudes, policies, practices, and systems. Moreover, Jamaican leaders and educators must not be afraid to "question existing paradigms" to "realign the education system by engaging all stakeholders in a great push to make education work for the future of Caribbean societies" (Smith, 2012, p. 26).

References

Altink, H. (2019). Public secrets: Race and colour in colonial and independent Jamaica. Liverpool: Liverpool University Press.

American Psychological Association (2022) *Parenting*. Available at: https://www.apa.org/topics/parenting (Accessed: 30 October 2022).

Barton, A. C., Drake, C., Perez, J.G., St.Louis, K. & George, M. (2004). Ecologies of parental engagement in urban education. *Educational Researcher*, 33(4), pp. 3–12. Available at https://doi.org/10.3102/0013189X033004003 (Accessed: 14 November 2022).

Bertheelsen, D., and Walker, S. (2008) Parents' involvement in their children's education. *Family Matters*, 79, pp. 34–41. Available at: https://search.informit.org/doi/10.3316/agispt.20091531.

Biddle, B. J., (1986). Recent developments in role theory. *Annual Review of Sociology*, 12, pp. 67–92.

Bourne, P. D., et al. (2015). The psychology of the Grade Six Achievement Test (G.S.A.T) in Jamaica. *Journal of Psychiatry*, 18(2), pp. 1–12. Available at: https://doi.org/10.4172/2378-5756.1000255 (Accessed: 31 May 2022).

Brown, L. H., and Beckett, K. S. (2007). Parent involvement in an alternative school for students at risk of educational failure. *Education and urban society*, 39(4), pp. 498–523.

Ceka, A., and Murati, R. (2016) The role of parents in the education of children. *Journal of Education and Practice*, 7(5), pp. 61–64.

Chung, G., Lanier, P., and Wong, P.Y.J. (2022) Mediating effects of parental stress on harsh parenting and parent-child relationship during coronavirus (COVID-19) pandemic in Singapore. *Journal of Family Violence*, 37(5), pp. 801–812. Available at: https://doi.org/10.1007/s10896-020-00200-1.

Cluver, L. et al. (2020) Parenting in a time of COVID-19. *The Lancet*, 395(10231), p. e64. Available at: https://doi.org/10.1016/S0140-6736(20)30736-4 (Accessed: 2 November 2022).

Connelly, F. M., & Clandinin, D. J. (1990). Stories of experience and narrative inquiry. *Educational Researcher*, 19(5), pp. 2–14. Available at: https://doi.org/10.3102/0013189X019005002 (Accessed: 14 November 2022).

Cooper, H. (1989). *Homework*. New York: Longman.

Dauber, S.L., and Epstein, J.L. (1993) Parents' attitudes and practices of involvement in inner-city elementary and middle schools. In N.F. Chavkin (Ed.), *Families and schools in a pluralistic society* (pp. 53–71). Albany: Sate University of New York Press.

Davidson P. M., and Hylton-Fraser K. (2021). Assessment, accountability, contextualization: Dilemmas in comparative education and educational leadership. In: English F., & English F. (Eds.), *The Palgrave Handbook of Educational Leadership and Management Discourse*. Palgrave Macmillan, Cham. Available at: https://doi.org/10.1007/978-3-030-39666-4_65-1.

Delgado-Gaitan, C. (1992). School matters in the Mexican-American home: Socializing children to education. *American Educational Research Journal*, 29(3), pp. 495–513.

Eccles, J.S., and Harold, R.D. (1993) Parent-school involvement during the early adolescent years. *Teachers College Record*, 94, pp. 568–587. Available at: http://doi.org/10.1177/016146819309400311.

European Union (2022). Jamaica: Multi-annual Indicative programme, 2021-2027. Available at: https://international-partnerships.ec.europa.eu/system/files/2022-01/mip-2021-c2021-9099-jamaica-annex_en.pdf (Accessed: 2 August 2023).

Haynes-Brown, T., Hordatt-Gentles, C., and Cole, S. (2021) Coping personally and professionally as a teacher during COVID-19. *Jamaica Gleaner*, January 17. Available at: https://jamaica-gleaner.com/article/art-leisure/20210117/coping-personally-and-professionally-teacher-during-covid-19 (Accessed: 10 November 2022).

Hibbert, K. (2020). Teachers share struggles of distance learning. *Jamaica Observer*, May 10. Available at: https://www.jamaicaobserver.com/news/teachers-share-struggles-of-distance-learning/ (Accessed: 2 August 2023).

Hickling-Hudson, A. (2015). Caribbean schooling and the social divide-what will it take to change neo-colonial education systems?. In Proceedings of the 59th Annual Comparative and International Education Society Conference (pp. 1–7). The Comparative and International Education Society (CIES).

Hoover-Dempsey, K., and Sandler, H. (1997) Why do parents become involved in their children's education? *Review of Educational Research*, 67(1), pp. 3–42. Available at: https://doi.org/10.2307/1170618.

Huang, Y., and Zhao, N. (2020) Generalized anxiety disorder, depressive symptoms and sleep quality during COVID-19 outbreak in China: A web-based cross-sectional survey. *Psychiatry Research*, 288, p. 112954. Available at: https://doi.org/10.1016/j.psychres.2020.112954.

Hylton K., and Hylton-Fraser, K. (2022). An evaluation of the "every child can learn, every child must learn" mantra's alignment with educational policies in Jamaica. *Equity in Education & Society*, 1(1), pp. 163–181. Available at: https://doi:10.1177/27526461211066497.

Jackson, D., and Heatherington, L. (2006). Young Jamaicans' attitudes toward mental illness: Experimental and demographic factors associated with social distance and stigmatizing opinions. *Journal of Community Psychology*, 34(5), pp. 563–576. Available at: https://doi.org/10.1002/jcop.20115 (Accessed: 14 November 2022).

Jackson Williams, D. (2012). Where do Jamaican adolescents turn for psychological help? *Child Youth Care Forum* 41, pp. 461–477. Available at: https://doi.org/10.1007/s10566-012-9177-7 (Accessed 12 November 2022).

Jamaica Education Transformation Commission (2021). *Reform of Education in Jamaica Report*. Kingston: MoEY.

Jamaica Gleaner. (2021) Teachers and parents are frustrated with online teaching. *Jamaica Gleaner*, October 4. Available at: https://jamaica-gleaner.com/article/esponsored/20211004/teachers-and-parents-are-frustrated-online-teaching#slideshow-0 (Accessed 10 November 2022).

Jamaica Gleaner. (2022) Cost of living in Jamaica among highest in Latam region. *Jamaica Gleaner*, September 9. Available at: https://jamaica-gleaner.com/article/business/20220909/cost-living-jamaica-among-highest-latam-region# (Accessed: 2 November 2022).

Jamaica Information Service. (2016) *National Parent-Teacher Association of Jamaica (NPTAJ) celebrates 10 years*. Available at: https://jis.gov.jm/national-parent-teacher-association-jamaica-nptaj-celebrates-10-years/ (Accessed: 2 November 2022).

Jamaica Observer. (2022a). Support for parents with special needs children. *Jamaica Observer*, April 10. Available at: https://www.jamaicaobserver.com/latest-news/support-for-parents-with-special-needs-children/. (Accessed: 2 August 2023).

Jamaica Observer. (2022b). Eight in eight days; two more teachers die in 24 hours. *Jamaica Observer*, May 19. Available at: https://www.jamaicaobserver.com/latest-news/8-in-8-days-two-more-teachers-die-in-24-hours/ (Accessed: May 30, 2022).

Jennings, Z. (2020). Social inclusion in education in the Commonwealth Caribbean. In R. Papa (Ed.), *Handbook on promoting social justice in education* (pp. 747–782). Cham: Springer.

Kotter, J.P. (1995) Leading change: Why transformation efforts fail. *Harvard Business Review*. Available at: https://hbr.org/1995/05/leading-change-why-transformation-efforts-fail-2 (Accessed 30 December 2022).

Ladson-Billings, G. (2001). *Crossing over to Canaan: The journey of new teachers in diverse classrooms*. San Francisco, CA: Jossey-Bass.

Lareau, A. (1987). Social class differences in family-school relationships: The importance of cultural capital. *Sociology of Education*, 60, pp. 73–85

Lareau, A., and Horvat, E. M. (1999). Moments of social inclusion and exclusion: Race, class, and cultural capital in family-school relationships. *Sociology of Education*, 72(1), pp. 37–53.

Lewin, K. (1943) Defining the field at a given time. *Psychological Review*, 50, pp. 293–310.

Lewin, K. (1948) *Resolving social conflicts*. New York: Harper & Row.

Lewis, K. (2016) Social justice leadership and inclusion: A genealogy. *Journal of Educational Administration and History*, 48(4), pp. 324–341.

Lyew, S. (2020) Pandemic parenting: Entertainers share their COVID-19 coping mechanisms. *Jamaica Gleaner*, April 8. Available at: https://jamaica-gleaner.com/article/entertainment/20200408/pandemic-parenting-entertainers-share-their-covid-19-coping#slideshow-0 (Accessed: 1 November 2022).

Menter, K., Ritchie, T., Ogg, J., Rogers, M., Shelleby, E.C., Santuzzi, A.M., and Wendel, M.J. (2022) Changes in parenting practices during the COVID-19 pandemic: Child behavior and mindful parenting as moderators. *School Psychology Review*, 51(2), pp. 132–149. Available at: https://doi.org/10.1080/2372966X.2020.1869497.

Merriam, S.B., and Tisdell, E.J. (2016). *Qualitative research: A guide to design and implementation* (4th edition). San Francisco, CA: Jossey-Bass.

Ministry of Education and Youth (MoEY). (2019). *Education statistics 2018-2019*. Kingston: MoEY.

Morelli, M., Cattelino, E., Baiocco, R., Trumello, C., Babore, A., Candelori, C., and Chirumbolo, A. (2020) Parents and children during the COVID-19 lockdown: The influence of parenting distress and parenting self-efficacy on children's emotional well-being. *Frontiers in Psychology*, pp. 1–10. Available at: https://doi.org/10.3389/fpsyg.2020.584645.

Murphy, J. (2022) Resource, parental shortfalls dampening morale, say teachers. *Jamaica Gleaner*, September 3. Available at: https://jamaica-gleaner.com/article/lead-stories/20220903/resource-parental-shortfalls-dampening-morale-say-teachers (Accessed: 2 November 2022).

Pierce M., Hope, H., Ford, T., Hatch, S., Hotopf, M., John, A., Kontopantelis, E., Webb, R. Wessely, S., McManus, S. & Abel, K.M. (2020) Mental health before and during the COVID-19 pandemic: A longitudinal probability sample survey of the UK population. *Lancet Psychiatry*, 7(10), pp. 883–892. Available at: https://doi.org/10.1016/s2215-0366(20)30308-4.

Purcell, L. (2002) Best practices in leading change. Presentation to Southern California SPIN, June 7, 2002.

Radio Jamaica. (2022) Teachers 'extremely frustrated' with indiscipline among students, June 8. Available at: http://radiojamaicanewsonline.com/local/teachers-extremely-frustrated-with-indiscipline-among-students (Accessed: 4 January, 2023).

Reynolds, A., and Clements, M. (2005) Parental involvement and children's school success. In E.N. Patrikakou, R.P. Weissberg, S. Redding, and H.J. Walberg (Eds.), *School-family partnerships: Promoting the social, emotional, and academic growth of children* (pp. 109–127). New York: Teachers College Press.

Ribeiro, L.M., Cunha, R.S., Silva, M.C.A., Carvalho, M., and Vital, M.L. (2021) Parental involvement during pandemic times: Challenges and opportunities. *Education Science*, 11(302), pp. 1–17. Available at: https://doi.org/10.3390/educsci11060302.

Roderique, T.W., Polloway, E.A., Cumblad, C., Epstein, M.H., and Bursuck, W.H. (1994) Homework: A survey of policies in the United States. *Journal of Learning Disabilities*, 27, pp. 481–487. Available at: https://doi.org/10.1177/002221949402700803.

Samms-Vaughan, M.E. (2006) *Children caught in the crossfire*. Kingston: Grace Kennedy Foundation.

Scott, S., and Webber, C. F. (2008) Evidence-based leadership development: The 4L framework. *Journal of Educational Administration*, 46(6), pp. 762–776.

Seaga, E. G. (2005) The folk roots of Jamaican cultural identity. *Caribbean Quarterly*, 51(2), pp. 79–95. https://doi.org/10.1080/00086495.2005.11672268.

Sergiovanni, T. J. (1984) Leadership and excellence in schooling. *Educational Leadership*, 41, pp. 4–13.

Sheldon, S. B. (2002) Parents' social networks and beliefs as predictors of parent involvement. *Elementary School Journal*, 102(4), pp. 301–316.

Shiel, R. (2020) *Young Jamaicans respond to domestic abuse in COVID-19*. Available at: https://www.unicef.org/jamaica/blog/young-jamaicans-respond-domestic-abuse-covid-19 (Accessed: 1 November 2022).

Smith, P.A. (2012) *Succession planning in London secondary schools: Implications for male African-Caribbean leaders*. MBA (Public Services) Dissertation, University of Warwick, Coventry, UK.

STATIN. (2013) *Population and housing census, 2011, Jamaica: Living conditions and household composition, Volume 11*. Kingston: Statistical Institute of Jamaica. Available at: https://census.statinja.gov.jm/wp-content/themes/futuriochild/Census2011Reports/Population%20and%20Housing%20Census%202011%20Jamaica%20Living%20Conditions%20and%20Household%20Composition%20Vol%2011.pdf (Accessed: 1 November 2022).

Storz, M. A. (2020). The COVID-19 pandemic: an unprecedented tragedy in the battle against childhood obesity. *Clinical and Experimental Pediatrics*, 63(12), p. 477.

Strauss, A. (1987) *Qualitative analysis for social scientists*. Cambridge: Cambridge University Press.

Theoharis, G., and Causton-Theoharis, J. (2008) Oppressors or emancipators: Critical dispositions for preparing inclusive school leaders. *Equity and Excellence in Education*, 41(2), pp. 230–246. Available at: https://doi.org/10.1080/10665680801973714.

Tuhiwai Smith, L. (2022). *Decolonizing methodologies* (3rd edition). London: Bloomsbury.

UNESCO. (2020). Education: From disruption to recovery. Available at: https://en.unesco.org/covid19/educationresponse (Accessed: 2 August 2023).

Wajdi, M. B. N., Iwan Kuswandi, Umar Al Faruq, Zulhijra, Z., Khairudin, K., & Khoiriyah, K. (2020). Education policy overcome coronavirus, a study of Indonesians. *EDUTEC: Journal of Education and Technology*, 3(2), pp. 96–106.

Walker, J. M. T., Wilkins, A. S., Dallaire, J. R., Sandler, H. M., & Hoover-Dempsey, K. V. (2005). Parental involvement: Model revision through scale development. *Elementary School Journal*, 106, pp. 85–104.

Williams, F. (2021) *What Jamaica is doing to end violence in schools*. Available at: https://www.unicef.org/jamaica/stories/what-jamaica-doing-end-violence-schools (Accessed: 2 November 2022).

World Bank. (2020) *Development projects: Jamaica early childhood development project*. Available at: https://projects.worldbank.org/en/projects-operations/project-detail/P095673?lang=en?cid=EXT_WBEmailShare_EXT (Accessed: 2 November 2022).

World Bank. (2023). The World Bank in Jamaica. Available at: https://www.worldbank.org/en/country/jamaica/overview#1 (Accessed: 2 August 2023).

11
STACKING STORIES AS INQUIRY INTO PRACTICE

Co-teaching an online literacy club for youth

Michelle A. Honeyford, Kelsey Collins-Kramble, and Jessica Neudorf-Wiebe

Story: the nervous leader

Creating a new experience for a group of teens can be overwhelming. There are so many questions:

What should the theme be? What types of activities should we do? Will they really enjoy that or are we just hoping they will? Will they come away gaining something new? Is it meaningful?

Now add on that we are doing this online, through Zoom—a platform quickly growing in popularity as we are all shifting and adapting and, dare I say, pivoting to this strange world the pandemic has forced upon us.

What activities can we adapt to this environment? Is it possible to build in multiple forms of engagement? Can we create experiences that get the participants up and moving? More importantly…how do we reach kids through a computer screen? How do we build community when we are all sitting in separate rooms, in separate buildings, on separate streets? How do we connect?

But wait… did we think about this *[email from a parent]*…"dyslexia…reading at a grade four level…**very worried about how her peers view her**…often afraid to try to read and write."

Did we build an experience that is welcoming for this participant? How do we make a meaningful reading and writing experience when we are unable to provide in-person support for our group? Are the books we plan to introduce going to be manageable? Do we have enough variety in our writing challenges and activities that we were planning? How do we make a space that is safe and encouraging for this participant to share their reading and writing?

Kelsey's internal monologue, "The nervous leader" conveys the excitement, uncertainty, possibility, concern, and doubt that swirled in and around us as we, a teacher educator and two teacher candidates, threw ourselves into designing an online writing and book club for a group of young teens in summer 2020. We wondered how meaningful a reading/writing club would be for youth in a summer leadership program; whether it would be possible to build a sense of belonging online; and if the novels and reading and writing invitations we had put together would appeal to a range of readers and writers. Posing these kinds of questions and exploring them together became an important part of our co-teaching practice. As Kelsey reflected:

Story: the nervous leader (continued)

I know what my first step is—it is reaching out to my team!

> I do not have to answer these questions alone. I have partners, collaborators, co-planners to bounce ideas off of. They may see solutions where I see questions and questions where I see solutions. They might take my ideas and strengthen them, improve them, build on them. I will do the same with their ideas. We are our own built-in support system. **We are a team**. And that makes this achievable and exciting, instead of overwhelming.

Our R/W/S Club collaboration grew from existing relationships: Jessica was a summer research assistant on a project Michelle was co-investigating related to the province's renewed English Language Arts (ELA) curriculum, and Kelsey was a project assistant for the writing project Michelle co-directs, having also been a student in Michelle's ELA methods course and practicum advisory cohort. Our conversations about literacy, curriculum, pedagogy, and assessment in those contexts were deep and far-ranging. In the year and a half since our R/W/S Club experience, the pandemic has continued to challenge and change us and our practice—in practicum and term teaching experiences in early years (Jessica) and middle years classrooms (Kelsey), and in literacies education courses and research (Michelle). We were eager to reconnect, revisit our experience in the Read/Write/Share Club (R/W/S Club), and re-engage with one another in professional inquiry and dialogue. But what might such an inquiry look like? How could we look back while also acknowledging our questions and experiences in this present moment? And what could we learn that would also move forward with us in our future practice?

In this chapter, we share what happened as we pursued these questions through a six-month inquiry, re-engaging with the data through methods of experimental writing—writing nomadically and open-endedly—(St. Pierre, 1997) and stacking stories (Burnett & Merchant, 2014, 2019, 2020), a method of writing stories in series through deep engagement with data and empirical materials. Like our experience co-teaching the R/W/S Club, this became a generative collaboration, with insights that have deepened and renewed our practice.

Co-teaching the Read/Write/Share Club

Story: a teacher's uncertainty; a co-planning strategy

A Google Doc as a guide. A Google Doc to share. We haven't done this before, but there's a first time for everything right? Today we will meet our students for our summer session and talk about how we can create an online community. *Community:* people wonder if it's possible at such a time as this. A pandemic. At a time when schools have shifted to online learning…. *Community* can seem like a beautiful word packaged for a later time when this is over. But here we are, preparing and envisioning an online community of summer students to R/W/S as they engage with one another and the books they read. Hope is our anchor as we dive into planning together. *Together:* yes, this is the beginning of community.

As with many things during the pandemic, the R/W/S Club was designed in response to the sudden need for online options as COVID restrictions threatened the summer leadership program planned for Grade 7–9 students in "Afterschool U."[1] When Afterschool U reached out to Michelle to ask about extending the Faculty of Education's participation into the summer months through providing an online experience, she contacted Kelsey and Jessica, who responded enthusiastically to the idea of co-planning and co-leading a book/writing club for the month of July.

We swiftly chose what felt like a relevant and open-ended theme for the Club, "What Matters Most," and nominated a short list of young adult novels that we selected for their diverse themes, characters, genres, plots, and relevance to the Winnipeg, Manitoba context—books written by authors who identify as mixed-race, Métis, and Cree, for example, about characters who dream to play basketball in a league that bans wearing a hijab; to become a jazz musician in a Guyanese Indian immigrant family with very different expectations; to learn to dance for the Pow Wow but keep it secret from the soccer team. The final list of nine Young Adult Literature choices included mystery novels, a futuristic dystopian novel, selections written in free verse, and a graphic novel. Many of our choices were available as e-books and audiobooks from the library, but we also used grant funds to purchase several copies of each book, and students' top two choices were delivered to their door by Afterschool U volunteers.

With choice and agency for readers and writers integral to our design, we generated a series of reading and writing challenges that R/W/S Club members could choose from, each exploring aspects of the "what matters most" theme. We posted these on Padlet along with the book selections and a curated list of tips for writers and readers. So that Afterschool U leaders could learn more about the Club, we hosted an information session, after which 15 students signed up. Throughout July, we hosted two sessions a week—a reading club on Mondays and a writing club on Wednesdays (1.5 h each). We organized a final meeting outdoors at a local park where we played games, took students on a poetry hike, read and celebrated our writing, announced the winners of our book awards, and presented each club member with a notebook, certificate, and their favorite R/W/S book to keep.

Perspectives and practices

Animating our work in the R/W/S Club—as we planned, debriefed, and as we inquired again into our R/W/S experience—is our belief in the possibility and potential of reading, writing, and sharing stories to build relationships, to listen to and learn from one another, and to engage with big questions about life, purpose, and our role—*Where do I come from? Who am I? Why am I here? Where am I going?* (Sinclair, 2016). We believe "all literatures matter," and that literature conveys

> what's important to a culture, the stories that are privileged and honoured, the narratives that people—often those in power, but also those resisting that power—believe to be central to their understanding of the world and their place in relation to it.
>
> *(Justice, 2018, p. 20)*

Stories have power and potential; they emerge out of lives, places, histories, cultures, and imaginations to *do* things. In other words, the texts we read, create, tell, and share are "not 'about' the world; rather, they are participants in the world" (Leander & Boldt, 2013, p. 25). With Leander and Boldt (2013) and others, we see the need for a philosophy of literacy "research and pedagogy as emergence" (p. 39), as they illustrate in the description of ten-year-old Lee's reading and play with two Japanese manga series on a Saturday. Lee surrounds himself with manga toys, costumes, and trading cards, acting things out while reading; playing games and watching cartoons; searching online for manga items; spending hours in manga fantasy play with a friend—reading and enacting scenes outside, drawing characters, and visiting fan sites. With abundant detail, Leander and Boldt point to how bodies, things, and affect come together, often in unexpected ways, and how literacy emerges through those relations, with multiple possibilities and potential.

Paying closer attention to materiality, affect, and the emergence of literacies can also contribute to better theorizing different kinds of classroom practice, forms of participation, and ways our pedagogies as educators might be reconfigured, reimagined, or transformed (Fenwick, 2012). Thinking about participation as including materials, objects, bodies, tools, and technologies, for instance, considers how "different forms of participation (and partial or non-participation)…are possible in holding together a practice" (Fenwick, 2012, p. 68) like an online discussion. This more expansive perspective suggests that as we reflect on our practice as teachers, we consider the innumerable and constantly changing dynamics at play in any and every moment. For us in the R/W/S Club, that included the moment-by-moment unfolding of activities in the virtual "Zoom room" as well as the dynamics at play in the spaces from which we and our club members were connecting. And, as Fenwick also reminds us, our locations also evoke how we feel positioned in relationship to practices (e.g., as insiders or outsiders)—practices like a timed writing prompt or an invitation to read aloud what we have written.

Thus, inquiring into practice and participation requires that we "see ourselves *inside pedagogy*" (Leander and Boldt, 2013, p. 42, italics in original), to consider how semiotic, discursive, and material forces may contribute to "change or dissolution of a practice" and to consider how different relations affect participation and learning (Fenwick, 2012, p. 68), including our own. As Kelsey compelled us to think about, for example, how using the chat function expands the time for a student to find the courage (and an older piece of writing) to share. And with Jessica's imaginative description of a club member in the Zoom waiting room, we wondered how our relations with students might begin before we even see and hear one another. We explore this further in the following sections.

An inquiry into our practice

Inquiry as stance is a theory of action, resistance, and knowledge that seeks the best interests of students and communities; centers the collective knowledge and intellectual capacity of practitioners; and assumes that the expertise needed to transform education emerges from teachers' interrogation of their own questions, theories, and practices as well as those of others (Cochran-Smith and Lytle, 2011). Inquiry as stance invites us to notice/think/wonder/feel inside pedagogy as "dynamic and fluid way[s] of knowing and being in the world of educational practice" that have the capacity to move/connect/relate across the space and time of "professional careers and educational settings" (Cochran-Smith and Lytle, 2011, p. 19).

Importantly, practitioner inquiry has the potential to contribute to the "creation of the *not yet* instead of the repetition of what *is*" (St. Pierre, 2019, p. 3) in educational research. As Lather and St. Pierre (2013) have described, post-qualitative research is a refusal—of representational and binary ways of thinking, of positivist and phenomenological ways of viewing the world, of privileging knowing over being, and of keeping language, the human, and the material largely separate from one another (pp. 629–630). Likewise, the limitations of humanist perspectives in education miss the potentialities of what *can be*. As Burnett and Merchant (2019) point out, "what isn't there, what has dispersed, and what has yet to come into being" is too "often disparaged, dismissed or simply missed" ("The problem with representation," para. 2). In our classrooms and in spaces like the R/W/S Club, inquiring into what comes to happen *and what doesn't* with/in/for our students is necessary if we wish to imagine and make possible the *not yet* and the *what can be*—if our research is to contribute knowledge beyond "apparent 'certainties' generated through an economy of testing, accountability and evidenced-based practice" ("The problem with representation," para. 2).

To be able to inquire into what is often ephemeral, elusive, felt, momentary, barely perceived, hidden, and emergent in assemblings of materials, things, and bodies in our teaching, practitioners need methods that can perform as "temporary structures"—able to move, morph, come, and go "while opening up new directions" (Koro-Ljungberg, 2016, p. xx). Experimental writing is a method of inquiry where the experience of writing and the texts that are produced are considered ongoing data collection (St. Pierre, 1995, 1997). Researchers use "text as a different kind of field" (St. Pierre, 1997, p. 408) for generating data, with the purpose of seeing and thinking differently. We hoped writing experimentally would open up new directions for inquiry into the R/W/S Club and also for our current practice. Nearing the end of another pandemic year, we were feeling somewhat worn out, depleted, stretched, and a little stuck, resonating with the idea that the "question of knowing if one *can* think differently than one thinks, and perceive differently than one sees, is absolutely necessary if one is to go on looking and reflecting at all" (Foucault, 1984/1985, p. 8, as cited in St. Pierre, 1997, p. 405; italics added for emphasis). Writing experimentally by stacking stories, writing stories with/from the data "and seeing what happens as they nudge up against one another—their continuities, contradictions and elisions" (p. 76)—generated new energy for us as practitioners. As methods for practitioner inquiry, experimental writing and stacking stories put our practice "in motion and under constant inquiry and questioning" (Koro-Ljungberg, 2016, p. xx). We describe our emergent process in the next couple sections.

Writing experimentally

Our collaboration leading up to the R/W/S Club and our planning and debriefing for each session generated all kinds of documentation. Data sources for this inquiry included a range of planning documents and communications, as well as student work and artifacts (see Table 11.1).

When we decided to re-engage in this inquiry, we approached it as a form of "wayfinding" (Ingold, 2007), working together to find our way in/with/alongside the data through writing. Applying the concept of wayfinding—from place to data—reminded us of our relations to the data, our "lived, inhabitant knowledge" of the data, and our need to "move mindfully

TABLE 11.1 Data sources, purpose, and examples

Data Source	Purpose and Description
Shared Google doc	*Planning space:* • Outline of plans for each workshop, with comments and resources
Google drive shared folder	*Creating and sharing documents:* • List of books and notes for selection process • Writing challenge ideas
Emails (internal)	*Making impromptu connections to:* • Share a resource, suggest ideas, and invite comment/response
Student questionnaires	*Learning from participants:* • Reading and writing interests, sampling of readerly/writerly activities (e.g., most recent book, best thing ever written), and goals
Padlet	*Providing an online hub for reading/writing resources and sharing:* • Summaries of books and author bios • Student writing challenge invitations • Resources for writing (samples created by leaders) • Responses to writing (by students and leaders) • Questions/FAQ
Program correspondence and feedback	*Engaging with RWS Club partners:* • Emails from parents, students, and partners (e.g., sharing a speech given by a participant about what they learned in the club)
Photos	*Celebrating moments:* • Zoom screenshots • Photos of in-person final meeting and celebration
Workshops	*Revisiting sessions:* • Two video recordings and saved chats
Writing	*Engaging and reflecting:* • Writing pieces created before, during, and after workshops • Teaching notes and observations • Reflective writing

alongside the nuances and interactivities of human and more-than-human" (McKenzie and Bieler, 2016, p. 67) in the data. To help us slow down and be attentive, we adapted the metacognitive Notice/Think/Wonder strategy that we have used in our classrooms, adding "Feel" to the frame and writing about what emerged through noticing, thinking, wondering, and feeling (and perhaps what did not). We met six times on Zoom and once in person for meetings that lasted anywhere from 1.5 h to a half-day. When we met, we shared our paths of movement (Ingold, 2007) with the data, referencing our notes, bits of writing, and specific moments in the data that were capturing our interest. As Michelle reflected on our first meeting in April:

> We were coming back to this; we were coming back together, re-connecting with one another. Kelsey and Jessica were in the midst of juggling the all-consuming responsibilities of their term positions near the end of an academic year that had been held (with some uncertainty at times) fully in person; I had just completed another online Afterschool U program with teacher candidates and was in the whirlwind of graduate progress reports. We needed to allow for conversation and dialogue about where we find ourselves now, and how that connects to what we are paying attention to—the noticings, insights, connections, and questions that are emerging. For Kelsey, silence in the R/W/S club became compelling in contrast to the loud energy of her current classroom; for Jessica, exploring ways of inviting and guiding younger children to engage with books and literature and meaningful writing was the slant; for me, an interest in this continues to be what I can learn about processes for collaborative professional inquiry that would be meaningful in a range of teaching and research contexts.

Our initial writings were quite descriptive and focused on sessions or particular activities, like our first introductory session with the student leaders. As Michelle wrote:

> "What matters most?" We ask. COVID has taken away so much, created so many concerns, introduced so many changes. We know so little about the lives of those whose names appear on the screen. We offer books, cover art, brief introductions to characters, conflicts, other adolescents' everyday routines, concerns, and relationships, events unfolding through significant challenges and changes....We wrap up this information session, with its invitations to get to know one another, write, have fun, build connections as readers. We have co-taught (if that's the right word) for the first time, taken turns facilitating, monitoring the chat, sharing, smiling, responding. We have imagined, planned, and as we say good-bye, we now hope there will be some who will press a button on a device and choose to join us next week.

We gravitated, in our writing and conversations, to instances that were readily recognizable as distinct events, like when we invited the youth to introduce themselves in that meeting by finding an object and writing about it. All three of us were inspired by various aspects of students' writing and sharing in that activity, and while it was a very predictable and defined place for our writing and inquiry to begin, we discussed what we were paying attention to and how, what might happen if we went back again with the questions we were raising about what had captured our interest and why, and to think about "what else"—what else was "going on too, engulfing these episodes, swirling in and out of them" (Burnett and Merchant, 2019, "Story 3," para. 1)?

Returning to the data after our conversations, Jessica shared that she found it helpful to repeat the question, "What do you notice, think, wonder, feel?" In fact, she wrote a piece, "The power of the question, 'What do you notice?'" that she shared in our subsequent research conversation:

> It's this constant...thinking about the strings of moments. We realize it's not so much about ourselves as teachers, but about what we are a part of with our students. It's about the unexpected...
> *the things of uncertainty lead to creation*
> *ideas, nuances, and the in-betweens*

Kelsey described how she was watching segments of Zoom video many times over, attempting to look differently each time so as to "avoid the obvious" (Burnett and Merchant, 2019, "Story 3," para. 2). She made an analogy to how the brain is able to block out the sight of our nose from our perception, even though it is constantly in our line of vision. As Kelsey described, "the more times I watched the same clip over and over, the more I stopped seeing the same things." While simple, our "notice, think, wonder, feel" frame drew us again to moments to ask "what *is happening*, and also...what *might happen/could have happened*" (Burnett and Merchant, 2020, p. 80, italics in original)?

But while we had spent significant time with the data, our writing felt flat, content to follow our noticing rather than step up and lead it—still comfortably representing rather than *re-presenting* (Burnett and Merchant, 2019). We returned to the approaches to stacking stories that Burnett and Merchant (2019) describe—playing with different points of view, narrative forms, and stages of a project—finding ourselves reading aloud their stories and becoming "wound" up in the assemblings as narratives and as craft for inquiry. How could we move from noticing the data to "storying and re-storying our data"? What orientations, perspectives, accounts, or forms might emerge in approaching the same scenes or learners (over time) playfully, letting go of the impulse "to unify or simplify" but instead add and complicate? ("Stacking stories," para. 4). Or, to take up Leander and Boldt's (2013) question,

"What happens when we consider literacy in 'and…and…and' relations" (p. 41)?

Stacking…and stacking stories

We created a shared document and began sharing drafts of our stories, each starting our own stack with three to four pieces. As we read and were inspired by each other's stories, we added to the stacks of one another. One stack was sub-divided into another (2 into 3). Table 11.2 provides a quick glance of the four-story stacks that emerged (36 pages). As well as perspective, the stories play with the format, genre (and mashups), mode, design, and semiotic systems.

In the meeting to share and discuss our stories, we posed the questions in Table 11.3. For each of us, writing the stories produced so much more than we anticipated—unexpected insights, connections to other data or to what was happening in our teaching, more questions, and new narrative forms— so we wanted to make time to share the "backstories" of our stories as well. In the discussion that follows, we highlight insights from our discussions of the "SummerTime Series" and "Opening Moments."

The SummerTime series

Stack 1 focused on SummerTime, a student who said little in the sessions (via text or mic) but whose contributions to the Padlet were some of the most memorable, particularly her Week 2 Challenge, a photo poem she wrote in response to our invitation to take a photo or paint/draw a picture to represent strength and perseverance. In "My Strength and Perseverance," SummerTime included two photos of herself in her Regalia with a poem that pays tribute to her mother for making it in honor of her spirit name as an Indigenous young woman. In her questionnaire, SummerTime shared that she enjoyed reading graphic novels, that her best writing to date was an essay and poem about her cat, and that her goal as a writer was to create a short graphic novel. Her first choice for the reading club was the graphic novel, *A Girl Called Echo (Vol 1, Pemmican Wars)* (2017), set in Winnipeg and written by Katherena Vermette, a poet, author, and Métis writer. On Padlet, SummerTime wrote about how she connected with Echo, remarking on their similarities, how she appreciated that the "story it tells is from history," told "in a way that makes it easy to understand, learn, and accept," and how the words connected to the "amazing" artwork (by illustrator Scott Henderson and colorist Donovan Yaciuk). When we invited the club to nominate the books they had read for awards, SummerTime nominated the graphic novel as "Most likely to become a motion picture," adding she thought it should be made into a short film and featured in a "Canadian Heritage Minute,"

TABLE 11.2 Stacking stories with R/W/S Club Data

Stack 1 SummerTime Series	Stack 2 Opening Moments	Stack 3 Introductions: A Hopeful Start	Stack 4 Silence Seen Again
"Four Readings: Message from Mom" (Re-presented email message)	"A Teacher's Uncertainty: A Co-Planning Strategy" (Reflective writing and excerpt from our shared planning doc)	"Perspectives of the Zoom Waiting Room" (A two-voice poem: teacher and student)	"What is Seen? What is Heard?" (Narrative)
"Across the Pages" (Imagined text conversation between SummerTime and Echo)	"Zoom Recording: On the Clock" (Time-stamped descriptive summary)	"What Are You Hoping to Get From This Group?" (Free verse poetry)	"The Chat Box" (Multimodal narrative essay)
"Children Are the Curriculum: One Student at a Time" (SummerTime: observations, notes, and reading/writing ideas)	"The File & The Muse" (Dramatic script)	"Notice, Think, Wonder: Welcoming Uncertainty & The In-Between" (Three-voice poem: student, text, and teacher)	"What About the Student?" (Provocation)
"Why Indigenous Young Adult Literature & Graphic Novels Matter" (A montage)	"Voice" (Soliloquy)		"The Collaborative Co-Teacher—My Thoughts in My Silence" (Reflective essay)
"My Echo: Why This Graphic Novel Matters to Me" (Imagined text-to-self conversation)	"The Chat Box and Tick Tocks: Lit!" (Recorded chat)		"Two Minute Scribbles" (Narrative)
"The Nervous Leader" (Internal monologue)	"Group Norms: Fridge Magnet Poetry" (List of most frequently used words)		
	"Norms by the Numbers" (Lists of numbers)		
	"Planning, Executing, Adapting—The Covert Leader Chat" (Hypothetical private chat)		

TABLE 11.3 Questions guiding our analysis

1. What data inspired you/caught your attention/pulled you/troubled you? Why?
2. How did the story come to be? What was your process? Thinking? What were you playing with/trying to do? What happened that you perhaps didn't expect or anticipate?
3. What does the story do? What does it make possible/visible/felt? What do you now notice, wonder, think, feel?
4. What is happening/unfolding as things/places/people come into relation?
5. What are we paying attention to? What happens when we unsettle our ways of noticing/knowing? What problems, questions, connections, fascinations, possibilities, potentialities emerge?
6. What relations are being nurtured or disrupted? What do we need to rethink, challenge, or pursue further? (Questions 4–6 adapted from Burnett & Merchant, 2020b)

a collection of bilingual short films featuring significant people, events, and stories in Canadian history.

The story stack is composed of five pieces, which include an email from SummerTime's mom describing SummerTime's complicated relationships with reading and the challenges reading posed for her socially, emotionally, and academically. SummerTime's mom also shared insights into her daughter's interests and qualities and outlined the kinds of supports that could contribute to her success as a reader. In this first story, the email is reproduced four times, each time emphasizing different words by increasing their font size, which creates four readings highlighting different aspects of SummerTime as a reader, learner, writer, and person. Another story, "Across the Pages," is a fictional text message conversation between SummerTime and Echo, written by playfully imagining a dialogue between the two by drawing upon SummerTime's questionnaire and Padlet contributions, along with the visual and written text of *A Girl Called Echo*. Also included in this stack is a story-in-a-table, a method of note-keeping for educators (jotting down quick notes from observations, conversations, and student's work) to support learning and assessment "one student at a time" (Gallagher and Kittle, 2018, p. 35). Inspired by the idea of "coaxing the brilliance" (Christensen, 2009) in every student and the dimensions of learning growth assessment framework in the Manitoba ELA curriculum (2020), the chart notes what we learn about SummerTime as a reader and writer from her contributions and submissions, with curricular ideas to expand and extend her learning and growth.

The initial stack also included a montage of quotes about "Why Indigenous Young Adult Literature and Graphic Novels Matter" inspired by SummerTime's writing and book choices (all written by and about Indigenous people), quotes from Indigenous writers and illustrators about the importance of Indigenous literatures, and an email from SummerTime's mom part way through the R/W/S club to let us know how much SummerTime was enjoying *A Girl Called Echo*. (The email inspired the idea to gift the club members with a book of their choice, as SummerTime had told her mom she wanted to keep the book *forever*). To this stack, Jessica added "My Echo: Why This Graphic Novel Matters to Me," an imagined series of text-to-self conversations exploring SummerTime's perspective at different moments of her participation in reading and writing club activities, including her hopes that Echo would find her "strength and perseverance" as she had. Kelsey wrote "The Nervous Leader," the internal monologue featured at the start of this chapter.

After reading aloud each piece and sharing the "writing stories" (Richardson, 1997) generated through/by our writing, we paused to consider what the story was doing thinking with the questions and concepts in Figure 11.1. Thus, our experimental writing opened a method of inquiry into the backstories of our writing, and our conversation created another "textual space" (St. Pierre, 1997, p. 408) for ongoing data collection. While we had planned for the stories to be the focal point of this chapter, the insights generated from our story conversations—exploring the creative and analytic processes of engaging with the data, with other stories, with texts, and with our current experiences—became more relevant for this purpose.

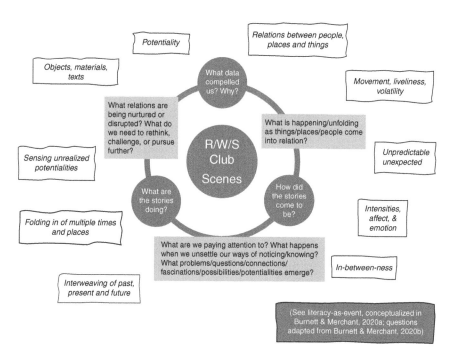

FIGURE 11.1 Questions and concepts in our conversations with stacking stories.

For Kelsey, the *SummerTime Series* drew attention to how teachers might re-evaluate the information that we are given about a learner and take a more holistic perspective in coming to know them as people. Given what seemed like just the "few little snippets" we knew about SummerTime, Michelle reflected on how it was quite astounding to see the snippets grow into 12 pages of documentation and how, in the process, "they weren't just bits anymore, they came into being in really interesting ways together." The documentation sparked the story writing, which in turn, Kelsey pointed out, contributed to making visible and feltfeeling the depth, breadth, independence, and transformation (the four dimensions of learning growth identified in the ELA curriculum framework) of SummerTime's language and literacy practices and identities as a reader, writer, and young Indigenous woman, even though the initial email from her mother and SummerTime's quietness in our sessions prompted some concern about whether the online environment would offer enough support and connections.

The stories in this series highlighted for us the potentiality of choice and agency in reading, writing, and sharing (i.e., what, when, and how); in the possibilities that emerge through assemblages of diverse texts whose characters, themes, images, and writing fire up affective intensities for readers; and in environments that are more conducive to sharing as things emerge and unfold (e.g., Padlet). Storying the data in these ways made more visible how affect produced new relations with/in/through SummerTime as a reader and writer. While such pedagogical moves in teaching language arts and literacy are not new, they have become all the more urgent for many of our students.

Further, allowing ourselves to stretch "beyond the 'evident'" as teachers and "into the realms of supposition and imagination" (Burnett and Merchant, 2019, "Stacking stories," para. 4) generated possibilities for transformation and change in our practice. Jessica, for example, felt compelled to consider the need to resist categories of assessment and think more holistically about her young students. Kelsey was generating ideas to expand the kinds of documentation she could use in middle and high school, where she already had a practice of keeping jot-notes of reading ideas for her students. She considered how adding quick notes emerging from observations, conversations, and artifacts would contribute to creating a body of "evidence of learning" that might include the more ephemeral, overlooked, or seemingly insignificant. Kelsey also wondered what students might point to as evidence of depth, breadth, independence, and transformation in their learning. What possibilities might emerge in stacking stories with students about their learning?

Opening moments

Stack 2 grew into the longest stack, initiated by several stories Jessica wrote about the 15 min or so we spent co-creating norms in our first R/W/S Club together. Given the limitations of space in this chapter, we cannot provide much more detail about the stories than is highlighted in Table 11.2, but our stacking of stories in this instance was an example of writing with different narrative forms and perspectives "to evoke the multiplicities" (Burnett and Merchant, 2019, "Stacking stories," para. 1) of co-creating norms, a participatory and collective practice common in Afterschool U and in many classrooms.

It was Jessica's intent to let the data speak for themselves. In putting excerpts from our planning document in juxtaposition with excerpts from the chat, for example, Jessica showed how the ideas we had as teachers were quite different from the norms suggested by the student leaders and reflected that perhaps what we set off to look for was too limited, something that we so often do as teachers. She included the Zoom chat verbatim to show how the conversation evolved and flowed as students gave ideas and suggestions. However, the chat alone, Jessica noted, did not show the complexity of all that was invisible, unheard, and happening in the cracks and in-betweens. While the task might seem simple and the gaps between the texts might be interpreted as times when nothing was happening, Jessica pointed out that

> even in the silence, you're not just waiting for them to speak, but you're trying to figure out the technology, you're trying to figure out if you are saying the right things, you're trying to figure out if maybe they can't hear you or maybe aren't sure how to unmute their microphones.

Thinking about silence as "grace space," as Jessica termed it, acknowledged that there was room for all of that, extended to everyone and everything—a compassionate, forgiving, and generative space for students and teachers where "you are not just positioned as the person knowing, but you also have this kind of vulnerability in *not knowing* what's all going to take place and happen."

The stories in this stack also explored Jessica's interest in voice. She reflected on how being told to "use your voice" or that "your voice matters" has almost become cliché, and that as someone who often prefers to be quiet, she sometimes feels that if she doesn't use her voice, she won't be noticed or people won't see the power that she has. In various contexts, we could agree that we have all felt "a little less heard if you're not speaking." But as Jessica pointed out, she loves to write, and the chat feature in Zoom inspired her to think about voice in different ways. In the story "Voice," Jessica wrote in first person as the voice, feeling ambivalent about being exercised in a different way through a chat conversation. She played with the initial frustration of the voice feeling disconnected from the actions of the body while simultaneously recognizing that it can be content to communicate through fingers/text instead.

Story: V o i c e

Ah, finally, I get to rest. I'm always waiting for you to use me, always curious what words you will use for my tones to dance and express, but now you are using your fingers to tap across keys rather than me to share your thoughts. Should I be jealous? Maybe furious? No, I feel content …. I see that you are using your words more. *Have faith in your abilities.* I always thought using me vocally was the way to show your capability, but I see now how you talk about the power of the pen. *Write for yourself, and not for others.* Could it be that resting your voice has given you a greater place to speak? The teacher asks a question. Your fingers continue to type quick and frequent responses. You're not using me vocally, but unequivocally, you are using me. I can feel it: the joy you have, I am dancing along with your fingertips, yet I feel at ease; there is a calmness about the way you share me. "Can we type?" you ask the teacher. In that moment, I know you feel strength and comfort in the way you express me through the keys.

Through the storying of these pieces, Jessica said the process also prompted her to wonder about how for these student leaders, the co-creation of norms was perhaps also viewed as an opportunity to encourage one another. In the context of the pandemic, messages of encouragement provided a way to connect. Referring to the "Norms by the Numbers" story that Michelle had added to the stack, Jessica suggested that perhaps one reason why particular students were so vocal was their desire to encourage one another and bring the group together.

Kelsey drew our attention to MysticRace, who was not the most vocal nor the first to share usually, but was the first to contribute to the chat and quickly followed his initial suggestion with a second one. We considered the significant variations in patterns/rhythms as we looked at when, how often, and how many words the student leaders volunteered, but we also considered the patterns and rhythms of listening, waiting, composing, and revising (perhaps multiple times before posting). We thought about affect as it relates to sharing—the needs and desires urging some to share as soon as something comes to mind and others to hold back. We considered how assemblings of technology, people, bandwidth, bodies, texts, and materials might open or close possibilities for participation—from the kinds of devices students might be on (and how that might impact the size of a keyboard or screen, the quality/presence of a microphone and speakers, how easy or difficult it might be to access various Zoom features), to what was happening around them at the moment (e.g., the level of noise and activity, what might be needing their attention). New questions also emerged from the data: How were the siblings in the club negotiating who got to write, and how were they mediating that? What sensations in this time and space were unfolding for leaders like SummerTime who didn't participate in the chat?

The relationship of silence and space also emerged as a potential for further inquiry, as Kelsey noticed she was not verbally present in the sharing and wished to explore her silence in a story: What was she worried about? What was she thinking about? Kelsey made connections to the awkwardness that silence seems to produce and the need we may feel in many social situations to fill silence. In thinking about classrooms, she wondered if that awkwardness interferes with providing ample time for students to prepare to share. As someone who really needed to think before they shared something, Kelsey said she was always passed by because she kept deliberating rather than sharing. Kelsey's story "The Chat Box" drew our attention to the fact that we were 12 min into our sharing time when MysticRace uploaded a piece he had written "a while ago" as an attachment in the chat and unmuted his mic to say, "I'll share." Would we have given students 12 min to share a quickwrite in a classroom? Kelsey asked. Yet, as Kelsey pointed out in her story, in all that is happening and unfolding, the movement of affect and emotion, relations and connections, the possibilities emerging and closing, that time "almost seems not enough."

Story: "Chat Box"

Twenty-six seconds. Less than half a minute. It doesn't seem like much time, but, in actuality, that is over 100 heartbeats or 1/3 of a song. It is enough time to write a grocery list or a short poem. In fact, when communicating verbally, we can say quite a bit in 26 seconds: 50 words on average. Twenty-six seconds is what it took for ten people to each share a single noun. In the moment, it felt like a particularly long time since we could not observe the process of the audience contemplating the question and forming a response—there was no body language to read. Instead, one must be patient in the silence and not be too quick to interrupt it out of discomfort. Twenty-six seconds to understand, consider, compose, and share. Viewed that way, it almost seems not enough.

Stacking stories as an ongoing practice in practitioner inquiry

Our collaborative inquiry talks back to research as a "subtractive process" by which "we view a scene, with an infinite number of moments, interactions, and possible rhizomatic lines, and we subtract from the scene all that makes the telling of a coherent post-hoc narrative difficult" (Leander and Boldt, 2013, p. 41). It is the complexity, multiplicity, and potential of small scenes from the R/W/S Club that have provoked our interest and imagination as practitioner researchers and, in this process, have reminded us that a subtractive story is a single story and a dangerous one (Adichie, 2009). We won't conclude with such a narrative either, but instead, consider how this experiment continues to move and change us, offering a few practices mindfully moving alongside us in the wayfinding of our ongoing work and practice.

Taking the "scenic" route

With a scenic perspective, we take in everything that is part of a scene—bodies, things, affect, texts—while realizing there is always more than we can see, feel, or imagine. Importantly, we can then see how we/our students/other humans are part of a larger assembling, an entangled coming together with various potentialities. From a scenic perspective, we can explore moment-by-moment what is happening, what might have happened, what emerges or gets produced, and what doesn't, what we noticed in the moment, what we didn't and why, what was opened, what was closed. A scenic perspective can make connections to multiple other scenes in different ways; as teachers, flexibly playing with "montages" of scenes together might help us in noticing, thinking, feeling, and wondering differently. This creates opportunities for teaching differently, for seeing different possibilities and potentialities.

Posing different kinds of questions

The kinds of questions we pose as we inquire into literacy and pedagogy also matter. The questions we have been thinking about remind us to consider what we are paying attention to and how—to what emerges when we unsettle our ways of noticing/knowing in relation to reading, writing, and sharing practices and spaces. Questioning what is happening/unfolding as things/bodies/emotions come into relation has expanded the ways we think about and notice literacy, as well as thinking about how we can bring things into a "composition of desire" (Deleuze and Guattari, 1987, p. 399) to produce meaningful literacy practices and engagements. Being attentive to the production of power in those relations, how/what relations are nurtured or disrupted, is also critical in this work, as is its ongoing nature—we are constantly in its flow and movement, considering what we need to rethink, challenge, or pursue further?

Writing creatively

Stacking stories as a method of practitioner inquiry enthused our love of writing again. In exploring those moments that attract our attention, we have been open to where the writing takes us, and we have enjoyed the process—the craft and play with genre and what it has produced. We've been reminded as language and literacy teachers of the importance of writing creatively ourselves. As Jessica pointed out, modes of professional writing (e.g., the constraints of writing parent emails and taking great care in presenting yourself as a first-year teacher to parents) can produce a bit of "writer's block." Being excited to pick up a journal and write creatively in relation to our practice jump-started other creative writing, made us feel like writers again, and contributed to "filling the well" again for other forms of professional communication, too.

Taking a relational perspective

Shifting from a representational to a relational perspective was an ongoing, but productive challenge. With the data, our conversations and writing, we continued to ask, "what else?" And there was always more. Writing, stacking, adding to, and then sharing our stories and engaging in the conversations they prompted was relational work—things moved, emerged, made themselves seen, disappeared, and took different form. Sharing the "origin" stories for each story in the stacks, we realized how many more were on the "cutting room floor," and how many others could be written. It has become all the more evident to us that there is never one story about a learner, never one story about a moment. In the same way that Massey (2005) has suggested that space might be redefined as the "simultaneity of stories-so-far" (p. 24, as cited in Leander and Boldt, p. 40), so we might say of our practice as teachers.

"What matters most?" We asked the student leaders in Afterschool U, and we continue to pose this question to ourselves. It's a question we need to take on and grapple with together, examining and questioning our beliefs and practices in ways that move toward differences and open up alternatives. As Short and Burke (2001) have argued, "Educators need to control their own inquiry so that they can ask questions that really matter in their lives as educators, just as students need to ask questions that are significant in their lives" (p. 39). In this moment, the simultaneity of stories-so-far all matter in the collective work needed to change our present and the future.

Note

1 Afterschool U is a long-standing university-community-school partnership that provides no-cost afterschool and summer programs for youth in Grades 5-12 on the campuses of the university. Through experiential programs offered by faculties, departments, and student organizations, mentorship, and scholarships, Afterschool U strives to break down barriers to accessing higher education

References

Adichie, C. N. (2009) The danger of a single story. TED. Available at: https://www.youtube.com/watch?v=D9Ihs241zeg.

Burnett, C., & Merchant, G. (2014) 'Points of view: reconceptualising literacies through an exploration of adult and child interactions in a virtual world', *Journal of Research in Reading*, 37(1), pp. 36–50.
Burnett, C., & Merchant, G. (2019) 'Stacking stories as method: research in early years' [author deposited version], available from Sheffield Hallam University Research Archive (SHURA) at: http://shura.shu.ac.uk/24923/.
Burnett, C., & Merchant, G. (2020) *Undoing the digital: sociomaterialism and literacy education*. London: Routledge.
Christensen, L. (2009) *Teaching for joy and justice: re-imagining the language arts classroom*. Milwaukee, WI: Rethinking Schools.
Cochran-Smith, M., & Lytle, S. (2011) 'Changing perspectives on practitioner research', *Learning Landscapes*, 4(2), pp. 17–23.
Deleuze, G., & Guattari, F. (1987) *A thousand plateaus: capitalism and schizophrenia* (B. Massumi, Trans.). Minneapolis: University of Minnesota Press.
Fenwick, T. (2012) 'Matterings of knowing and doing: sociomaterial approaches to understanding practice', In Hager, P. et al. (eds.) *Practice, learning and change: practice-theory perspectives on professional learning*. Singapore: Springer, pp. 67–83.
Foucault, M. (1985) *The history of sexuality: vol. 3: the care of the self* (R. Hurley, Trans.). New York: Vintage. (Original work published 1984).
Gallagher, K., & Kittle, P. (2018) *180 days: two teachers and the quest to engage and empower adolescents*. New York: Heinemann.
Justice, D. H. (2018) *Why Indigenous literatures matter*. Waterloo, ON: Wilfrid Laurier Press.
Ingold, T. (2007) *Lines: a brief history*. New York: Routledge.
Koro-Ljungberg, M. (2016) *Reconceptualizing qualitative research: methodologies without methodology*. Thousand Oaks, CA: SAGE Publications, Inc.
Lather, P., & St. Pierre, E. A. (2013) 'Post-qualitative research', *International Journal of Qualitative Studies in Education*, 26(6), pp. 629–633.
Leander, K., & Boldt, G. (2013) 'Rereading "a pedagogy of multiliteracies": bodies, texts, and emergence', *Journal of Literacy Research*, 45(1), pp. 22–46.
Manitoba Education (2020). *English language arts curriculum framework: a living document*. Available from: https://www.edu.gov.mb.ca/k12/cur/ela/framework/index.html.
Massey, D. (2005) *For space*. Thousand Oaks, CA: Sage.
McKenzie, M., & Bieler, A. (2016) *Critical education and sociomaterial practice: narration, place, and the social*. New York: Peter Lang.
Richardson, L. (1997) *Fields of play: constructing an academic life*. New Brunswick, NJ: Rutgers University Press.
Sinclair, M. (2016, March 22) 'An evening with Justice Murray Sinclair', *Re-visioning teacher education: responding to the TRC Calls to Action* (symposium). Winnipeg: University of Manitoba.
Short, K., & Burke, C. (2001) 'Curriculum as inquiry', In Boran, S., & Comber, B. (eds.) *Critiquing whole language and classroom inquiry*. Urbana, IL: National Council of Teachers of English, pp. 18–41.
St. Pierre, E. A. (1995) *Arts of existence: the construction of subjectivity in older, White southern women*. Unpublished doctoral dissertation, Ohio State University, Columbus.

St. Pierre, E. A. (1997) 'Circling the text: nomadic writing practices', *Qualitative Inquiry*, 3(4), pp. 403–417.

St. Pierre, E. A. (2019) 'Post qualitative inquiry in an ontology of immanence', *Qualitative Inquiry*, 25(1), pp. 3–16.

Vermette, K., Henderson, S., & Yaciuk, D. (2017) *A girl called Echo (vol 1, pemmican wars)*. Winnipeg: Highwater Press.

Reimaginings

New Ways of Teaching and Being a Teacher

12
WHAT THE COVID-19 PANDEMIC HAS TAUGHT US ABOUT BECOMING A TEACHER

Lessons for post-pandemic realities

Benjamin Luke Moorhouse and My C. Tiet

Introduction

The COVID-19 pandemic has been a destabilizing event. It has affected almost every aspect of human life in every corner of the globe. In education, the effects have been profound. At one point, during the pandemic, over one billion students, representing more than 98% of the world's population, were affected by government-mandated school closures initiated to reduce the spread of the virus (UNESCO, 2020). This was something very few people, including teachers, were prepared or trained for (Cutri et al., 2020). Teachers around the world were required to reconceptualize their role and practices as they were in a kind of 'survival mode' of teaching. They were learning on-the-spot how to shift modalities and stay connected with their students despite physical distances and personal challenges (Moorhouse & Kohnke, 2021).

The extreme instability and uncertainty of the pandemic period can provide us with important insights into becoming a teacher. First, it has reinforced the notion that 'being' a teacher, as part of a teacher's identity, is a dynamic construct that is unequivocally affected by personal as well as contextual factors (Pennington & Richards, 2016) and one which is continuously evolving and negotiated through experiences with those environmental changes (Sachs, 2005). Second, it has reminded us of the core role teachers ought to play in our communities: not just as disseminators of knowledge or assessors of skills, but as caretakers – someone whom children within their care can trust and get support from in challenging times.

However, it is often the concept of 'being a teacher' and the role of caretaker that can put a heavy toll on beginning teachers (Burrow et al., 2020).

DOI: 10.4324/9781003352129-16

Beginning teachers are teachers who have just graduated from ITE programmes and started working in schools (du Plessis & Sunde, 2017). They can spend years, training to become a teacher, yet the transition to the profession can be both exciting and overwhelming with many beginning teachers experiencing a 'reality shock' (Aspfors & Bondas, 2013). The 'sanitized' and 'safe' experiences they receive in their initial teacher education (ITE) programmes mean they can miss out on getting a full understanding of the complexities of teaching and feel they are 'missing' something when they are given responsibility over a group of students for the first time (du Plessis & Sunde, 2017). The sense of feeling ill-prepared and lacking required knowledge and skills has worsened under the COVID-19 pandemic realities (Moorhouse, 2021a, 2021b) – leading to active debates about the essential knowledge, skills, and attributes beginning teachers need to enter the profession and calls for change in how ITE programmes prepare pre-service teachers (PSTs) for the realities of teaching now and in the future. To date, many of these calls have related to the need for teachers to develop greater professional digital competence. Indeed, Benjamin (the first author) (e.g. Moorhouse et al., 2022) and many others (e.g. Diz-Otero et al., 2022; Kidd & Murray, 2022; Kohnke, 2022) have highlighted the knowledge and skills teachers need to use technology for teaching. However, in this chapter, we want to go beyond the often-discussed competencies needed for teaching and look at the 'soft skills' of teaching.

In this conceptual chapter, drawing on our own lived experiences as teachers and teacher educators, we argue that the pandemic has highlighted the need for beginning teachers to understand the personal and contextual factors associated with 'being' a teacher and are ready for their role as caretakers. The chapter begins by presenting the pre-pandemic ITE landscape in Hong Kong, where both of us are situated. This is followed by a reflection on our lived experiences during the pandemic and how it led us to question our previous practices and ITE generally. Finally, we propose three interrelated pedagogical priorities for teacher education in the post-pandemic realities: (1) pedagogy of care (and self-care); (2) pedagogy of autonomy and partnership; and (3) pedagogy of reflective practice. We suggest that a focus on these pedagogies is essential in a post-pandemic world in which beginning teachers could be teaching in increasingly diverse, rapidly changing, complex, and digitally infused environments (Moorhouse, 2021a). We argue that it is often times of crisis that provide us with opportunities to re-examine and reconsider alternative ways of being, thinking, doing, and relating.

Pre-pandemic realities

We have been involved in education, both as primary school teachers, and more recently as teacher educators for over fifteen years. We feel lucky to have experienced teacher education as students, mentors, and teacher educators and feel this has helped us relate to our students' lived experiences as they move through their ITE. However, we have also faced many internal struggles trying to understand the role of teacher education and consider what the PSTs under our guidance need in terms of skills, knowledge, and attributes to be 'workplace ready' (Clark & Newberry, 2019) or even understand what 'workplace ready' means at all. We were keenly aware of the need to prepare teachers for the reality of schooling, but also felt a responsibility to help them imagine and consider other, hopefully better, ways of thinking about education and the concept of a teacher. But how can we address these aims? And if we do not know what graduates need to be workplace ready, how can we know what they need for an imagined reality?

These internal struggles have been exacerbated by the teaching and ITE environment we found ourselves in during the pre-pandemic years. In Hong Kong, ITE is offered in three different modes: Full-time Postgraduate Diploma of Education (F/T PGDE), Part-time Postgraduate Diploma of Education (P/T PGDE), and Full-time Bachelor of Education (BEd). The F/T PGDE is conducted over one academic year, and the P/T PGDE spans over two years and is designed for in-service teachers who are permitted to teach but not yet qualified teachers. The BEd is conducted over five years usually in combination with a subject-specific degree (e.g. a BEd and Bachelor of Arts in English), creating a double degree. Each programme involves taught courses and professional practicums in schools. Each focusses on teaching subject specialists for either primary and/or secondary school contexts.

Due to the subject-specific nature of teaching in both Hong Kong primary and secondary schools, all the programmes placed great emphasis on knowledge and skills development focussing on learning and demonstrating subject-specific teaching competencies. As teacher-educators focussed on English-language education, our curriculum, and teaching aimed to develop English-language pedagogical content knowledge (PCK). When we observed students during their professional teaching practicum (a period of time PSTs spend teaching in schools during their ITE), we were primarily concerned with how they implemented the knowledge in practice. While broader social, political, and cultural issues in education (e.g. aims of education, social justice and equity, global education, teacher development, etc.) are explored, their emphasis remains relatively peripheral compared to the prioritized focus on PCK. Fundamentally, we were preparing our students to be 'English-language teachers' *first* and 'teachers' second. This is a common focus of ITE (De Costa & Norton, 2017).

We believe this does not reflect the realities that our graduates experience when they become teachers. Pedagogical competence may aid PSTs to face the initial reality shock of teaching, but we believe it alone cannot sustain teachers' efforts as they tackle ongoing challenges and negotiations needed throughout their careers nor is it enough to reap job satisfaction. Often when we talk to graduates, their main concerns and challenges but also rewards and satisfactions are not about their students' language development or academic performance, but rather about the rapport and relationships they build in their classrooms. It is the relational aspect of teaching that both drives them forward and holds them back (Cochran-Smith, 2003). Teachers who struggle with this can feel frustrated and unmotivated, while those who succeed often feel personally and professionally fulfiled.

As teacher education in Hong Kong is positioned within universities, programmes and processes are generally based on academic norms where 'fairness' is a core value. What we mean is, our programmes focussed on maintaining 'equality' and not 'equity'. Students were treated the same regardless of their specific backgrounds, needs, and interests. Each course is given a credit weighting, and once students pass a course, they can move on to the next course in their programme of study. All courses are measured by objectives and quantifiable outcomes (Ball, 2004). While this leads to efficiency and clarity in practices, it can equally lead to standardization of practices and assessment tasks that can benefit certain learners over others – neglecting to consider students' individual needs. Moreover, it can cause teacher educators to design courses and teach content that can be more easily assessed, such as knowledge and technical teaching skills, and neglect less tangible but important attributes or soft skills, such as 'care.' It can also mean that students move on to a subsequent course even if they get a marginal pass in their courses. When our programmes and processes are structured in this way, our PSTs can develop misconceptions about 'good' practices and fail to gain a deeper and more holistic understanding of their development as teachers over time.

In our classrooms, while we were aware of the issues evident in our context, we succumbed to them. Our courses prioritized the development of PCK, and we assessed our students against programme and course outcomes. As much as we made efforts to build rapport and show care for our students, we did it in a 'taken for granted' way without explicit thought into what we were doing nor why (Moorhouse & Tiet, 2021). Although we emphasized reflective practice in our teaching, we too felt bound by our role and context, which seem to have prevented us from moving our teaching forward. Then in 2020, the pandemic descended on us. It disrupted the status quo (Shoffner & Webb, 2022) and created an impetus to look at ourselves and our context in a new light.

Pandemic realities

Before the pandemic, the 2019-2020 academic year had already been a challenging one for Hong Kong. The academic year started in September during widespread civil unrest triggered by the now-suspended '2019 Hong Kong extradition bill' which led to campus occupations and the suspension of face-to-face classes in mid-November 2019. Face-to-face classes resumed in January 2020, only to be suspended again in February 2020 due to the rapid spread of the virus (Zhao, 2020). Despite weathering the early protest-induced disruptions, and the psychological effect it had on us and everyone living in Hong Kong, we were still not prepared for the COVID-19 pandemic. As if with a wave of a wand, the virus brought about a sudden psychological and pedagogical disruption, unlike anything either of us had ever experienced before, which instantly levelled the playing field for *all* educators alike. Besides PSTs, long-time veteran teachers were also confronted with a COVID-induced 'reality shock' which thrusted us into a 'survival mode' of compulsory online teaching. In Hong Kong, the government initiated a policy entitled 'Suspend classes without suspending learning' (Yeung, 2020), which required teachers at all levels to find ways to continue to support student learning remotely. Years of experience did not do much to prepare teachers (Moorhouse & Wong, 2022) or ourselves for the unprecedented impact of the pandemic. We as teacher educators also felt lost and insecure. In hindsight, it was a combination of contextual (i.e. an incidental increase of teacher autonomy within our institutions) and personal factors (i.e. our commitment to a pedagogy of care) which grounded and guided us through the volatility of unsettling changes.

Contextually, the day-to-day uncertainties destabilized administrative processes and infrastructure in businesses, organizations, and institutions (Yang & Huang, 2021). In the two higher education institutions in which we worked, the prolonged disruption of the pandemic seems to have loosened entrenched practices and ruffled existing hierarchical relations. Systems in place proved inadequate to promptly and effectively deal with the sudden and incessant changes. This situation opened up space and provided legitimacy for more agency from teachers and students. The unprecedented situation led teachers to be asked to assess students' realm of needs (i.e. academic, social, emotional, psychological, access to e-learning resources, etc.) and propose coping measures and solutions. We welcomed these more encompassing considerations of our students' needs as they better align with our view of ourselves as caretakers and teachers. During normal times, executing duties of our professional role may not necessarily agree with our own personal beliefs and philosophy in education (Argyris & Schon, 1974). However, the pandemic thwarted institutional enforcement of traditionally held expectations of our teacher role, thus affording a degree of autonomy for us to exercise our own subjectivity and decision-making in response to it in the workplace. We found greater space to be the kind of teacher we wanted to be. Arguably, this reduced managerialism was a blessing in disguise and made possible the merging of our teacher *role* and *identity*. While our teacher role subjects us to the situated responsibilities and accountability in our organizations (De Vries et al., 2014; Valli & Buese, 2007), our teacher beliefs exert some degree of agency towards influencing the way we conceive and enact our classroom practice (Danielewicz, 2001; Eccles, 2009). In this way, our beliefs of our role as caretakers put us in a better position to capitalize on emerging opportunities to prioritize such relational aspects of our teaching.

Besides the permitting institutional context, the needed response to the 'reality shock' was happening on an individual level as well. Educators all over the world were suddenly overwhelmed by the global predicament which made planning for instruction and learning difficult. A look around the many existing resources seemed futile as they were not fitful for the current situation at hand. The learning outcomes in course syllabi provided little guidance on how we could provide care for our students and be responsive to their needs remotely. In Hong Kong, higher education teachers were highly recommended to teach our classes synchronously online through video-conferencing software (e.g. Zoom). At the onset, we certainly were not equipped or ready for this unfamiliar mode (Moorhouse & Tiet, 2021). Our past reliance on our daily face-to-face interactions with students (e.g. showing up to class with a smile, being well-prepared for class, showing patience in answering students' questions, exercising compassion to change an assignment deadline, etc.) as adequate manifestations of care led us into false content. It prevented us from critically evaluating the pedagogy of care in our practice and continually exploring what it entails or alternative forms it could be embodied. It came to our realization that many professional hours were spent improving course content, delivery, and assessments, yet relatively little time was allocated to this supposedly prized aspect of our work. So, when the pandemic came, we too experienced a crisis with our own professional identity, leaving us ill-prepared to address this core component of care in our role as teachers.

In the hopes of providing more stability to our students, we felt obligated to teach with a forced sense of normalcy. However, it did not take long for us to notice that it was not 'business as usual'. The pandemic was more than a health emergency; it was a social and emotional one as well (Mehrotra, 2021). Enacting the pedagogy of care at the time seemed to require us to be transparent and candid with our students, revealing our vulnerabilities to them as well as acknowledging theirs. Whether or not we could identify and define the type of care our students needed, we found ways to *practice* and *express* it so our students can *feel* it. We experimented with different instruction delivery modes, adjusted ways of assessing, attempted innovations to 'humanize' the synchronous online classroom, and attempted various digital tools to help us connect and communicate with our students in hopes to let our teacher presence and care be felt (Moorhouse & Tiet, 2021; Moorhouse & Wong, 2022). Although our experimentations were ad hoc and imperfect, it felt 'perfect' enough at the time as we believed that every little bit of care had to be prioritized above all. It was like steering a ship through a storm without the full knowledge of how to do so. Yet unexpectedly, the messy tortuous process provided interesting insights on the bilateral relationship between teacher identity and teacher actions.

During the pandemic, we did not have enough time to think too thoroughly about what to do, how to teach, and respond to our students. It was not feasible to ponder about the situation, gain a sufficient understanding of what we were confronting, and plan adequately before we act. Such extent and intentions of proactivity were not plausible. We had to react and react quickly as best as we could. The abrupt change of teaching mode had us so busy that we felt like we were not prioritizing pedagogy of care, but subverting it to more urgent and practical concerns of teaching, such as appropriating the course content for the online mode, making lecture videos for asynchronous learning, setting up expeditious communication channels with students for possible short-notice changes, etc. We wanted to care but did not feel we had the time to do so, let alone intentionally or proactively plan for it. Paradoxically, for some reason, our actions exuded a sense of care and our students responded favourably to what we did.

This made us think that our personal belief of what a 'good teacher' should be was at work without us even knowing. The 'doing' was initially guided by a subconscious 'knowing', and the actions forged realities that subsequently helped reinforce our narratives as teachers (conscious 'knowing'). In a way, the 'doing' without the fully aware and complete 'knowing' can be effective in clarifying and reinforcing the conscious 'knowing' of one's teacher identity. Traditionally, teacher action is deemed as a way to express one's own teacher identity, implying that the 'knowing' comes before the 'doing'. However, our experiences seem to suggest that the 'doing' could precede and feed into the conscious 'knowing', especially in uncertain times when complete 'knowing' might not be possible. The seemingly undeliberate 'doing' was in fact intuitively deliberate, guided by our underlying beliefs of who we are ourselves as caretakers first and teachers second.

If nothing else, the pandemic has educated us to rethink, recognize, and reorient our priorities in our professional as well as personal lives. In the absence of crisis, there is a tendency to savour the comfort of maintaining the status quo and cater to urgent matters over important ones. Lives may be lived and things may be done as if there are still many tomorrows. But what if tomorrow never comes? Then, there is a need to live and act truthfully and vigorously now! As teacher educators, we need to revitalize the essence and soul of what it means to 'be' a teacher – the passion, connectivity, and meaning associated with our work. How might we strive to achieve this in the post-pandemic world?

Post-pandemic 'Imagined' realities and priorities

Our experiences and our reflections on our experiences have taught us that we need to think again about the ways we are preparing teachers for the field. While we acknowledge the value of equipping PSTs with the knowledge and skills needed to teach their subject specialism, we hope to convince ITE providers, education department officials, and teacher educators that an overemphasis on PCK may not adequately prepare PSTs for their role as teachers. We feel they need to be 'teachers' first and 'subject specialists' second. The focus should be on preparing them to be caring, autonomous, and reflective professionals who can respond to the psychological and holistic needs and development of their students. To do this, we feel that teacher education should be reorientated and structured around three interrelated pedagogical priorities: (1) pedagogy of care (and self-care); (2) pedagogy of autonomy and partnership; and (3) pedagogy of reflective practice.

Pedagogy of care (and self-care)

The basic premise of a 'pedagogy of care' is that we place care of others and ourselves (self-care) as central to our ITE programmes and teaching practices (Nicol et al., 2010). First, we need to recognize that we are caretakers – a central tenet of being a teacher is to care for our students. Through this, we can model the kind of care we wish our students to show to their students. This means that when we design programmes, courses, learning activities, and assessments, we need to look at them through our students' eyes. Second, we need to understand that 'care' may seem to come naturally to many teachers and teacher educators, but it is likely a learned behaviour, something, developed over time that requires ongoing reinforcement through shared experiences with learners. It is an openness to understanding why and how our learners may act or feel a certain thing that can help us 'care'. Third, we need to remember that integral to pedagogy of care is self-care. Teachers and teacher educators can struggle to 'switch off' and look after themselves. There can be an inherent feeling of guilt if a message from a student does not get an instant response from us, or we do not mark something straight away. However, learning how to look after ourselves and building our awareness of our own psychological well-being is crucial. By understanding our own needs and developing strategies to care for ourselves, we can better care for others. Indeed, a key piece of advice from a group of newly qualified Hong Kong teachers who graduated from ITE in 2020 suggested that taking care of our own mental well-being should be a priority. As this teacher stated:

> Take care of your mental well-being. Don't put all of yourself into work only because it will only stress you out and you will not get joy out of the things you do. It is okay to take a break.
> *(Moorhouse, 2021b, p. 2)*

Care has long been assumed as an integral part of 'being' a teacher. However, how this humanistic and relational teacher quality is conceptualized and incorporated into teachers' professional identity is still very much work-in-progress. In pre-COVID times, it was an agenda subverted to other initiatives that dealt with more tangible, observable, and measurable aspects of teacher practice. Pedagogy of care was deemed essential and important, but lacked the perceived urgency to be prioritized or properly entertained. To this end, we argue that the pandemic is a blessing in disguise to teacher education in a sense that it made way for uncomfortable yet important dialogues about teacher identity and the role of care in the profession (Shoffner & Webb, 2022). The pandemic has brought to the forefront the pedagogy of care as a taken-for-granted concept in pre-COVID times with daily face-to-face instruction. Such a realization permitted and fostered individual agency to take a more active role in reconceptualizing pedagogy of care during the uncertain times. More importantly, it invited teachers' experimentation with how it could be implemented and manifested in one's practice. And ironically, it is this seemingly haphazard hodgepodge experimentation that brought clarity to the ambiguous construct of care in teachers' work.

Teaching is both a science and an art that necessarily involves instructional as well as relational responsibilities. While the scientific aspect of teachers' work involving the more explicit 'harder skills' (i.e. subject and pedagogical content knowledge) is readily found in teacher professional qualifications, the more artistic intangible aspects of 'being' a teacher (i.e. dispositional and emotional competence) are rather difficult to define and less obviously stated in professional teaching standards. These 'softer' expectations are assumed to be conveniently embedded in broader classroom practice guidelines, such as cultivating a positive caring learning environment, supporting student learning, attending to students' social and emotional needs, etc. However, teachers' acquisitions of them are left to individual discretion and capabilities than a required professional goal pursuit (O'Connor, 2008). Furthermore, these 'soft' affective competencies are rarely explained in terms of *how* teachers could go about developing and negotiating them into their professional identity for their particular classroom realities which may prevent or hinder their enactment in practice. Over the years, different scholars have brought these important skills to the forefront, for example, Schon's (1983, 1987) notion of teacher intuition, Hostetler's (2016) case of teachers' perceptual 'ethical insights', and Korthagen's (2017) call for a more holistic 'professional development 3.0' version which goes beyond mere teacher competencies (e.g. classroom management, lesson planning, assessment, etc.) to account for the relational, affective, and character traits of being a teacher (e.g. relatedness, creativity, courage, kindness, humour, honesty, love, etc). Still, the artistry of teaching seems to remain under-explored and under-utilized to guide teacher training and professional development in ITE programmes. There is a need to not just create, but prioritize constructive dialogues that contribute to a common language which we can use to explicate this more tacit yet equally powerful teacher skill set.

Pedagogy of autonomy and partnership

The pandemic has reminded us that stability is not inevitable and we need to be prepared for different eventualities. It seems very few of us were in 2020. Of course, teacher education cannot prepare students for every eventuality (Goodwin, 2010). Nonetheless, we can build and normalize a culture that respects individuality and capitalizes on the collective wisdom and support from the community. The two together can better prepare our students to be able to respond to possible eventualities. Thus, the need to prioritise a pedagogy of autonomy and partnership in our practices is deemed essential.

Teacher autonomy is understood as the degree of freedom teachers have to develop and implement practices to meet the needs of their learners (Benson, 2010; Parker, 2015). However, to be able to act on the autonomy afforded, teachers need the ability to critically reflect and engage in evidence-based decision-making and independent actions. Autonomous teachers are able to assume responsibility for the purpose, content, method of their teaching, as well as being able to monitor their learners' progress and evaluate outcomes. To cultivate teacher autonomy, we can draw on theories pertaining to learner autonomy as by developing our PSTs autonomy, we can prepare them with the skills and knowledge needed to be autonomous teachers. Huang and Benson (2013) explain that learner autonomy can be understood as a learners' desire or motivation to take an active role in their learning (i.e. they need to want to have a role over their own learning); their ability to take an active role in their learning (i.e. they need the knowledge and skills needed to engage in autonomous learning); and the freedom to do so (i.e. they need time and space to engage in active learning). Hence, a pedagogy of autonomy prioritizes the development of these capacities. For example, PSTs can be encouraged to develop their own development goals, design plans to help them achieve them, and monitor their progress towards them. Teachers can support PSTs' ability by modelling and providing space and opportunities for students to take greater ownership of their learning.

Importantly, a pedagogy of autonomy requires the need for a community or at least an 'other' where we can find support, guidance, mutual understanding, and critical friends. This is why we suggest that 'autonomy' and 'partnership' need to be seen as *one* pedagogical priority. As dichotomous as the two might seem, they complement each other and work in synergy. A collaborative partnership with colleagues, students, parents, and other key stakeholders allows teachers to position themselves within a larger system with shared common aims but with different, yet equal, contributions. A partnership allows for co-construction and co-accountability. It also allows for the pooling of strengths and the support of weaknesses. In teacher education, we can implement the principles of partnership by involving students in different levels of decision-making, curriculum design, learning activity preparation, and assessment practices. Through these kinds of partnerships, PSTs can gain autonomous learning abilities and an awareness of the value close partnerships with students and others can provide. Personally, we found the partnership we forged during the pandemic sustained us and allowed us to tackle the challenges of the time (Moorhouse & Tiet, 2021).

Pedagogy of reflective practice

It can be seen from this chapter that reflection is very important to us. The ability to reflect on our lived experiences allows us to better understand ourselves and our actions leading to continuous adaptation and learning. As Grayling (2003) argues, 'the best thing any education can bequeath is the habit of reflection and questioning' (p.179). Obviously, the focus on reflective practice and calls for it to be included in teacher education are not new. We regularly included reflective tasks in our courses and professional practicum. But looking back, the reflective tasks were more performative than developmental in nature and neglected some of the complexities of 'real' reflective practice.

We propose that reflection be integrated in ITE in such a way that is more developmental, dispositional, and personalized to the individual PST's identity formation equips them with emotional resilience for the workplace and offers a tool to facilitate long-term professional growth. To do that, reflection needs to take into account and address the cognitive *and* emotional demands of teaching. Dewey (1933) is widely credited for highlighting the importance of experiential learning and reflective thought as the 'sole method of escape from the purely impulsive or purely routine action' (p.15). Compared to his ideas on the cognitive processes of reflection, the affective aspects mentioned in his work (i.e. 'wholeheartedness' and 'open-mindedness') received slower attention. This resulted in an initial cognitive-domain-dominated construct of reflection which was later balanced by more exploration and increased awareness of the affective features operant in the reflective process. Thus, teacher reflection involves *both* cognitive and affective capabilities (Day & Leitch, 2001; Tiet, 2019; Zembylas, 2014).

For reflection to not merely be used as an evaluative thinking tool to examine practice, it is vital to help PSTs develop affective and dispositional capabilities to welcome and invite reflection. Reflection is in fact uncomfortable to the mind (cognition) and heart (affect) because it necessarily involves a disruption (state of disequilibrium) to what one is thinking and feeling. It is cognitively uncomfortable as one grapples with 'new' noticings which may not fit nicely into one's existing knowing (Rodgers, 2002). These 'other' thoughts and ideas create distance from one's usual way of thinking and viewing to trigger a cognitive impetus (dissonance) for reflection to take place. Affectively, teachers may encounter conflicts between their beliefs and actions in the workplace which result in a tug of war between their personal 'self' and professional 'self'. Such internal struggle of the selves summons reflection as a narrative tool to reconcile and find meaning in what one does, thinks, and acts with respect to one's internal self (Tiet, 2019). In this way, reflection can help PSTs become critical reflective thinkers equipped with the emotional resiliency to confront the complex social, moral, and ethical nature of teachers' work.

Affective capabilities of reflection also entail our ability to continually reflect and adapt ourselves to meet the needs of the changes of our context, students, and society but also critique the ways these changes are also affecting our beliefs and practices. It seems more than ever the ability of teachers to view changes as opportunities, weather uncertainties with courage, and make adjustments accordingly is paramount. To do this, reflective teachers may need more than an open mind, heightened self-awareness, or strong social and moral commitments. We need to embrace imperfection and vulnerability as an integral part of teaching and creating shared experiences with our students, especially in the post-pandemic world in which instability might be the norm rather than the exception.

Our own experiences during the pandemic testify to this proposition. It seems that amid the busyness and the myriad attempts to deliver our 'ideal' instruction, we inadvertently reinstated our professional identity in the process. For example, rather than starting from a clear construction of what pedagogy of care is and entails, we forged, constructed, and expressed it in the process of exploring it (Moorhouse & Tiet, 2021). We had to acknowledge our own vulnerability in the situation and accept the imperfect experimentations in finding ways to serve and connect with our students. In the end, we were not defeated by feelings of exhaustion, guilt, or hopelessness, but empowered and energized with a revitality of our identity as caretakers and teachers.

Therefore, it is important that ITE focusses on developing our students' awareness of the value of reflective practice, devising tools to support them to become reflective practitioners, and helping to develop their cognitive and affective capacities to reflect on their practices and experiences. The use of videos, teaching materials, students' work, and shared experiences can serve as useful data for teacher educators to model reflection and for students to engage in dialogic reflection. Students need to make the process of reflection their own, but teacher educators can make space for reflection and provide scaffolding to help them explore their honest and true conceptions, thoughts, and ideas. We echo Darling-Hammond and Bransford's (2005) call for the need to prepare teachers as reflective lifelong learners (not merely as competent practitioners) in the profession. Teaching is context-specific, dynamic, and ever-evolving. Perhaps the best preparation we can offer goes back to a famous Chinese proverb – teach them *how* to fish and various ways to cook fish rather than feeding them the fish.

Conclusion

It can be seen that there is considerable overlap between the proposed pedagogical priorities. Essentially, they focus on the humanistic aspect of teacher development and teaching, moving away from standardization of practice, and an over-emphasis on discipline-specific knowledge and PCK. We understand this could create considerable challenges for ITE in contexts, such as ours, where a focus on standardization and knowledge acquisition are prioritized. Issues, such as how do we assess soft skills, and sometimes abstract concepts, such as care, autonomy, and reflective practice, will naturally arise and are already concerns of scholars and practitioners (e.g. Hargreaves, 2009). One extreme course of action would be to rethink how we conduct and assess ITE in the first place – moving towards a system where credits and grades are not the outcomes of courses – but rather evidence of knowledge, skills, and attributes Rather than a grade-based system, we would have a system focusing on mastery – where students are provided multiple opportunities to demonstrate their competencies. Of course, their voice and opinions would need to form part of this process too. This may make the process and attainment of goals more transparent and allow PSTs greater ownership over the process than current practices afford. Importantly though, our PSTs must leave ITE with the recognition that 'becoming' and 'being' a teacher is a 'never-ending endeavour' (Yazan, 2019, p. 4). As Freire puts it:

> [I]t is in our incompleteness, of which we are aware, that education as a permanent process is grounded. Women and men are capable of being educated only to the extent that are capable of seeing themselves as unfinished. Education does not make us educable. It is our awareness of being unfinished that makes us educated. And the same awareness in which we are inserted makes us eternal seekers.
>
> *(1998, p. 58)*

We, therefore, need to equip our students with the skills needed to continue to learn, be self-aware, and adapt to the possible contexts in which they find themselves. As teaching continues to evolve and become more diverse, rapidly complex, and digitally infused, this seems to be the best way we can prepare them.

In this chapter, we have shared our lessons from the COVID-19 disruptions that focus on the human side of teaching and the essential but often overlooked role of teachers as caretakers. We have argued that the relational role of teaching is what often defines a teacher's identity and can affect their sense of 'being' which in turn can affect their 'doing', 'thinking', and 'relating'. Our professional experiences during the pandemic inform us of the need to reorientate ITE around three pedagogical priorities that would help equip our students with essential attributes for them to 'be' teachers. We are under no illusion that these are new ideas, nor that we are the only teacher educators thinking this way. In fact, there is now a growing amount of scholarship exploring what we can learn from this unprecedented period. We hope by adding our perspectives and voice, we can see more discussion and debate around the topic of becoming a teacher. We will try our best to enact the pedagogical priorities we propose here in our practices.

References

Argyris, C., & Schon, D. (1974). *Theory in practice: Increasing professional effectiveness.* San Francisco: Jossey Bass.

Aspfors, J., & Bondas, T. (2013). Caring about caring: Newly qualified teachers' experiences of their relationships within the school community. *Teachers and Teaching, 19*(3), 243–259. DOI:10.1080/13540602.2012.754158.

Ball, S. J. (2004). Education for sale! The commodification of everything? King's Annual Education Lecture, University of London. Available from: https://nepc.colorado.edu/sites/default/files/CERU-0410-253-OWI.pdf (Accessed 24 January 2023).

Benson, P. (2010). Teacher education and teacher autonomy: Creating spaces for experimentation in secondary school English language teaching. *Language Teaching Research, 14*(3), 259–275.

Burrow, R., Williams, R., & Thomas, D. (2020). Stressed, depressed and exhausted: Six years as a teacher in UK state education. *Work, Employment and Society, 34*(5), 949–958. DOI:10.1177/0950017020903040.

Clark, S., & Newberry, M. (2019). Are we building preservice teacher self-efficacy? A large-scale study examining teacher education experiences. *Asia-Pacific Journal of Teacher Education, 47*(1), 32–47. DOI:10.1080/1359866X.2018.1497772.

Cochran-Smith, M. (2003). Sometimes it's not about the money: Teaching and heart. *Journal of Teacher Education, 54*(5), 371–375.

Cutri, R. M., Mena, J., & Whiting, E. F. (2020). Faculty readiness for online crisis teaching: Transitioning to online teaching during the COVID-19 pandemic. *European Journal of Teacher Education, 43*(4), 523–541. DOI:10.1080/02619768.2020.1815702.

Danielewicz, J. (2001). *Teaching selves: Identity, pedagogy, and teacher education.* Albany, NY: Suny Press.

Darling-Hammond, L., & Bransford, J. (2005). *Preface.* In L. Darling-Hammond, & J. Bransford (eds.), *Preparing teachers for a changing world: What teachers should learn and be able to do* (pp. vii–x). San Francisco: Jossey-Bass.

Day, C., & Leitch, R. (2001). Teachers' and teacher educators' lives: The role of emotion. *Teaching and Teacher Education, 17*(4), 403–415.

De Costa, P. I., & Norton, B. (2017). Introduction: Identity, transdisciplinarity, and the good language teacher. *The Modern Language Journal, 101*(S1), 3–14.

De Vries, S., van de Grift, W. J., & Jansen, E. P. (2014). How teachers' beliefs about learning and teaching relate to their continuing professional development. *Teachers and Teaching, 20*(3), 338–357.

Dewey, J. (1933). *How we think: A restatement of the relation of reflective thinking to the educative process*. New York: D.C. Health and Company.

Diz-Otero, M., Portela-Pino, I., Domínguez-Lloria, S., & Pino-Juste, M. (2022). Digital competence in secondary education teachers during the COVID-19-derived pandemic: Comparative analysis. *Education + Training*, ahead-of-print. DOI:10.1108/ET-01-2022-0001.

du Plessis, A. E., & Sunde, E. (2017). The workplace experiences of beginning teachers in three countries: A message for initial teacher education from the field. *Journal of Education for Teaching, 43*(2), 132–150. DOI:10.1080/02607476.2017.1286759.

Eccles, J. (2009). Who am I and what am I going to do with my life? Personal and collective identities as motivators of action. *Educational Psychologist, 44*(2), 78–89.

Freire, P. (1998). *Teachers as cultural workers: Letters to those who dare to teach*. Boulder, CO: Westview Press.

Goodwin, A. L. (2010). Globalization and the preparation of quality teachers: Rethinking knowledge domains for teaching. *Teaching Education, 21*(1), 19–32. DOI:10.1080/10476210903466901.

Grayling, A. (2003). *Meditations for the humanist: Ethics for a secular age*. Oxford: Oxford University Press.

Hargreaves, A. (2009). A decade of educational change and a defining moment of opportunity—an introduction. *Journal of Educational Change, 10*, 89–100.

Hostetler, K. D. (2016). Beyond reflection: Perception, virtue, and teacher knowledge. *Educational Philosophy and Theory, 48*(2), 179–190. https://doi.org/10.1080/00131857.2014.989950

Huang, J. P., & Benson, P. (2013). Autonomy, agency and identity in foreign and second language education. *CJAL, 36*(1), 7–28.

Kidd, W., & Murray, J. (2022). Educators' perspectives of online teaching during the pandemic: Implications for initial teacher education. *Journal of Education for Teaching, 48*(4), 393–406. DOI:10.1080/02607476.2022.2082273.

Kohnke, L. (2022). A qualitative exploration of student perspectives of chatbot use during emergency remote teaching. *International Journal of Mobile Learning and Organisation, 16*(4), 475–488.

Korthagen, F. A. J. (2017). Inconvenient truths about teacher learning: Towards professional development 3.0. *Teachers and Teaching: Theory and Practice, 23*(4), 387–405.

Mehrotra, G. R. (2021). Centering a pedagogy of care in the pandemic. *Qualitative Social Work, 20*(1–2), 537–543. DOI:10.1177/1473325020981079.

Moorhouse, B. L. (2021a). Beginning teaching during COVID-19: Newly qualified Hong Kong teachers' preparedness for online teaching. *Educational Studies*, Online First. DOI:10.1080/03055698.2021.1964939.

Moorhouse, B. L. (2021b). Beginning teaching during COVID-19: Advice from newly qualified teachers. *Journal of Education for Teaching, 47*(5), 749–751. DOI:10.1080/02607476.2021.1952844.

Moorhouse, B. L., & Kohnke, L. (2021). Thriving or surviving emergency remote teaching necessitated by COVID-19: University Teachers' Perspectives. *Asia-Pacific Education Researcher, 30*(3), 279–287. DOI:10.1007/s40299-021-00567-9.

Moorhouse, B. L., & Tiet, M. C. (2021). Attempting to implement a pedagogy of care during the disruptions to teacher education caused by COVID-19: A collaborative self-study. *Studying Teacher Education, 17*(2), 208–227. DOI:10.1080/17425964.2021.1925644.

Moorhouse, B. L., & Wong, K. M. (2022). Reconceptualising teacher education courses for online teaching: The experiences of two teacher educators. In J. K. H. Pun et al. (eds.), *The use of technology in English medium education*, English Language Education 27 (pp. 109–117). Singapore: Springer. DOI:10.1007/978-3-030-99622-2_8.

Moorhouse, B. L., Walsh, S., Li, Y., & Wong, L. L. C. (2022). Assisting and mediating interaction during synchronous online language lessons: Teachers' professional practices. *TESOL Quarterly, 56*, 934–960. DOI:10.1002/tesq.3144.

Nicol, C., Novakowski, J., Ghaleb, F., & Beairsto, S. (2010). Interweaving pedagogies of care and inquiry: Tensions, dilemmas and possibilities. *Studying Teacher Education, 6*(3), 235–244. DOI:10.1080/17425964.2010.518494.

O'Connor, K. E. (2008). "You Choose to Care": Teachers, emotions and professional identity. *Teaching and Teacher Education, 24*(1), 117–126. DOI:10.1016/j.tate.2006.11.008.

Parker, G. (2015). Teachers' autonomy. *Research in Education, 93*(1), 19. DOI:10.7227/RIE.0008.

Pennington, M. C., & Richards, J. C. (2016). Teacher identity in language teaching: Integrating personal, contextual, and professional factors. *RELC Journal, 47*(1), 1–19.

Rodgers, C. R. (2002). Seeing student learning: Teacher change and the role of reflection. *Harvard Educational Review, 72*(2), 230–253.

Sachs, J. (2005). Teacher education and the development of professional identity. In P. M. Denicolo, & M. Kompf (eds.), *Connecting policy and practice: Challenges for teaching and learning in schools and universities* (pp. 5–21). Routledge. DOI:10.4324/9780203012529.

Schon, D. A. (1983). *The reflective practitioner: How professional think in action*. New York: Basic Books.

Schon, D. A. (1987). *Educating the reflective practitioner*. San Francisco, CA: Jossey-Bass.

Shoffner, M., & Webb, A. W. (Eds.). (2022). *Reconstructing care in teacher education after COVID-19: Caring enough to change*. New York: Routledge.

Tiet, M. C. (2019). *Let's get real! – Exploring in-service English teachers' reflective practices in a Hong Kong Primary School*. Hong Kong, SAR: Unpublished doctoral thesis, The University of Hong Kong.

UNESCO. (2020). Education: From disruption to recovery UNESCO. Available at: https://en.unesco.org/covid19/educationresponse (Accessed 24 May 2020).

Valli, L., & Buese, D. (2007). The changing roles of teachers in an era of high-stakes accountability. *American Educational Research Journal, 44*(3), 519–558.

Yang, B., & Huang, C. (2021). Turn crisis into opportunity in response to COVID-19: Experience from a Chinese University and future prospects. *Studies in Higher Education*, 46(1), 121–132. DOI:10.1080/03075079.2020.1859687.

Yazan, B. (2019). Toward identity-oriented teacher education: Critical autoethnographic narrative. *Tesol Journal*, 10(1), e00388.

Yeung, K. (2020). *Suspending classes without suspending learning*. Hong Kong Education Bureau. Available from: https://www.edb.gov.hk/en/about-edb/press/insiderperspective/insiderperspective20200212.html (Accessed 12 February 2020).

Zembylas, M. (2014). The place of emotion in teacher reflection: Elias, Foucault and 'critical emotional reflexivity'. *Power and Education*, 6(2), 210–222.

Zhao, R. (2020). Hong Kong universities suspend on-campus classes. *China Daily Online*, January 31. https://www.chinadailyhk.com/article/119792.

13

OPPORTUNITIES FOR MODERNISING AND REVOLUTIONISING EDUCATION SYSTEMS POST-COVID

Drawing on an international survey of teachers' experiences during the COVID-19 pandemic

Carol Hordatt Gentles, Marilyn Leask, and Mark Williams

Introduction

The COVID-19 pandemic created challenges for education that were unprecedented with implications for significant changes in how we think about and practise the work of teaching and learning. The International Teachers Task Force (ITTF, 2020) estimated in 2020 that around 63 million primary and secondary teachers around the world were affected by school closures in 165 countries due to the pandemic. This placed teachers "on the frontlines of the response to ensure that learning continued". UNESCO estimates 1.6 billion learners in 190 countries lost schooling during this period (UNESCO, 2020). In rising to this challenge many teachers had to shift rapidly from accustomed ways of teaching in physical classrooms to teaching online or through the radio, television, or telephone or in community spaces. In many contexts, teachers had to figure out unconventional ways to reach vulnerable and marginalised students.

Initial reports (EI, 2020; ITTF, 2020) suggest that while the response of teachers in the first stages of the pandemic was seen as heroic and praiseworthy, it also affected them psychologically, financially, and professionally. In many instances, for example, teachers worked during school closures without adequate socio-emotional support. Many functioned in a climate of fear and anxiety around their own safety and that of their families, while adapting to working from home. Teachers also had to figure out how to adjust curricula, their pedagogy and practice for online or other delivery without professional training or support. They had to change how they conducted assessments. They had to change their mindsets about accustomed ways of practice and ways in which they understood and wielded power

DOI: 10.4324/9781003352129-17

and authority. Their workloads expanded in scope and weight. Measures of accountability became more onerous. They began interacting differently with students and their families. As countries moved towards reopening schools even while the pandemic continued, expectations for teacher work changed again. Not only were they expected to return to physical classrooms and continue providing quality learning for all students, but they were also expected, at the same time, to play key roles in making schools into safe spaces (Leask and Younie, 2021).

The pandemic also highlighted extant inequities such as infrastructure needs, inequitable access to connectivity, equipment, and thus online learning. This led to widespread marginalisation of learners. As the world moves forward to a post-COVID-19 era, governments, learners, communities, and teachers will benefit if we capitalise on the lessons learnt about teaching and learning during the lockdowns. We consider and discuss these as post-COVID-19 opportunities for modernising and revolutionising education systems. First, we document teachers' and learners' experiences and then examine the implications and opportunities for all stakeholders. We begin by outlining the project.

The teacher's experiences and practices during the COVID-19 project

This chapter is based on the research report from the Teacher Voice Series -*Teacher Experiences and Practices during Covid-19* (Hordatt Gentles and Leask, 2021) undertaken on behalf of the International Council on Education for Teaching and the MESHGuides/Education Futures Collaboration charity. It also draws on desk research (Hammond, 2021; Leask and Younie, 2021) into practices which support the continuity of teaching and learning during crises. The report documents the many challenges teachers faced when schools were closed and solutions that were developed to address these to ensure continuity of schooling during the COVID-19 pandemic.

The *Teacher Experiences and Practices during Covid-19* research were guided by five main questions.

- How has your job changed since the pandemic?
- What new strategies/practices did you develop?
- What strategies/practices do you want to continue using?
- What do you see yourself doing differently in the future?
- What do you see as challenges for sustaining education during times of crisis?

Data were gathered by thirty-five researchers across 40 countries and 500 educators at all levels of education via focus groups and interviews (Hordatt

Gentles and Leask, 2021). Two international webinars were held during June and December 2020 in which teachers were invited to talk about their experiences and share the knowledge, understanding and insight they had with respect to the changes, concerns and challenges arising due to the COVID-19 pandemic.

Data were analysed by the lead researchers using coding and categorisation to generate initial themes. A second round of analysis was done to collate the data around the themes which emerged. Peer review of the results and report by the thirty-five researchers provided credibility.

Findings

As might be expected, factors which impacted teachers' experiences and practices during COVID-19 included the economic status of the country, time of year, size of the population, degree of centralisation of the education sector and teachers' relationship with the government: whether the government had a collaborative approach to working with the education sector or a top-down management approach. Yet despite differences in culture and context, we found several common themes emerged across countries in relation to –how teachers addressed the challenges brought on by school closures, teachers' experiences with using technology, and the new practices they employed to manage teaching and learning. We outline these below. (In this chapter our intention is to draw out commonalities in teachers' views across countries. There is not enough space here to provide details of all the local, regional and/or national contexts that shaped these teachers' experiences).

Teachers became drivers of change

It became clear that teachers can and will drive educational change if they see it as helpful in meeting their students' learning needs. When schools were closed down at the start of the pandemic, many teachers were basically on their own, with little guidance or support from school leaders or policymakers. Teachers worried about their student's well-being and learning losses. They could not reach their students. To manage the situation, teachers bravely navigated technology they were not familiar with, dived into unknown virtual teaching and learning spaces, adjusted their pedagogy, and found new ways to secure support from parents. In responding to our interviews, teachers shared a variety of strategies and practices they had developed to reach students both remotely and/ or online.

Teachers engaged with technology differently

In all countries in our study including the wealthiest, teachers struggled to manage the problem of limited or nonexistent internet connectivity. Families without internet access and devices were prevalent in high, medium, and low-income countries. They could not afford online access costs or provide devices for their children. Our research (2021, p. 26) showed that where families had to buy data to support online learning, "particular children in families were prioritised as were subjects. Previously for schooling, parents just had to provide school uniforms and lunch, now they had to find money to buy data, so they made choices". This was frustrating for teachers –often the children who were considered the most promising in a family were afforded all or more access time. This meant other children –those considered less intelligent, or with less promise, were marginalised. Many teachers themselves lacked devices, reliable WIFI access, or even electricity. Some described how difficult it was to teach from their homes. They described how they had to teach classes using a cell phone. These difficulties pushed teachers to reorganise their finances so they could buy data and purchase equipment such as laptops, desks and chairs. For many, this was financially burdensome and stressful, because they could not afford such purchases. Technology was now no longer a choice – it was a necessity for teaching and learning.

Teachers reported they began to see technology use differently. Many had lacked confidence prior to the pandemic in integrating technology into their lessons and teaching. But, as offsetting learning losses became a priority, they began to see the value of changing how they viewed technology. As one teacher shared, *A new mindset was emerging: Previously technology was used as a side dish – now digital tools are the main dish"*. Another teacher reported "*I have embraced the online platform that has been developed and find the actual delivery of classes enjoyable. I have learned new skills and have fully immersed myself in this new way of delivering*". Teachers described multiple ways in which they engaged technology to reach and engage students.

Many, especially in developing countries, used WhatsApp and a variety of other apps to come up with new ways to communicate with students and parents, to keep records, and to devise techniques for engaging students. In many instances where students had no devices other than a cellular phone, WhatsApp became the only means of maintaining contact. Some teachers even uploaded lessons and recorded themselves teaching so students could hear them. Teachers also employed the use of one-on-one meetings on the Microsoft Teams platform during lessons where students had to "screen share" their work for discussion. This was found to be a useful strategy to enhance student accountability. Screen sharing replaced walking around the class as a method of gauging learner performance on an ongoing basis.

Teachers also recognised how valuable it was to record lessons and share these recordings with students. They told interviewers that many of their students loved this option as they could review the lessons at their own pace. Sharing applications and diagrams in the virtual classroom was beneficial and enhanced teaching. Additionally, online teaching and learning made it easy to collaborate after hours with learners who needed extra help with lesson concepts after the lesson had ended. The ability to save all information on their laptops was very useful for both teachers and students. This helped teachers with accountability and record-keeping.

Various technologies were identified as very useful. For example, using and then sharing PowerPoint presentations was described as helpful for online teaching. Students could read and discuss the electronic slides with their classmates. For many teachers, it was the first time they had engaged with PowerPoint as a teaching tool. Students were encouraged to use PowerPoints for their presentations. A maths teacher reported she found the interactive whiteboard to be the best teaching tool available on the online learning platform. Another teacher recommended the use of flipped classroom teaching as a useful strategy. She set students the task to research a topic offline. Students had to collaborate offline and then present live and online as if they were the teacher. The teacher then encouraged constructive criticism from peers. Some teachers delegated lesson topics for students to prepare and deliver. Teachers would then recap key learning points. The strategy of online group work using breakout rooms in the Teams/Zoom type software was also recommended. Students had to come on live to the whole group, show their faces and give feedback on their group's work. Teachers could "pop in" to the breakout rooms to advise/see progress. This was considered a useful strategy to get students to interact with each other and the learning materials.

Teachers' technology use was not, however, only digital. In situations where access to the internet was limited, teachers "rediscovered" the value of long-standing technologies and pedagogies used by radio schools and open/virtual schools. In some countries like Mexico, teachers found innovative ways to distribute handouts to their students who had no WIFI access. One teacher recounted they relied on the local egg vendor to give worksheets to students, who completed them and returned them to the vendor. The teachers marked the worksheets, and the egg vendor returned them to the students. In Jamaica, one teacher in an inner-city area launched an innovative project to paint building walls with blackboard paint, upon which she and other teachers wrote daily lessons and assignments for children in the community. As they engaged with all types of technology, teachers also made changes to how they taught.

Teachers made changes to pedagogy

To survive and manage in virtual spaces teachers made changes to their pedagogy. They reported that they began to see the value of pedagogies, approaches, and models for learning that were already being used but had previously not been used as effectively as they could be. For example, moving away from the traditional lecturing mode was found to be easier in the virtual classroom. As one English teacher described *"I have begun to engage my students increasingly into self-exploration and independent learning. Before the pandemic 60% of my classes were information input through lecture. Today, information input in the form of a lecture is almost 0%"*. In their interviews, teachers described a multitude of strategies and techniques that they had been trying out, including the use of different questioning techniques, or allowing students to conduct research online while in class. As a teacher from South Africa reported, *"encouraging students to explore on their own and asking them to share their observations/understandings of concepts/skills/knowledge have been found to be very useful"*. A high school teacher shared that for her, *"forum discussion seems to be much more engaging on Facebook than VLE, and video presentations allowed students to show their creativity"*. Teachers reported that they provided the students with more independent work to do, to keep them active all the time, and so that students felt more responsible for their own progress. Less assessment-based teaching was a result. Some teachers welcomed this as they found as there was now more contact time for discussion and learning.

Teachers explained that they became more mindful of the need to use their pedagogy to ensure the inclusion of all their students. In online spaces, it was difficult to know if students were paying attention or if they were still in the class. Thus, two teachers described a useful strategy they devised to get students engaged during virtual classes, as well as to monitor their participation. They used a "Rolodex" method where they would go methodically through the students' names, calling each student out, to elicit responses. Pedagogy also focused more on meeting students' differentiated learning needs. A Brazilian teacher said, *"I intend to continue facilitating students in their learning through exploration. I will also put in more effort into encouraging my students to build independent learning and study skills"*. Another teacher was excited to share her discovery that

> *A combination of synchronous and asynchronous methods seems to be most effective for me. While recorded video seems to help, I have realised some students need the guided face-to-face Zoom meeting to keep them focused and serious about their studies. Some content like grammar rules are actually easier to record and share – this seems to give students plenty of time to watch the video as well as practise.*

An interesting outcome of what teachers reported was they realised that some children prefer online learning and that the array of online resources –software, apps, and learning management platforms, available offered invaluable support for teaching effectively and enhancing students' engagement. Teachers also saw they can be flexible in how they cater for different learning needs. Teachers reported that some children preferred online learning and indeed that some children performed better during remote teaching than in classroom settings.

Teachers grappled with shifting power relations

As teachers started using technology and changing their pedagogy, many found traditional classroom behaviour management techniques did not necessarily work online. There was a decentring of power relations as the teacher moved from a central role to a facilitating role. Teachers spoke about experiencing anxiety as they felt themselves losing authority over students in virtual classrooms. They struggled to maintain control because students had more choices about paying more attention. As one teacher from Panama realised, *"The teacher cannot make students turn on the video or speak"*. Teachers felt disempowered by not being able to insist on student attendance. *"Some students have access to the internet but they use the reason of 'cannot access the internet' as an excuse NOT to attend online classes"*. Teachers lost the capacity to manage and reach students through body language. They lost the power of the walls of a classroom to confine students and co-opt their attention. It became difficult because power and authority were now shared. A challenge for one teacher was class control. She struggled to stop random questions and keep students on track. She eventually found that using the "raise hand tool" was effective to manage this problem. Sometimes students disrupted the lesson by interfering with the technology. To manage this one teacher used an external whiteboard app instead of an internal Microsoft Teams whiteboard app, to ensure that students could not delete work as the teacher progressed. Teachers also struggled to share power with parents. As a teacher from Barbados complained *"Parents are in the classroom and monitoring"* *"Parents are there seeing what you do"*. This was a huge problem for teachers in many countries as parents began trying to "help" teachers by monitoring their children's online schooling at home.

Coming from these challenges, a powerful lesson for some teachers was realising that it was acceptable to share power in the classroom with their students. Some spoke of recording lessons taught online and making these accessible to students and parents. This was a new experience for them. Before the pandemic, this would have been seen as invasive and threatening to their authority in the classroom. Now this became a powerful way of allowing students to review what had been taught in class. The pandemic also precipitated more flexible ways of thinking about assessment. Teachers were able to give students more autonomy in choosing how they learn best.

Discussion

There is no doubt that the pandemic experience influenced many teachers to rethink their pedagogy and practice. They recognised that many of the changes they had to make during the pandemic were worth keeping. As one teacher said, *"Altogether, this pandemic has changed the course of our job for the better. It taught us lessons that will prepare us for a better future"*.

What is important to recognise is that most of what was learnt or described as valuable for improving teaching and learning was not new. It is ironic that in proposing strategies and paradigmatic shifts for modernising and revolutionising education in a post-COVID time, we are essentially suggesting nothing unique or groundbreaking. What is revolutionary is our suggestions for building on the knowledge that we already have and for reframing how we think about and use extant ideas about pedagogy, policy, and technology use. More specifically, some key lessons are that teachers will drive change if their ideas and innovations are included in decision and policymaking. It was evident from our research that teachers value when their voice and professional autonomy and intelligence for navigating change policies are respected. This has important implications for motivating teachers to change their pedagogy from traditional teacher-led to learner-led practice. Technology integration and new ways of teaching can be achieved if we recognise the capacity of teachers to lead and be strategic and forward-thinking. There is also great potential in supporting teachers as they innovate with and rediscover culturally relevant and useful non-digital technologies like extant forms of remote schooling such as virtual schools –open schools and radio schools. Equity of access to quality schooling for students with different learning styles, different abilities and diverse backgrounds is possible if we capitalise on opportunities for differentiated teaching and learning offered by technology.

These lessons learnt support our suggestions for moving educational change forward in the post-pandemic era. We suggest this can be accomplished if politicians and civil servants support teachers by upgrading infrastructure and resources for teaching and by acknowledging the value of teachers' voices and intelligence. If we want to capitalise on what teachers experienced during the pandemic, we must ensure that we use what we have learnt to inform policy as we move forward. Key questions to ask are, how do we forge supportive and collaborative partnerships between governments and teachers that are beneficial to learners and communities and the country as a whole? How might the step change in teacher skills and knowledge about the use of technologies during the COVID-19 pandemic be harnessed to improve teaching and learners' outcomes in a post-pandemic world? Key strategies should focus on opening up resources so that teachers can continue to capitalise on what they learnt, during COVID-19, about technology use for enhancing student learning. This suggests a democratisation of access to resources that can support equity of access for all students. We must also insist that policymakers work with teachers as genuine partners in planning for educational innovation. We look at these more closely below and offer our recommendations.

Opening up resources

During the pandemic, many companies and governments made free offers and provided resources. There were great examples in our findings of governments providing high-quality support for teaching with various technologies –using radio, TV and online and offline internet. But what about small and low-income countries with much less capacity than wealthier countries? Might some combine their efforts for the common good? What would it take to open up the resources that are there already in some countries, but closed to teachers in other countries? Universal access to public broadband should be considered a basic human right! Might at least some of the governments with good online resources behind firewalls pull together to support teachers across the world so there is equitable access for all? Teachers spoke a lot about how they benefitted from the goodwill shown by tech companies during the pandemic, in offering free access to digital tools and learning platforms. Why can this not be sustained?

In some countries, existing remote or home-schooling systems and networks were already in place, and these continued to provide largely uninterrupted schooling throughout the pandemic. In some of these countries, the rapid extension of programmes using existing widely accessible technologies such as radio –including solar-powered radios, and television took place. This points to the potential of developing the concept of "open schools". The definition of an open school used here is for a state-funded mainstream school for people, young and old, who cannot access or who missed out on accessing a bricks-and-mortar institution. What is proposed is not correspondence schooling but a form of mainstream online school with active engagement between teachers and students (Brighouse and Moon, 2020; Sutton et al., 2020). This would be a mainstream alternative for the millions of students who either cannot access physical schooling or who find online schooling fits better with their learning needs. For example, academics found that one-in-three young people say their mental health and well-being improved during COVID-19 lockdown measures. Neurodiverse individuals, those who face barriers to attendance, and those who were bullied or anxious preferred the online schooling they experienced to their traditional schools (Soneson et al., 2022).

Teachers we interviewed found students who were previously silent in the class contributed more with online teaching by typing questions into "chat windows". In the UK, a 2020 study by the University of Sussex (Shepherd and Hancock, 2022, p. 3) found that in England, "the majority of children with special educational needs and disabilities (SEND) felt less stress and anxiety away from school and at home during lockdown". It also stated that

> three out of five parent carers felt their children with SEND were less stressed, as lockdown allowed greater time spent with families, increased

one-to-one time and provided greater flexibility to pursue own interests at home while removing the social pressures of school, the requirement to wear uniform and experiences with bullies.

The concept of open schooling can also be useful at all levels. For example, for further and vocational education, Australia's virtual TAFE provides an example of an "Open Vocational College" able to provide upskilling across all sectors of workers in remote locations (See References: web links). Tertiary-level teachers we interviewed said many of their adult students, especially women, preferred online classes to physical classes because it allowed them more flexibility with childcare. The Open School fits into a vision of national education systems that are flexible and pluralistic. Along these lines, the secondary, tertiary, and further education systems become more adaptable and able to serve the needs of more young people in all their myriad different ways. Central to this is an understanding that the classroom is not the only definition of a space for learning and that different forms of teaching work for different people at different times. Target cohorts might be students in remote areas, refugee and asylum-seeking children, children facing long-term absence from school, learners with various disabilities, neurodiverse students, and travellers. What is important is that the Open School is a natural and timely evolution for existing education systems which currently do not have such provisions, or which now have embryonic provisions from COVID period investments. We must build on and develop what we learnt about teaching and learning during the pandemic as these lessons are invaluable for improving the quality of education possible both in future crises and a post-pandemic world.

Working with teachers as genuine partners in planning for educational innovation

It was evident that teachers demonstrated remarkable commitment and resilience in trying to sustain student learning during the pandemic. This was accomplished at great personal (emotional and psychological) and professional costs for teachers. If this could be recognised and valued by decisive government leadership in regard to planning and policy for teaching, the resilience and new knowledge of teachers could be harnessed for a wider national benefit. In moving forward teachers could be supported to work flexibly with local communities on solutions to ensuring continuity of schooling for all, as local conditions are so variable. Critical to the success of planning for and managing potential crises in education, is the development of policies guided by the firsthand experiences of teachers. This view is supported by the call from the ITTF (2020) to "include teachers in developing Covid-19 education responses… at all steps of education policy-making and planning". It speaks to the notion that "teacher voice is a critical element in any successful approach" (Doucet, Netolicky, Timmers and Tuscano, 2020, p. 2) to delivering quality education in the time of COVID-19, and indeed in times of any future national or global crises. This is so because it is teachers who know their students and know where they were academically when schools shut down. It is teachers who have monitored their students' social-emotional and mental health (ibid, 2020), communicated with students' parents, and tried to support their students' transition to online learning. In situations where online delivery has been problematic and students could not be reached, it was teachers who noted and monitored the increasing marginalisation of their students. It was teachers who strategised and led the search for ways to connect with students. It is also teachers who experienced having to function without proper support.

A common concern was that most teachers were unprepared for online teaching. Teachers from across the world –from low, medium, and high-income countries reported that as they coped with the crisis of school closures, they experienced rapid upskilling in the use of technologies to support remote learning –and that they wanted to continue to use technologies for teaching. They also gained useful insights into their own capacity for professional learning. positive professional development and a key lesson from the pandemic experience is that it is teachers who are best positioned to offer insight into the types of professional learning opportunities and training they need to function effectively now and in the future. For example, teachers found the increased professional collaboration they experienced during COVID, through education partnerships, webinars, and COVID-focused research projects was extremely beneficial. It motivated them to move out of spaces of professional isolation they inhabited before COVID-19. Teachers described emerging and strengthening professional autonomy and confidence in their capacity to be innovative. They experienced many initial challenges with using technology due to their own lack of skills and preparation but moving forward, teachers found they quickly developed confidence and the skills and competencies to be dynamic, fluid, and flexible.

We must acknowledge that a shift in teachers' understanding and skills, professional autonomy, and confidence in the use of educational technologies to support learning and changed dispositions towards professional collaboration has taken place. This step change is a phenomenon which could be of long-term benefit to societies, teachers, and learners worldwide. Policymakers need to recognise and value the capacity of teachers to drive and manage change. As was witnessed during the pandemic as teachers began to manage their remote teaching better and where leadership and policy on transitioning to remote teaching were lacking, many teachers took the initiative in organising knowledge-sharing with colleagues and the remote teaching of young people in partnership with their local communities. This capacity for innovation, if recognised, if nurtured through professional preparation, valued, and capitalised upon, may provide meaningful support for governments wishing to reform and update educational practices.

Conclusions

Our findings suggested that the school lockdowns during the pandemic pushed teachers into changing rapidly. As they tried to continue meeting their students' learning needs, teachers in many places experienced rapid professional learning and rapid upskilling. In the face of the slow response by school leaders and policymakers to figure out how to manage schooling in virtual rather than physical spaces, teachers exerted professional autonomy and confidence in innovating, thus gaining confidence in their capacity to manage change. The pandemic pushed teachers to use technologies and there was a step change in blended teaching and learning. The ways in which teachers responded to challenges arising from school closures, the strategies they used, their changing mindsets about technology use, and how they innovated, provide us with valuable lessons about what is possible when teachers are genuinely invested in educational change. The pandemic and its enforced lockdowns launched possibilities for schooling at all levels, years into the future. With access to schools restricted mainly to children of key workers and learners classed as "vulnerable", accepted concepts about where students learn and how they learn had to change overnight. For thousands of students, the very space in which they learnt was transformed.

Teachers' response to the pandemic, employing a diverse set of existing tools with some determination arguably saved mass education. Teachers and students demonstrated that the online space was a valid one for learning. Their efforts were proof that online-based education not only works at scale, but for some students, it can even be superior. Yet as society struggles to get back to normal, those bold strides into a technologically inspired educational future have been checked. Traditional classroom teaching may work well for many but there is a sizable minority for whom this model of teaching and learning is not productive. The major opportunity post-COVID for all involved in education systems is to capitalise on the knowledge and receptivity of the education sector and the population at large to the use of technologies for education. The benefits of COVID driven changes that teachers identified point to the role teachers can play in envisaging and managing change in their own settings –if administrators and policymakers can work with teachers.

The rapid professional development undertaken to enable teachers to teach remotely shows what can be done to upskill the profession quickly if there is the will to do so and trust in teachers' abilities to innovate and adapt to local circumstances and challenges. Through "open schools" initiatives and remote professional development for teachers (see the MESHGuides model www.meshguides.org); governments now have opportunities to address long-standing problems of learners' access to specialist subject teaching and access to education for groups for whom traditional schools are not accessible. This is enabled because there is widespread understanding about how to use technology for learning together with plenty of resources and examples of innovative use of traditional media as well as online and offline tools.

The UN's Sustainable Development Goal 4c is focused on improving the quality of education for all children, by providing quality teaching and teachers. The COVID-19 period has shown what can be done with remote and online learning to support this goal. It has also shown how educators can take ownership of their practice and learning in times of crisis to provide innovative solutions. The question is whether the lessons learnt from teachers' experiences during this pandemic will be understood and used by those charged with planning for education in the future.

References

Brighouse, T., and Moon, B. (2020) *Like the Open University, We now Need an Open School for the Whole Country.* https://www.theguardian.com/education/2020/may/12/like-the-open-university-we-now-need-an-open-school-for-the-whole-country. Accessed 21 November 2022.

Doucet, A., Netolicky, D., Timmers, K., and Tuscano, F.J. (2020) *Thinking about Pedagogy in an Unfolding Pandemic. An Independent Report on Approaches to Distance Learning During Covid19 School Closures.* Independent Report written to inform the work of Education International and UNESCO. Version 2.0 | 29 March 2020. https://teachertaskforce.org/knowledge-hub/thinking-about-pedagogy-unfolding-pandemic. Accessed 21 November 2022.

EI - Education International (2020) *International Summit on the Teaching Profession 2020: Teachers Recognised as the Heroes of the Covid-19 Crisis in Education.* https://www.ei-ie.org/en/detail/16814/international-summit-on-the-teaching-profession-2020-teachers-recognised-as-the-heroes-of-the-Covid-19-crisis-in-education. Accessed 21 November 2022.

Hammond, M. (ed) (2021) *Supporting Remote Teaching and Learning in Developing Countries: From the Global to the Local.* Kathmandu, Nepal: British Council. https://www.britishcouncil.org.np/sites/default/files/teaching_learning_book.pdf. Accessed 21 November 2022.

Hordatt Gentles, C., and Leask, M. (2021) *Teachers' Experiences and Practices during Covid-19.* International Council on Education for Teaching and MESHGuides ISSN 0799-6624 https://www.icet4u.org/docs/ICET_MESH_REPORT_AUGUST_2021.pdf. Accessed 21 November 2022.

ITTF - International Teachers Task Force (2020) *Response to the Covid-19 Outbreak - Call for Action on Teachers.* https://teachertaskforce.org/knowledge-hub/response-Covid-19-outbreak-call-action-teachers-0. Accessible to subscribers. Accessed 21 November 2022.

Leask, M., and Younie, S. (2021) *Ensuring Schooling for All in Times of Crisis - Lessons from Covid-19.* London: Routledge.

Shepherd, J., and Hancock, C. (2022) *Education and Covid-19: Perspectives from Parent Carers of Children with SEND*. UK. University of Sussex. https://www.sussex.ac.uk/webteam/gateway/file.php?name=education-and-Covid-19---perspectives-from-parent-carers-of-children-with-send.pdf&site=26. Accessed 21 November 2022.

Soneson, E., Puntis, S., Chapman, N. et al. (2022) *Happier during Lockdown: A Descriptive Analysis of Self-Reported Wellbeing in 17,000 UK School Students during Covid-19 Lockdown.* European Child Adolescent Psychiatry. https://doi.org/10.1007/s00787-021-01934-z (summary on https://www.cam.ac.uk/research/news/one-in-three-young-people-say-they-felt-happier-during-lockdown). Accessed 21 November 2022.

Sutton, K., Sunderland, E., Holmes, W., Pau, S., and Bower, K. (2020) *An Open School for the Post-Covid World*. Slough: NFER/NESTA. https://www.nesta.org.uk/project-updates/open-school-post-Covid-world/ and https://docs.google.com/presentation/d/1w4P1KUlcW1DsVYdzuy8zjmChaxKVC0XJvz44IwzA_bo/edit#slide=id.g9c813a9bce_0_30. Accessed 21 November 2022.

UNESCO (2020) *Covid-19 Learning Disruption Recovery Snapshot*. https://en.unesco.org/news/Covid-19-learning-disruption-recovery-snapshot-unescos-work-education-2020. Accessed 21 November 2022.

Web Links

Australia: Alice Springs School of the Air. https://assoa.nt.edu.au
Australia: Victorian Open School. https://www.vsv.vic.edu.au
Canada: Manitoba Education (n.d.) Distance learning [online]. https://www.edu.gov.mb.ca/k12/dl/

14
SOCIOMATERIAL PERSPECTIVES ON HYBRID LEARNING IN PRIMARY CLASSROOMS DURING THE COVID-19 PANDEMIC

Noreen Dunnett

Introduction

During the COVID-19 pandemic, with many school buildings closed, traditional concepts of the 'classroom' and school as a physical environment for learning were disrupted, and teachers and students had to adapt to learning in new, hybrid environments. There are many different takes on hybridity in education and it is often confused with blended learning. In blended learning models, the primary model is face-to-face learning coupled with online tasks, often set as 'home' work (Hrastinski, 2019). In this model, online resources are not a substitute for in-person class time but are intended to enhance and build on classroom activities. Hybrid learning environments, however, are more complex, fusing together dichotomies such as physical–digital, formal–informal contexts, and synchronous and asynchronous activity (Bøjer & Brøns, 2022). As such they offer opportunities to experiment with existing pedagogy and intervene in familiar practices in new and interesting ways. Some of these opportunities are explored in this chapter through drawing on vignettes drawn from a study of two primary schools in England.

According to the UN Educational, Scientific and Cultural Organisation, 107 countries implemented national school closures at some point during the pandemic (Defeyter et al., 2020). Teachers were left with the choice of trying to sustain a version of their face-to-face delivery remotely through 'live' online lessons, in essence, a blended learning model, or accept the reality of very different social and material relations and adapt their approach accordingly. In most schooling systems there is a strong impetus towards stability and predictability, an impetus which continued in the hybrid environments created during the COVID-19 pandemic. Schools continued to put processes in

DOI: 10.4324/9781003352129-18

place to re-order and negotiate the continuation of school practices (Alirezabeigi et al., 2020) and establish a sense of 'togetherness' through routines or 'rituals'. The continuation of these familiar practices, which control space and time and govern bodies, movement, talk and interaction, could be seen as an attempt to replicate the face-to-face, 'embodied' experience of schooling. Schooling is habitually assembled for students through a range of social and material elements – uniform, furniture, signage, resources and physical transportation from home to school environment, the transition from the 'playground' into the school buildings. These assemblages, which we label and recognise as 'school' and 'classroom', change relations between children and adults. Identities are assigned – children become students and adults become teachers. Humans are entangled with technology, objects and the physical school environment.

However, few schools had the capability to replicate their entire face-to-face teaching offer although many transferred aspects of their teaching activity to online environments such as Google Classroom and Microsoft Teams sites.[1] The majority of English schools responded by offering a mixture of synchronous and asynchronous activities and a range of resources, from digital materials to physical packs of work (DFE Guidance, 2020b; Howard et al., 2021). Parents were expected to step into the 'teacher' role at home, despite many having to work from home and take care of several children simultaneously. New online teaching practices were debated – for example, should cameras be turned on or off in virtual lessons. Terms such as 'remote learning', 'home learning' and 'online learning' were used interchangeably, when in practice, they are very different things (Hrastinski, 2019). Technology itself was a major issue from the start and continued to be so, albeit to a lesser extent. Getting devices and connectivity into every household, during March and April 2020 became the main pre-occupation of the Department for Education in England.

Despite teachers' efforts to sustain habitual ways of 'doing school', existing notions of 'school' and 'classroom' started to become blurred as teachers, parents and students began to question the necessity of school day timings and behaviour expectations in online spaces. It became apparent that a homogeneous, hybrid, educational experience was not going to materialise. However, rather than using the opportunities presented by the hybrid environment, a deficit model emerged, which saw this new situation as a set of problems to be overcome. Post-COVID, this manifested itself in terms such as 'learning loss' and 'back on track' (Lee & Wenham, 2021; Newton, 2021).

In the next section, a more affirmative approach is adopted to discuss what might be learned from the experience of teaching online. I suggest that adopting a sociomaterial sensibility when reflecting on hybrid teaching and learning might help teachers explore and expand their practice to support a wider range of student needs. I use a series of vignettes to argue that sociomaterial practices co-constitute the concept of 'classroomness' adding to our understanding of practice and pedagogy in hybrid learning environments.

A sociomaterial take on hybrid learning spaces

Between 2020 and 2022 many international empirical studies reviewed the effect of COVID-19 lockdowns on education: in the UK (Coleman, 2021; Kim & Asbury, 2020; Kim et al., 2021); in Europe and Asia (Iivari et al., 2020); Norway (Bubb & Jones, 2020); New Zealand and Australia (Bond, 2021). These studies tended to focus on human perception, experience and reaction to hybrid learning, using methodologies such as teacher interviews, student surveys and parental diaries. Sociomaterial approaches shift away from human-centred views of learning which emphasise the personal and social, to include material actors such as objects, bodies, technologies and settings and consider the implications for education. In classrooms, furniture, Interactive WhiteBoards (IWB) and other equipment, for example, combine with children and teachers to produce activities, speech and ways of learning. Sociomaterial approaches can help us look systematically at how social and material elements 'assemble' and how power relations emerge from these assemblages so that we can intervene, disturb or understand these networks (Fenwick, 2015).

Schools exist within a wider network of governmental and societal expectations. What happens in them is a result of a network of regulation and accountability including curriculum and assessment as well as social and cultural values. In England, the National Curriculum (DfE, 2015) and external assessments such as Standard Assessment Tests (SATs), GCSE and A Level examinations exert a strong influence over the organisation of time in schools, creating a dominant narrative or imagined single trajectory for teaching and learning (Massey, 2005). During COVID-19 Lockdown 1 (March–June 2020), the traditional trajectory for school activity was severely disrupted. All national testing in England, in the form of examinations and Standard Assessment Tests (SATs), was suspended in favour of teacher-assessed grades (TAGs). Suddenly, the expectations for the way in which schools organised terms, weeks and days – the school 'timetable' – became irrelevant. Instead, the organisation of the school curriculum varied according to the phase of education and the proximity of major assessment points such as SATs, GCSE and A Level assessments. DfE (2020b) guidance recognised that the new 'remote learning' model could not sustain the traditional, sequential approach to curriculum delivery and stated:

> Many schools are finding they need to take a pragmatic approach to covering the curriculum, prioritising important concepts and particular groups of pupils where necessary…

…Some schools are postponing the introduction of new curriculum content until remote education practices are better embedded. They're spending the first few weeks reinforcing long-term memory by consolidating topics and concepts already taught.

(DfE Guidance, May 2020, n.p.)

The organisation of time was not the only aspect of normal school activity which was disrupted by COVID-19 lockdowns. Learning 'spaces' were no longer confined to physical school buildings. Usefully, spatial theory frames education as a spatial practice rather than taking place in any particular context. The spatial metaphor moves away from container-like notions of the classroom as 'bounded contexts' (Fenwick, 2015, p. 83). 'Space' is something which is always under construction, continually being constituted through interactions and embedded in material practices (Massey, 2005). More fluid notions of space provide a lens through which emergent social and material practices can be mapped. Learning can, therefore, be seen as part of relational networks embedded in different social practices in classrooms, online learning platforms, the outdoors, gaming environments and homes.

The sociomaterial approach that is used in this chapter is influenced by Latour's (2005) Actor Network Theory (ANT) which provides a spatial account of 'how relations in an assemblage are drawn together and stabilised' (Müller & Schurr, 2016, p. 218). Hybrid spaces, perhaps even more than other spaces, bring together and draw attention to what Massey (2005) calls 'unconnected narratives', stories about how learning happens in school and home, classroom and online platforms. They encourage us to consider how boundaries are created, crossed and fused, and how personal and public lives with different timelines can co-exist and collaborate. Exploring the way hybrid spaces are constituted allows us to question why school time/space might expect to impose itself on home time/space, and how boundaries are redrawn through practices such as the imposed wearing of school uniform during online learning sessions. Such intersections – between personal and public, physical and virtual, official and unofficial, spaces and how they were constituted and negotiated by two primary schools – form the basis of the empirical work in this chapter.

I draw on three key concepts around spatial practice, 'siting' (Leander & McKim, 2003); 'practice meshwork' (Schatzki, 2010) and 'classroom-ness' (Burnett, 2014), to explore how concepts of 'school' and 'classroom' are created and maintained by two teachers during COVID-19 lockdowns between March 2020 and March 2021. The first of these concepts, 'siting', refers to the processes through which spaces are produced (Leander & McKim, 2003). Leander and McKim discuss research sites, not as physical locations in which to conduct research but as the following and interpreting of 'space-constituting practices' (p. 225). This challenges the notion of the classroom as a single space instead constituted through co-existing spaces, or what Burnett (2014) labels 'official' and 'unofficial' spaces. Classrooms are seen as emergent spaces enacted by a network of human and non-human actors (McGregor, 2004).

Burnett (2016) also uses Schatzki's (2010) notion of a 'practice meshwork' or 'assemblage of practice' (Antczak & Beaudry, 2021) to describe the variety of practices which 'mesh' together in the physical classroom – schooling, friendship and community practices developed within and outside school. I captured some of these moments as they occurred during the COVID-19 lockdowns, through data collection methods such as screen capture, photos and interviews. Using these data I was able to explore how a range of hybrid practices establish 'classroom-ness' (Burnett, 2014), interrogate the problematic nature of 'being together' (Burnett, 2016) and investigate how 'togetherness' may be achieved through assemblages of people, technology, objects and environments such as Microsoft Teams virtual breakout spaces, YouTube and Oak National Academy.[2] In subsequent sections of this chapter, I analyse how spatio-temporal relations within assemblages both established, adapted and disrupted traditional school practices during and post-COVID-19 lockdowns and how togetherness in hybrid learning environments might have been achieved through differing assemblages of people, technology, objects and environment.

Context

At the end of February 2020, several weeks prior to the school lockdowns in March 2020, I was asked, by a Church of England Multi-Academy Trust (MAT)[3] in the English Midlands, to set up Microsoft Teams sites (Figure 14.1) for twelve primary schools; to provide some rapid training for teachers and to set up an online support desk in Teams providing 24/7 technical and pedagogical support in online learning approaches and software.

As an academic researcher, I recognised that my temporary role as MAT online learning advisor offered me a unique opportunity to observe the 'live' online activities of teachers and students across a range of schools, classes and age groups in the unprecedented situation we all faced in March 2020. I developed relationships with teachers and schools whilst supporting schools' day-to-day online practices, both advising and discussing with teachers, on a daily basis, how they were creating their 'learning spaces' in this new hybrid environment. Following these daily professional conversations with teachers and observations of their activity on Teams Posts, chats and resource areas, I sought formal ethical approval for an ethnographic study of the hybrid practices of two teachers in different schools within the MAT whose approaches to organising student learning experiences on their Teams sites appeared to differ.

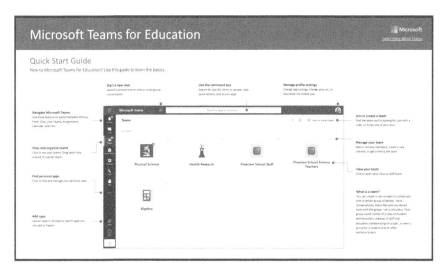

FIGURE 14.1 Microsoft Teams sites (screenshot MicrosoftTeamsforEducation_QuickGuide_EN-US.pdf (azureedge.net) used with permission from Microsoft).

School W is a medium-sized primary school on the outskirts of a small market town. The school has eight classes, organised in separate year groups (including Early Years). The teacher, whom I will refer to as Teacher WJ, taught the Year 6 class (11–12-year-olds). School E is a much smaller school in a Nottinghamshire village, with only four mixed-year classes. During the COVID-19 pandemic Teacher EK taught Class 3 which contained students in Years 3 and 4 (seven to nine-year-olds).

In order to compare online classroom practices with wholly face-to-face classroom practice I analysed the posts, documents, video and recordings of live class Teams meetings uploaded to each teacher's Microsoft Teams site and post-lockdown and observed each teacher in their physical classrooms over a period of one day. During observations, photographs were taken and field notes were made to aid analysis. Participants and schools have been anonymised.

Discussion for methodological approaches

Traditional school ethnographies are largely concerned with the experiences and interactions of *people* as agents, surrounded by passive objects such as desks, boards and computers, in the physical school building, which acts as a 'container' for educational activity. In contrast, a sociomaterial sensibility that is influenced by Actor Network Theory (Latour, 2005) regards desks and school buildings as actors, capable of acting on and being enacted by other actors whether they be people, objects, technology, environment. Rather than focusing on human experiences and interactions in an ethnographic study, the sociomaterial researcher maps and analyses how all actors come together, stabilise and interact. Alirezabeigi et al. (2020) argue that the digital actors which are part of hybrid learning environments configure school activities and spatio-temporal organisation into a mode of 'doing' called 'digital pedagogics' (p. 203). Digital actors have specific influences in hybrid learning environments which can be observed through patterns of use and interaction (McGregor, 2003). By mapping participant experiences, movements, timings through interviews, observations, field notes and the collection of artefacts such as photographs and drawings, the sociomaterial ethnographer is able to interpret how learning spaces are constituted through social and material practices. Spatial strategies such as room layouts, for example, work to manage behaviour and the way that power is negotiated between teachers and students (Pike, 2010).

Certain ethical issues are inherent in ethnographies which incorporate online environments. As an active participant as well as a researcher, I was entangled in the practices which I was attempting to map and document. As an online learning consultant employed by the MAT, I had access to all Teams sites used by schools within the Trust. This ability to 'lurk' (Leander & McKim, 2003) on the Teams sites of all schools in the MAT simultaneously, allowed a unique insight into online practices during COVID-19 lockdowns but ethically, required a 'heightened level of disclosure' (Yadlin-Segal et al., 2020). I took care to remind teachers of my continuing online presence on their Teams site, as my identity was 'negotiated and sustained by the situation' (Hine, 2000). I was part of a 'practice meshwork' (Schatzki, 2010) where I was helping to shape what happened in the online Teams environment. I developed relationships with teachers and schools whilst supporting schools' day-to-day online practices, both advising and discussing with teachers, on a daily basis, how they were creating their 'learning spaces' in this new hybrid environment, taking place simultaneously in the physical school buildings and online in Microsoft Teams.

In the next section, I draw on data collected through observations, interviews and documentation of activity on Teams sites. Individual consent was gained for the explicit use of specific data which I use to present a series of vignettes analysing spatio-temporal practices in the hybrid learning environment created by the two schools in my study.

'Classroomness' and temporal practices

Schools often organised on the assumption that all students within a classroom tend to learn the same thing, at the same time and at roughly the same pace. Learning activities are organised to be sequential. As Burnett (2016) points out 'Official markings of time are important here in privileging certain ways of ordering and demarcating ideas about success, failure and progress' (p. 11). In hybrid learning environments, however, ease of movement between online materials, applications and websites produces a different lesson 'flow' and raises questions about how teachers' and students' time is related, ordered and bounded.

Within the schooling assemblage time is organised socially and materially through a number of different mechanisms: clocks, representing chronological time mark out the progress of the school 'day'; timetables, both whole school and classroom, exert agency organising and regulating the assembling of people, resources and environment to ensure coverage of the curriculum. However, despite the assumption of sequential learning, most learning environments support multiple temporal frames that may both overlap or occur sequentially (Zagal & Mateas, 2015), such as the discussion of the primary school year in a Church of England MAT later in this chapter.

In Lockdown 1 (March–June 2020), teacher participants' different social and material circumstances afforded a variety of opportunities to re-constitute the 'classroom' in the hybrid environment (see Table 14.1 for details of online/offline teacher and student locations).

In hybrid learning environments, learning activities can be both synchronous and asynchronous. The first vignette discusses some of the ways in which synchronous activity and practices in hybrid learning environments provide a sense of togetherness through co-existing official and unofficial spaces.

TABLE 14.1 Teacher/student spaces and devices in Lockdown 1 (physical locations shaded)

Spaces	Home	Microsoft Teams	Website Blogs	School Classroom	Devices
SCHOOL W					
Teacher WJ	x	x	x		Chromebook iPad
Students WJ	x	x	x	x	Chromebooks
SCHOOL E					
Teacher EK		x		x	Laptop iPad
Students EK	x	x			Personal devices – mobile phone, tablet, laptop

Vignette 1 Synchronous encounters in hybrid environments

In this study, the Microsoft Teams site (see Figure 14.1) became a meeting point for previously unrelated occurrences – stored online texts and materials, home and school locations, communication and technological devices. The Teams Channel posts area evolved into the 'official' school space, the focus on dynamic, daily teacher–student dialogue. This hybrid space, like the physical classroom, had its own constraints and affordances which set off new social processes – dialogue, sharing, emotional reaction, and establishing of online identities.

School W Year 6 Teams Channel Messages area was similar to the structure shown in the main panel in Figure 14.1. My study looked at the textual interactions between teachers and students on a single day in Lockdown 1 (March 2020), the 'site' (Leander & McKim, 2003) of 'space-constituting practices'. On the surface, the dialogue appeared to be a 'virtual' replication of the daily 'meet and greet' routine which normally takes place at the physical classroom door. This daily interchange, when performed face-to-face, is an important part of establishing 'school' and classroom boundaries, or as Burnett (2014) put it, the co-existence of 'official' and 'unofficial' spaces'. The Teams Channel area assembles 'space' through text, images, emoticons and through the organisation of time. Although time appeared to be ordered chronologically and sequentially through dated and timed posts and replies, there were three separate 'threads' of conversation happening simultaneously. Multiple conversation threads between the teacher and different groups of students overlap and involve both people and affordances. Affordances refer to the possibilities or constraints an object provides for action in particular situations.

In Conversation 1, Student 1 initiated an informal conversation about the weather with the teacher. Another student (Student 3, Conversation 2) started a separate conversation a few minutes earlier. After a short delay, a third student and the teacher respond to her, to discuss their weekend. The language, although written, is informal and speech-like e.g 'Morning girls, have you had a good weekend'. Teachers and students use emoticons to replace the non-verbal communication which would have been apparent in a face-to-face conversation. Finally the teacher posted a separate, general, formal greeting to the whole class. In this post, language was formal, technically accurate, conveying clear information about the 'work' for that day. She dealt with queries and used capital letters for the word 'DON'T' to emphasise her instruction.

The Microsoft Teams channel affords the teacher the opportunity to take part in two conversations simultaneously, as was shown by the timing of her replies in each thread. Chat conversations can happen without one interfering with another as simultaneous spoken conversations would. This pattern, of entangled and overlapping conversation, continues throughout the day on the Teams site, as teachers and students 'narrativise and create the classroom 'space time' through their discourse' (Leander & McKim, 2003). The teacher can respond to student's questions when convenient and students can refer to her answers at any time – there is a permanent record of the interchange. In the physical classroom setting such interchanges are ephemeral. If a student does not listen or hear correctly, the message is lost.

Another example of synchronous communication was the use of the Teams Meeting tool which enables 'live' videoconferencing. School W's Teams meeting recordings show students took part in Teams meetings from a variety of physical locations within student homes – sitting on the floor, on sofas, and in bedrooms. Indeed, during the daily group reading of the class 'novel' students would often lie on their beds to listen to the teacher read. The variety of available spaces in student homes was both an advantage and disadvantage. Choosing your own space and bodily arrangement to suit the activity and your own comfort could be said to be conducive to learning and attention. However, the need for technology, in the shape of a computer or device, and a quiet location did offer constraints (Coleman, 2021), with some students being forced to sit on the stairs, in utility rooms and conservatories or to contend with younger siblings, parents and others in the same room, often very disruptive in terms of concentration (Brink et al., 2020).

> …home environments are often chaotic…not muted…you can see it all playing out on screen…we've got adults …parents who think they're co-medians and want to get the attention on them, which wasn't appropriate in the slightest…got the dog barking and the birds chirping in the background and the washing machine banging…
>
> *(Teacher WJ interview, Nov 2021)*

Synchronous communication is the norm in physical classrooms. Synchronous communication in Teams meetings, on the other hand, offered teachers a unique opportunity to reflect on how assemblages of bodies, furniture, physical context might affect different learning activities, both positively and negatively.

Microsoft Teams meetings performed a very positive role in preserving a sense of the primary school year in a Church of England MAT, through online versions of communal activities or rituals such as Harvest Festival celebrations, Nativity plays, and assemblies. Online, these rituals were often polysynchronous, conducted in 'live' Teams meetings but also recorded for future reference, and themselves containing pre-recorded performances.

Vignette 2 Asynchronous and polysynchronous time

Learning activity, in the Teams Channel area (Figure 14.1) mentioned earlier was often polysynchronous – a mixture of asynchronous and synchronous tasks. On the 1st April, 2020, Teacher WJ set an Industrial Revolution task for her Year 6 class. An electronic version of the task sheet is provided in the Files area of the Year 6 Teams site (Figure 14.2).

Two Teams meetings are scheduled at 11.00 and 13.45 for students to join, ask questions and discuss the task. Students are expected to read through the task sheet prior to the Teams meeting. This meeting is recorded for others to watch later. The teacher advises that students can stay in the virtual meeting for as long as they want.

Spatio-temporally this one teaching activity operated in a polysemic manner. There was no dominant 'narrative' or organisational rationale for the learning which took place each day. Students in multiple physical locations accessed this task at different points in the day, through a range of devices. Depending on when they noticed the post in the Teams Channel, downloaded and read the task sheet, they were able to participate simultaneously in the videoconference with other students and staff. The disadvantage of this asynchronous approach was that some students were too late 'spotting' the task and missed the live meetings which meant watching the recording of the meeting rather than having 'live' access to teacher support. On the other hand, the presence of a 'recording' meant that absent students did not miss out on the activity entirely.

In teacher interviews, it became apparent that asynchronous learning also allowed children with different learning needs to access more one-to-one

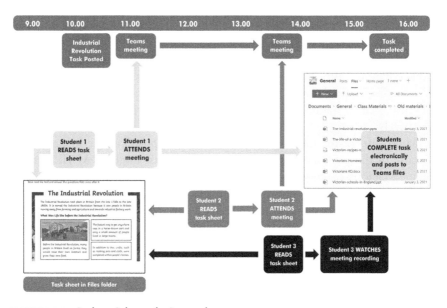

FIGURE 14.2 Industrial revolution task.

support pre- and post-class activity and to do their learning in different 'sites' such as the outdoors, which would not be available onsite.

> ...one little boy...didn't have a diagnosis but he had autistic tendencies...he would do his own little projects linked to what we've done...he'd do some extra learning on, I don't know, what he'd been busy doing the garden.

There are real opportunities here to re-examine the nature of boundaries between formal–informal learning and the concept of 'homework', particularly at the primary school level. Boundaries are not simply spatial but also temporal. Leander (2007, p. 27) has argued that space-time in schools usually involves sequential activity with a single space for each task. In contrast, for an individual to be involved in several *simultaneous* activities at a time is common in online environments such as digital gaming but is seen as potentially 'disruptive' in the classroom. The opportunity to extend and allow students to follow their own interests without detracting from whole class activity or progress demonstrates that 'multiple narratives' of learning are possible once the temporal convening of space can move beyond the single trajectory of the 'school day' in the physical classroom.

Teacher EK comments on this in her interview:

> So, we were doing...a bit of work on... protecting the planet and this boy had done some work, inspired by the film Wall-E and made a persuasive campaign if you like, based on that learning, based on that film...wasn't what we were doing strictly, but it lent itself and it was something that he was really passionate about...it was nice for him to be able to share that... whereas if you are sticking to a rigid timetable in school it would be 'Come on we're doing this, I've not asked you do to that'.

More individual, personalised approaches enabled certain students to bloom – students identified as having autism, ADHD and English as an additional language had the time and space to practise and work on extra material with one-to-one attention from teaching assistants and parents.

Vignette 3 Spaces and places

This blurring of boundaries or permeability of the hybrid space was well demonstrated on Teams Channel posts, spatially and temporally with students and teachers often posting in the early hours of the morning and late at night. During the lockdown periods, boundaries between school and home became increasingly blurred:

> To begin with...ones in the first lockdown they'd be on at half six, 'Hi Miss, are you awake?" ...I want to keep them, don't want them to switch

off, don't want them to go away, stop being on, so I'd rather do that…I'm a night owl anyway… I've got ones…with family issues…really just wants somebody to say goodnight to them.

(Teacher WJ interview)

Although Teams Channel posts were an 'official' space, frequent references to personal and family activities were made, particularly during Lockdown 1, where teachers were actively encouraging family activities such as physical exercise, baking and musical performances. In addition to posting textual comments, students and their families were sharing pictures and videos of their formal and informal activities, with both classmates and the teacher. The flow of activity was continuous and unbounded by the physical walls or timings of the classroom. The distributed agency and the permeability of this space were also demonstrated through the ability to share links to material outside of official resources. The online environment gave both teachers and students access to a range of online materials not accessible in the physical classroom environment due to the lack of individual devices. Students and teachers shared agency by finding and sharing links to interesting material which other students were able to explore without disturbing the 'visible pedagogy' (Bernstein, 2004) of the rest of their class.

This shared agency was demonstrated further in the Autumn of 2020 when Teacher WJ, physically present in the school building, was no longer an active agent in the Teams channel, although still occasionally monitoring and commenting there. Students colonised the Teams Channel space – dropping in to play Minecraft together, to socialise and to give information – turning it into an 'unofficial' space, existing within or alongside the 'official' classroom space.

Although there were constraints during COVID-19 lockdowns, which other authors have documented (Lee & Wenham, 2021), such as lack of engagement and access to wifi and devices, hybrid learning environments did offer affordances unavailable in the physical classroom setting. For example, the 'timetables' in each study school differed according to the 'narrative' created in Teams Channel Posts around the dispersed and diverse timelines which individual students were creating from themselves the daily 'menu'. Initially, Teacher WJ encouraged her older, Year 6 students (aged ten to 11) to take control of the organisation and timing of their daily learning activity. However, students and their parents appeared uncomfortable with this level of agency and the teacher was forced to provide a daily 'menu' of activities on the school website, in a Class Blog and in OneNote Class Notebook. However, the over-arching 'story' or 'narrative' which 'emerged' from the Posts timeline is demonstrated in the dialogue between Teacher WJ and her students (Figure 14.1) and the manner in which she took account of different home environments and the resources available to students. By providing multiple ways to approach tasks – through video, visually, and on paper – and demonstrate learning, the teacher acknowledged the differing social and material affordances in the hybrid learning environment compared to the physical classroom. Students' agency over the timing and duration of 'official' tasks meant that they could also take part in leisure and creative activities during the 'school day' e.g. videogames, baking, making music, going for walks, gymnastics and helping family with chores.

Teacher EK (School E) in contrast, with her class of younger Y3/4 students, used Microsoft Sway[4] presentations, posted daily on her Microsoft Teams channel. Her video explanations of Maths and English activities were embedded in the Sway presentation which encouraged linear progress through a daily 'timetable'. Sway's 'timeline' feature also allowed students to 'dip' into the presentation in a non-chronological way. Whilst Teacher EK's video explanations appeared to directly replicate face-to-face explanations at the IWB in the physical classroom, the hybrid environment afforded differing ways to interact with them. Students could watch and complete activities through hyperlinked, individual worksheets stored in Teams site Files or to websites such as *TTRockstars*, but also had the ability to pause and replay the teacher's explanations or to do the work alongside the teacher. Even within the relatively linear structure of the Sway presentations, multiple timescales co-existed – weekly as well as daily or hourly tasks such as reading and spelling were set within each 'Sway'.

In asynchronous learning tasks, objects such as textbooks and worksheets often became the 'agents' for sequential activity. Exercise books appeared as powerful actors in a specific 'lesson' or activity, working with other actors such as pens, teacher instructions and so on to materialise an outcome, often in the form of a written response, which was photographed and posted on the class timeline.

Handwriting is still highly valued in primary education, where the ability to produce legible, cursive handwriting is a formal expectation, not least because in England it is the focus for high stakes assessment[5] at Key Stage 2.[6] Hours are spent practising the physical skills required to produce legible, handwritten responses, with the vast majority of student responses being handwritten. This, despite an adult working world where the electronic document reigns supreme and where it could be argued that teaching typing skills alongside handwriting would be equally valuable. In the hybrid learning environments, discussed in this chapter, tasks could be done in OneNote Class Notebook or responses within the online Word document which contained the task content. However, there was very limited use of either the Teams Assignment tool or OneNote. Electronic 'objects' did not generally become 'schooled resources' in the same way as physical objects such as the exercise book or even other online educational environments to which students were referred – commercial online learning sites such as *Big Maths*,

WhiteRose Maths, *Testbase* or *Oak National Academy* – which required online responses and often provided online feedback on tasks.

Conclusion

This chapter has challenged the notion of the classroom as a single 'space' (Burnett, 2014). Sociomaterial perspectives on hybrid learning environments can help us to re-imagine the 'classroom as a physical, bounded space, instead encouraging us to consider it as emerging from "space-constituting practices"' (Leander & McKim, 2003, p. 225). By following, mapping and analysing some of the hybrid practices of two teachers in primary schools during the COVID-19 lockdown periods, I have explored: how 'official' and 'unofficial' spaces co-exist and create 'togetherness'; how the agency might be negotiated between students and teachers; and how consideration of differing spatio-temporal relations might offer opportunities for supporting the needs of individual students, for feedback, student interest and motivation.

Hybrid learning during COVID-19 lockdowns foregrounded the boundaries between home and school, formal and informal and encouraged us to regard learning situations as constituted through assemblages of human, non-human, technology and environment. If hybrid learning is to have a real chance of success in school settings, it needs to be regarded as an opportunity rather than a deficit version of in-person learning. It can be an opportunity to implement pedagogy which does not just integrate technology but pedagogy which helps generate different spatio-temporal relations.

Whilst teachers in this study were familiar with and happy to refer students to complete online teaching schemes such as *Classroom Secrets*, *WhiteRose Maths*, *TT Maths Rockstars* and used applications such as *Explain Everything* to produce teaching materials, they were significantly less familiar or confident about **students** using such software in learning activities. Teacher EK, who made significant use of *Explain Everything*™ to produce video explanations for her SWAY presentations, was surprised and interested in my suggestion that *Explain Everything*™ could also be used as a 'learning tool', with students making collaborative presentations to explain their Maths problem-solving processes, for example. Another example was the use of *Minecraft Education*™ with students who were difficult to engage in routine online activities. *Minecraft Education*™ offered free remote access to their 'game' during COVID and with my support and online collaboration, we had two after-school sessions with Class 4 (Years 5 & 6) 'in-world'. However, lack of confidence and familiarity with *Minecraft Education*™ meant that it was never successfully integrated into formal learning activities although the *Minecraft Education*™ website includes large banks of lesson plans for every subject.

Technical constraints to the use of such software in the physical classroom setting, even in non-lockdown circumstances both pre- and post-COVID, include: the lack of one-to-one student access to suitable devices and the very small budgets which small schools have to pay for the purchase and licensing of the software. Primary schools, in particular, can really benefit from centralised technical and pedagogical support available in multi-academy trusts, as in the MAT used in this study, at least during COVID-19 lockdown periods.

The pedagogical model of 'direct instruction' and assessment pressures from Standard Assessment Tests may be the underlying reason for the 'deficit model' which plagues hybrid learning environments. In the packed primary curriculum, the sheer amount of content causes significant time constraints. Hybrid learning environments offer real opportunities to deviate from this and offer students a more enriched and interesting curriculum. For example, outside visitors such as authors, experts, and teachers from other schools can be a serious expense and disruption to a small school's daily or weekly routine. In Lockdown 2, School E provided their students with links to an online 'live' session provided by the Literacy Trust to celebrate National Storytelling Week, where a speaker read football-themed stories. In the 'hybrid' classroom, Teams Meetings and Zoom could offer such opportunities regularly, with much smaller costs and less inconvenience for authors and speakers.

The vignettes in this chapter demonstrate that when teachers took advantage of opportunities provided in the hybrid 'classroom', such as flexible time and greater access to outside resources, there were demonstrable benefits for students. Interviews conducted post-COVID lockdowns revealed that teachers recognised the opportunities offered by hybrid learning environments, still routinely posting their daily activities menu and resources in Teams for absent students, for example. However, teachers felt that as long as online and hybrid learning is seen as a 'deficit' model and the emphasis on assessment and inspection continues, it is unlikely that they or their schools will be able to embrace new practices or take time to reflect and build on their experiences of hybrid learning environments.

Notes

1 Microsoft Teams for Education offers an online collaboration space in which teachers and students can share notes, chats, meetings, assignments – see Figure 14.1. https://edudownloads.azureedge.net/msdownloads/MicrosoftTeamsforEducation_QuickGuide_EN-US.pdf.
2 UK-based online classroom and resource hub providing teachers with free lessons and resources for pupils four to 16 years. Originally created by the Reach Foundation (a UK educational charity) during the first COVID-19 school lockdown in 2020, it was relaunched in Sept 2022 as a 'curriculum resources quango' (TES, 2022) sponsored by the UK Department for Education.

3 A multi-academy trust (MAT) is a group of aligned educational academies that come together to form a trust. Academies in the UK school system are educational institutions that rely on state funding directly from the Department for Education (DfE).
4 Microsoft Sway is similar to PowerPoint but web-based. It enables more than one person to edit and work on a presentation and online materials are immediately accessible and searchable from within the programme.
5 Key Stage 2 teacher assessment guidance 2022-23 - GOV.UK (www.gov.uk), 6.4 Handwriting.
6 Key Stage 2 is the legal term for the four years of schooling in maintained schools in England and Wales when the pupils are aged between seven and 11 years.

References

Alirezabeigi, S., Masschelein, J. and Decuypere, M. (2020) 'Investigating digital doings through breakdowns: A sociomaterial ethnography of a Bring Your Own Device school', *Learning, Media and Technology*, 45(2), pp. 193–207.

Antczak, K. A., & Beaudry, M. C. (2019). Assemblages of practice. A conceptual framework for exploring human–thing relations in archaeology. *Archaeological Dialogues*, 26(2), 87–110.Bøjer, B. H. and Brøns, M. G. (2022) 'How co-design can contribute to the ongoing development of hybrid learning spaces by empowering the users'. In Gil, E., Mor, Y.,& Köppe, C. (eds) *Understanding Teaching-Learning Practice*. Springer International Publishing, pp. 45–60.

Bond, M. (2021) 'Schools and emergency remote education during the COVID-19 pandemic: A living rapid systematic review', *Asian Journal of Distance Education*, 15(2), pp. 191–247.

Bubb, S. and Jones, M.-A. (2020) 'Learning from the COVID-19 home-schooling experience: Listening to pupils, parents/carers and teachers', *Improving Schools*, 23(3), pp. 209–222.

Burnett, C. (2014) 'Investigating pupils' interactions around digital texts: A spatial perspective on the "classroom-ness" of digital literacy practices in schools', *Educational Review*, 66(2), pp. 192–209.

Burnett, C. (2016) 'Being together in classrooms at the interface of the physical and virtual: Implications for collaboration in on/off-screen sites', *Learning, Media and Technology*, 41(4), pp. 566–589.

Coleman, V. (2021) 'Digital divide in UK education during COVID-19 pandemic: Literature review. Research report', *Cambridge Assessment*.

Defeyter, M., Von Hippel, P., Shinwell, J., Mann, E., Henderson, E., Brownlee, I., Pepper, G., Stretesky, P., Long, M. and McKenna, J. (2020) 'Covid-19: Back to school, rebuilding a better future for all children', *Education Select Committee*.

Department For Education (2015). National curriculum in England: Primary curriculum. Available online at: https://www.gov.uk/government/publications/national-curriculum-in-england-primary-curriculum. Accessed December 9, 2022,

Department For Education (2020a) *Guidance: Adapting teaching practice for remote education*. Department of Education (UK).

Department For Education (2020b) *Adapting the curriculum for remote education*. Department for Education Guidance. (UK).

Fenwick, T. (2015). Sociomateriality and learning: a critical approach. In Scott, D. & Hargreaves, E. (eds.), *The SAGE Handbook of learning*. London: SAGE Publications Ltd, pp. 83–93. https://dx.doi.org/10.4135/9781473915213.n8

Fenwick, T., Edwards, R., Sawchuk, P. (2015). *Emerging Approaches to Educational Research: Tracing the Socio-Material.* London: Taylor & Francis.
[AU: Please provide publisher location (city name).]Howard, E., Khan, A., & Lockyer, C. (2021). *Learning during the pandemic: Review of research from England* (Ofqual/21/6803/4). Ofqual.
Hrastinski, S (2019) 'What do we mean by blended learning?', *TechTrends*, Springer Science and Business Media LLC, 63(5), pp. 564–569.
Iivari, N., Sharma, S. and Ventä-Olkkonen, L. (2020) 'Digital transformation of everyday life–How COVID-19 pandemic transformed the basic education of the young generation and why information management research should care?', *International Journal of Information Management*, 55, pp. 102183.
Kim, L. E. and Asbury, K. (2020) "Like a rug had been pulled from under you': The impact of COVID-19 on teachers in England during the first six weeks of the UK lockdown', *British Journal of Educational Psychology*, 90(4), pp. 1062–1083.
Kim, L. E., Dundas, S. and Asbury, K. (2021) "I think it's been difficult for the ones that haven't got as many resources in their homes': Teacher concerns about the impact of COVID-19 on pupil learning and wellbeing', *Teachers and Teaching*, 1–16. doi: 10.1080/13540602.2021.1982690
Latour, B. (2005). *Reassembling the social: An introduction to actor-network-theory.* Oxford University Press.
Leander, K. M. and McKim, K. K. (2003) 'Tracing the everyday 'sitings' of adolescents on the internet: A strategic adaptation of ethnography across online and offline spaces', *Education, Communication & Information*, 3(2), pp. 211–240.
Lee, C. and Wenham, L. (2021) 'We just have to sail this sea all together until we find a shore': Parents' accounts of home-educating primary-school children in England during COVID-19', *Education 3-13*, 51(2), 276–291.
Massey, D. B. (2005). *For space.* Sage Publications Ltd.
McGregor, J. (2003). 'Making spaces: Teacher workplace topologies,' *Pedagogy, Culture and Society*, 11, 353–377.
McGregor, J. (2004). 'Spatiality and the place of the material in schools,' *Pedagogy, Culture and Society*, 12, 347–372.
Müller, M. & Schurr, C. (2016). 'Assemblage thinking and actor-network theory: conjunctions, disjunctions, cross-fertilisations,' *Transactions of the Institute of British Geographers*, 41, 217–229.
Newton, P. (2021). 'Learning during the pandemic: Quantifying lost learning'. *Ofqual's Strategy*.
Pike, J. (2010). "I don't have to listen to you! You're just a dinner lady!': power and resistance at lunchtimes in primary schools', *Children's Geographies*, 8(3), 275–287.
Schatzki, T. (2010). 'Materiality and social life,' *Nature and Culture*, 5(2) 123+. *Gale Academic OneFile*, link.gale.com/apps/doc/A233045546/AONE?u=ed_itw&sid=bookmark-AONE&xid=91716934. Accessed 30 December 2022.
Yadlin-Segal, A., Tsuria, R., & Bellar, W. (2020). 'The ethics of studying digital contexts: Reflections from three empirical case studies', *Human Behavior and Emerging Technologies*, 2(2), pp. 168–178.

15

LEARNING TO READ THE (DIGITAL) ROOM DURING THE COVID-19 PANDEMIC

Teacher perspectives

Linda Laidlaw and Suzanna So Har Wong

Introduction

The shift from "the before times" to the pandemic landscape that emerged starting in March 2020 has marked a time of change and significant impacts for many. For teachers across the globe, the arrival of COVID-19 also brought massive changes to conditions of instruction. Teachers experienced unprecedented challenges including those that were directly pandemic related and where pandemic modes of instruction uncovered gaps in institutional systems as well as inequities for students. In some regions, the pandemic also revealed a lack of political willingness to support safer conditions in schools and what seemed a devaluing of the well-being of both students and their teachers. In our own context in the province of Alberta, Canada, school safety has at times been sacrificed for "let 'er rip" political agendas where there were moves to discontinue COVID prevention measures in schools when government officials made decisions that were not based on science or health data.

School closures are not unusual for localized events such as extreme weather and, less commonly, for other sorts of disease outbreaks. These types of school closures are typically temporary and involve instruction shutting down for a few days with no other particular adaptions. However, with the emergence of the COVID-19 pandemic, many schools were forced to transition their classes to online and remote instruction for months at a time. In the province of Alberta, and indeed, across Canada, teachers were required to rapidly shift from face-to-face instruction to online and/or remote teaching, and in many areas, teachers were given only a few days' notice.

While existing literature and analyses at the time of our writing are still relatively scarce on the topic of schooling, teaching, and learning during the

DOI: 10.4324/9781003352129-19

COVID-19 pandemic, a number of research examples underline how K-12 school systems were caught off guard in the quick switch to online and/or remote teaching. According to the Alberta Teachers Association's survey report (ATA Research, 2020), most respondents (teachers in the province of Alberta) were unprepared for this transition and encountered challenges in creating high-quality learning experiences for their students, and particularly, in the context of the requirement to teach in online environments. The ATA survey report results are similar to the findings from the Organization for Economic Cooperation and Development (Schleicher, 2020) in which "teachers have reported a high need for training in the use of information and communication technologies (ICT)" (p. 16). As Canadian educational theorist, Andy Hargreaves (2021) notes, not only were conditions for teaching changed, teachers also lacked their usual social and teaching community supports and connections to "school life" as they taught during periods of remote instruction.

Unintended pandemic research

Our study of teacher experiences during the COVID-19 pandemic was an unintentional diversion from our original research plans. Prior to the pandemic closures of schools that occurred in March 2020, we had invited a group of teachers to engage with our ongoing study examining literacies and maker space pedagogies in early years classrooms. As we embarked on the original project in 2019, our research and study activities were informed by notions from complexity thinking (Davis and Sumara, 2008) and theories of literacy and multimodality (Pahl and Rowsell, 2012; Scott and Marsh, 2018). We used qualitative research methods informed by ethnography (Kvale, 1996; Purcell-Gates, 2011) in our work with the focus group for our "maker" meetings and activities. We have continued to embrace a three-dimensional literacy framework that bring together an operational dimension (facility with literacy tools), a cultural dimension (understanding of literacy contexts), and a critical dimension (interpreting and assessing information), following from Green (1988, 2012). While these approaches were maintained in the revised pandemic study, we needed to make considerable changes to our research methods, given the in-person research activities were not possible for a considerable length of time.

Our focus group was comprised of eight teachers who ranged in levels of experience (newer teachers to mid-career educators) and who worked in various school locations (urban, suburban, rural, English language learner settings, and alternative teaching settings). All of the teachers were working in elementary years schools, at the kindergarten to grade/year six level, including those who were consultants. The teachers also varied in their comfort level with technology, from several who had worked in technology leadership roles in their districts to teachers who were interested in learning more but saw themselves as novices.

After March 2020, as the pandemic arrived, we were unable to work with the teachers and potential student participants in the ways we had planned, that is, in face-to-face focus groups, school visits, and makerspace workshops. All of the teachers in the focus group initially switched to online and remote learning and teaching, as required by their districts, aside from two teachers who were on maternity leaves but who returned to the classroom over the first year of the pandemic. Schools were inaccessible for research purposes during times of pandemic restrictions in our region, and the university was closed to in-person work as well as placing restrictions on human participant research. Even when face-to-face learning returned in schools more widely in Fall 2021, access for university researchers still remained limited, as many schools, while open for students and teachers, were closed to visitors. Over the past year (from 2021- to Fall 2022), restrictions have eased, schools and teachers have often been focused on dealing with repercussions from the pandemic, lacking the time and energy to participate in research projects.

In spite of these setbacks, we remained in contact with our focus group teachers informally, starting from when we were all at home during the first few months of the pandemic period. These teachers had much to say about pandemic impacts on their own teaching practices, their students, and other aspects of their teaching lives, and several of them mentioned that they would be interested in exploring topics connected to our pre-pandemic focus group meetings but looking more closely at how these had been influenced by the pandemic. Through email messages and phone conversations, they expressed that they wanted to talk about their pandemic experiences, challenges, and new learning as they unpacked new and unfamiliar experiences. Thus, we shifted the focus of our project to examine digital practices for teachers and students during the COVID-19 pandemic, with seven of our original eight teachers agreeing to continue in the revised pandemic-focused study.

We set up a pilot survey early in 2021, looking at digital experiences during online and remote teaching since the start of the pandemic. The 14 teachers in our initial survey were working as elementary school teachers, literacy consultants who were supporting teachers, or teachers providing student learning assistance or other supports. The remote and distance learning taking place in their schools ranged from online instruction using platforms such as Google Classroom and Google Meets, or Zoom, or as distance learning with physical lesson packages delivered to students and supported by online meetings. The pilot survey was followed up by a series of teacher interviews and included five teachers in addition to the seven focus group participants, including two teachers who were located in the province of British Columbia and one in the province of Ontario. Teachers clearly expressed a desire to talk about and consider their experiences—including their shifting practices in the digital realm, as well as their other pandemic-related experiences in schools.

In our pilot survey, we had naively assumed that the circumstances and impacts of COVID-19 would be over within a year—however, as impacts from the pandemic have continued to provide ongoing challenges and unexpected situations for teachers (and researchers!), we decided to redevelop our survey in order to gather a wider diversity of teacher perspectives. As this new survey is still ongoing, our chapter relies more centrally on findings from our initial pilot survey, the teacher interviews, and one in-person focus group meeting that took place in June 2022. For these teachers, most of them were teaching "in person" in schools for at least some periods of time from Spring 2021 onward, with schools generally returning to "in person" instruction by Fall 2021. However, some of the consultants were still working remotely, and students in some areas still had the choice to continue in an online option. By June 2022, all of the participants we met with in the focus group had returned to in-person teaching or consulting. Participants included rural and urban teachers in the province of Alberta, several participants from British Columbia and Ontario, and several teacher participants from Yukon Territory and the Northwest Territories.

Struggles and challenges: "It was tough!"

During the early phase of the pandemic (March 2020-June 2021), teachers across our studies frequently commented on their struggles in switching to digital, online modes of instruction. Many of the teachers struggled with gaining an accurate sense of student engagement and spoke about students being disconnected and their difficulties in knowing which students might not be fully "present" or were struggling even though they had logged into the online instructional platform. They also remarked on student difficulties with technology due to a lack of provision of devices or technical problems such as poor Wi-Fi connectivity. As one of the literacy consultants mentioned, referring to the teachers she was supporting through offering professional development sessions, "It is hard to 'read the room' online, and especially when some keep cameras off." This was echoed even more strongly in comments about students.

> H, an experienced teacher working in the province of Ontario, summarizes:
> We [teachers] were all thrust into this situation. Nobody really knew how serious it was and … we just didn't have the technical know-how, the kids didn't have the skills, we did the best we could… It was tough, it was really, really tough! We had never had any training on using the online

platform [Microsoft Teams]. We didn't know what we were doing.... The parents had no training. The teachers had no training. The kids didn't have devices. It was just a schmozzle.

In addition to her worries about getting sick during the first waves of the pandemic, H also felt that her school policy-makers devalued and disrespected her teaching professionalism. For example, her school division told the teachers that they were required to deliver their teaching in four different ways/modes to their students:

In September 2020... you could choose to be in person, you could choose to have paper copies sent home to you. You could choose to be synchronous [and] digital where you were at a virtual school, or you could be asynchronous [and] digital, where your work was posted digitally. They [members of the school board leadership team] brought us together, and they told us—the teachers are responsible for all four models of delivery.... People [my colleagues] were crying. I have never in all my 30 years of teaching in that school have I seen people [teachers] break down like that...never, never, and people just collapsed, while we were just in full throttle pandemic. It was crushing!

H's experience with being required to address multiple modes and time arrangements for instruction stands out as particularly difficult. Other regions and school districts addressed instruction differently. After initial periods of everyone working remotely (March to June 2020), rather than having individual teachers work in multiple ways, in some regions, teachers were assigned classrooms that were solely online *or* in-person instruction as parents were able to make the choice between online or school-based instruction for their children. "In person" teachers, however, often experienced pandemic-related disruptions as various student quarantines and absences or their own or family illness resulted in needing to problem-solve options for instruction, particularly when there were shortages of substitute teachers. Thus, "in person" teachers were still required to make additional effort and, at times, offer additional modes of instruction.

M was a newly graduated teacher who was teaching in the online option, working with eight to nine-year-old children. This was his first full-time teaching job. As these students were from different parts of the city, they did not know each other prior to attending the online classroom. This presented challenges for M in helping students to get to know one another and feel as though they were part of a classroom. Many of his struggles were experiences that were typical for a new teacher, but heightened by the remote nature of his teaching—where he lacked the ability to talk to other classroom teachers, as he was assigned centrally with all the other online teachers who taught students from across the school division. He worked from either his own home or alone in an empty classroom. While he was exploring his own pedagogical approaches and beliefs as a beginning teacher, he generally had to do this in isolation and experienced online teaching as quite stressful. While he did not experience too many challenges related to working within the school district's digital platform, his struggles were more connected to a lack of experience with student diversity and differences and the ability to make connections with students he had never met in person and who had not previously met one another. As he stated, "I've got to notice the students. Also … to build the trust with students."

While M and H were both far apart in terms of years of teaching and geography, their experiences overlapped in terms of being faced with stressful conditions for instruction, a lack of support for new or unfamiliar teaching methods, and their own pandemic-related worries. They are representative of many of our interviewees, survey respondents, and our teacher focus group members.

While the first waves (and year) of the pandemic created what was experienced as the most significant upheavals for teachers and classrooms, teachers also encountered other uncertainties during the second pandemic school year (Fall 2020 to June 2021). C, an Indigenous teacher who worked in a First Nation community, noted that her school was shut down multiple times:

> Because we taught in the First Nation community, there was a certain number [of COVID-19 cases] that we would shut down the schools completely. Most of the time it was shut down for a period of time. Absolutely nothing. And then we would open up the Google classrooms and then send home the learning packages, send home food. And then we opened up again to cohorts. So, it was kind of like up and down, up and down, depending on the wave.

As C noted, the pandemic impacts on her teaching community went beyond shifting approaches to instruction—children and families also relied on support programs for more basic needs such as meal programs, which became inaccessible at times of school closures. Inequities for students and larger burdens due to COVID were also made visible to her. As she noted:

> It was really hard because our students didn't come online, and that was just part of being on the reserve. You know like, these kids have lost, like, members of their family … and COVID… hit the whole household. I remember coming back and then a student already told me, "I had COVID twice."

I really saw the economic barriers when it came to COVID.

Digital inequity was also an issue that teachers saw impacting student participation in less affluent communities. In C's teaching environment in the First Nations community, this was another area of learning for her:

> [A] hard lesson I learned was ... a lot of [families], like maybe a family had one phone to 10 people. Or else one iPod to a family of five.
> We were lending out Chromebooks (laptops) too... I remember ... this kid just wouldn't listen to me but I would see her walk by the school ... just to use the wifi. 'cause some homes don't have wifi. Third world.

As other teachers noted, even when students were able to access devices and the internet, teaching online often revealed other challenging aspects of children's lives, where parents were working remotely at the same time their children had online school and so were unable to help or support their child's instruction. Some children simply "disappeared" from online instruction for weeks.

After a 26-month gap in our focus group meetings, in June 2022 we were finally able to meet in person with our teacher focus group. We met in an airy café, as our usual university setting was still shifting back from various restrictions. While the teachers were excited to meet with us and one another—they work across three different school districts in the city—they all spoke about feeling deeply tired and the word "burned out" was mentioned by several, as they shared their experiences in schools since the start of the pandemic. Across this group of seven teachers, all but one had been infected at least once with COVID, some had been infected twice or more, and one was still dealing with ongoing fatigue and struggling with long COVID. Since the return to in-person learning, they had all experienced various periods of upheaval in their teaching, with classroom or school quarantine shut-downs, their own episodes of being sick and/or dealing with illness in their own families, and having to stay at home off and on due to being a "close contact" when this was still a requirement. And, it is important to underline all teachers who missed school — regardless of the reason — still had preparation responsibilities and work to set up for substitute teachers. Some of the teachers had also been required to take on other teachers' classroom responsibilities when there was a shortage of substitute teachers in their schools—an occurrence that was not unusual during the pandemic. They all spoke of the responsibilities of additional cleaning, sanitizing, and health and safety policies that classroom teachers were tasked with, particularly those who were working with younger children. For example, at one point, books in the classroom libraries were required to be quarantined after use, which presented an additional burden on teachers, so that some simply stopped sending books home with students. To address this, some of the focus group teachers developed new lending approaches. One of the teachers sent larger collections of ten books that each child could keep at home for several weeks. Some school districts purchased access to online reading platforms such as Raz Kids, Epic, Sora, and other options. However, teachers mentioned that these digital platforms worked best for children in more affluent families where there was access to digital devices and highspeed internet. For some students, the online reading platforms were simply inaccessible.

Change, innovation, and resilience: "I've become a better teacher in some ways"

While the teachers in our project were all very clear that the pandemic presented many challenges to their teaching practice, many also articulated that they discovered unexpected benefits, often connected to integration of technology for instruction. Teachers reported learning new skills and seeing new opportunities for classroom literacy and digital communication modes. For example, some teachers were able to find creative ways to reach out to virtually connect with community experts—such as inviting guest speakers to participate remotely and taking students on virtual field trips. H, who had had to teach in a variety of challenging situations and conditions, noted that she also strived to explore innovative approaches and was still determined to do her best for her students. H describes some of her changes in digital practices:

> I think one of the things [connected] to the pandemic has been kind of a bonus.... Virtually, we had opportunities to access things, but if we were in a position where we had to physically go to these things, we couldn't have done it. Because you know, we don't have the budget to take kids out for field trip experiences.... So, I had a lot of online experiences with the students and I think those are going to continue. I think that would be good, because literally it gives us access to things we did not have access to before.

J is an experienced teacher who teaches in an urban school district in a multicultural school that includes students who have come to Canada from many different countries. Although she and her students experienced challenges, she was able to use her teaching skills and knowledge of her students to develop new practices in periods of online remote instruction. She approached all challenges as opportunities to expand her own professional learning and gain new understandings about her students:

> Two of my students blossomed in online learning, I wasn't hearing a peep out of them in the classroom. One of them became this exuberant [student] dancing around [and] chatting up a storm with the kids online, where in person I didn't hear a peep out of her. So maybe just like the comfort zone

of being in her own home, in her own space, with her parents there, maybe there was a certain level of feelings of safety.

When J missed seeing her students face-to-face, she decided to deliver her students' weekly learning packages to their sidewalks in front of their homes. This gave her an opportunity to see her students' neighborhood and their families and to reconnect with her students:

> Those pandemic kids and I, the online kids, we were linked in a special way because I got to know them on their own ground. This was a bonus to me.

She also learned to be more flexible in her pedagogical approaches when teaching online:

> We've had to be so flexible which is good for the brain, but exhausting for the body. However, it shifted my teaching. I think that I've become a better teacher in some ways. I'm using different teaching strategies now in the classroom than I did before [the pandemic] just because of that scarcity mindset—scarcity of time, and the need to be more effective as a teacher…

She also remarked that she found the connection to children's home lives during remote online learning to be significant:

> …I was looking into peoples' living rooms and I was seeing the kids in their pajamas sitting on their bed on a Friday morning. Like, it was very intimate…. And so it felt like those families and I, I still feel like we're linked in a way.

Many of the teachers commented that while the experience of teaching remotely or online was challenging, it also created new opportunities and connections and forced them to learn new approaches and gain familiarity with digital technologies. As one teacher stated, "I was able to use more innovative practices, the pandemic pushed me to learn and be acquainted with different technologies out of necessity." One of the literacy consultants noted that, while there was a large learning curve for some teachers, "I was impressed with the growth and perseverance of teachers who call themselves technologically challenged." What also became apparent across the teacher participants was how much variation in support they received in relation to their own professional learning—ranging from very little or none, to mismatches where school administration seemed to have little understanding of what teachers were faced with, to supports that took place in innovative ways and those that considered the challenges and learning needs of teachers in the unusual circumstances of a pandemic.

Pandemic professional development: emergency learning

The topic of support for teachers switching to different modes of instruction during the pandemic and the need to learn new digital skills was frequently mentioned by the teachers in our study. According to teachers in an OECD (2019) report on leadership and lifelong learning, the most impactful and helpful professional development (PD) programs are those that take up collaborative approaches to address both student learning and to provide a network of teacher support. As well, PD programs that involve a strong focus on curriculum content or subject areas were cited as most beneficial. With the arrival of the pandemic, typical practices for teacher professional development were disrupted. The usual after-school sessions located in schools, district sessions that would draw educators from across school districts, and in-person teachers' conventions and conferences all ceased in the first two years of the pandemic in many places. Yet the need for additional learning opportunities for teachers was high, as Schleicher's (2020) OECD report outlines that even prior to COVID-19, teachers around the globe reported a high need for additional training in computer and information technologies, creating challenges during pandemic instruction. He states, "most of the education systems covered by the OECD's … (PISA) [Programme for International Assessment] were not ready for the world of digital learning opportunities" (p. 16).

One of the literacy consultants who responded to our survey noted that she and other consultants were able to work remotely with teachers and offer supports to help with shifting to online remote instruction. She stated that some teachers had appreciated not having to dash away at the end of the school day to attend in-person workshops when they could participate virtually, something also mentioned by several survey respondents. However, generally, the teachers in our survey and interviews reported that they were more likely to participate in workshops or seminars that involved collaborative approaches such as peer support or working with literacy coaches connected to their schools. With a certain degree of more isolation for many teachers, they expressed a desire for approaches that involved more personal engagement and collegiality. We suspect that collaborative approaches were more popular with our participants because it both provided personal connections as well as helping to strengthen or support professional learning networks they could draw upon in the future. Some teachers received professional development opportunities within their own school districts, but other participants had to seek out professional learning on their own.

In one teacher's example, C did not have a lot of support from her school district. Her professional development during the first wave of the pandemic mostly involved searching for resources online by herself. In a contrasting example, J had many professional development opportunities provided by her school division and felt very supported by her principal and the literacy consultants connected to her school in the shift to online instruction. H noted that her school district, while lacking in some aspects of support for assisting teachers in learning a new instructional platform, did offer helpful technology troubleshooting services that could be called upon immediately, which allowed her to focus more on the pedagogical aspects of her classes rather than be sidelined by trying to sort out student technical issues.

The teacher participants in our study who were literacy consultants or literacy "coaches" who provided professional development workshops and seminars to the teachers in their school districts were presented with significant challenges in trying to meet the needs of many teachers during the pandemic. "Just in time" formats for professional development workshops that were responsive to immediate needs and were flexibly structured, as well as peer support from teachers in their own network, appeared to provide the most useful learning supports for many teachers in our study. However, as needs were high and literacy consultants or coaches were relatively few, the consultants struggled with trying to create models of support that would work for all. Teachers' needs for learning how to deal with technologies involved in remote and/or online learning were urgent, yet as Hargreaves (2021) suggests, improving teachers' digital expertise in the pandemic,

> should not only include knowledge of apps, tabs, platforms, and other technical resources, but also the ability to determine when digitally-based resources do and do not provide unique added value for effective learning compared to other resources.
>
> (p. 1853)

From operational-technical to critical considerations: changing practices

Most of the teachers in our study moved beyond simply learning how to use new platforms or applications. In our analysis of teachers' comments about their digital literacy instruction, we noticed that many mentioned they were shifting their practices from what they had been focusing on at the start of pandemic teaching. As mentioned earlier, we used Green's (1988, 2012) three-dimensional (3D) model of literacy to assist with our analyses because it provides a flexible framework which recognizes that literacy, communication, and technology practices are multidimensional, interconnected, and nonlinear. In Green's (2012) model, the three overlapping dimensions work together simultaneously and can be used to understand communication in the digital era. The *operational-technical* dimension involves the skills and competencies required to read and write printed texts or use specific technology tools such as alphabets, tablets, or computers. The *cultural-discursive* dimension involves a deeper understanding of literacy contexts, for example, the ability to understand various meanings of digital media or understand genres. The *critical-reflexive* dimension refers to the capacity to interpret multiple and/or conflicting sources of information, to transform and synthesize understanding, and to ask critical questions about intentions and points of view of various texts.

Teacher participants' responses indicated that at the start of the pandemic, when they suddenly switched to remote and online instruction, they were primarily focusing on the operational-technical aspects of digital literacy practices. In this phase, the teachers' concerns were centered on how to operate specific digital platforms and applications. C shared her approach with her students:

> I just took it very slow. I just said, "Hey guys, we are gonna try Google Classroom today," and then I said "For today we're just going to look at the website. We're going to see how far we can go through." And then the next day I'd be like, "Alright—today we're going to practice downloading documents." And then, I just went baby steps with that one class.

For C, the operational-technical "baby steps," highlighting the digital literacy practices her students needed to learn, was also important in helping her manage instruction at the beginning of her online experiences. Another teacher, H, at the start of her pandemic teaching, needed to make sure that she could operate the Microsoft Teams platform, which presented "a steep learning curve" for her. She stated in her interview that "the technical issues that were experienced in those [students'] homes could be very different ones…" noting issues like learning how to share screens. Basic technical problem-solving and learning how the platform functioned was key to her teaching during this time.

After the teacher participants gained competency and became more familiar with operating the technical aspects of their online teaching, some began to engage more with cultural-discursive dimensions of literacy in their instruction. J focused on building relationships with her students online. As she recognized that linguistic diversity of her students impacted many aspects of her teaching, she noted that being better able to understand her students' home language and literacy practices was important. She had students who were newcomers to Canada and whose parents were not fluent in English, and she needed to find additional ways to communicate with this group of students in her online classroom. Using language that was culturally relevant and accessible to her students (and their parents) was crucial for J, and she acknowledged that her literacy practices needed to change:

> Yes, it's the pandemic time but it's also a point of privilege as well. I really think that we[teachers] have these privileges to communicate with others easily and others who don't. The gap between these two … the pandemic has really elbowed that gap wider, I think.

Across our teacher participants, as they became more familiar with online structures, apps, and digital tools, they also became more critical about the affordances of different structures and how online and offline formats impacted different children. J noted that some of her students participated more actively in the online remote classroom than they had initially in her "regular" pre-pandemic classroom, leading her to consider how both approaches of teaching supported different students in different ways. Another teacher stated, "I worked with technology in a way I never would have, if I had not been forced to by COVID." Several of the teachers admitted that because they were required to rapidly gain experience in using digital tools and strategies, they were now looking more closely at which applications and approaches were more pedagogically beneficial for their students and had shifted their teaching to include more digital practices even after students had returned to their usual classrooms: "[I am] using more digital supports than before and recognizing the need for more digital skills for my students."

Beyond learning new digital skills—from more basic operational knowledge to becoming more critically aware of how different digital practices may or may not impact student learning and classroom practices—the teacher participants also shared their thoughts on the larger impacts of pandemic learning for their classrooms. Some of the teachers expressed perspectives that were more critical of educational authorities—their school administration, government educational authorities, or school district officials—citing pedagogical mismatches or a lack of real understanding regarding what teachers were being asked to do, or regarding students' needs:

> The district was least helpful as their consultants had not had the same experiences teaching online and were not fully aware of the challenges we faced. The district did a great deal of work with creating videos and lessons for the 2020–21 year, but they were not put into a useful format for my students.

Within the focus group and across some of the interviews, after students had returned to classrooms and to in-person learning, some teachers were skeptical about common media panics about "learning loss" and government assessment plans to track this, noting that, generally, their own students had made considerable progress and were catching up academically. They expressed a sense of pride in the student resilience and growth they had observed, in the face of many difficult pandemic-related experiences. However, they also expressed being surprised to see little focus from the media or their own school authorities on what they saw as an enduring consequence of the pandemic—children's overall lack of social experiences and opportunities. Their students had missed out on many activities and experiences of childhood — going shopping with parents, participating in after-school activities and sports, and more frequent play opportunities with peers that would have typically happened prior to the pandemic. One teacher remarked that their students "just seemed younger" and lacked the social skills she would have usually seen in pre-pandemic years with previous students at the same grade level. This comment elicited full agreement across our focus group, and many of the interview participants mentioned similar observations. Other teachers wondered whether some of the government and district efforts to focus on "learning loss" might be counterproductive, as social development was not being supported in the same ways, and instead, in some school districts, students were undergoing many hours of extra literacy and mathematics assessment at the start of the 2022 school year, which also took away significant time from what they saw as more valuable classroom activities and community building. Such perspectives are supported by Hargreaves (2021), who suggests that the "narrative of lost learning" has a number of flaws, suggesting that often they are focused on "arbitrary norms" and, do not recognize that under pandemic conditions, schooling has been disrupted for all (p. 1836). Rather than an emphasis on striving to "make up" learning time—a perspective that sees students as deficient and teachers as required to fill the gaps—shifting to look at the impacts on teaching and learning in a more holistic and interconnected way might offer more productive opportunities to re-envision post-pandemic classrooms.

Toward a post-pandemic future: what now?

As schools have shifted back to more typical in-person classroom learning, and a kind of "new normal," the teachers we have interviewed or surveyed more recently have continued to reflect on their pandemic experiences as well as looking toward a future that still holds some uncertainty. One teacher sums it up, "I think I am still processing many of these things, 'cause it was so different." Another stated, "I found myself coming back this year with lots of questions." Conditions in schools, in the province of Alberta, and indeed in other areas across Canada, have continued to present challenges for teachers and students. In reflecting on the perspectives shared by the teachers in our study, we see the need to move beyond the dichotomies outlined by Hargreaves (2021), of "post-pandemic narratives of educational doom" and "jubilant celebrations of bright spots and silver linings" (p. 1835) acknowledging the messy uncertainties that lie ahead. Existing research on the impacts of the pandemic on teachers and students, at the time of this writing, has focused primarily on the first year of COVID-19 realities, looking at situations of lockdowns, more significant schooling closures and restrictions, and online and remote instruction (see, e.g., Greenhow and Lewin, 2021; Sánchez-Cruzado et al., 2021; Sosa Díaz, 2021). As well, as we have mentioned earlier, the topic of "learning loss in the pandemic" seems to be an area of rapid growth, with a quick Google Scholar search returning hundreds of recent publication results, including many with rather speculative titles such as "estimated learning loss" or "projecting the pandemic impacts of learning loss." With much research (like our own project), also impacted by pandemic restrictions, we expect to see more publications emerging globally on the pandemic impacts on schools, learners, and teachers and including post-pandemic analyses to help guide the way forward. We suspect that collecting the "batting scores" resulting from what appears to be a surge in testing may, in the end, be less useful than looking ahead to creating responsive practices and listening to teachers. We shall see.

For educators, educational stakeholders, government policy-makers, and curriculum designers, while the pandemic has presented many challenges, it has also revealed that practices can change rapidly, particularly when the political will to do so is present. Yet, "top down" decision-making, as reported by some of the teachers in our study, was not always in tune with the experiences in classrooms or the needs of teachers and students. "Bottom up" actions and what Hargreaves (2021) labels "an immense asset of teachers' professional capital" was essential to creating instruction that responded to rapidly changing circumstances.

While the pandemic presented a disruptive influence, disruption can also present opportunities for innovation and change. In our earlier research looking at the disruptions and tensions posed by shifts into new digital media practices (Laidlaw, O'Mara, and Wong, 2022), we suggest that, "what might be initially experienced as a disruption… may in fact present opportunities for more innovative teaching and learning experiences for all" (p. 74) and perhaps invite a more critical stance on established practices. While the pandemic has presented as a global, systemic phenomenon, with many nonlinear impacts typical of complex processes (Davis and Sumara, 2008; Doll, 1993), it has also presented openings for change and ways of working differently. Many of the teachers expressed their hope that while the pandemic was difficult, the skills and knowledge that were gained "[W]ill slowly enhance our school cultures by building institutional knowledge and expertise."

We conclude our chapter with questions. As we enter into a post-pandemic future, will we see more systemic changes to support teachers' (and students') digital literacy practices? Will education systems make changes to support technology provision and equity for all students? We wonder, too, if we will see more strategic learning arising from the pandemic conditions in education systems over time. Perhaps the experiences of the pandemic might create options for more flexibility for learners who may benefit from some of the alternate modes of instruction that were introduced during online and remote learning. We wonder, as well, whether "lessons learned" from the pandemic will lead to changes that will better respond to student needs. We are curious about how teachers will be encouraged (or forced?) to respond to pandemic-provoked systemic changes. In our own research, we are planning for ongoing follow-up with participants, and we will continue to survey teachers. We see that examining the long-term impacts of the COVID-19 pandemic, on teachers as well as students, is important and critical work as we move forward.

References

ATA Research (2020) Alberta Teachers Responding to Coronavirus (COVID-19): Pandemic Research Study Initial Report. [online] Available at: https://legacy.teachers.ab.ca/SiteCollectionDocuments/ATA/News%20and%20Info/Issues/COVID-19/Alberta%20Teachers%20Responding%20to%20Coronavirus%20(COVID-19)%20-%20ATA%20Pandemic%20Research%20Study%20(INITIAL%20REPORT)-ExSum.pdf (Accessed 17 October 2022).

Davis, B. and Sumara, D.J. (2008) *Complexity and education: inquiries into learning, teaching, and research*. New York: Routledge.

Doll, W.E. (1993) *A post-modern perspective on curriculum*. New York: Teachers College Press.

Green, B. (1988) Subject-specific literacy and school learning: A focus on writing. *Australian Journal of Education*, 32(2), pp. 156–179. doi:10.1177/000494418803200203

Green, B. (2012) Subject-specific literacy and school learning: a revised account. In: B. Green and C. Beavis, eds., *Literacy in 3D: An integrated perspective in theory and practice*. Melbourne: ACER, pp. 2–21.

Greenhow, C. and Lewin, C. (2021) Online and blended learning: Contexts and conditions for education in an emergency. *British Journal of Educational Technology*, 52(4), pp. 1301–1305. doi:10.1111/bjet.13130

Hargreaves, A. (2021) What the COVID-19 pandemic has taught us about teachers and teaching. *FACETS*, 6, pp. 1835–1863. doi:10.1139/facets-2021-0084

Kvale, S. (1996) *Interviews: An introduction to qualitative research interviewing*. Thousand Oaks, CA: Sage Publications.

Laidlaw, L., O'Mara, J., and Wong, S. (2022) *Secret lives of children in the digital age: disruptive devices and resourceful learners*. Gorham, ME: Myers Educational Press.

OECD (2019) *TALIS 2018 Results (Volume I): Teachers and school leaders as lifelong learners*, TALIS, OECD Publishing, Paris. https://doi.org/10.1787/1d0bc92a-en

Pahl, K. and Rowsell, J. (2012) *Literacy and education*. London: SAGE.

Purcell-Gates, V. (2011) Ethnographic research. In: N. Duke and M. Mallette, eds., *Literacy research methodologies*. New York: Guildford.

Sánchez-Cruzado, C., Santiago Campión, R., and Sánchez-Compaña, M.T. (2021) Teacher digital literacy: the indisputable challenge after COVID-19. *Sustainability*, 13(4), p. 1858. https://doi.org/10.3390/su13041858

Schleicher, A. (2020) *The impact of COVID-19 on education: insights from education at a glance*. Available at https://www.oecd.org/education/the-impact-of-covid-19-on-education-insights-education-at-a-glance-2020.pdf (Accessed 17 October 2022).

Scott, F. and Marsh, J. (2018) Digital literacies in early childhood. *Oxford Research Encyclopedia of Education*. https://doi.org/10.1093/acrefore/9780190264093.013.97

Sosa Díaz, M.J. (2021) Emergency remote education, family support and the digital divide in the context of the COVID-19 lockdown. *International Journal of Environmental Research and Public Health*, 18(15), p. 7956. doi:10.3390/ijerph18157956

16
POST-COVID PEDAGOGY

Intersectional identities and technological spaces

Ahmet Atay

Introduction

Teaching is hard, but some find it harder than others. Most of us do not think about why teaching is hard, while others spend a significant portion of their academic careers considering the reasons behind this hardship. As our cultural identities cause us to have different experiences in the classroom and in higher education, our ideas about what makes teaching difficult also differ. This is the case in the U.S-American higher education context. Our identities matter in the classroom although we are often encouraged to disregard them as educators when we are in the classroom. Therefore, my transnational and intersectional immigrant queer identity shaped my experiences in the classroom and the larger educational context perhaps a bit differently than the mainstream instructors. Hence, my identities are both visible and invisible in the classroom, as they shape my teaching and presence in educational contexts.

This autoethnographic essay is not about one particular research project and its findings. Instead, it is about my personal experiences teaching during the COVID times. I am employing a personal writing style, which might be a bit less familiar to some. Autoethnography as a research method focuses on our personal experiences within a cultural context or a situation or groups of contexts. Autoethnography as ethnographic and performative writing (Ellis & Bochner, 2000; Pelias, 2000) aims to help scholars to bridge from a critical ethnographic lens to cultural and performative writing. Through this type of academic exploration, they can offer a cultural critique through personal stories. I structured this essay in a way where I present my stories; I blend them with existing literature. Hence, it will read as unconventional

DOI: 10.4324/9781003352129-20

for some of you. During the early days of the COVID-19 pandemic and the subsequent months, we incorporated online learning into our teaching or created digital classrooms; consequently, some faculty members contended that they missed the normal—the good old days of teaching. Some were even nostalgic about an in-classroom experience that had never been there. There was a yearning for the "normal"—whatever that was. Classroom spaces had their issues well before the pandemic. Some chose to recognize those issues, while others ignored them. However, the pandemic made such issues more visible and nuanced. In *Teaching to Transgress*, hooks (1994b) recognized the crisis in education decades before the COVID-19 pandemic:

> There is a serious crisis in education. Students often do not want to learn and teachers do not want to teach. More than ever before in the recent history of this nation, educators are compelled to confront the biases that have shaped teaching practices in our society and to create new ways of knowing, different strategies for the sharing of knowledge.
>
> *(p. 12)*

What hooks observed in the early 1990s was the beginning of a crisis that many did not want to acknowledge or address. Others were clinging to a myth or fantasy, afraid to make revisions that would turn the classroom into a more just place and make our experiences more equitable, humane, and welcoming as well as less oppressive. However, some acknowledged the issues hooks was articulating and worked toward challenging the oppressive structures in the classroom and fighting for the voice of the marginalized.

While the COVID-19 pandemic made teaching harder, it also provided new opportunities and possibilities. In this chapter, in addition to presenting my story using a fusion of autoethnographic and narrative methods, I discuss how post-COVID faculty and administrators must understand the role and lives of intersectional and transnational scholars as well as the role of media technologies in teaching and learning. We must consider these issues collectively, as new technologies have presented new freedoms, opportunities, and possibilities for educating students but also provided alternative and perhaps more equitable and inclusive spaces for historically marginalized scholars.

Before I present my stories to you, the reader, I must articulate my positionality as the author. I am a transnational queer scholar who teaches courses on communication and media studies as well as gender and sexuality studies at a small private liberal arts university in the middle of Ohio. Our state is conservative, and the county where our institution is situated is even more so. While, as a transnational queer cosmopolitan, I work at a relatively progressive institution, we live and work in a conservative environment. Why does any of this information matter? It matters because this shapes how I teach in the classroom as well as how I live my life outside of it. This context will also help you gain a better sense of my individual and collective stories.

I would like to begin by narrating three stories, which will help me situate my experiences while inviting you to understand how our experiences may be drastically different because of our cultural identities, even though we may be working at the same or similar institutions. In this unconventional essay, I use autoethnographic writing (Adams & Holman Jones, 2008; Alexander, 2008, 2014; Bhattacharya, 2018; Chawla & Atay, 2018; Homan Jones, 2010, 2016) to illustrate my experiences and also offer insights into how social and cultural forces (such as the COVID-19 pandemic and technological developments) shape the teaching experiences of historically marginalized instructors. In particular, I focus on how media technologies, online platforms, quick media applications, and digital culture at large impact our teaching and learning. Furthermore, I discuss the kind of possibilities these may present for historically marginalized faculty.

New media technologies and pedagogies

As Jenkins (2006) stated, we live in a convergence culture. We are surrounded by a digital ecosystem and visual culture that impact our daily lives. In addition to using new media technologies, online platforms, and quick media applications to communicate, we use these to perform daily tasks, such as paying bills, booking hotels and flights, buying groceries, watching our favorite shows or films, listening to music, and even looking for love and sex in digital spaces. A significant portion of our everyday lives are digitalized, and there is no denying how much these technologies consume our time and also provide a source of escape from the physical world. Hence, denying their role and importance in our everyday lives would be foolish.

We live in a highly digitalized world. Most social and cultural institutions, such as health, transportation, and government, have, either successfully or unsuccessfully, embraced the role of new media technologies and are aiming to incorporate them into their functioning. For example, the health industry is highly dependent on robotics and digital technologies for scanning human bodies and complicated surgeries. As educators, we like technologies, but most of us remain wary, keeping these technologies at arm's length.

Considering that we are educating a highly technologically savvy and diverse generation, we must carefully examine their cultures to understand how they learn and interact with one another within and outside of the class. Members of Generation Z were born into these technologies and grew up with them (Atay & Ashlock, 2022). While they are shaped by the digital culture, they also shape the culture that we, as educators, are situated in. Failing to acknowledge this reality would be like swimming against the tide, and it would not benefit learners or teachers who see value in these technologies.

We use new media technologies and digital platforms for different reasons, with one of the primary reasons being to access or share information; in essence, we use them to learn. I love reading physical books because I love holding a book and smelling the pages, old and new; however, lately, a significant portion of my reading, both for academic purposes and pleasure, occurs online. Moreover, I use online libraries or digital archives to access reading materials that are not easily available to me in a physical format, at least in the middle of small-town Ohio. Here, my intended argument is that online technologies and digital platforms provide new opportunities for learning and accessing information. Hence, they are a crucial part of our learning experiences. Then why are we hesitant to incorporate new media technologies or online platforms into our teaching? I will return to this question and further interrogate it through my stories.

There are two ways of explaining the presence of new media technologies or online platforms in everyday teaching and learning in academia: (a) the incorporation of new media technologies into face-to-face classrooms and online teaching and learning via digital platforms and (b) a complete shift toward the cyber or digital space to facilitate learning. Online classes have been around for some time now, at least in the bigger state-funded universities in the United States. While these universities have already embraced online learning to serve students who learn differently or non-traditional students who work in addition to attending their studies, liberal arts universities and privately funded universities are reluctant to adopt this model because they offer a different type of education. They are residential campuses (i.e., students live and learn on the campus). Hence, online technology is often deemed a less desirable form of education. In the virtual model, learning takes place solely on online platforms, either synchronically or otherwise (some hybrid models offer limited face-to-face interactions). Students complete their modules online, take their exams online, and upload their written work to the online system that becomes the digital classroom. Online classes incorporate videos, blogs, discussion boards, and other interactive content and assignments.

Most of us are comfortable with the first idea. I believe in the power of face-to-face teaching and learning, and I am not against those who do not want to abandon traditional ways of teaching. The physical classroom can be a magical place where positive transformation can happen. For example, we can observe our students, watch their facial expressions, and, perhaps, feel their emotions. However, the classroom can also be an oppressive space for some (Atay, 2021a, 2021b; Calafell, 2007; Fassett & Warren, 2007; Freire, 1972; hooks, 1994a, 1994b; Toyosaki, 2013). Those who are nostalgic about pre-COVID-19 classrooms often miss the mark and ignore that the teaching spaces we enjoy could function as a painful and oppressive environment for some. I am not throwing the baby out with the bathwater here; I am not arguing for the demolition of face-to-face teaching and a shift toward completely online learning. Instead, I am suggesting that we need to understand how technology and online platforms facilitate learning for some and offer new ways of empowerment for others who are actively teaching in highly oppressive academic structures. The stories that I present below embody these tensions.

Story 1: The pre-COVID-19 times

I love teaching. I love interacting with students and teaching new materials as well as suggesting new or alternative ways of looking at or engaging with social, cultural, political, economic, and even personal issues, problems, situations, and contexts. At the same time, I find teaching exhausting, especially when it comes to teaching material that personally resonates with me. I often teach courses on the intersections of culture, media, and identity (i.e., intercultural communication, mediated gender, race, sexuality, and transnational queer cinema). Due to the nature of what I teach, I often attract particular types of students, namely those who see themselves in the curriculum and identify with the course materials or assignments in different ways. There is a personal dimension to the type of courses I teach. Perhaps this is one of the reasons my students and I build mentoring relationships that transcend the classroom. Teaching certain topics is hard, but it is even harder for those of us who embody or live the topics we teach. They are personal. Hence, as instructors, we become vulnerable. For example, teaching topics on race, ethnicity, gender, sexuality, and immigration is particularly challenging for me because often, the conversations that occur in the classroom leak into non-educational spaces, and I continue to live and relive these topics. For some educators, teaching such topics may be easier because they do not embody the issues or identities that they teach. When they turn the lights off and go home, they have the luxury of leaving these topics behind. Others, like me, continue to dwell on these topics as we face our everyday challenges.

***

It was just an ordinary Thursday in late February. The students in my Intercultural Communication course had already been tackling complicated topics in the class, namely the intersections of gender, race, nationality, and sexuality in everyday life contexts. Since the class syllabus followed a topical pattern, at that point in the semester, we had already defined crucial concepts, such as race, ethnicity, gender, sexual orientation, and intersectionality, to discuss the intersections of race, ethnicity, and gender in everyday life encounters (Gonzalez & Chen, 2015; Martin et al., 1998). The class took an intersectional approach and interrogated how different cultural identity markers were constructed and performed in everyday life encounters, ranging from interpersonal relationships to education and media. For example, the students understood that racial and/or sexual minorities had a complicated history to reckon with regarding the construction of race and ethnicity in politics, the legal system, and higher education. When the representations and everyday interactions were not racist, sexist, or homophobic, racial, ethnic, and sexual minorities were visibly absent from everyday imagination, media, and popular culture. One of the learning goals of this course involved connecting everyday stories and academic work with students' lives and engaging in difficult conversations using these written and visual texts as case studies.

In the last two weeks of the course, we added more layers and grappled with "thicker intersectionalities" through our class material (Yep, 2016). Hence, we dedicated some time to the construction, performance, and representations of race, ethnicity, and queerness. While unpacking these representations and discussing the ways in which these representations may be mirroring our own lived experiences, some of the students were visibly restless. On that particular Thursday, we were discussing Calafell's (2007) "Mentoring and Love: An Open Letter." In this article, Calafell has beautifully and evocatively written about the hurdles she faced in U.S. academia as a minority faculty member. She has discussed the connections that she established with her Latinx/a/o students to survive. Following hooks' arguments (1994b), Calafell has argued that higher education institutions were designed for mainstream White individuals and never really meant for minorities; essentially, the structure itself and all of the practices within the structure were designed with White individuals in mind. Hence, the main goal was to allow White individuals to thrive. As racial minorities entered the system, they were forced to grapple with failure, loneliness, and a sense of not-belonging. As Calafell has articulated, this is true for hierarchically marginalized faculty members. Scholars such as myself, Chen (2014), and Toyosaki (2018) argue that this is also true for minoritized faculty members.

I assign this article as part of this course because I want to have honest conversations with my students about the higher education environment in which we are deeply invested and situated. However, these conversations are never easy. As a transnational queer faculty member, I identify with Calafell's story because I see so much of myself in it. Surviving academia as a junior faculty member is hard, but it is even harder for those of us who have historically been marginalized or accented. We often take jobs at locations far away from our family and close friends; consequently, we often endure loneliness in addition to other discriminatory behaviors directed at our race, ethnicity, accent, sexual orientation, or ability/disability. These experiences often leave their marks in the shape of academic scars, and they often linger with us for a long time.

I began the class with a general question: "What did you all think of Calafell's story and ideas about surviving in academia?" Some might think that general questions are an easy way out, but this question matters to me; hence, I lead with it. As soon as I had finished talking, several hands went up—students who wanted to offer their opinions. I called on the students one by one, and Chelsea and Leila raised their hands last. I was wondering if they would answer my question. I often refuse to cold call students out of respect for their silence, especially the historically marginalized students. I want to protect them but also protect their voices and stories. If they are willing to share, which they often are, they know that the classroom space is always invitational, and they have the opportunity to speak up. In particular, some of the international students who come from cultures that do not encourage them to speak out in the classroom or who fear saying the wrong word may choose not to actively respond to the oral participation invitations in the classroom. Their voices matter, but so does their choice to remain silent. I had often appreciated Chelsea's and Leila's voices as well as their contributions to our classroom discussions. Thus, I was quite curious about what they would say, and what stories they were willing to share. To my surprise, when I called on them, their voices were cracking. As they shared their stories, they did not shy away from expressing their raw emotions. As marginalized students, they often face discrimination, ranging from blunt racism to microaggressions that mainstream individuals may not recognize on the surface level. The first one to speak up was Chelsea. She shared her story with great detail. She talked about needing to use her computer or cellphone in the classroom for two reasons: she needed to be online and accessible to her family as they were undergoing some hardships, and she needed a safe space to retreat to in case of classroom microaggressions. Classrooms can be liberatory for some but aggressive and hurtful for others. Leila's story was different. She hated being called out in the classroom for technology usage and being expected to either speak on behalf of her culture or share an opinion that she had no cultural reference for. Similar to Chelsea, she used her cellphone or laptop in class to search for information or, sometimes, to say goodnight to her parents who lived on another continent, in a different time zone.

Chelsea: I hate it when professors call me out when I am online. I am not really doing anything on the Internet, nor I am playing video games. I am just online. Just in case.

Leila: My family is eight hours ahead of here. Some days, we cannot even talk because I am always busy. I just want to say hi or good night, so I go online during the class. Professors either give me a look or remind me of their computer policies. (Here their voices are appropriated to capture the essence of their sentiments instead of using a direct quotation).

Both Chelsea and Leila connected their stories back to Calafell's article. Similar to Calafell, they also find ways to survive in academic settings. Their chosen survival strategies provide them with opportunities and, sometimes, escape. Such strategies may be different from those of mainstream individuals; furthermore, these students may be viewed as disrespectful or not sufficiently engaged. Nevertheless, these are strategies to learn in the classroom, even though the classroom may not be invitational and may even be hostile.

Story 2: Pandemic times: empowering students

March 2020 changed our realities. In so many ways, nothing is the same, nor will it be. The news of the COVID-19 epidemic (which later became a pandemic) began circulating in late February. First, the crisis was limited to China and Asia, but subsequently, it became a dire situation in Europe; as we watched, European cities and towns implemented lockdowns one by one. It was only a matter of time before the same situation occurred in the United States.

During the last days of February, my department was conducting job interviews for a non-tenure track, visiting assistant professor position, and one of our candidates hailed from the West Coast. One of my colleagues and I took this candidate to dinner, and some of our dinner conversations revolved around the emerging health crisis and how we might handle teaching in the midst of it. It was the early days of the situation, so no one had any idea. Afterward, the candidate returned to the West Coast, while we resumed our routine for a short period; our two-week spring break began a couple of days later. During this time, Seattle became ground zero for the pandemic, and lockdown orders were issued. During the second week of the break, we were notified that we would be teaching online synchronously for the next two weeks until more clarity about the health situation could be obtained.

Being a small liberal arts university, our institution did not consider online teaching to be acceptable; thus, we were caught off-guard and very unprepared. Most faculty members had never taught online courses, and the vast majority were not accustomed to using online education platforms. Fortunately, I had taught online prior to my current job, and I had been using Moodle, our required online education platform since I began my job. I had been uploading documents, keeping a grade book, and communicating with students via the platform. I was lucky, but I needed to learn more tricks and new approaches if we were about to use the platform as our new venue of education. The rest of the college, however, was not as lucky. Most faculty members had never used Moodle, and online pedagogies were not something they had ever considered. There was both silence and chaos. People were concerned about students' well-being, but they were also concerned about themselves and doubted their ability to finish the semester online.

In the end, we completed the semester online, but the pandemic took a turn for the worse in the summer, and the university began exploring online education opportunities for the fall term. While some faculty members were excited and willing to teach face-to-face, others—including me—had no desire to teach face-to-face while we faced the direst challenge of the century. Instead of seeing teaching online as a burden, I saw it as an opportunity. As a media scholar studying media education, the situation we were facing became my academic lab—a phenomenon that I was interested in further examining. As faculty members were planning to teach online and preparing for the possibility of further lockdowns, we were asked to take workshops during the summer of 2020. While the workshops covered the basics, as well as an introduction to online teaching, we were asking larger and more pressing questions about access to technologies, equity issues, and issues that international students may face regarding time differences. We surely had challenges ahead of us, but this was also an opportunity to rethink the role played by technology in the classroom and our pedagogical approaches.

***

February 2022, Tuesday night

As a graduate student, I took several night courses. However, during my time at university, I only taught a single night course with a colleague on serial narratives and social justice. Night courses were not common at my university until very recently. During the pandemic, I decided to offer a night course to accommodate students who were in different time zones in the United States while also allowing international students in Asian countries in particular to take it. Thus, the Horror Cinema class was born out of necessity but also my interest in the genre. The class was scheduled to be taught once a week at night, allowing us to meet on Microsoft Teams as a class and discuss different aspects of the genre.

After a long day, I was ready to meet my students online at 7:30 p.m. Since this was going to be a long night, I made a strong cup of coffee and set it next to a glass of water. One of the perks of teaching at home online synchronically was that I could drink coffee and water and munch on snacks freely. It is not common for teachers to eat in the physical classroom; however, online classrooms have different rules and expectations, especially if you are teaching a night course for just 24 students. I signed in and started the meeting ten minutes before the start time. I try to arrive five to ten minutes early to my classrooms so that I can chat with my students and get to know them. I decided to keep the tradition alive online. Most students logged in to the class right at 7:30, but some of them periodically came in earlier to chat and connect. We indulged in random conversations in which they told me about their lives and everyday interactions. Some of them were living on campus because they were taking science classes that required or encouraged them to attend in person. Others were all over the place, ranging from Alaska to China. Regardless of our locations, we managed to create a social and supportive classroom. These random conversations before the class helped me cultivate a sense of community among my learners.

People have complicated relationships with cameras. While some instructors required their students to turn their cameras on, I did not. I highly encouraged them to do so if they felt comfortable with it; some did turn their cameras on, sometimes revealing their pets resting next to them, while others were having an early breakfast or late dinner and therefore chose not to. Some were in their pajamas, and so was I. Regardless of our attires, our food and beverages, and the presence of our household members, we were in the cyber classroom, ready and eager to learn.

I started the session with a simple, yet effective, question: "How are you all doing tonight?" We took roughly ten minutes to connect and take care of the housekeeping business, such as talking about upcoming assignments or clarifying questions, before diving into the course material. We were covering the early golden age of horror films. *Cat People* (1942), directed by Jacques Tourneur was one of the films in that day's course content. After I gave a brief lecture on the film's producer, Val Lewton, we began discussing the film. My international students were quiet that night. I knew they were awake and present, but they were not participating orally. Their cameras were off as well. These facts did not bother me much, but they would have bothered some of the faculty. Hence, I reminded all of them to use the chatroom if they wanted to participate through other means. Within minutes, there were several messages on the board. One after another, they reported how much they liked the film. While they did not watch older films and never thought they would appreciate them, *Cat People* was a nice surprise for them.

Students learn differently and participate differently. While we heavily emphasize the importance of talking in the classroom in U.S. higher education, we do not consider active listening as participation. Students who are shy, afraid of talking in front of others, or insecure about their language abilities are often quiet in the classroom. However, the chatroom function provided my students with an alternative way to participate, which is not an option in the physical classroom. They were more active, willing, and sometimes eager to participate. They also self-reported that, sometimes, they looked up information about the films or era under discussion since they—especially international students—lacked information on these topics. Therefore, using Google and Wikipedia as part of the classroom experience became a new reality—a rather productive one at that. Freire (2000), hooks (1994a), and Fassett and Warren (2007) all highlight the need to empower students to be more active and in charge of their learning. Hence, I believe that allowing students, especially historically marginalized students, to use media technologies in the classroom is a form of empowerment. This empowerment may not be in the form of the environment envisioned by the aforementioned authors; nevertheless, it is a type of empowerment that allows students access to our classes and their contexts differently, in addition to providing a new opportunity for meaningful classroom participation.

Story 3: Online teaching and faculty

I have always wanted to experiment with online teaching, but there has not been any place for it in my university's conceptualization of what education means. Our administrators consider online education to be a lesser form of education; hence, it has never been allowed or appreciated. As I am a media scholar who believes in media education and in developing new media pedagogies, this approach goes directly against my beliefs. We must incorporate technology into our teaching, including various aspects of online learning. After all, we are educating the members of a generation, Generation Z, who were born into these technologies and global digital cultures (Atay & Ashlock, 2022). Moreover, I want to experiment with online education to allow myself a break from being physically present on campus or heavily involved with our high college-wide academic service expectations, including academic advising. As there are only a handful of BIPOC (Black, indigenous, and people of color), queer, and international faculty on campus, our service loads and expectations are higher than those of the mainstream faculty. This clearly marginalizes already marginalized groups of people by demanding more of their time and setting up expectations that are not sustainable in the long run. I hoped that online teaching would shield me from these expectations, which are continuously perpetuated by neoliberal higher education (Giroux, 2014).

***

My body is always on display. I teach courses that are in high demand and also emotionally taxing. I chair departments, work on elected and appointed university committees, and serve as an academic advisor for several students in an official capacity; the number of students I supervise is considerably higher than that of 95% of my colleagues at the university. Furthermore, I mentor historically marginalized students and faculty members. In essence, I carry out visible and invisible labor. I am not listing these to show that I am a busy individual. Rather, I intend to make a point: when there are only a handful of BIPOC, international, and queer faculty members on a university campus, we can be in high demand, with little appreciation for the work we are asked or expected to do. When we are absent, we are visible. When our bodies are not in meetings or everywhere all the time, we are more visible than when our bodies are present. Essentially, we are expected to be physically present all the time. The COVID-19 pandemic added more layers to this complex situation. At the same time, when online meetings became the norm and we were given permission to teach online, we found the much-appreciated breathing room to exist in a different way.

Convincing the university administrators to let me teach remotely during the pandemic was truly an ordeal. They only permitted faculty members who had health conditions to do so, and I was not in that category. Being someone who lives alone in the United States, I attempted to get them to see reason. If I were to fall sick, I would not have a support system or a family unit to take care of me. Finally, they gave in. I taught my courses during the 2020–2021 academic year online synchronously. I held virtual office hours and attended meetings online. I was present, even though it was only digitally for some.

Like every morning during the lockdown, I woke up at 7:30 a.m. Two cups of coffee and a light breakfast prepared me to face my daily duties. That day, Thursday, October, like every other day, I had a series of meetings spread throughout the day. We live in a culture of excessive meetings, and I am accustomed to having three to six meetings a day. Prior to the pandemic, I would run from building to building and teach my courses in between. Attending meetings in my living room or studying while wearing my pajama bottoms and a sweater was a nice change of pace. I had back-to-back meetings at 10.00 a.m. and 11.00 a.m. A student wanted to meet at noon, but I had to say "not today" since I was teaching at 1.00 p.m., and I needed to have lunch. After teaching my classes and attending a short meeting, I ran (digitally) to my long committee meeting. In between these activities, I was able to have coffee or tea and snacks, indulge my cat's affectionate interruptions, and take care of house chores that I hardly ever attend to during the semester. It felt like I was being a regular person, instead of an academic who is starved for personal time.

While I had very few in-person interactions, it was nice to have a routine that allowed me to be a human being, whatever that really means in academia. It was nice to hide while still being present in the midst of the digital culture. I felt human —digitally human.

Conclusion

We live in a global digital culture. We live in a media convergence culture (Jenkins, 2006), where we consume and produce information and services. Technology has infiltrated every single aspect of our lives. We communicate with others through text messages, social media posts, chats, blogs, and images. We maintain familial relationships through these technologies. We buy and sell things online. We scan and upload or download aspects of our lives on any given day. We learn online by reading newspapers and online encyclopedias, and we consume news and stories online. We watch television on our gadgets; document our lives and take photos via our smartphones;

and represent parts of our identities for others in multiple ways. We are digital beings; there is no denying this.

The digitalization of education, incorporation of new media technologies and quick media applications, and inclusion of online education or aspects of it in our teaching or pedagogy are inevitable. It is important that we recognize the role of technology in our lives and its link to our learning. This will allow us to generate new pedagogies and strategies for educating members of future generations and helping them understand the role of media in our everyday lives.

While some vilify online learning or view it as a lesser form of education, online teaching and learning present various new opportunities and possibilities for students and faculty members alike. In this chapter, I have argued in favor of this point. Rather than reminiscing about the good old days of teaching and being nostalgic about classroom experiences and cultures that may or may not have been there to begin with we need to understand the role of media and technology in the classroom and closely examine some of the merits and demerits of online education or hybrid education (which blends in-person and online experiences).

To consolidate my argument, I will now touch on three points that I have repeatedly highlighted in this essay. Online learning and the incorporation of technologies into our pedagogies present new opportunities. First, this provides different types of access for students who learn differently, have different realities and personal situations, or have families outside of the United States. Online learning will allow them to attend classes more easily. They can talk to their families while learning online, if needed, allowing them to feel connected and less alone. Second, online learning and new media technology usage could help us reimagine what it means to be a minority student or faculty member in higher education. At times, both faculty and students hailing from historically marginalized backgrounds grapple with the oppressive structures within the physical classroom and other academic environments. Online classes or hybrid models could allow students and faculty to remove themselves from this structure with the aid of digital realities and technologies while still teaching and learning. Hence, we can see these forms of learning and teaching as a different type of empowerment. Finally, online teaching and learning can be used as a retention tool. For example, I would much prefer to live somewhere else for a semester or a year and still be able to teach my classes and participate in faculty governance via online or digital means. These technologies could also be used to retain students. Often, real-life challenges may prevent students from attending class regularly. If the classes are hybrid or online, they can still learn.

I am not proposing that we demolish schools and move entirely to online domains. Rather, I contend that the pandemic experiences have proved that we can have different forms of learning and teaching and that universities should support faculty and students who want to explore these opportunities and options. Online teaching and learning may not be for everyone, but we should have the freedom to participate in this form of education if we so choose. Finally, if we want to teach online or use hybrid models, we need to develop new digital or online pedagogies. We cannot simply apply our in-class teaching pedagogies to online experiences. We must develop new skills, tactics, and approaches.

References

Adams, T. E. & Holman Jones, S. (2008). Autoethnography is queer. In N. K. Denzin, Y. S. Lincoln, & L. T. Smith (Eds.), *Handbook of critical and indigenous methodologies* (pp. 373–390). Thousand Oaks, CA: Sage.

Alexander, B. K. (2008). Queer(y)ing the postcolonial through the West(ern). In N. K. Denzin, Y. S. Lincoln, & L. T. Smith (Eds.), *Handbook or critical and indigenous methodologies* (pp. 101–133). Thousand Oaks, CA: Sage.

Alexander, B. K. (2014). Bodies yearning on the borders of becoming: A performative reflection on three embodied axes of social difference. *Qualitative Inquiry*, 20(10), 1169–1178.

Atay, A. (2018). Digital life writing: The failure of a diasporic, queer, blue Tinker Bell. *Interactions: Studies in Communication & Culture*, 9(2), 183–193.

Atay, A. (2021a). Challenging the discourse of post-truth in media classes: Digital media and cultural pedagogies. In D. Kahl, Jr. & A. Atay (Eds.), *Pedagogies of post truth* (pp. 39–53). Lanham, MD: Lexington Books.

Atay, A. (2021b). Reflection, revision, resistance. *Communication Education*, 70(3), 342–346.

Atay, A. & Ashlock, M. Z. (2022). New media technologies, social media, millennials, and generation z: An introduction. In A. Atay & M. Z. Ashlock (Eds.), *Social media, technology and new generations: Digital millennial generation and generation z* (pp. 1–19). Lanham, MD: Lexington Books.

Bhattacharya, K. (2018). Coloring memories and imaginations of "home": Crafting a decolonizing autoethnography. *Cultural Studies <=> Critical Methodologies*, 18(1), 9–15. doi: 10.1177/1532708617734010.

Calafell, B. M. (2007). Mentoring and love: An open letter. *Cultural Studies <=> Critical Methodologies*, 7(4), 425–441. doi: 10.1177/1532708607305123.

Chen, Y.-W. (2014). "Are you an immigrant?": Identity-based critical reflections of teaching intercultural communication. In K. G. Hendrix & A. Hebbani (Eds.), *Hidden roads: Nonnative Englishspeaking international professors in the classroom* (pp. 5–16). San Francisco, CA: Jossey-Bass. doi: 10.1002/tl.20091.

Ellis, C. & Bochner, A. P. (2000). Autoethnography, personal narrative, reflexivity. In N. K. Denzin & Y. S. Lincoln (Eds.), *Handbook of qualitative research* (2nd ed., pp. 733–768). Thousand Oaks, CA: Sage.

Fassett, D. L. & Warren, J. T. (2007). *Critical communication pedagogy*. Thousand Oaks, CA: Sage.

Freire, P. (2000). *Pedagogy of the oppressed*. New York: Continuum.

Giroux, H. (2014). *Neoliberalism's war on higher education*. Chicago, IL: Heymarket Books.

Gonzalez, A. & Chen, Y.-W. (Eds.). (2015). *Our voices: Essays in culture, ethnicity and communication*. Oxford: Oxford University Press.

Holman Jones, S. (2010). Burnt: Writing torch singers and torch singing. *Cultural Studies/Critical Methodologies*, 10(4), 283–294.

Holman Jones, S. (2016). Living bodies of thought. *Qualitative Inquiry*, 22(4), 228–237.

hooks, b. (1994a). Homeplace: A site of resistance. In D. S. Madison (Ed.), *The women that I am: The literature and culture of contemporary women of color* (pp. 448–454). New York: St Martin's.

hooks, b. (1994b). *Teaching to transgress: Education as the practice of freedom*. New York: Routledge.

Jenkins, H. (2006). *Convergence culture: Where old and new media collide*. New York: New York University Press.

Martin, J. N., Nakayama, T. K., & Flores, L. A. (Eds.). (1998). *Readings in intercultural communication: Experiences and contexts*. Boston, MA: McGraw Hill.

Pelias, R. J. (2000). The critical life. *Communication Education*, 49(3), 220–228. doi: 10.1080/03634520009379210.

Tourneur, J. (1942). *Cat people*. RKO Radio Pictures.

Toyosaki, S. (2013). Pedagogical love as critical labor: Relational pedagogy of whiteness. *Qualitative Communication Research*, 2, 411–433.

Toyosaki, S. (2018). Toward de/postcolonial autoethnography: Critical relationality with the academic second persona. *Cultural Studies <=> Critical Methodologies*, 18(1), 32–42. doi: 10.1177/1532708617735133.

Yep, G. A. (2016). Toward thick(er) intersectionalities: Theorizing, researching, and activating the complexities of communication and identities. In K. Sorrells & S. Sekimoto (Eds.), *Globalizing intercultural communication: A reader* (pp. 86–94). Thousand Oaks, CA: Sage.

Conclusion

17

COVID-19

A catalyst for change

Katy Marsh-Davies and Suzanne Brown

Introduction

In 2020, Morin's (2020) maxim 'expect the unexpected' proliferated. For teachers, this meant rapidly adapting their lives and practices to ensure they remained effective during the COVID-19 pandemic, whilst guidance was often emergent. In this book, we have presented examples of the 'pandemic pedagogies' utilised by teachers in a variety of educational contexts in several different countries. These often incorporated digital technologies to facilitate remote teaching and learning, which was necessary to limit the spread of the virus.

Through the accounts of educators featured in the preceding parts of the book around *Priorities*, *Alliances*, and *Re-imaginings*, we can see that over time, some teachers were able to experiment and find innovative solutions to the challenges posed by the unforeseen predicament, even enhancing their practice and rekindling the joy of teaching. For others, outcomes were less positive, echoing Donitsa-Schmidt & Ramot's (2020) finding that teachers worked harder than even before during the pandemic, leading to stress and burnout.

As discussed in our introductory chapter, neoliberalist systems of schooling are characterised by outdated and inappropriate notions and practices, which fail to serve children well and have detrimental impacts on teachers' well-being and professional agency (Lakes & Carter, 2011). This, we suggest, has contributed to a retention crisis (alongside factors such as unfavourable working conditions and stagnating pay – as Weale (2022) reports of the English context). Whilst the attrition challenge paused during the pandemic, as teachers sought to remain in relatively stable employment during a social and economic crisis where few alternative options presented themselves, the issue is now returning to pre-pandemic proportions (this at least is the situation in England – see Worth, 2023).

Teacher recruitment difficulties also resolved themselves temporarily in England during the pandemic (ibid). People from different walks of life had reason and time to reflect on their ambitions and/or experienced the loss of existing employment, so may have had a different sense of risk around career change. Additionally, the experience of supporting their own children's learning during lockdowns seems to have spurred an attraction to the profession for some (Adams, 2020). But again, increased interest in teaching careers was short-lived, and 2022 saw a substantial dip in people registering for ITE (Initial Teacher Education) courses in England, taking registrations to below pre-COVID levels (Worth, 2023).

Without substantial change, the resourcing challenge seems insurmountable. Benhenda and Macmillan (2021) report how the most recent OECD TALIS Survey (OECD, 2018) revealed that 15% of teachers aged 50 years or under were intending to leave teaching within the next five years. Of course, the pandemic might have dampened this exit figure, but the intent is still of great concern with implications for the profession and individuals. Lower quality teaching and lower student achievement are the consequences of frequent staffing changes (ibid). In turn, this makes attracting high-quality teachers to schools more difficult (Sorensen & Ladd, 2020). This is particularly pertinent in schools with higher levels of disadvantage and helps educational inequalities to persist (Gershenson, 2021) because teacher turnover is especially problematic in those settings (Allen et al., 2018).

Teachers are not interchangeable, and so recruitment and retention of teacher talent are not just about numbers. The quality of teachers and their teaching have been found to be the most important factor in student outcomes, with differences in student performance being greater within schools than between schools (OECD, 2005). It is therefore necessary for effort to be focused toward improving working conditions to retain experienced teachers. In the report 'Teachers Matter' (OECD, 2005), the point is made that the quality of teaching is not just linked to the quality of teachers, although this is clearly important, but is determined by the environment in which their work takes place: 'able teachers are not necessarily going to reach their potential in settings that do not provide appropriate support or sufficient challenge and reward' (ibid, p. 7). Managing attrition will reduce the need for recruitment activity – and the associated time and cost this entails – but even where recruitment is required, change is still needed for the profession to be appealing, accessible, and sustainable for a broad range of individuals.

As Collet-Sabé & Ball (2022, p. 1) comment, 'the COVID pandemic has been both a catalyst for the end of things traditional and a disruption in which fundamental questions about the continuation of things, indeed of our species, have been raised'. There is diversity in opinion around what should happen with regard to teachers and teaching post-COVID. Responses have ranged from calls for a return to pre-pandemic 'normality' and for pupils to be supported to swiftly catch up on the so-called 'lost learning' (EPI, 2021) to proclamations that the 'death of the school' should be a consequence of the pandemic – in other words, there should be a radical re-organisation of education in its wake (see for example Ball & Collet-Sabé, 2022; Robinson, 2020). Others call for 'lessons to be learned' and for some changes to be made within existing structures of schooling. Nóvoa & Alvim (2020), for example, call for a 'metamorphosis', stating 'we do not want the disintegration of the school but, rather, its profound transformation in the context of new relations with society and knowledge, always valuing teachers and a humanist vision of education' (ibid, p. 38).

This book has provided opportunities for scholars to present their ideas for how the profession and practices of education might be re-imagined as a result of the experiences of teachers during the COVID-19 pandemic. As Robinson (2020, p. 7) commented, the pandemic 'pressed pause on many of our social systems', it is also a chance, he said, to press 'reset'. Through their chapters, our contributors have given platform to the voices of teachers, who continued to practice during the unprecedented and challenging experience of the COVID-19 crisis. Moving forward without 'adequate inclusion of teacher perspectives', job-related stress may, Robinson et al. (2022, p. 1) write, lead to further 'teacher shortages, deterioration of teacher mental health, and ultimately worse outcomes for students'.

In this chapter, we present a call for action, drawing from the preceding chapters to present a series of proposals for teaching post-COVID. Together these express what teachers need and deserve if the profession is to be attractive, professionally empowering, personally fulfilling, and effective post-COVID. We stress the timeliness and importance of these recommendations and consider some of the limitations around what we propose. First, we lay the groundwork by discussing two key themes that emerged within and across the chapters to make visible the deliberations that led to our proposals.

Complex lives and shifting identities

Teachers' lives can be considered complex (Elbaz-Luwisch, 2007). This is manifest in the frequent requirements for teachers to make decisions about how to prioritise their time and efforts. Whilst this might be said of many professionals, some dilemmas are consequences of the specific working contexts and patterns that most teachers experience. For example, in many countries, childcare that facilitates early starts to the working day is not available, and as Brown's chapter explored, this leads to some teachers who are parents (most often mothers) working reduced hours in an attempt to make combining family and job roles manageable.

There are emotional and practical challenges faced by teachers, including trainee teachers (as explored in Woodhouse's chapter), implicit in trying to balance professional and domestic lives. Both Woodhouse and Brown highlight expressions of guilt by mothers in particular. Woodhouse's sample of student teacher mothers reported feeling that they were not doing well enough as parents during their ITE studies. She found that that ITE providers do not routinely consider parents' challenges, such as the need to plan ahead for childcare. Consequently, Woodhouse concludes student teacher mothers have to be particularly well-organised, resilient, agentic and determined if they are to complete their ITE programme successfully and enter the teaching profession. Both Brown and Woodhouse's chapters focus exclusively on the experiences of female teachers (as does Steffan & Potočnik's on menopause), but teaching continues to be a female-dominated profession (OECD, 2023), so supporting this demographic is important in efforts to retain teachers.

The day-to-day 'rhythms' (as Cameron & Abrams put it in their chapter) of teachers altered profoundly during the pandemic as they were required to manage conflicting roles and recalibrate their lives. Jones et al.'s (2022) survey results suggest that the nature of the work of teachers changed significantly – there was 'a large reduction in teachers' daily instructional minutes […] which were replaced with increased planning, paperwork, and interactions with colleagues and parents' (p. 1). Chapters in the part of this book about *Alliances* also note the increased prominence of the relational aspects of teachers' work during the crisis (we discuss this further in the following section). Furthermore, chapters throughout the book support the thesis that COVID brought dilemmas about priorities into sharp focus as teachers had to make often urgent, painful, and sometimes profoundly life-affecting decisions about, for example, whether to prioritise time for the children in their classes or their own offspring; their students' well-being or their own; or the meeting of state-prescribed targets or the more broadly defined learning, engagement, and enjoyment of those they teach.

Coleman et al., in their chapter, propose that the pandemic shifted all aspects of educators' lives; furthermore, for some, it offered 'a moment, a space, in which we might think of ourselves, others, and the world differently' (Collet-Sabé & Ball, 2022, p. 1). Forde et al.'s chapter discusses how issues that were already over-stretching teachers (e.g. poor management and heavy or misaligned workloads) were exacerbated during the pandemic. It also rendered the complex, sometimes 'messy',[1] lives of teachers more likely to be visible to others as digital learning provided a window into home-spaces, and interruptions from family, pets, delivery workers, etc. could not always be averted (Dunnett's chapter provides an insightful deconstruction of the sociomaterial aspects of teaching from home). This increased apparency/scrutiny of teachers as whole and complex people brought issues of identity to the fore, as Atay reflects on in his chapter. He proposes that the move to online learning could be experienced as empowering, but also not without difficulty, especially for teachers (and students) from historically marginalised groups.

As a punctuating moment in recent human history, the pandemic was an opportunity for some to pause and reflect (Robinson, 2020). As the background noise of face-to-face socialising fell away, teachers like many people may have had chance to consider their own lives and what is important to them, engaging in the identity work classically defined by Sveningsson & Alvesson (2003) as the ways human beings are 'engaged in forming, repairing, maintaining, strengthening or revising the constructions that are productive of a sense of coherence and distinctiveness' (p. 1165). Caza et al. (2018) propose that identity work is an ongoing process that can be accelerated and brought to the fore by significant or traumatic events such as a change in work contexts. A pandemic requiring the closure of schools, displacing teachers and requiring them to work in new ways, is an apt example. Whilst Alvesson & Willmott (2002) consider an employee's sense of self 'a significant medium and outcome of organizational control' (p. 622), they also propose it as a possible space for 'forms of micro-emancipation' (p. 624). In other words, by considering issues of identity, we might observe instances of social change, which, no matter how small, can signal a loosening of control and indicate transformation. This chimes in with Atay's proposal and is indicative of the impact of the pandemic for some teachers' identities.

Reflecting on identity might sound like a trivial, abstract or even indulgent activity (Mykhalovskiy, 1996), but it has concrete consequences for the lives of teachers including choices around whether to continue in the profession – thereby it also impacts upon pupils' educational and life chances (OECD, 2018). We propose therefore that it is crucial to acknowledge and explore how COVID has changed the social role[2] of a teacher and how individual teachers find consonance with this. Beauchamp & Thomas (2009, p. 175) suggest that identity can be seen as 'an organising element in teachers' professional lives' – an opportunity to think about oneself and changes that one might wish to make to their lives and practice. Hong & Cross Francis (2020, p. 208) agree with the impactful quality of identity work, stating that teacher identity is a significant concept with regard to 'efforts at unpacking teachers' professional lives, understanding teaching quality, motivation to teach, and career decision making'.

Looking beyond fundamental career decisions to the day-to-day activities of teachers, identity is also relevant. Coleman et al. propose in their chapter that a teacher's values and standpoint are entwined in their pedagogies and practices – for example, whether they feel proficient in face-to-face or online teaching can form part of their professional identity. So the forced engagement with digital technologies during the pandemic – which became the primary source of connecting with students for many teachers – led to some educators' professional identities being shaken, they say, as previously confident academics felt like novices due to this new sense of deficiency. This loss of confidence and changed perception of self are also noted in Laidlaw & Wong's chapter, as illustrated in their participants' struggles to relate to and engage students who would not use video in online sessions, and speaks to the 'precarity' (to borrow Coleman et al.'s eloquent phrasing) that the pandemic brought for teacher identity.

Other chapters present accounts of teachers (only eventually, in some cases) finding new confidence with technology, including experimenting with new ways of teaching (Hordatt Gentles et al.) and connecting (Honeyford et al.), finding new ways to balance roles (Woodhouse), and experience renewed joy in teaching (Forde et al.), as well as having chance to reflect on the purposes of teaching (Moorehouse & Tiet). No clear conclusion emerged from the chapters about whether the pandemic made teachers' lives less or more complex, or somehow easier to manage – it is likely that 'all of the above' were the case, dependent on the intricate web of circumstances in which individual teachers' found themselves – but the message that the COVID-19 crisis has had profound implications for teachers' lives and identities resonates throughout this book. This suggests a need for ongoing reflexivity from practitioners around what it means to be a teacher, as well as careful consideration of how to adjust their practices and organise their lives to remain cognisant of their priorities. This will require support from teacher educators, school leaders, and policy-makers in terms of appropriate mechanisms and resourcing. As we discuss below, no teacher works in isolation, and individual efforts are unlikely to lead to comprehensive change.

Care & co-dependence

As Cain et al. write post-COVID (2022), 'teaching is inherently a social practice, and care is integral to successful teaching' (p. 4). In this section, we reflect on these two associated aspects of teaching (i.e. teaching as relational and care as a crucial part of the role), which emerge in this book as central to the pandemic experience for many educators. Chapters have pointed to ways in which teachers collaborated with and supported one another during the pandemic. The act of opening up teaching and learning resources for other practitioners to share, for example, was highlighted in Hordatt Gentles et al.'s chapter, and can be viewed as a simple act (when facilitated by digital and social media) with great implications in easing the daily burden of fellow teachers.

Honeyford et al.'s chapter builds on the experience of conducting an online writing and book club for young teens and reveals the careful considerations of the authors around how to collaboratively design, deliver, and reflect upon the unique summer 2020 session. Co-author Kelsey reflected at the time '*we are our own built-in support system. We are a team. And that makes this achievable and exciting, instead of overwhelming*'. This is a sentiment mirrored in Cameron & Abram's chapter where a participating teacher describes weekly professional learning sessions during COVID with the intent '*to just come together as a staff, to build camaraderie, and to also develop whatever skills need to be*'.

Hargreaves' (2019) review of research on collaboration found that teachers who work in collaborative cultures tend to secure higher student results than colleagues who work in cultures of individualism. This highlights the paradox of neoliberal attempts to demarcate individual teacher performance for the ends of simplifying data (Bradbury & Roberts-Holmes, 2017). The experiences reported in this book of how teachers collaborated with one another gladly and effectively during the pandemic suggest that cultivating cultures of 'collaborative professionalism' (see Hargreaves, 2019) in teaching could reap benefits and enable transformation.

Through the preceding chapters, we have also heard about teachers negotiating new relationships and dependencies with broader stakeholders. Pokhrel & Mehta (2021) propose that the COVID experience has forged a strong connection between teachers and parents. Practitioners working in new ways with families is evident in Boyd et al.'s chapter and their example from early childhood education and in the chapter by Hylton-Fraser & Hylton, where they discuss the importance of parental involvement in children's learning.

Accounts of relationships with leaders highlighted in the book illuminate contrasting experiences. We hear examples of these being strong, supportive, and pivotal for educators during the pandemic (as in Boyd et al.'s chapter) but also ambivalent, even detrimental (Kinkead-Clarke & Abdul-Majied). The ecological systems model (Bronfenbrenner & Morris, 2006) that Boyd et al. draw upon in their chapter illustrates the importance of congruence between the approach of early childhood leaders, the early childhood service, and the home learning environment and highlights the co-dependencies entailed in ensuring that learning was effective during lockdowns. A holistic community approach to supporting teachers and learning is important beyond the early childhood phase and beyond the pandemic period (Iyengar, 2021).

As we have already touched on, pupils' perceptions of their educators changed during the pandemic as teachers became humanised and more relatable, visibly having similar lives and problems to them, and teachers gleaned a more holistic sense of the circumstances of their students' lives (Gourlay et al., 2021). Coleman et al. claim that academic teachers continue to have greater responsibility for student care post-COVID. They suggest that due to pandemic-induced anxiety and students' declining self-efficacy, it became a central part of a teacher's role during the pandemic and continues to be so. Forde et al. report that as the focus moved to the nurturing aspects of the role, some teachers rediscovered their positive emotions around teaching. They proclaim that this return to the core principles of education contributed to enhanced teacher well-being and motivation during the crisis and may form part of the solution with regard to retaining teachers in the profession going forward. Likewise, Moorhouse & Tiet, looking at the context of ITE, suggest that it is vital for teachers to incorporate care as part of their teacher identity, from the very beginning of their training.

In their chapter, Cameron & Abrams present examples of care emerging from their data as significant in teachers' experiences of the pandemic and something they do not wish to lose from their roles going forward. But foregrounding care as a key aspect of the work of teachers is not without costs. There are worrying examples in the book of teachers sacrificing their own well-being to ensure their pupils' (see Forde et al.'s chapter). Furthermore, care is a gendered notion that can undermine professionalism by being framed in opposition to it and considered 'women's work' (Poole & Isaacs, 1997). As Kinkead-Clark & Abdul-Majied discuss, in their chapter about early childhood settings, where care is seen as the main or only part of a role professional status remains elusive. This is echoed by Boyd et al. They report that in Australia, early childhood practitioners were not recognised as essential workers during the pandemic when other teachers were. They say the early childhood field is at a disadvantage as anyone is perceived as able to rear children, and caring for children can be done by teenage babysitters. But, they stress that early childhood educators were not just carers during the pandemic – they provided important early learning experiences for children, supported families, and worked hard to provide an environment that was safe and hygienic – and this continues post-COVID.

Cameron & Abrams, through the research reported in their chapter, observe that teachers have modified their practices since COVID-19 '*to meet their students' needs and, eventually, their own needs*'. They propose that caring for students is related to an educator's own well-being and call for future research and practice to focus on the relationship between students' needs and teachers' needs. Their findings hint at a move from self-sacrifice as an aspect of teacher role identity (Jin & Cortazzi, 2016) to a recognition that (1) caring, as part of a teacher's work, can be enriching – good for their well-being as well as that of their students; and (2) looking after themselves means teachers are more likely to remain present and able to provide care and consistency for their students (OECD, 2018). A cultural change in this direction seems promising for teacher retention (as well as student outcomes), but for impacts to be realised, this needs to be acknowledged by every stakeholder in the 'ecosystem' of learning – and working practices need to be adapted accordingly.

Call for action

Whilst undoubtedly difficult, the pandemic also provided an opportunity to shine a light on the achievements of teachers and the complexity of their lives. It highlighted the tensions that many teachers experience between professional and personal concerns due to heavy workloads and inflexible working conditions. For many, it was a time when their dedication to learners and their families was reinforced as they gained new understandings of those they taught. Many of the chapters speak of reaffirmations of long-held beliefs, of re-invigorated commitments, and of renewed enthusiasm for the work of teaching. At the same time, they spotlight the difficulties entailed in managing the complex demands of the personal and professional lives of teachers and to incompatibilities between what matters to them and the demands of contemporary educational systems. Drawing on these rich insights, we make four recommendations for teachers and teaching post-COVID:

Develop and nurture the professional autonomy of teachers

As the chapters of this book have illustrated, the COVID-19 pandemic led to many teachers working with more autonomy and flexibility around what and how to teach, where and when to work, and how to combine their teaching roles with other concerns, such as their own wellness, caring for others, and enjoyment of life.

The pandemic disrupted educational policy agendas and practices situated within the dominant and widely circulating discourses of globalisation and neoliberalism (see Adams and Povey, 2018; Goodson, 2014). With the break from some of the mechanisms that control the work and lives of teachers (e.g. fixed working hours and spaces, classroom observations, school inspections, and a target-driven curriculum), some found their practice re-invigorated, as they worked with greater creativity and collaboration, ultimately resulting in improved well-being and enjoyment of teaching.

The 'age of the autonomous professional' (Hargreaves, 2000) was prevalent in developed nations during the 1960s to the mid-1980s, where teachers 'enjoyed unprecedented autonomy over curriculum development and decision making' (ibid, p. 158). However, this changed in many jurisdictions in the late 1980s–2000 as demands increased for teachers to teach in prescribed ways, develop new skills, and comply with new initiatives. This approach left teachers with less personal resource for engagement with the more creative and moral purposes of education (Adams & Povey, 2018). Instead, the focus on 'quality' judgements diverted teachers' attention toward an endless quest for progress, which involved teachers competing with both themselves and against others in the profession (ibid).

For newer teachers, the COVID-19 pandemic arguably provided a taste of the autonomy (re)experienced by their more seasoned colleagues. The insights provided by chapters in this book reinforce the necessity for teachers' professionalism to be protected, and for their autonomy to be ensured and acknowledged within teacher education and curriculum policies (Nóvoa & Alvim, 2022). Part of such autonomy is for teachers to be trusted and to be confident and supported in their decision-making. This requires teachers to be adaptable in response to finding solutions to the challenges posed by their day-to-day lives as teachers. Whilst the pandemic provided plenty of opportunities for teachers to demonstrate this skill, it also highlighted the importance of autonomy being situated within a more flexible school environment so that capacity for initiative, adaptation, and change (ibid) are enabled.

Running parallel to this is a need for more flexibility in working patterns. Flexibility is important in enabling teachers to combine interests and responsibilities beyond the school gate with those at work. Working part-time is often considered to be effective in providing work–life balance and enhanced well-being (Shiri et al., 2022), but Brown's chapter suggests otherwise for the teaching profession. Beyond rigid part-time hours, what is required post-COVID are creative context-specific solutions offering genuine flexibility that work for, not against, teachers and are arrived at through negotiation with them. Research in this area is limited and will be required in order to iron out the practical challenges that this may present and make adoption of flexible working straightforward for teachers and their settings.

Incorporate reflexive practice into teacher development

Through our second recommendation, we wish to add to calls (from Husu et al., 2008 and others) for emerging and more experienced teachers to have the time and tools to engage effectively in reflexive practice (commonly cited as originally propagated by Dewey, 1933, and Schön, 1983). This would build on much existing work in initial and continuing education. Here we expand on why it is so crucial to continue and expand this beyond COVID.

As explored throughout this book, COVID raised questions about what it means to be a teacher, but of course, there is no singular purpose of teaching, which leads us to be concerned by neoliberalist efforts to shape visions of education through narrow market-driven values (Gilbert, 2021). Being reflexive about the purposes of education should be a 'situated practice' (Stîngu, 2012) by the individual teacher in relation to their context including phase, setting (structural and cultural components), and regional political and socio-economic factors. And, as COVID has shown us, what it means to be a teacher shifts over time, as well as from place to place. For example, Cameron & Abram's chapter suggests that the pandemic brought a movement toward a culture of 'caring not scoring' (hinting at a loosening grip of neoliberal agendas), as they noted 'a seismic shift in cultural practices' in the charter school they observed, 'away from the charter's protocol to use benchmark-based assessments to embrace in-the-moment intuitive assessments and acceptance of well-being'.

Moorehouse & Tiet provide insightful discussion of the value of reflexive activity for new teachers within their chapter. They write of the pandemic as a 'reality shock' that led teachers to ask 'what if tomorrow never comes?' and to react by intuitively aligning their practice to their personal values. These centred on care, truth, vigour, and connectedness. Moorehouse & Tiet urge teachers to enact a habit of reflection and questioning and work with 'open-mindedness' and 'wholeheartedness' (Dewey, 1933). More research around the purposes, forms, and outcomes of teachers' reflexive practice post-COVID would provide both a wider evidence base and specific examples/ideas for actions to aid teacher reflexivity, which holds promise as a valuable means of developing, motivating, and retaining education professionals.

Cultivate cultures of care and empathy for all

In the preceding sections of this chapter, we explored how the pandemic has heightened the significance of care for teachers, and in teaching, but that this can be at the expense of teacher well-being and/or professional integrity. Here we develop an argument for cultivating cultures of care and empathy post-COVID for all involved in the process of education and propose approaches to change that are mindful of these difficulties.

In 2011, Barr called for teacher development activities to focus more on training teachers 'to recognise and exercise their cognitive and emotional empathic capacities' (ibid). It may well be that for many teachers, the pandemic required them to draw on these qualities more than at any other moment in many of their careers. Whilst remote learning rendered this challenging, the chapters of this book present many examples of considerate and empathetic practice. Cultivating empathetic cultures closely relates to our prior call for increased opportunity and support for individual teachers to engage in reflexive practice. It also connects with our call for increased and concerted collaboration in support of teaching and learning (which we discuss further in the following section). It furthermore requires professional autonomy (our first recommendation) – for teachers to be able to choose how to respond to specific instances of student need and provide appropriate support. In short, our four recommendations work together as pillars for transformation in education, prioritising care and empathy and ensuring that these extend to attitudes toward teachers and leaders, as well as to students. The co-dependency of student and teacher well-being should be explicit and safeguarded in such cultures.

DeCampos et al. (2017) propose that cultural initiatives must be coupled with structural change in order to be successful. Teacher performance and school performance in neoliberalism are often reduced to blunt data which can dehumanise the experience of education (Bradbury & Roberts-Holmes, 2017), 'remodelling learners as a compliant proto workforce' (Humphreys, 2017, p. 41) and subduing teachers into serving market-driven strategies of accountability and competition (Loh & Hu, 2014) rather than allowing them the freedom to innovate and adapt to support learning and well-being in specific contexts. For cultures of care, empathy, and inclusion to thrive, we concur with DeCampos et al. (2017) that corresponding structural change is simultaneously required. This entails carefully reconsidering, amongst other things, quality standards, school inspection foci, and how teachers and pupils are assessed in the post-COVID era.

Work collaboratively to achieve transformation

As Niesz (2007) reflects, the way Western schools are organised serves to limit opportunities for teachers to work collaboratively. She discusses the Japanese model that incorporates time to discuss practice and plan lessons with other teachers within the working day. Looking beyond networks within schools, and writing before the pandemic, Niesz (2007) postulates that 'communities of practice, in which learning and teaching are interwoven in social networks, may someday lead to a movement to put thoughtful professional expertise back into schooling' (ibid, p. 605).

Ritchie (2012, p. 120) proposes that

> education has increasingly become more technical and instrumental, with a primary focus on the economic outcomes of education [...]. These changes push teacher education away from social justice teacher preparation and toward preparing teachers as technicians to raise students' standardized test scores.

He presents insightful examples that demonstrate the importance of collaborating in networks beyond and between schools to support teachers to 'enact critical pedagogical practices that seek to make school a place that is equitable, democratic, collaborative, just, and humane' (ibid).

Stank et al. (2001, p. 31) define collaboration as 'a process of decision making among interdependent parties ... [it] involves joint ownership of decisions and collective responsibility for outcomes'. Collaboration can be a vehicle for change (Senge et al., 2007), but building collective capacity for change entails careful considerations around culture and reciprocity (Jones & Harris, 2014). Furthermore, infrastructure 'that connects people together in a meaningful, productive and compelling way' (ibid, p. 475) is required. This reinforces our call for changes to culture and systems to be considered as equally important and mutually reinforcing.

The chapters of this book have shown that working in collaboration with others (e.g. parents, colleagues, other education professionals, and students) enabled learning to continue during a pandemic that presented imminent danger to life and closed schools. Collaboration can also be a pathway to achieving transformation post-COVID. Like Sharrat & Fullan (2009), we recognise that this will require motivation and organisation. Having opportunities to be reflexive with regard to the purposes of education, being empowered to act with autonomy and flexibility, and having a supportive network are, we propose, *all* vital in enabling change.

Final reflections

In this chapter, we have argued for change to the structures and cultures of teaching in order to support autonomous, reflexive, caring, and collaborative teachers. Of course, none of this is new, and change is not a simple process (Hayes, 2022). It is also important to recognise that this book offers only a partial view. Our chapters do not represent all phases of education or geographical regions and inevitably feature only those teacher participants with the time, motivation, and capacity to contribute, even during a global health emergency. By foregrounding the experiences and perspectives of teachers, we have largely excluded those of others (perhaps most notably, those they teach). The teachers' voices are filtered through the words of the researcher-author/s, many of whom have a similar standpoint to our own, informed by Western-centric academia and inspired by critical studies of education and organisation. The research methods utilised to capture data were also shaped by the preference and circumstances of the researcher during the pandemic. And we cover a limited range of topics – we do not consider in any depth important issues such as the remuneration of teachers, budgets for education, and safeguarding of children, for example, which for others might have been the starting points for contemplating teaching post-COVID. Additionally, we are not blind to the unequal distribution of privilege and capacities for change in the global educational context, which we see largely as enduring consequences of national histories and policy contexts. This speaks to a need for allies for teachers, both from within and outside of the education profession – and across national boundaries.

Educational institutions 'have a unique opportunity to positively and proactively change as a result of COVID-19' (Zhao & Watterson, 2021, p. 10). The pandemic has shown us that change in working environments, patterns, and practices is possible and can be made to happen quickly when there is a necessity, a will, and support. We should not lose the momentum of this catalyst for change if we wish to combat the ill-effects of neoliberalism and avoid the loss of valued teacher talent. Fullan (2020, p. 27) proposes that 'the change transition – pandemic and beyond – will play itself out over the next decade' and as Sir Ken Robinson (2020, p. 9) stated shortly before his death, 'to create a new sort of world, and a new kind of normal that generations to follow will add to and shape for themselves … it starts with education, it always has done'.

Notes

1 This word was used by participants in our research with teachers during COVID (Marsh-Davies & Burnett, 2021).
2 Here we are drawing upon Burke & Stets (2009) definition of a social role as 'a set of expectations tied to a social position' (p. 114).

References

Adams, R. (2020) 'Homeschooling boosts parents' interest in teaching as a career', *The Guardian*. Available at: https://www.theguardian.com/education/2020/may/30/home-schooling-boosts-parents-interest-in-teaching-as-a-career.

Adams, G. and Povey, H. (2018) '"Now There's Everything to Stop You": Teacher autonomy then and now' in Jurdak, M. & Vithal, R. (eds.) Socio-political dimensions of mathematics education: Voices from margin to mainstream. ICME-13 Monographs. Springer, pp. 209–230. Available at: https://shura.shu.ac.uk/16437/.

Allen, R., Burgess, S., & Mayo, J. (2018) The teacher labour market, teacher turnover and disadvantaged schools: New evidence for England. *Education Economics*, 26 (1), pp. 4–23. Available at: https://doi.org/10.1080/09645292.2017.1366425.

Alvesson, M. & Willmott, H. (2002) Identity regulation as organisational control: Producing the appropriate individual. *Journal of Management Studies*, 39, pp. 619–644.

Ball, S. & Collet-Sabé, J. (2022) Against school: An epistemological critique. *Discourse: Studies in the Cultural Politics of Education*, 43(6), pp. 985–999. https://doi.org/10.1080/01596306.2021.1947780.

Barr, J. (2011) The relationship between teachers' empathy and perceptions of school culture. *Educational Studies*, 37(3), pp. 365–369. https://doi.org/10.1080/03055698.2010.506342.

Beauchamp, C. & Thomas, L. (2009) Understanding teacher identity: An overview of issues in the literature and implications for teacher education. *Cambridge Journal of Education*, 39(2), pp. 175–189. https://doi.org/10.1080/03057640902902252.

Benhenda, A. & Macmillan, L. (2021) 'How to Attract and Retain Teachers', *CEPEO Briefing Note Series 13*, UCL Centre for Education Policy and Equalising Opportunities, revised May 2021.

Bradbury, A. & Roberts-Holmes, G. (2017) *The datafication of primary and early years education*. London: Routledge.

Bronfenbrenner, U. & Morris, P. A. (2006) 'The Bioecological Model of Human Development' in Lerner, R. M. & Damon, W. (eds.) Handbook of child psychology: Theoretical models of human development. Hoboken, NJ: John Wiley & Sons, pp. 793–828.

Burke, P. J. & Stets, J. E. (2009) *Identity theory*. New York: Oxford University Press.

Cain, M., Campbell, C., & Coleman, K. (2022) Kindness and empathy beyond all else': Challenges to professional identities of Higher Education teachers during COVID-19 times. *The Australian Educational Researcher.* Available at: https://doi.org/10.1007/s13384-022-00552-1

Caza, B. B., Vough, H., & Puranik H. (2018) Identity work in organizations and occupations: Definitions, theories, and pathways forward. *Journal of Organizational Behaviour*, 39, pp. 889–910.

Collet-Sabé, J. & Ball, S. J. (2022) Beyond school. The challenge of co-producing and commoning a different episteme for education. *Journal of Education Policy.* https://doi.org/10.1080/02680939.2022.2157890.

DeCampos, H. A., Fawcett, A. M., & Fawcett, S. E. (2017) Cultural and structural forces: A potentially symbiotic or dysfunctional relationship in the journey towards supply chain collaboration. *Journal of Transportation Management*, 27(1), pp. 23–38. https://doi.org/10.22237/jotm/1498867380

Dewey, J. (1933) *How we think: A restatement of the relation of reflective thinking to the educative process.* Boston, MA: D.C. Heath & Co Publishers.

Donitsa-Schmidt, S. & Ramot, R. (2020) Opportunities and challenges: teacher education in Israel in the Covid-19 pandemic. *Journal of Education for Teaching*, 46 (4), pp. 586–595. https://doi.org/10.1080/02607476.2020.1799708.

Elbaz-Luwisch, F. (2007) 'Studying Teachers' Lives and Experience: Narrative Inquiry Into K-12 Teaching' in Clandinin, D. J. (ed.) *Handbook of narrative inquiry: mapping a methodology*, Thousand Oaks, CA: Sage Publications, Inc., pp. 357–382.

EPI (2021) epi.org.uk. Available at: https://epi.org.uk/publications-and-research/epi-research-for-the-department-for-education-on-pupil-learning-loss/ (Accessed: 07 March 2023).

Fullan, M. (2020) Learning and the pandemic: What's next? *Prospects*, 49, pp. 25–28. Available at: https://doi.org/10.1007/s11125-020-09502-0

Gershenson, S. (2021) 'Identifying and Producing Effective Teachers', *IZA DP*, 14096. Available at: https://www.iza.org/publications/dp/14096/identifying-and-producing-effective-teachers (Accessed 10 May 2021).

Gilbert, C. (2021) Punching the clock: A Foucauldian analysis of teacher time clock use. *Critical Studies in Education*, 62(4), pp. 439–454.

Goodson, I. (2014) *Curriculum, personal narrative and the social future.* Abingdon: Routledge.

Gourlay, L., Littlejohn, A., Oliver, M., & Potter, J. (2021) Lockdown literacies and semiotic assemblages: Academic boundary work in the Covid-19 crisis. *Learning, Media and Technology.* https://doi.org/10.1080/17439884.2021.1900242.

Hargreaves, A. (2019) Teacher collaboration: 30 years of research on its nature, forms, limitations and effects. *Teachers and Teaching*, 25(5), pp. 603–621. https://doi.org/10.1080/13540602.2019.1639499.

Hargreaves, A. (2000) Four ages of professionalism and professional learning. *Teachers and Teaching*, 6(2), pp. 151–182.

Hayes, J. (2022) *The theory & practice of change management.* London: Red Globe Press.

Husu, J., Toom, A., & Patrikainen, S. (2008) Guided reflection as a means to demonstrate and develop student teachers' reflective competencies. *Reflective Practice*, 9(1), pp. 37–51. https://doi.org/10.1080/14623940701816642

Hong, J. & Cross Francis, D. (2020) Unpacking complex phenomena through qualitative inquiry: The case of teacher identity research. *Educational Psychologist*, 55(4), pp. 208–219. https://doi.org/10.1080/00461520.2020.1783265

Humphreys, P. (2017) 'Neoliberal Schooling, Dehumanisation and an Education' in Rudd, T., Goodson, I.F. (eds.) *Negotiating neoliberalism. Studies in professional life and work*, vol 3. Rotterdam: Sense Publishers.

Iyengar, R. (2021) Rethinking community participation in education post Covid-19. *Prospects*, 51, pp. 437–447. https://doi.org/10.1007/s11125-020-09538-2

Jin, L. & Cortazzi, M. (2016) *Engineering the soul*. London: Routledge

Jones, M. & Harris, A. (2014) Principals leading successful organizational change. *Journal of Organizational Change Management*, 27(3), pp. 473–485.

Jones, N. D., Camburn, E. M., Kelcey, B., & Quintero, E. (2022) 'Teachers' time use and affect before and after COVID-19 school closures. *AERA Open*, 8(1), pp. 1–14. https://doi.org/10.1177/23328584211068068.

Lakes, R. D. & Carter, P. A. (2011) Neoliberalism and education: An introduction march. *Educational Studies*, 47(2), pp. 107–110. https://doi.org/10.1080/00131946.2011.556387

Loh, J. & Hu, G. (2014) Subdued by the system: Neoliberalism and the beginning teacher. *Teaching and Teacher Education*, 41, pp. 13–21.

Marsh-Davies, K. & Burnett, C. (2021) 'Being a Teacher during COVID-19', *British Academy of Management 2021: Virtual Conference Proceedings*. Available at: https://virtual.oxfordabstracts.com/#/event/1821/submission/207 (Accessed: 15 January 2023).

Morin, E. (2020) *Un festival d'incertitudes*. Tracts de crise: Un virus et des hommes (pp. 404–419). Paris: Gallimard.

Mykhalovskiy, E. (1996) Reconsidering table talk: Critical thoughts on the relationship between sociology, autobiography and self-indulgence. *Qual Sociol*, 19, pp. 131–151. https://doi.org/10.1007/BF02393251

Niesz, T. (2007) Why teacher networks (can) work. *Phi Delta Kappan*, pp. 605–610.

Nóvoa, A. & Alvim, Y. (2020) Nothing is new, but everything has changed: A viewpoint on the future school. *Prospects*, 49, pp. 35–41.

OECD (2005) 'Teachers matter: Attracting, developing and retaining effective teachers'. Available at: https://www.oecd.org/education/school/34990905.pdf

OECD (2018) 'TALIS Survey 2018'. Available at: https://www.oecd.org/education/talis/

OECD (2023) 'Distribution of Teachers by age and gender'. Available at: stats.oecd.org

Pokhrel, S. & Mehta, K. S. (2021) 'COVID-19: Educational challenges in Nepal', *SSRN*, Available at: http://dx.doi.org/10.2139/ssrn.3856948

Poole, M. & Isaacs, D. (1997) Caring: A gendered concept. *Women's Studies International Forum*, 20 (4), pp. 524–536. Available at: https://www.sciencedirect.com/science/article/abs/pii/S0277539597000411

Ritchie, S. (2012) Incubating and sustaining: How teacher networks enable and support social justice education. *Journal of Teacher Education*, 63(2), pp. 120–131.

Robinson, K. (2020) A global reset of education. *Prospects*, 49, pp. 7–9. Available at: https://doi.org/10.1007/s11125-020-09493-y

Robinson, L. E., Valido, A., & Drescher, A. (2022) Teachers, stress, and the COVID-19 pandemic: A qualitative analysis. *School Mental Health*. Available at: https://doi.org/10.1007/s12310-022-09533-2

Schön, D. A. (1983) *The reflective practitioner. How professionals think in action*. New York: Basic Books.

Senge, P. M., Lichtenstein, B. B., Kaeufer, K., Bradbury, H. & Carroll, J. S. (2007) Collaborating for systemic change. *MIT Sloan Management Review*, 48(2), p. 44.

Sharrat, L. & Fullan, M. (2009) *Realization: The change imperative for deepening district wide reform*. Corwin Press: Thousand Oaks.

Shiri, R., Turunen, J., & Kausto, J. (2022) The effect of employee-oriented flexible work on mental health: a systematic review. *Healthcare*, 10(883), pp. 1–14. Available at: https://doi.org/10.3390/healthcare10050883

Sorensen, L. C., & Ladd, H. F. (2020) The hidden costs of teacher turnover. *AERA Open*, 6(1). Available at: https://doi.org/10.1177/2332858420905812

Stank, T. P., Keller, S. B., & Daugherty, P. J. (2001) Supply chain collaboration and logistical service performance. *Journal of Business Logistics*, 22(1), pp. 29–48.

Stîngu, M. M. (2012) Reflexive practice in teacher education: facts and trends. *Procedia-Social and Behavioral Sciences*, 33, pp. 617–621.

Sveningsson, S. & Alvesson, M. (2003) Managing managerial identities: organizational fragmentation, discourse and identity struggle. *Human Relations*, 56(10), pp. 1163–1193.

Weale, S. (2022) Teachers and Social Workers suffer most from lost decade for pay growth in UK, *The Guardian*. Available at: https://www.theguardian.com/education/2022/dec/21/teachers-and-social-workers-suffer-most-from-lost-decade-for-pay-growth-in-uk

Worth, J. (2023) *Short Supply: Addressing the Post-Pandemic Teacher Supply Challenge in England, National Foundation for Educational Research*. Slough: NFER. Available at: https://www.nfer.ac.uk/media/5210/addressing_the_post_pandemic_teacher_supply_challenge.pdf (Accessed 28th February 2023)

Zhao, Y. & Watterson, J. (2021) The changes we need: Education post COVID-19. *Journal of Educational Change*, 22, pp. 3–12.

INDEX

adaptive behavioural strategies 67
ageism 81
alliances 14–15, 312
anxiety 34, 58, 80, 92
Australia 106–109, 163–165
Autoethnography 291
Autonomy 81, 87, 234, 248–249, 317–318

behaviour management 248
blended learning 62, 256
bullying 250–251

Canada 15, 109, 274, 281–287
career break 26
Caribbean 127–134
change management 187–189
childcare 32, 45, 53, 164, 311–312
classroom observations 96, 317
classroomness 262–263
communities 136–138
communities of practice 107, 109
creative writing 111, 220

datafication 7
democratisation 16, 249, 320
deprivation 91
digital literacy 121, 284–285, 289
dissonance 12, 147, 236

early childhood phase, including ECCE, ECE 127, 163
empathy 44, 118, 147, 173, 319–320

empowerment 295, 300–301, 303
exhaustion 78–79, 117, 146, 158–159, 189, 236
experiential learning 57, 112–113, 187, 235
experimental writing 204, 207, 214

family-friendly 44, 63
feminism 25
flexible working 25, 27, 33, 64–70, 102, 318
flipped learning 121
Foucault, M. 207

gay/lesbian/queer teachers 9, 291–293, 296, 301
gender pay gap 9
guilt 30, 34–35, 50–51, 232, 236, 312

higher education 44, 107–109, 229–230, 291, 296, 301
homeostasis 181, 195
Hong Kong 226–230
hooks, B. 292, 296
human resource management (HRM) 89, 92
hybrid learning 194, 256–259, 304

identity work 313
inequalities 9, 26, 57, 131, 310
initial teacher education (ITE) 43–44, 226, 310

Index

intersectionality 295
isolation 182, 252, 279, 314

Jamaica 131–132, 134–138, 183–186, 189–192, 195–197
job security 89, 117, 190

kindness 118, 233

Latour, B. 259, 261
life history research 25
lifelong learning 160, 283
literacy 205–206, 219, 271, 275–281, 284–289
lost learning / learning loss 41, 153, 287, 244–247, 286–288, 311

managerialism 90, 279
marketisation 8
menopause 13, 65–68, 82–84
mentoring 58, 96, 99, 227, 295, 301

narrative inquiry 111–112, 187
neoliberalism 7, 301, 309, 315, 317–318, 321
neurodiversity 250, 251
newly qualified teachers (NQTs) 58, 82, 93, 99

parent teachers 26–28, 191
parental involvement 138. 182, 184, 196–197, 315
part-time working 12, 25–28, 62, 67, 318
pastoral care 95, 100
performance management 13, 87, 89, 90, 95–96
performativity 8
professional learning 94, 108, 114, 156–159, 252, 281–283

professionalisation 90, 137
psychological safety 67–68, 77–84

randomised control trials 8
reflexivity 111, 148, 157–160, 314, 319
refugees and asylum seekers 251
remuneration 127, 139, 321
resilience 70, 89, 107, 118–122, 177, 281

safeguarding 3, 94, 321
school inspections 317, 320
self-care 118, 157, 232–234
semiotics 206, 211
slow scholarship 119–120
social constructivism 147–149, 157
social justice 196, 227, 299, 320
special educational needs and disabilities (SEND) 250
sustainable development goals 131
systems theory 166

teacher educators 226–230
teacher identity 9, 231, 313–316
timetabling 58, 79–81, 94, 258, 267–269
trauma 120, 313

university *see* higher education

voice 11, 68, 93, 216–217, 252, 292
vulnerability 128–129, 135–137, 216, 236

widening participation 43, 44
work life balance 12, 33, 54, 67, 89, 118
working hours 27, 33, 134